# EUROPE SINCE 1989

# EUROPE SINCE 1989

*a history*

## PHILIPP THER

*Translated by Charlotte Hughes-Kreutzmüller*

Princeton University Press

Princeton and Oxford

English translation copyright © 2016 by Princeton University Press

Originally published as *Die neue Ordnung auf dem alten Kontinent: eine Geschichte des neoliberalen Europa.*

Copyright © Suhrkamp Verlag Berlin 2014

Published by Princeton University Press, 41 William Street, Princeton, New Jersey 08540

In the United Kingdom: Princeton University Press, 6 Oxford Street, Woodstock, Oxfordshire OX20 1TR

press.princeton.edu

Jacket photograph courtesy of Przemysław Zacharuk

All Rights Reserved

ISBN 978-0-691-16737-4
Library of Congress Control Number: 2016931665

British Library Cataloging-in-Publication Data is available

The translation of this work was funded by Geisteswissenschaften International—Translation Funding for Humanities and Social Sciences from Germany, a joint initiative of the Fritz Thyssen Foundation, the German Federal Foreign Office, the collecting society VG WORT and the Börsenverein des Deutschen Buchhandels (German Publishers & Booksellers Association).

This book has been composed in Baskerville 120 Pro and Swiss 721

Printed on acid-free paper. ∞

Printed in the United States of America

10 9 8 7 6 5 4 3 2 1

# CONTENTS

# PREFACE TO THE ENGLISH EDITION

Britain's decision to leave the European Union confronts it with a very uncertain future, but is also another strong signal that a period of European history has come to a close. The British plebiscite against the EU confirms the fragility of the neoliberal order that emerged in the 1980s. The first big blow came with the stock market crash of 2008–9 and the subsequent economic crisis. Some countries, like Germany, have recovered from the crisis, but southern Europe and the lower middle classes across large parts of the continent have not.

The political responses to neoliberalism are proving even more explosive than its economic consequences. Populists all over Europe are exploiting the general discontent with high unemployment, insecure and badly paid jobs for the young, and intensifying economic competition due to free trade and labor migrants. As Brexit shows, the old specter of nationalism is back again, and has greater popular appeal than the EU, which has been made the scapegoat for all sorts of social and economic problems. The populists promise to safeguard their ethnically defined nation from the ills of global competition, labor competition at home, rising criminality, foreign terrorists, and the decay of traditional national values. But their more fundamental allure lies in the fact that they have successfully contradicted the Thatcherite slogan "There is no alternative," once mocked as TINA. This antipolitical mode of argumentation was misused to press through several major economic and social reforms, and unfortunately even European integration and the EU project. The Brexit campaign succeeded because it insisted there is an alternative, even if it is detrimental to large parts of the population and might in fact lead to the dissolution of the United Kingdom.

Though the Brexit vote occurred seven years after the crisis of 2008–9, there is another connection between the two events. In several postcommunist countries, the crisis was so severe that it resulted in unprecedented mass migration. In 2015 Europe was preoccupied with the arrival of more than one million refugees from the Middle East (and blatantly failed to find a common response to this challenge) but, contrary to the popular view, this influx was considerably less than the labor migration triggered by the crisis of 2008–9. Between 2009 and 2011, Romania lost 2.4 million inhabitants, or more than 10 percent of its population; Latvia and Lithuania lost several hundred thousand, mostly through labor migration. These people left their homes not only to escape the deep recession, but also in reaction to the drastic social cuts demanded by the International Monetary Fund and its various "rescue packages." The United Kingdom was the most important receiving country for labor migrants from Eastern Europe. This immigration helped the UK to recover economically from the crisis, but also increased the job competition for the lower middle class. The right-wing populists of the UK Independence Party (UKIP) built their campaign on popular dissatisfaction with the growing economic pressure, especially on the labor market. Will Denmark, the Netherlands, France, and other countries with strong right-wing populist movements follow the English example? The rise of Donald Trump shows that this is not merely a European problem. Such questions about the future are beyond the ambit of historians. But by analyzing the past, one might better understand the present tendency toward closed societies, as opposed to the open societies once conceptualized by Karl Popper and realized in large parts of Europe after 1989.

Another proponent of closed societies and a major external challenge for the European Union and the West at large is Vladimir Putin. Russian aggression against Ukraine has ended a long phase of peace on the continent, one that had helped to strengthen the postcommunist economies and sustain social spending in Western Europe after the end of the Cold War. The authoritarian turn in Eastern Europe is not confined to Russia; it has infected Hungary and is threatening to grip Poland. New splits have appeared not only between the East and West of Europe, but also between the North and South. Another large country and a founding member of the EU, Italy, has not yet recovered from the crisis.

In fact, labor migration from Italy is on the rise, and from Greece even more so. In the long run, these imbalances and the growing economic and social gaps between countries and especially within societies are jeopardizing the achievements of European integration, such as open borders, more than the challenge posed by the refugees from the Middle East and Africa.

The only consolation in this gloomy picture is the fact that at certain moments in recent history the situation was worse. This was true in the early 1990s, when Yugoslavia fell apart in a bloody and protracted civil war, resulting in a refugee crisis even more severe than the present one. The Soviet Union and its most important successor state, the Russian Federation, were plunged into chaos, and the standard Western economic recipes did not seem to work. In fact, even the expert bets on Poland were mixed in those years: unemployment was constantly rising, social protests threatened to derail reforms, the postcommunists won the elections in 1993, and it was not clear whether the economy had already hit bottom. Moreover, the European Union was divided between further integration and enlargement, and it failed miserably to bring order to its own backyard in Yugoslavia or devise a new Marshall Plan for the Eastern neighbors knocking at its doors.

And yet nowadays commentators look back calmly at the turbulent early 1990s, and even idealize the economic reforms enacted then. This tendency shaped the self-affirming debate in the United States about the postcommunist transformation at the twenty-fifth anniversary of 1989. In 2014 a pair of American scholars writing for *Foreign Affairs* made the bold claim that the postcommunist states had become "normal countries." These neoliberal success stories glossed over Russia in the 1990s, where the depression was as deep as the one in the United States in the 1930s. And one should not forget that the disintegration of Yugoslavia and of Czechoslovakia was caused in part by conflicts over whether to enact radical or gradual reforms. Even in relatively "successful" countries such as Poland, the economic reforms brought suffering to millions of people in rural and old industrial regions. The hardship experienced by transformation's losers and disillusionment with neoliberal capitalism have created fertile ground for populist parties, authoritarian tendencies, and even neo-fascist movements. As a result of the crisis, Western Europe is now facing similar challenges.

Hence the "dual transition"—from planned to market economy and from dictatorship to democracy—that many observers in 1989–90 expected to occur did not materialize. There was no universal "end of history" resulting in liberal democracy, because capitalism, as German historian Jürgen Kocka has pointed out, can exist without democracy. This may even be true for the United States, where left- and right-wing populists are on the rise as well. All these current problems have multiple causes, but they certainly include the growing gap between rich and poor, increased pressure on the middle class, the loss of the European equivalent of the "American dream," and the diminishing capability of states and their governments to alleviate social and economic woes.

It would be simplistic to blame neoliberalism for all these problems. Instead, this book proposes to use it as a neutral, analytical term, and to distinguish between its intellectual history, its implementation (which always depended on the given context), and its social and political consequences. But certainly the main pillars of this ideology—blind belief in the market as an adjudicator in almost all human affairs, irrational reliance on the rationality of market participants, disdain for the state as expressed in the myth of "big government," and the uniform application of the economic recipes of the Washington Consensus (which was also passed in 1989 and shows the global dimension of this caesura)—have had grave side effects. Therefore, one cannot claim that the shock therapy came first and was followed by growth and prosperity. Such a simple causal correlation cannot be proven. Still, this does not imply that the gradualists were right: countries that tried to avoid reforms in the early 1990s, such as Romania and Ukraine, fared even worse.

The main argument of this book is that the economic performance of the postcommunist countries, including Germany after its 1990 unification, depended above all on their social capital. This also best explains Poland's unexpected success. Due to the dysfunction of their nation's planned economy, millions of Poles had learned how to run businesses and survive in a market economy prior to 1989. They took up the many opportunities offered by the new order. To explain this properly requires a social history perspective focusing not only on reform policies, but also on "transformation from below." Thus, this book adds to the growing historiography on neoliberalism, which so far has concentrated on its intellectual roots and breakthrough up to the 1980s. Here, the main issue is how neoliberalism was implemented in Europe in a first wave after 1989, and in a second wave starting in the late 1990s and ending with the disaster of 2008–9 (the Eastern European bubble which burst then had some commonalities with the American real estate bubble). The impact on various societies, social groups, regions, and cities is another important topic. This impact should not be painted in somber colors only. The new order also created opportunities for certain groups within society; as in the United States, neoliberalism had a popular dimension. The comparative analysis moves from East to West, and not the other way around, as is common in the traditional, occidentalist historiography of Europe. Tony Judt has already stressed the significance of changes in the East on the West in his masterly history of postwar Europe. This book tries to continue his work in terms of time and with a stronger focus on social and economic history.

PHILIPP THER
VIENNA, JUNE 2016

# EUROPE SINCE 1989

# 1

# Introduction

## On the Road to 1989

The origins of this book lie in the golden summer of 1977. It was a bright time in Europe, both politically and meteorologically. The first oil crisis had passed, and a policy of détente prevailed. The Helsinki Accords of 1975 had built confidence; the West German government propagated "change through rapprochement." The East-West standoff seemed to have calmed. It was in this political climate that my parents decided to take a summer vacation in the "Eastern Bloc." The phrase was spoken with a note of apprehension, despite the new optimism. "Eastern" meant communist; "bloc" suggested self-imposed seclusion and military threat. Various members of our family had bad personal memories of the Red Army in 1945, and in 1968, when it had crushed the Prague Spring. The itinerary for our vacation, then, was worked out with due caution. The first stop was to be Hungary, for it was known as the "happiest barracks in the communist camp." Then we would travel to southern Poland, from there to the beautiful Krkonoše Mountains lining the Polish-Czech border and, lastly, to Prague to visit relatives. Our journey started well. There was no iron curtain across the border; the Hungarian guards greeted us cheerfully. We were not fazed by passport and custom controls, as they were still common at Western European borders. Budapest was quite close and the Danube glittered in the evening light. The goulash we ate at a restaurant, namesake of Hungarian communism, was far spicier than anything at home in bland West Germany.

The first incident that hinted at the events to come in 1989 occurred after nightfall at the campsite in Budapest. At the gate, there were two entry booths and two lines of people—one long, one short. The long line, which did not seem to be moving, was made up of Germans. But they spoke an unfamiliar, eastern dialect, and scowled as they stood empty-handed, waiting. Germans also made up the fast-moving, short line next to them. They were dressed more like us and held valuable West German deutschmarks in their hands. It was embarrassing to me, a teenager at my father's side, to march past others waiting in line. I was told that we were in the line to pay with West German marks and so would be allotted a space immediately, while those in the other line had to wait until the end of the day and take what was left, because they could pay only in East German marks. If no spaces were left, they would have to sleep in their cars. Outraged, I asked my father why the poor East Germans did not benefit from the special friendship between Eastern Bloc countries that was trumpeted by communist propaganda. My father replied that the Eastern Bloc countries suffered from a shortage of foreign exchange and were eager to get their hands on deutschmarks. This was also the reason why Western tourists were required to exchange a certain amount of money, at that time twenty-five West German marks (around twelve US dollars), for every day of their stay. I suggested giving the East Germans in the long line some deutschmarks; exchanging them as we did schillings in Austria. Another discussion followed, continued later with our campsite neighbors from Karl-Marx-Stadt, about why the Eastern Bloc only permitted changing money in a bank and what an official rate of exchange was.

That night at the campsite in Budapest was like a crash course in international finance and economics: Eastern currencies, Western currencies, foreign exchange, export, import, foreign debt, and—touching on "economics from below"—unofficial rates of exchange and the black market. The obvious injustice of the two lines and the scowls of those cooling their heels for hours preyed on my mind. A week later, after a long wait and extensive checks at the Hungarian-Slovak border, and again at the Czech-Polish border, which did not tally at all with the official image of socialist friendship, I gained the opportunity to put my newly acquired financial knowledge to use in Kraków. The Polish friends we had met the previous summer as they were hitchhiking through Germany on their first trip to the West—another journey made possible by the détente—wanted to buy deutschmarks from us. They told us of the rising prices, empty stores, and falling value of the złoty. Clearly, West German marks and US dollars were worth far more than the national currency in Poland. Thus ordinary Polish citizens were already demonstrating the kind of market savvy that later helped their country's economy to flourish. But back in 1977, nobody imagined that the Eastern Bloc would ever collapse, or that a neoliberal train was being put on track in the United Kingdom and the United States that was set to cross Europe in 1989.

However, the 1977 slump in the black market price of the złoty presaged the massive economic problems that soon confronted the People's Republic of Poland. As we now know, it marked the beginning of a five-year downward slide for the Polish economy.[1] The modernization the country had hoped to achieve by importing Western technology had failed, leaving only foreign debts that it struggled to pay off. For me, as a teenage visitor, Poland's rising inflation (which the planned economy should theoretically have prevented) was not an acute problem. On the contrary, I received three times as many złotys from our host family for my saved-up pocket money than my father got for the same number of deutschmarks at the bank's official rate of exchange. For the pile of aluminum coins and bills as paper-thin as play money I could send postcards to all my friends and buy unlimited amounts of ice cream for a week. I was not, however, able to buy ballpoint pens or ink cartridges. Nevertheless, I had unconsciously become a privileged Westerner in Poland. But this good fortune under "real existing socialism"—a step on the way to communist paradise, as the ideologues would have it—was not without alloy. I soon noticed that the local youngsters could not afford to buy any ice cream, or jeans, or sneakers for that matter. Furthermore, although there was no standing in line for campsites in Kraków, as there had been in Budapest, there were long queues for meat, sugar, cream, and other goods that we Westerners took utterly for granted.

In Czechoslovakia, the third stop on our journey, scarcity was not a problem. Our relatives in Prague drove a new Škoda, lived in a modern detached house in an idyllic spot overlooking the Vltava River, and had a delightful weekend home, too. The standard of living of our West German family of six was no higher. But behind closed doors, my great-uncle and his son complained about the political situation. They were dismayed by the so-called normalization (*normalizace*) instituted after the crushing of the Prague Spring (which every specialist in Eastern European studies should bear in mind before using the word "normal") and the inefficiency of national industries, with which they, both engineers, were acquainted from personal experience. They could see that their country was falling behind on a technological level, and it hurt their professional and national pride. Even we tourists sensed the leaden atmosphere in the Czech capital: the site of Jan Palach's self-immolation in January 1969 in protest against the Warsaw Pact invasion (which ended the Prague Spring) and other symbolic places were oppressively monitored.

Not everybody was resigned to the status quo. There were courageous dissidents in the East, and in the West, including my high school's Prague-born headmaster. When the Polish regime cracked down on the Solidarność (Solidarity) movement in fall 1981, our headmaster organized a food parcel campaign to benefit the needy in Poland. When the Czech dissidents involved in Charta 77 were hit by a wave of arrests, the school sent intellectual sustenance to Czechoslovakia: parcels of books containing banned literature, collected and packed by our class. Contrary to Czech author Milan Kundera's accusation in his 1983 essay "The Tragedy of Central Europe," then, the countries beyond the bloc boundary had not been completely forgotten.[2] But more important than this Western aid, in a historical perspective, was the fact that the Eastern Bloc societies were shifting ever closer to the West. An increasing number of Poles, Hungarians, and Czechs traveled to Western Europe under the policy of détente, some as tourists, like our friends from Kraków, and others on business.

Although they saw how much richer the West was, the postwar boom had, in fact, already ended. Some countries in the West were wrestling with currency vagaries (the US dollar came under strong pressure in the 1970s; Great Britain needed to be bailed out by an IMF rescue package in 1976), rising unemployment, and spiraling national deficits, which in turn fueled inflation. Economists in the East closely observed the crisis of the West. As the later reform politicians Václav Klaus and Leszek Balcerowicz noted with interest, it prompted an international paradigm shift in economic policy away from Keynesianism, which was considered to have failed, and toward monetarism—steering the economy by means of money supply, controlled by central banks. Following the election victories of Margaret Thatcher and Ronald Reagan, the UK and US governments set about privatizing state enterprises, liberalizing previously regulated sectors (such as banks and the stock exchange), and generally withdrawing from the economy.[3] Their actions serve as a rough definition of neoliberalism, which then became a major factor driving European history, first in the United Kingdom, then in the postcommunist East, reaching Western Europe after a slight delay and eventually the Mediterranean South. In the eighties even Social Democrat–ruled countries such as West Germany started discussing cuts in social spending. After two severe recessions, there was a growing sense of crisis in all Western countries.

But the Eastern Bloc's problems were more obvious and more fundamental. The constant shortfalls in supply, the conspicuous injustices, and the growing economic gulf between East and West were among the factors that confounded communism (the ideology) and state socialism (the practice). But before 1989, neither the experts on Eastern Europe, who will play an important part in this book, nor the acquaintances I made on further trips behind the Iron Curtain predicted that the end was near. As a student, I advanced from investing in ice cream to selling or bartering packets of nylon pantyhose and music cassettes. This enabled me to finance a number of carefree "East-side" vacations spent in interesting conversation. Even in the summer of 1989, almost all Western Sovietologists were convinced of the permanence of the Cold War constellation and the Soviet Union. It is easy to criticize this misjudgment with the wisdom of hindsight. But it is more rewarding to think back to explore the complexities and contingencies of the period. The challenge is to take from these an explanation for the sudden collapse of the old order in 1989–91 and its consequences for Western Europe.

Underneath the surface, political unrest was brewing throughout the Eastern Bloc. It was perceptible even in oppressively controlled Czechoslovakia. During one of my visits, timed to coincide with the May 1 celebrations in 1989, a counterdemonstration suddenly emerged from the official rally on Prague's Václavské Náměstí (Wenceslas Square) when protesters started shouting antiregime slogans. But before the security forces could intervene, the renegades had merged back into the ranks behind the red flags and banners of Marx, Engels, and Lenin. That evening there was heavy rioting; the police cracked down with brute force on the demonstrators. Nevertheless, the opposition kept up its strategy of nonviolence, and fortunately did so again in the fall. Although the city centers were full of security forces, militia, and secret police, many of whom were recognizable by their leather jackets and alcohol-puffed faces, there were not enough of them to subdue or arrest several hundred thousand demonstrators. That fall more than a quarter of a century ago, the crowd had an irresistible, magnetic force.

Yet in early November the Wenceslas Square protesters and I, their Western guest, could not be certain that all the men in uniform and leather jackets would continue to simply look on. The intense atmosphere of tension bonded complete strangers. In late November, when a happy end was on the horizon, the collective sense of relief and joy was correspondingly huge. The mood in Prague was like that of a school graduation party: we had passed the test; the old authorities had no more to say; the world was our oyster. It seemed as if anything was possible.[4]

But the exhilaration soon gave way to disillusionment. This was especially noticeable in the winter of 1989–90 in Berlin, which I visited after the revolution in Prague. West Berliners complained about all the newcomers from the East, jamming the streets with their stinking cars and buying up all the supermarket stock. Suddenly the tables were turned—Westerners now had to stand in line themselves. Meanwhile, postcommunist societies faced a different category of problems. In Poland, hyperinflation obliterated the population's złoty savings and reduced real incomes—the "real" aspect in this case being their value in foreign currencies—to the equivalent of less than fifty dollars a month. With less foreign debt, Czechoslovakia was not immediately compelled to introduce radical reforms. But the cancellation of food subsidies caused 50-percent price rises for dairy products and vegetables, and around 30 percent for bread.[5] In East Germany (GDR), hundreds of factories stopped production and dismissed their staff. Yet economic collapse did not lead to the "third way" between capitalism and socialism that some former dissidents had hoped for. In 1990, socialism was too unpopular to win any elections or loans from the West.

By the early nineties, a political and economic movement toward neoliberal economic policy had emerged in almost all postcommunist countries. It was supported by the countries west of the now-perforated Iron Curtain, whose societies were not aware of the far-reaching implications of this paradigm shift. Their governments glossed over the potential pitfalls with grand promises of prosperity for all. A good example was German chancellor Helmut Kohl's promise of "flourishing landscapes" in East Germany. This slogan helped him to win the first federal elections in 1990, but became the butt of jokes in later years in view of all the difficulties besetting the East, and soon the former West of Germany. As far as Western observers were concerned, the countries in transition were still on the other side of the Iron Curtain, which had perhaps thinned but not yet been raised. Social science scholarship reserved the term "transition" and the more encompassing "transformation" for the eastern half of Europe. Thus Western governments, scholars, and commentators implied that Eastern Europe needed to profoundly change, whereas the West could remain more or less as it was. In the light of earlier revolutionary periods, such as those after 1789, 1848, and 1917, they were effectively pursuing a strategy of containment.

This book narrates and analyzes contemporary European history from a different vantage point. Instead of dealing with

Eastern Europe as a territorial container and enclosed system, it shows how the changes after the fall of the Berlin Wall affected and "cotransformed" Western and eventually southern Europe. This has also informed the intinerary by which the reader travels through Europe and its most recent history. This is not an occidentalist history of Europe like a great number of older books, which Norman Davies once mocked as "Euro-history." It is, rather, a European history narrated from an Eastern angle, from the perspective of the peoples who ended communism, tore down the Wall, and then underwent unprecedented political, social, and economic change. Hence the reader will find more information on the history of Poland and Germany than on, for instance, France. But obviously no history of Europe can cover the entire continent equally and exhaustively.

While the West lived under the illusion that it would remain more or less unchanged by the breakdown of state socialism, the effects of the "shock therapy" in Eastern Europe soon became apparent in Poland. On a visit to my Kraków friends in fall 1991, I found the city with its half a million inhabitants shrouded in an acrid brown haze. The cause was the Nowa Huta steelworks. But people were glad the chimneys were puffing away because the factory was at least a source of employment. There were only three restaurants open in the evening in the city center, as few residents could afford to eat out. Stores were empty, no longer because of a lack of supplies, but because of low demand. Hardly anybody had money to spend. The only thriving segment was the farmers' markets, offering onions, potatoes, and other basic foodstuffs at low prices. Was this the new order that the proponents of free market economy had promised? Where were the economic reforms supposed to be heading?

Let's take one last leap in time to the boom years after EU enlargement: Warsaw, Kraków, Prague, and Berlin all have consumer palaces, seas of illuminated advertisements, and a constant hum of background noise from the heavy traffic and music emanating from bars and stores, open until well into the night. Is this still Eastern Europe, or has it blended into the West? The soundscapes are the same; so are the visual stimuli. But driving cross-country between the cities, one sees a different picture. Empty apartment blocks and derelict factories bear witness to earlier attempts to create a socialist modernity. Aging and shrinking village populations give little cause for optimism about the future.

This close juxtaposition of affluence and poverty, urban boom and rural stagnation, is no longer a feature of the former Eastern Bloc alone. Europe is rife with growing regional and social disparities in the West as in the East (as is also true of the United States). Many towns in (West) Germany's former industrial heart, the Ruhr region, are as gray today as the stereotypical image of communist towns. Is there a connection between the upswing in parts of Eastern Europe and the crisis in regions of the West? This issue is also addressed below: United Germany, Austria, Sweden, and Finland were all directly affected by the post-1989 reforms and resultant economic competition from Eastern Europe. To an extent, these countries were compelled to reinvent themselves. Germany in particular underwent a process of cotransformation that transcended the Cold War boundaries.

The aftershocks were weaker in the countries of southern Europe. At first they seemed largely unaffected by the opening of Europe, riding out the 1990s and the introduction of the euro in 2001. But since the euro crisis that erupted in 2010, developments there have echoed those in Eastern Europe. Many reforms prescribed to Greece, Italy, Spain, and Portugal for privatization, liberalization, and deregulation recall the neoliberal cuts in postcommunist Europe. Will the South become the new East? This question addresses the very recent past, which is usually avoided by historians. But the extent and duration of the great recession after the stock market crash of 2008–9 and its consequences for society are comparable with the situation in Eastern Europe in the nineties. One difference is that rising unemployment and increasing poverty in Southern Europe have so far affected the young much more than the older generations. Exploring such contrasts and analogies has been a motivation to continue this book's exploration into the recent past.

Since the crisis of 2008–9, neoliberal doctrine has come under widespread criticism. But it should not be forgotten that the

economic changes in the former Eastern Bloc created many opportunities, especially in the urban centers. It would be wrong,
then, to polemically write off the entire project. Nevertheless, it
is undeniable that the situation in rural areas and in the successor
states of the Soviet Union took a dramatic downturn. (The Baltic
states have undergone a unique development; they must be considered separately and not as part of the post-Soviet world.)

Because of the wide range of regional differences, it is not easy
to come to a general conclusion about the neoliberal reforms in
Europe. And any contemporary balance sheet would certainly be
different from one drawn before the outbreak of the great recession sparked in 2008–9. While postcommunist transformation was
regarded as a success some years ago—and a requirement for accession to the European Union in 2004—the economies of countries such as Latvia, Lithuania, Hungary, Romania, and Bulgaria
were in deep decline. Yet so was neoliberal doctrine. In the early
nineties, Western experts assumed that the development of market economy and democracy were interconnected and interdepen-
dent. Now this premise is challenged. Perhaps neoliberal reforms
and "shock therapy" could only be implemented in the postcommunist countries precisely because they were not yet full-fledged
democracies. These nations encountered little organized protest;
if one did arise, it was quickly quashed. Although there was no
scenario to compare with Pinochet's Chile, neoliberalism in Eastern Europe was not entirely democratic. Of course, the new order
had its supporters. The younger generation in 1989 had unimag-
ined opportunities for advancement and profited from the newly
opened borders in Europe. By contrast, the over-forties, who were
tied down by family commitments and less flexible about employment, often struggled to adapt, or were immediately hit by social
cuts and layoffs.

Individual experience and exposure are key to forming opinions and a basic requirement for good academic work. Yet it is
often hidden behind a façade of objectivity and rarely made explicit in the fields of economics or political science. Contemporary
history, in particular, is influenced by the personal experiences
and memories of those writing it. Hence the eyewitness is not the

historian's foe, as is sometimes claimed. First-hand experience such as the present author gained can shed a different light on seemingly universal developments and conventional wisdom. I am therefore making my experiences explicit, in the light of ethnological and anthropological writings on "fieldwork."

A specificity of this form of participating historical observation is the passage of time. Temporal distance brings mixed blessings: on the one hand, memories become increasingly blurred the further the processes and events in question recede into the past. While I remember the black market exchange rate for the Czechoslovakian crown in 1988, I have forgotten the conversion rate for the Polish "ice cream currency" of 1977. But on the other hand, it is much easier to understand and evaluate completed processes. When Tony Judt wrote *Postwar*, his masterful synthesis of recent European history, it was clear that the Cold War and other central factors defining the period had ended more than a decade earlier. Temporal proximity certainly helped him to conceptualize the book as he did. Writing about an epoch soon after its close is also helpful for conducting oral history interviews. Yet where contemporary events are concerned, the historian acts only as a chronicler. The best practice is probably to combine the analysis of recent and more distant periods of time, or at least to keep "deep" historical knowledge in mind.

What appear to be new and even exciting developments often turn out to be a repetition of previous patterns. Consider this example: Since the crisis of 2008–9, which Europe has not yet overcome, economic cuts and reforms have often been presented to the public as "necessary," "unavoidable," and "the only alternative." The echoes of the Thatcherite slogan "There is no alternative" (parodied with the acronym TINA) will be unmistakable to anyone who lived in England in the eighties, or Poland in the nineties, or Germany in the new millennium. This mode of public debate can be situated within the larger context of neoliberal discourses. They are of course familiar to the West, but were particularly pronounced in postcommunist transition countries, which therefore deserve special attention in this consideration of the most recent period of European history. Neoliberalism has relied on a certain rhetorical toolkit to legitimize radical reforms, social cuts, and other controversial policies. This book devotes much attention to neoliberal discourse, the analysis of which can be more revealing than the assessment of quantitative data. Percentages and growth statistics should always be interpreted with a grain of salt.

The manner in which systems changed from the 1980s on depended to a large degree on the way societies, social groups, and individuals adjusted to enormous challenges. Individual adaptation to the new neoliberal order can also be termed "self-transformation." The "heroes" of the present book are not the handful of reform politicians, but the millions of individuals who managed to cope with the rapidly changing environment, support their families on monthly incomes of the equivalent of one or two hundred US dollars, and still look ahead with vitality and optimism. Europe today seems almost to have lost this sense of possibility and confidence in the future. Perhaps the Eastern European experiences of the early nineties can be useful for dealing with the present-day economic and social crises. Although these are certainly severe, especially in Greece, other societies can be shown to have overcome similar circumstances in quite recent history.

## Postrevolutionary Europe

At what point does a period of time become an epoch in history? When does it leave the present and become historical? Though contemporary history can be defined as the "epoch of the still living,"[6] the death of pertinent actors can also be a reference point. Margaret Thatcher and Ronald Reagan, the earlier protagonists of neoliberalism, have died. So has Milton Friedman, the economist who paved the way for their policies. The ranks of 1989's revolutionaries are thinning out. The prominent civil rights activists Václav Havel, Jiří Dienstbier, Bronisław Geremek, and Tadeusz Mazowiecki have all passed away in recent years. The political leaders who allowed the turnaround to happen are also passing into history. Mikhail Gorbachev is over eighty; many other former reform communists have already died. Younger generations

Fig. 1.1. Fall of the Berlin Wall on November 9, 1989: people celebrating by the Brandenburg Gate. Photo: ullstein bild / imageBROKER / Norbert Michalke.

are, of course, also affected by the inexorable passing of time. Those who filled the streets of Warsaw, Budapest, East Berlin, and Prague in fall 1989, and Kyiv (as the Ukrainian capital has been named since the country gained independence) and Moscow in 1991, have now entered middle age. The demonstrations in fall 1989, the rejoicing when the communists stepped down, the excitement at the first free elections—this all seems very distant, not least because so much changed during the nineties, not only in the lives of the over 330 million citizens of postcommunist countries in Europe but ultimately for all Europeans.

The gaps left by actors' passing and memories fading are filled with political interpretations of history. At the 2009 celebrations marking the twentieth anniversary of the revolution, the political elites across Europe paid respect to the courage of the dissidents and demonstrators in 1989 and their achievements of liberty and democracy. In Berlin, a symbolic wall was created out of polystyrene blocks, decorated by artists, that were then knocked down consecutively like falling dominos. In this way, 1989 was staged as a foundational moment for united Germany and a united Europe.[7]

Some years ago, academic discussion of the events of 1989 and the subsequent reforms entered the realm of historical debate. Twenty years after the Iron Curtain was torn down, scholars began discussing whether the changes thus initiated could be considered a revolution at all. They also asked which approach to reforms had been more successful: "shock therapy" or the gradual reorganization of economy, government, and society. These historical inquiries have gained contemporary relevance because the same repertoire of reforms has been revived by the European Union, the International Monetary Fund (IMF), the World Bank, and local experts for use in crisis-torn Southern Europe. Germany's cotransformation began as early as 2001, when social-democratic chancellor Gerhard Schröder was in power.

As a university lecturer, I have noticed the topic's transition into history because of my students' questions and backgrounds. Almost all of my students in recent years were born after 1989. They do not remember the Berlin Wall, the border lined with spring guns, the hundreds of thousands of secret service spies, or a political system to rival liberal democracy. Although the subsequent neoliberal reforms changed Europeans' lives in many ways, bringing freedom to travel, open borders, increased—though unequally distributed—affluence, and stronger economic competition in many fields, historical research on the epoch is still in its infancy.

This book starts by tracing the chronological development of neoliberal Europe. The ground was prepared for 1989 by the reform debates of the eighties in Eastern and Western Europe. The book proposes that the combination of these debates, the failure of gradual reforms in the Eastern Bloc, and the end of system rivalry resulted in a hegemony of neoliberalism, first among economic experts, and later in a wider political arena. The Cold War and its end in Europe are explored in a separate section. The revolutions that occurred in 1989–91 are analyzed in the light of their specific qualities and causes (see chapter 3). Next, the focus is placed on the course and results of the subsequent transformation—a term that is usually used in the singular even though the postcommunist countries evolved in quite different ways. This is not surprising in view of their number, their varying precommunist histories, and the differences in the duration and character of communist rule within them. It is more surprising that the area referred to as Eastern Europe or the "Eastern Bloc" during the Cold War is still often treated as a cohesive unit in the social sciences.

The fifth chapter of this book explores the growing differences within the postcommunist countries caused by the new neoliberal order.[8] The urban economic growth centers and the rural areas that fell far behind as a result of the reforms are literally worlds apart. This discrepancy is considered in a section titled "Rich Cities, Poor Regions." Even today, one need only drive fifty miles beyond Berlin, Warsaw, or Budapest into the country to see the differences. But appearances can be misleading. By way of comparison, the book also refers to extensive statistical material, including information from the EU statistical agency Eurostat, the World Bank, the Organisation for Economic Co-operation and Development (OECD), the IMF, and various government agencies and national banks. A list of all the databases consulted would outstretch the book's scope, but they are referenced in the endnotes, mostly with keywords to facilitate further research on the internet.[9] Processing the—sometimes conflicting—information from these databases is complicated by the fact that they are based on different premises, and tend to be constructed along strictly national lines. In any case, statistics do not say much about people's everyday lives. Hence, they are combined here with archival material (from city administrations, for example), expert opinions, newspaper reports, and other media sources, as well as personal observations by the author.[10]

Regional divergence has been accompanied by convergence on an international level. This is demonstrated by a comparison of the cities of Warsaw, Prague, Budapest, Berlin, and Vienna. Bratislava (despite its smaller population of around four hundred thousand) and the Ukrainian capital Kyiv are also considered, as post-Soviet examples. West Berlin and Vienna were not part of the Eastern Bloc but are included here nevertheless. More than twenty-five years after the end of the Cold War, the mental mapping it generated should be revised and new spatial perspectives allowed. It is time to jump the wall that divided Europe for many decades.

The city comparison also reveals that the German capital, which believed itself to be fast evolving from "a city to a global city to a metropolis,"[11] was outpaced in the East Central European economic stakes by Prague and Warsaw in 2007–8. This is shown by various indicators such as per capita gross domestic product, unemployment rates, and population development.[12] Yet the same indicators show that in the early nineties Berlin had been well ahead of the capital cities in Eastern Europe. Why did it fall behind for two decades? What does this tell us about Germany's *Sonderweg*, or special path of transformation? Berlin-bashing, a popular sport in unified Germany, is not a concern of the present author. Rather, the aim of this book is to critically examine this transformation. As developments in the various capital cities are analyzed, a picture emerges of very different consequences of neoliberalism from country to country, region to region, and even town to town. It also emerges that the impact of reforms was by no means confined to Eastern Europe, but caused major changes west of the former Iron Curtain as well.

## Neoliberalism on the Rise

The origins of neoliberalism lie in the late interwar and early postwar period. In 1947, the liberal economist Friedrich von Hayek gathered together a group of like-minded acquaintances near Mont Pèlerin at Lake Geneva in Switzerland to devise an alternative economic model to Soviet planned economy and the Keynesian welfare state. The enigmatic international circle of thinkers that became the Mont Pèlerin Society agreed on the central goals of promoting free market economy, free competition (it applied the concept of freedom primarily to the economy), and limiting government to its basic functions. It developed its standpoint in reaction to the nascent Cold War—the influential public intellectual Walter Lippmann, who had coined this term, was among the founding members—and the long-term dominance of the Roosevelt New Deal and state interventionism in Western economic policy.[13] Initially, the Mont Pèlerin Society was widely viewed as renegade.

Until the 1970s, economics were shaped by Paul Samuelson's "neoclassical synthesis"—his writings still count among the standard reference works on economics today—which followed on from Keynesian theory.[14] But "stagflation" (low economic growth rates in combination with high inflation) after the oil crisis and rising national budget deficits put the Keynesians in the United States and the United Kingdom, and, a little later, in continental Europe, on the defensive. An increasing number of economists challenged the idea of state interventionism and advocated a supply-oriented economic policy and monetarism. Under this system, independent central banks were supposed to steer the economy and combat inflation by controlling the supply of money.

This paradigm shift was largely propelled by the Chicago School following Milton Friedman, a supporter of Hayek and longtime member of the Mont Pèlerin Society. The Chicago School's theories hinge on belief in the efficiency of the markets and the rationality of market participants. These tenets were inscribed in the Washington Consensus, devised in 1989 as a form of crisis intervention to stabilize the economies of debt-ridden countries by means of strict austerity policies. The architects included the World Bank, the IMF, the US Treasury Department, and senior members of the US Congress. Originally tailored for the economically ailing countries of Latin America, it was later applied dogmatically to the postcommunist countries. It would go beyond the scope of this book to reproduce all ten economic commandments contained in the Washington Consensus (in a Decalogue written by economist John Williamson). In summation, the central goal was the triad of liberalization, deregulation, and privatization. Foreign direct investments and financial capitalism were also important ingredients in its global economic recipe.[15] Of course, even in the nineties there were critics of the Washington Consensus and the Chicago School. But they were firmly in the minority—until the New York stock market crash of

2008 and the outbreak of the world economic crisis. Joseph E. Stiglitz has attacked what he branded "market fundamentalism" (the belief in self-regulating and balancing markets) and the over-emphasis on private property and faith in the rationality of market participants.[16]

Yet neoliberalism is a hard concept to define. Having coined the term by means of the prefix "neo," to indicate a departure from the failed laissez-faire liberalism of the interwar period and the world economic crisis of 1929, its proponents did not identify with it beyond the early postwar period. Even Milton Friedman distanced himself from the term; John Williamson, too, dismissed it as nothing more than a political battle cry.[17] Critics of neoliberalism are, then, attacking a slippery fish that contemporary economists and politicians do not like to be associated with. However, neoliberal theory and policies have been advocated by a range of different actors, from professors at small colleges and renowned universities to major think tanks such as the conservative Heritage Foundation in the United States, and powerful politicians. Dieter Plehwe has asserted, "hegemonial neoliberalism must be conceived of in plural terms as a political philosophy and a political practice."[18] It is a moving target that is constantly being changed and adapted, which is precisely why it is so effective.

It would be wrong, then, to portray neoliberalism in a historical perspective as a homogenous, coherent concept. Its chief proponents frequently disagreed on issues such as the role of central banks (which is central to monetarism but hard to reconcile with minimal state intervention) and the implementation of shock therapies. As well as disagreements on theory, deviations in practice had perhaps an even greater impact. Even Thatcherism and Reaganomics showed unintended effects, as did the radical reforms in postcommunist Europe, which had to be followed by a number of corrections and adjustments. Neoliberal theory and rhetoric is one thing, neoliberal practice quite another. Many soapbox speeches were held in postcommunist Europe in order to entice—or pacify—international creditors and investors. But in practice, economies were driven largely by compromise and pragmatism. Nevertheless, all postcommunist countries eventually jumped on the neoliberal bandwagon and introduced radical economic reforms, some earlier, some (such as unified Germany) later.

This neoliberal hegemony can be compared on an abstract level with nationalism, the most successful ideology of the nineteenth century. Nationalism was also ideologically nebulous, advocated by a wide range of actors, and adaptable to completely different setups: to the requirements of stateless national movements as well as to those of large empires; to rural and industrial societies. Yet two ideological goals always remained central: the creation of statehood (or reinforcing the power of the extant state) and the greatest possible congruence between the state and the nation. Neoliberalism's ideological benchmarks were the primacy of the economy, minimal government intervention in business (one of the motives behind extensive privatization), and a concept of humans as *homo oeconomicus*. In another parallel, few advocates of these ideologies called themselves nationalists or neoliberals, respectively. These attributes were considered pejorative. But nationalism research, which uses the term in a neutral sense, has made an important contribution to our understanding of the ideology that shaped an epoch of history (the "long" nineteenth century). Like research into neoliberalism, it began contemporaneously, with the first scholarly studies on nationalism appearing in the 1930s. Those early publications are of course now outdated, as one day this book will be. But regardless of what the future brings, historical inquiries and surveys are useful tools for orientation. Without them, it would be difficult to understand contemporary Europe and its most recent history.

Today, the term "neoliberalism" is often used as a catchall for aggressive, right-wing economic policy. Sometimes neoliberalism is confused with neoconservatism, which George W. Bush advocated during his controversial presidency. He stood for the postwar, Anglo-Saxon Protestant ideal of traditional family values and small-town life—a worldview that would have been quite alien to European neoliberals such as Friedrich von Hayek. But neoliberals and neoconservatives such as Francis Fukuyama have one thing in common: the teleological conviction that a democratic order based on Western-style market economy marks the "end of history."

This book is not a fashionably fundamental critique of neoliberalism but a study of its application and social consequences. The postcommunist countries served as experimentation sites for neoliberal policy. This is not to say that they faithfully swallowed all neoliberal prescriptions.[19] The governments of Eastern Europe developed their own neoliberal methods and put them into practice. The history of "transformation" can therefore provide insight into how neoliberalism was implemented and how it eventually changed the actions, values, and everyday lives of the people affected.

## Europe in Transformation

In the United States today, it is still more common to refer to postcommunist change as a transition than a transformation. In some respects interchangeable, the two terms nevertheless accentuate different aspects. The term transition is borrowed from the Spanish word "transición" as used by Juan Linz and other political scientists to refer to the establishment of democracy after dictatorship and the demise of the military regimes in post-Franco Spain and South America.[20] An academic discipline of transitology has emerged, focusing on democratic consolidation and political value changes in societies formerly ruled by dictators. After the events of 1989, economists David Lipton and Jeffrey Sachs published an article in the magazine *Foreign Affairs* pleading the case for "dual transition" in Eastern Europe following Poland's example. By this, they meant establishing market economy, which they regarded as essential for democracy.[21] This dual telos of planned economy to market economy (the first dimension of transition) and dictatorship to democracy (the second dimension) reflected the dominant trend in contemporary thought, also represented by Francis Fukuyama's aforementioned essay.

The changes began to be termed transformation by social scientists, mostly in Europe, who were more skeptical of untrammeled market economy and wanted to draw attention to the social dimensions of the changes. As this book aims to explore the bigger picture, it, too, uses the term transformation. The state of research in the field cannot be given in a nutshell; suffice it to say that its focus has shifted over time. Initially, political system change and the consolidation of democracy were the main objects of investigation. Later, economic reforms and privatization with all its side effects, such as corruption and mass unemployment, began to garner scholarly interest. During the nineties, the processes by which states were rebuilt (the third dimension of the transformation) were more intensively researched. Most recently, the focus has shifted to the fourth dimension: the influence of external actors such as the World Bank, the IMF and the European Union.[22]

This broad field of research has produced an enormous yield of facts, data, and analyses that are invaluable to historical study. But it should be borne in mind that contemporary writers were at least indirectly influenced by the hegemony of neoliberalism, if not always convinced by it as an ideology. These scholars and theorists were often employed as political and economic advisers and played their part in steering the course of transformation. Publications of the time should therefore be regarded as part of the transformation discourse and as historical sources requiring critical appraisal.

As well as considering neighboring disciplines in the social sciences, this book extends the conventional timescale. The year 1989 is often regarded as a kind of "year zero." Indeed, it was one of the most important caesuras in modern European history. But successful businessmen and convinced supporters of democracy did not suddenly mushroom in Eastern Europe that year. The dysfunctionality of planned economy, resulting in widespread scarcity, forced growing sections of Eastern Bloc societies to start playing the market some time before 1989. The human capital comprising these actors cannot be measured in the same way as economic data. Yet it was crucial for transformation and helps to explain why, for example, Poland experienced an "economic miracle" and other countries did not. Hence it seems a good idea not to fixate on the caesura of 1989, which was just the start of a

revolutionary phase that lasted de facto until 1991. Taking continuities and longer-term influences from the period of state socialism and even the precommunist era into consideration helps us
to understand the different paths of development, some far more
dynamic than others, of the various countries and regions.

The book will also endeavor to broaden some spatial horizons.
Previously, the transformation has been viewed within a territorial
container, defined by spatial concepts such as "Eastern Europe." A
few scholars, chiefly political scientists, have compared the political system change in Eastern Europe with developments in South
America and other parts of the world. (See, for example, Samuel
Huntington's *The Third Wave*, a classic work on the three waves of
democratization.)[23] But by and large, the Cold War boundary dividing Europe into East and West has remained strangely intact in
the minds of academics. Only East Germany got out of the box,
because it was absorbed into the prosperous West when Germany
unified. Yet it is more accurate to regard the Federal Republic of
Germany (FRG) as another country in economic transformation,
even if neoliberal reform debates reached West Germany only in
the late 1990s—around a decade later than in the postcommunist
world.

As the reforms progressed and the European Union enlarged,
the terms transformation and transition lost some of their earlier
allure. Padraic Kenney was the first historian to draw a provisional
balance sheet of the transformation era.[24] For historians, whose
métier is analyzing the changes that occur over time, the term
transformation is only useful when applied in a specific sense. In
a historical perspective, transformation denotes the especially far-
reaching, extensive, and accelerated change of a political system,
economy, and society.

As mentioned above, such changes began before the revolutions of 1989. Yet this caesura should not be played down. Charles
Tilly, like the sociologist Theda Skocpol, ranks it among the great
European revolutions.[25] The essential difference between 1989
and 1789, 1848, and 1917 was its predominant lack of violence
and willful destruction. Insofar as violence was used in 1989, as in
Romania, Soviet Lithuania, and Georgia and, most notoriously,

on Tiananmen Square in Beijing, it was used as an instrument of power, wielded by counterrevolutionaries. In some respects, then, the radical changes of 1989–91, which ended with the collapse of the Soviet Union and the independence of its constituent republics, conflicted with the traditional concept of revolution.

The sociologist Zygmunt Bauman has linked the two phases of revolution and transformation by emphasizing the strong drive for political and social nation-building among the revolutionary elites of 1989.[26] In this way, he places the transformation in a temporal continuum of sequential action, following on from the preceding revolutions in all their different guises. Hence the transformation can be regarded as a process of postrevolutionary change. Of course, the results of this change differed within the Eastern Bloc, from country to country, and especially within each country. That is the main subject of this book.

Such variance also existed in earlier revolutionary periods, such as the late eighteenth century and after World War I. The American Revolution is an example of a partial change. The founding fathers of the United States created a new state and political system but only slightly altered the social order. Nevertheless, according to Hannah Arendt, among others, there is good cause to regard the War for American Independence as a revolution.[27] Despite the considerable distance in time and space, the events of 1776 show a certain similarity with developments in 1989 on the other side of the Atlantic. Both revolutions marked the establishment of constitutional democracies as one of their most important results. Neither ended in orgies of violence or mass terror, as in France after 1789 or Russia after 1917. The price for this was the survival, relatively unharmed, of some sections of the old elites. In some countries they were even able to return to positions of power. But this does not mean that revolution must entail extreme violence to be real. The bloody French and Russian revolutions, for example, produced surprising continuities with regard to imperial, autocratic rule. While such aspects are open to debate, it remains undisputable that the revolutions of 1989–91 and the postrevolutionary transformation are comparable with earlier processes of similar importance.

As in the case of earlier revolutions, it does not make much sense to identify a certain point in time as the zero hour. To understand the American Revolution, one must consider the period before 1776 and the British Empire's ongoing struggle with political representation and participation in its transatlantic colonies, which were developing economically and socially at a dynamic pace. Alexis de Tocqueville's and Edmund Burke's observations on the French Revolution also begin with comprehensive analyses of the preceding regimes.[28] Transformation was, then, never exclusively postrevolutionary, but gained a new dynamic with each revolutionary upheaval.

German sociologist Claus Offe has proposed that the synchrony of change in the state, economy, and society is an additional element defining transformation.[29] Offe in turn owed a certain debt to Reinhart Koselleck, one of the most distinguished German historians of the postwar era, who dealt intensively with the (a)synchrony and temporality of historical processes. Indeed, a distinctive concept of time prevailed in the transformation epoch—the sense of time racing, and one historic moment following the next. History unfolded at a breathtaking pace between 1989 and 1991, similarly to the years following World War I, when Polish writer Maria Dąbrowska noted a sense of acceleration. In her Warsaw diary of 1918–19, she wrote: "One wakes up and finds oneself in another state, another life."[30]

It is striking how often politicians and intellectuals spoke of *historic* moments, events, missions, and breaks with the past in 1989. The Canadian writer Douglas Coupland parodied what he saw as tediously frequent references to history as "historical overdosing"[31] in his novel *Generation X*, published in 1991. Commentators went into overdrive in an attempt to capture the increasingly transient present. But for most of the postcommunist elites, history was no more than a negative background to contemporary developments. The communist era was demonized in the same way as the ancien régime in France after 1789 and the Habsburg, Romanov, and Ottoman Empires after their falls in 1918.

Equally, the period after 1989 was full of visions of future glory. The general tone of contemporary discourse was that the historic opportunity to usher in a future of liberty and prosperity was there to be seized. Ultimately, this call to historic action served to gloss over the rather gloomy present. Like all revolutionary events, those of 1989 occurred in connection with, and almost inevitably compounded, economic crises. The prevalent concept of time in 1989 and the early nineties is part of the transformation discourse that this book seeks to investigate in the context of neoliberal developments. As well as the course of reforms, growth statistics, and other "hard facts" of transformation, it will consider legitimizing strategies, semantics, and meanings in the sense of New Cultural History.[32]

This book is the product of years of scholarly interest.[33] It builds on my own personal experience of the Velvet Revolution, my many years' professional activity in the Czech Republic and Poland in the nineties, my extended research visits and trips to Ukraine, Russia, and the Caucasus, and academic cooperation with Eastern European colleagues. It was thanks to the changes of 1989–91 that this wide world was open to me at all. Strangely, no concept of a generation of 1989 has emerged, although many young protesters from that fall and the ensuing months of high hopes and idealism certainly perceived themselves as such. Unlike the generation of 1968 or 1848, they have not been immortalized in print. Any sense of generational community has since been weakened by the rapid pace of change, the divergent experiences of transformation depending on individuals' gender and social background, and the sobering results of the changes in the early 1990s. It is the task of contemporary history to explore these subjective, individual experiences more closely than does mainstream transformation research, which has dealt primarily with states and economies on a macro level.

What does it mean for a historian to tackle a domain of social science? The more recent the historical period in question, the more sociologists, political scientists, anthropologists and proponents of other branches of the social sciences will be investigating it. This changes the role of historical science, and especially hermeneutics, the methodology of text interpretation. On the premise that reality in the modern world is a construct, the media are an important source. Neoliberalism, which has ideological characteristics but not the coherence of Marxism or other "classic" ideologies, was made and conveyed by the media. A critical examination of neoliberal discourses is therefore essential for any historical survey. Reviewing past research, such as interviews conducted by social scientists thirty or forty years ago, can also be very fruitful. A closer look at everyday life in the 1970s and 1980s shows "real existing socialism" to have been not as gray or stagnant as the politburos of the time but the seedbed of a long period of change.

While some things become clearer as the events recede further into the past, other aspects are clouded. It seems to go without saying that the opinions of today's historians on neoliberal transformation have no impact on the process itself. But this was not true of earlier social-scientific transformation research, which has now become historical, too. Many economists and sociologists dealing with postcommunist Europe in the nineties acted as political advisers and influenced the course of reforms with their expert opinions. The US economist Jeffrey Sachs was the archetypal analyst-reformer. Active first in Poland, then Russia (officially named the Russian Federation since 1991) and elsewhere as an economic adviser, he was one of the architects of the "shock therapy." Sachs and the *Brygada Marriotta*, as the Western experts were ironically dubbed (after the swish Warsaw hotel in which they resided), stood out for their disarming self-confidence. A Harvard professor, Sachs's absolute faith in the market made his prescription for improving the present and the future irresistible. It was characteristic of the neoliberal epoch that one country after the next adopted very similar economic models and reform packages, as Sachs advised. He and his fellow experts obviously expected the standard formulae to work equally well wherever they were applied.

But the reforms had very different outcomes. For around the last fifteen years, the various resultant economic orders have been analyzed under the banner of "varieties of capitalism." They are considered here in chapter 4.[34] Rather than following the social-science model of investigation, taking a top-down approach to focus on the ideology's embeddedness in institutions and abstract economic data, the aim here is to provide a historical narrative of transformation from the bottom up. The book sets out to guide the reader through neoliberal Europe, for the most part chronologically, and across various spatial configurations (transnational regions, states, intranational regions, and cities).

Another characteristic of neoliberalism is the aforementioned fixation on private ownership. Considered an essential pillar of market economy,[35] it went hand in hand with an aversion to big government, which was regarded as stifling and oppressive—as state socialism had demonstrated on the extreme end of the scale. While privatization became a top political priority in the former GDR and Czechoslovak Socialist Republic (ČSSR), with the former country pursuing restitution rather than the sale of nationalized property wherever possible, it was slowed down in Poland in the mid-nineties. To this day, much of the property nationalized by the communists remains in state hands. But Poland is nevertheless a functioning market economy. The history of the last twenty-five years, then, seems to challenge the dogma of privatization. When addressing questions such as these, contemporary history should resist the temptation to simply invert arguments. Russia is a reminder that this does not always work: here, the purchase and sale of state-owned real estate was delayed until the Land Act of 2003, resulting in the neglect and decline of large stretches of rural Russia.[36]

The Budapest-based political scientists Dorothee Bohle and Béla Greskovits have identified three distinct types of systems that became established in the new European Union member states as a result of different transformational processes and outcomes: "neoliberal capitalist," "embedded neoliberal," and "corporatist."[37] Each type corresponds with a specific geographical area, namely the Baltic states, the Visegrad countries (Poland, Czechoslovakia, and Hungary, which forged an economic and political alliance in the Hungarian town of Visegrad in early 1991), and Slovenia, respectively. If one extends the model to Russia, Ukraine, Belarus, and Moldavia—that is, the European successor states of the Soviet Union—the number of neoliberal-capitalist market economies with at most rudimentary welfare states is even larger. Hence the reforms can be seen to have had a predominantly neoliberal outcome. Russia and Ukraine did not establish stable democracies; their economies are dominated by oligarchs. The "oligarchic-neoliberal" system could, then, be added to the above typology.

Since Bohle and Greskovits identified more or less neoliberal system types in all postcommunist countries, with the exception of Slovenia, the question is raised of how precise the concept is. Does it not overstretch the concept of neoliberalism to apply it to almost the entire former Eastern Bloc and beyond, indeed to the global order since the mid-eighties?[38] Have the outcomes of political and economic system change not been too various to be covered by one neoliberal umbrella? The course of reforms and the intentions of the actors involved certainly varied greatly, from country to country and year to year. Yet the basic principles inscribed in the Washington Consensus were applied across the board. Every postcommunist country in Europe attempted liberalization, deregulation, and privatization, often with unexpected consequences and ripple effects. The one common outcome in all countries prior to European Union enlargement was growing inequality on a social and spatial level. As this common ground was so predominant, it is accurate to speak of the establishment of a new, neoliberal order, despite the many differences.

While postcommunist countries and English-language scholarship continued to take a skeptical view of the welfare state, some continental European transitologists began to regard fully functioning government as a precondition for successful system change. In 2007, the most prominent German expert, Wolfgang Merkel, proposed that state continuity, especially with respect to education and social security, facilitated transformation. The Harvard-based political scientist Grzegorz Ekiert considers government reforms, such as the building of local and regional administration, to have been a key factor in Poland's rise since 1989.[39]

In this regard, one can differentiate between three groups of countries: those that enjoyed territorial continuity and whose statehood remained largely intact throughout the period 1989–91; those that emerged from collapsed empires and multinational states and had to first consolidate their (mostly weak) new statehood; and a third group struck by ethnic conflicts and violence. The civil wars in the Caucasus and the former Yugoslavia, and the bloodshed they caused among the civilian populations, overshadowed all other transformational experiences.[40] But Yugoslavia must nevertheless be included in the history of the transformation era. After all, the collapse of this multinational state was linked to disagreements over reforms. Yugoslavia, like the entire Eastern Bloc, had been in the midst of a deep economic crisis since the mid-eighties. The IMF and international creditors prescribed reforms which only some sections of the political elites accepted. Because the country was federally organized, the reforms could not be implemented. It was in the subsequent dispute over whether to extend federalization or to return to centralization that the battle lines of the future armed conflict were drawn.[41] Romania was also on the brink of civil war in 1990. In Bucharest, regime-loyal miners clashed with students and intellectuals in violent riots known as *mineriads*; interethnic conflicts also helped the postcommunists to stay in power.[42] These conflicts should not be missing from any balance sheet of transformation.

A central focus of transitology is how democracy is consolidated and political values change in postdictatorial societies. The state of research on these issues is excellent. This book will therefore concentrate mostly on questions of social history. But it also aims to shed some light on the strikingly divergent developments on the road to democracy. In East Central and Southeastern Europe, and in the Baltic states, the dominant trend was to orientate political change toward the German system of parliamentary democracy. Presidential power was curtailed and parliaments accorded greater authority. Poland, which had been at the vanguard of regime change in 1989, took a leading role again. In the countries of the former Soviet Union, by contrast, presidential systems have come to predominate. In Russia, Vladimir Putin has established an authoritarian regime.[43] This discrepancy in the outcomes of political system change shows that Samuel Huntington's "third wave of democratization" occurred unevenly, giving rise to new forms of governance that had not been anticipated in the early nineties. China and Vietnam are particularly striking examples.[44] The establishment of market economy in these countries did not lead to comprehensive democratization. Does this mean that post-communist capitalism can work without democracy? Russia, in spite of its structural problems and high dependency on oil and gas exports, seems to point in this direction. Authoritarian state capitalism has certainly become a serious rival to the West since the crisis of 2008–9 (see chapters 5 and 10).

Transitologists have approached their core fields of interest—political system change, the adoption of market economy, and the transformation of statehood—almost exclusively from a nation-state perspective. Journals such as the *Economist* and various think tanks have orchestrated a kind of international competition between nations battling toward democracy and market economy. Points are awarded for the degree to which the respective governments have achieved the targets advocated by the IMF and neoliberal think tanks. In the early nineties, the Czech Republic and Hungary were considered model transformation countries while Poland was criticized for its reliance on agriculture and general backwardness. Hence a country's level of modernization or perceived lack of sophistication was a second, rarely overtly expressed criterion for evaluation. Ironically, this continued a tendency of state socialism. The communists had made great efforts to catapult Eastern Europe to a Western level of development by forced industrialization, collectivization, and other means.[45] After 1989, "catch-up modernization" remained the primary goal, but without the utopian promise of communist paradise. The ideal now was wealth and consumerism.

At the Copenhagen summit of 2002, the European Union candidate countries were commended for having achieved the transition to market economies and democracies. This success, and European Union enlargement in the years 2004–7, posed a problem for transformation studies. It rendered a number of its research objects irrelevant, insofar as it adhered to the old backwardness paradigm. In terms of gross domestic product per capita (which is of course only one of many indicators), the wealthiest post-communist countries had already overtaken the poorest old EU member states by 2002–3. Taking only capital cities into consideration, the East caught up at an even faster pace. Far less scholarly attention was paid to this upswing than to the previous transformation crises. Perhaps contemporary academia had internalized the journalistic rule of thumb that only bad news is good news.

With the crisis of 2008–9 came the anticipated bad news. Some postcommunist countries went into recessions almost as deep as the economic collapse of 1990 or 1991, with negative growth rates of up to 18 percent. The former Eastern Bloc countries managed to overcome the crisis faster than the Southeastern European countries, albeit at the cost of more radical social cuts. The IMF now exemplifies states like Latvia as crisis-beaters to be imitated by countries such as Greece. Whether neoliberal reforms actually generated any economic growth is a question that runs through this entire book, and is discussed by the example of a number of case studies in various periods. Germany felt the impact of the second wave of neoliberalism not only from without—in economic competition from its easterly neighbor countries—but also in its adjoined Eastern half, the former GDR. Postcommunist reforms here created many new problems for the unified German state and its social security system. Strangely, this cotransformation in Germany and Europe as a whole has been very little researched. Transformation research has by and large remained a field of "area study," restricted to Eastern Europe. Even if one were to regard postcommunist transformation as completed by certain key years, such as 2004 or 2009, neoliberal reforms and post–welfare state transformation continue to be topical issues, pertinent to Southern Europe and the entire eurozone.

In this book, elements of cotransformation, or East-West transfer (terms such as "influence" and "diffusion" are too simplistic since they suggest the straightforward adoption of foreign models), are discussed predominantly in the context of contemporary German history and three main points of inquiry: political transformation discourses before and during Germany's pension and labor market reforms of 2001–5; academic and public debate on the concept of "civil society"; and the role of politicians from the former GDR (such as Angela Merkel), whose political identities were formed during German transformation. Transfer history is not only made up of "successful" transfers, in which one culture adopts and adapts elements from another, but also processes of demarcation. They occurred not only in postcommunist states, especially Putin's Russia, but also in the West.

As mentioned above, transitologists as well as traditional historians of Europe tend to adopt a nation-state perspective. There are certainly plausible arguments for this: Nation-states steer macroeconomic development, adopt reforms, organize social security systems, and are the most important framework for democratic decision-making. But as is shown below, there can be tremendous intrastate divergence—growing gulfs between rich and poor, large cities and rural regions—which has a particular impact on the everyday lives of the populations.[46] Research on urban transformation after 1989 has focused on the geographical and social metamorphoses of cities and urban areas.[47] This book will further zoom in on the cities, because they bear striking witness to the rapid changes of the past twenty-five years. Literature, information, or source material on individual urban districts, villages, or streets, and the groups, families, and individuals who inhabit them is hard to come by. But social anthropologists and ethnologists have begun to close this gap with studies of factory communities, small social groups, and specific environments, which are of great interest to historians.[48] The state of literature on the transformation era is low (with the exception of the aforementioned short book by Padraic Kenney). Tony Judt, Hartmut Kaelble, Harold James, and most recently Konrad Jarausch have discussed the 1990s in the respective last chapters of their major surveys of twentieth century or postwar European history.[49] But there is still no book conceptualizing the quarter-century since 1989 as a distinct historical epoch.[50] Neoliberalism was the guiding ideology of this epoch, so it deserves to be the center of attention. Knowledge of its history is the precondition for understanding the present, in Europe and beyond.

# 2

# Where the East Meets the West

## Crisis and Reform Debates in the 1980s

### The Demise of State Socialism

The collapse of communist rule and the Eastern Bloc took the world of international politics and most Western observers completely by surprise. In the United States, especially, socialist countries had been widely regarded as totalitarian states where communists reigned supreme over "atomized," passive societies. Schoolchildren in the West learned from their atlases that the Soviet empire was all the countries behind the Iron Curtain, swathed in a blanket of foreboding red and juxtaposed against the Western states in their light and airy blue. But the Eastern Bloc under late state socialism was not such a static, homogenous unit. Only a few experts, such as the German political scientist Klaus Segbers and the Swedish economist Anders Åslund, recognized the force of the social dynamics and implications of the economic crisis in the Soviet Union before 1989.[1]

/ The protracted demise of state socialism had begun many years previously, in the late 1960s. The brutal suppression of the Prague Spring destroyed any hopes for "socialism with a human face" or reforming the system. True, Poland and Hungary opened economically in the 1970s) But rather than improve the performance of their planned economies, the import of Western technology (for instance, for auto manufacturers "Polski Fiat" and the shipbuilding industry on the Baltic Coast) only resulted in massive foreign debt. The Soviet Union, which appeared so formidable to the outside world, was stagnating economically. All of the Eastern Bloc countries missed the "digital revolution" that not only marked the dawn of new technologies but also increased the importance of productivity gains and international trade.

As the economic gulf between East and West widened, the legitimacy of communist rule was increasingly undermined. In the GDR in 1956, the First Secretary of the Socialist Unity Party (SED), Walter Ulbricht, had famously promised to "overtake, not catch up" (überholen, ohne einzuholen).[2] Some decades later, his slogan had a hollow ring. In the GDR as much as in the other Eastern Bloc countries, the communists were unable to fulfill the unofficial *contrat social* of a better supply of consumer goods in exchange for political compliance.[3] Many items were rarely or never available; if at all, they could only be purchased in foreign currencies from special stores: Intershop in the GDR, Tuzex in the ČSSR, Pewex in Poland, and Beriozka in the Soviet Union. Hence the importance of black-market deals, bartering, and currency smuggling as described in the introduction. (My Bohemian grandmother invented a fail-safe solution for the latter: three West German one-hundred-mark notes could be folded to the same size as one rectangular Bahlsen butter cookie. The cookie packet was carefully unglued using steam, the notes inserted, and the packet resealed.) The communists were held responsible for the scarcity because they had a monopoly on political power.

(The situation escalated in Poland first. In 1979–80, the Polish government tried to reduce the country's budget deficit by raising the prices for consumer goods and even basic foodstuffs. The public responded with mass protests and other forms of unrest. This led to the founding of the independent trade union Solidarność (Solidarity), the first mass movement to emerge beyond the party or official state organizations in a communist-ruled country. Mikhail Gorbachev later tried to alleviate the ongoing crisis of the planned economy by instituting glasnost and perestroika, but to no greater avail than the efforts of the reform communists in Hungary and Poland.

( Contrary to expectations, communist rule was undermined by the East-West détente and, in particular, the Helsinki Conference on Security and Cooperation in Europe in 1975.[4] The leaders of the Eastern Bloc countries initially took the Final Act of the CSCE to be a resounding success. Agreeing to respect the coexistence of the different systems and abide by the principle of nonintervention, the signatory states seemed to confirm the status quo for decades to come. But the communist regimes underestimated the impetus that the conference gave. The opposition in many countries took advantage of the legal provisions of the Helsinki Accords to formulate their demands. One result was Charta 77 in Czechoslovakia, which referred explicitly to the text of the accords and called on the government to respect human rights.

Another result of the détente and the CSCE was the partial opening of the Iron Curtain for individual travelers. The Poles, Hungarians, Czechs, and Slovaks who were permitted to travel could in this way gain firsthand impressions of the rival system. The West—including former "archenemy" West Germany—exuded a magnetic attraction, not only on account of its much more colorful consumer world but also its greater freedoms in most other areas of life. While the majority of GDR citizens were not permitted to cross the Iron Curtain, they were close enough to receive West German television signals and thus get a tantalizing idea of the West. In the second half of the 1980s, my Czech relatives visited West Germany at least once a year in order to purchase durable electronic appliances, water faucets that did not drip, and textiles of all kinds. Tens of thousands of Poles worked as harvest hands in West Germany and Sweden. Poland also sent between ten thousand and thirty thousand contract laborers to the GDR each year. As well as performing their regular tasks, these seasonal laborers and guest workers traded popular Western products and items from other socialist countries as a sideline. Commercial tourism became such a widespread phenomenon among Poles that sociological studies were written on the subject, dubbed *turizm zarobkowy*. Even diplomats participated in the mass-scale smuggling, much to the annoyance of the GDR border authorities who were obliged to let them pass. Warsaw evolved into a hub of trade, where Western products were illicitly sold and distributed across Eastern Europe, right up to the USSR.[5]

Communist propaganda suggested that international contact within the Eastern Bloc consolidated the brotherly ties between socialist nations. But often enough, the opposite was true. The cautious increase in commercial opportunities bred rivalry and misunderstandings that seemed to confirm personal prejudices (as, for instance, when Polish "tourists" in Frankfurt an der Oder snapped up the last available frying pan or pair of children's shoes, as residents of the East German border town recalled with indignation as late as 2004). It also enabled growing sections of the Polish population to acquire capitalist skills.

The same can be said of government functionaries engaged in the economic sphere. In 1989–90, they had the choice of using their skills and contacts to ease their way into capitalism or trying to uphold the old order by force. Many managed to maintain a comfortable lifestyle after their regime's collapse. Back in the seventies Egon Bahr, the main architect of West Germany's social-democratic *Ostpolitik* (policy toward the Eastern Bloc), had trusted in "change through rapprochement" ("Wandel durch Annäherung"). Although the Eastern Bloc changed too little to prove him right, rapprochement between the East and West certainly occurred on a popular level, through trade, travelling, and tourism.

At the same time, the front lines between communist authorities and opposition forces in Eastern Europe began to yield. Over the course of bitter and extended disputes, the regimes and their opponents came to form Janus-like units. In the USSR, Poland, and Hungary in the second half of the eighties, reform communists adopted some of the opposition's arguments and became increasingly open to change. Even in the reform-averse GDR and ČSSR, the official press started disseminating ideas that had originated with the opposition. The vision of Europe on which Gorbachev's concept of a "common European home" was based is one example.[6] Cold War historians have questioned the seriousness and impact of these visions. In any case, like the ideas of the international peace movement, they testify to trans-bloc thinking.

Meanwhile, the official economic cooperation between East and West gathered its own momentum. In the wake of the oil crises of 1973 and 1979 and the subsequent recessions, the West turned increasingly to the Eastern Bloc as a supplier of raw materials, a trade partner, and even a potential sales market. Despite having inflamed tensions by invading Afghanistan, the Soviet Union was still able to clinch the "deal of the century" with West Germany: they agreed to supply Russian natural gas to the Federal Republic in exchange for steel pipes, compressors (which were subject to export restrictions according to the Coordinating Committee for Multilateral Export Controls, or CoCom), and turbines to transmit the gas. The Austrian company VÖEST constructed an entire steel mill in the East German Eisenhüttenstadt steelworks combine; the banking group Raiffeisenbank founded its first Eastern European subsidiary in Hungary; IKEA and other major Western companies contracted with factories in Poland and the GDR to manufacture their products.[7] These transactions were indeed "confidence-building measures," and they deepened the East's dependence on the West.

## An Alternative Reading of the Cold War

All these changes before 1989 can be woven together into an alternative reading of the Cold War. Mainstream American Cold War historiography explains the end of the East-West conflict in confrontational terms. The doyen of this school of thought, John Lewis Gaddis, basically argues that Ronald Reagan's arms race brought the Soviet Union to its knees in the eighties.[8] The realization that the USSR could not keep pace with military rearmament supposedly convinced Gorbachev to introduce the reforms that ultimately led to the collapse of the Soviet empire. But there are a number of arguments to challenge this view. On a global level, for one, the ongoing confrontation with the West has served to consolidate the communist regimes in North Korea and Cuba until today, and reaffirmed their disapproval of reforms.

The policy of détente, by contrast, contributed significantly to ending the Cold War. This is especially evident when the East-West conflict is seen from a "Eurocentric" perspective. As outlined above, the rapprochement on the old continent gave rise to crucial confidence-building measures, dependencies, and entanglements. The problem with this narrative is that it is not based on a clear juxtaposition of good and evil and does not produce any heroes. On the contrary, it shows that the West German government under social-democratic chancellor Helmut Schmidt neglected to support the Solidarność movement in Poland. With the benefit of hindsight, one might ask why the West supplied the GDR and other Eastern Bloc countries with loans of billions for many years. This alternative reading of the end of the Cold War, then, explores a political and moral gray zone of interaction and compromise between East and West and between the regimes and their respective oppositions.

Whatever significance changing perceptions, dependencies, and entanglements had for ending the Cold War, these factors certainly shaped the manner in which regime changes were effected in the years 1989–91. The use of military or physical force had declined since the end of Stalinism. True, the Red Army had marched into Hungary in 1956, Czechoslovakia in 1968, and Afghanistan in 1979. But the Soviet Union had subsequently paid a high political and financial price. Partly for this reason, it tried to avoid repeating the occurrence in Poland in 1980–81. Another, equally important factor was the communists' relaxation of violence against their own citizens. The thaw in 1956 marked the end both of mass terror in the USSR and the Gulag system, which had never become fully established on the fringes of the Soviet empire anyway. By the 1970s and '80s, although demonstrations were still violently suppressed and dissidents tortured, political mass murder had been stopped. Paradoxically, this is illustrated by the case of a Polish priest, Jerzy Popiełuszko, who was abducted and murdered by security forces in 1984. The incident provoked such an outcry that the henchmen were subsequently indicted by their own regime. Despite the nominal sentences they received, their indictment signaled to police agents and spies to exercise greater restraint. Overall, the police and security forces in the Eastern Bloc stopped inspiring the intense fear they had in the 1950s and '60s. The open discussions about the political and economic situation my family engaged in during our summer vacation in Poland in 1977, and conversations I had in the streets, bars, and restaurants in the eighties, testified to this.

Of course, the situation differed from country to country. In Poland, people spoke openly and freely; Czechs looked over their shoulders in cafés and restaurants, checking for unwanted listeners; East German citizens avoided talking about "real existing socialism" or communist party leader Erich Honecker in public. But in general terms, the citizens of Eastern Bloc countries were not as "atomized" as totalitarianism theory—previously a major influence on Cold War studies—has claimed.

## The Neoliberal Turn in East and West

Viewing Europe in the latter years of the Cold War as a system of interconnected conduits casts a different light on the reform debates of the 1980s. Some developments occurred almost in parallel in Western and Eastern Europe. Margaret Thatcher responded to the United Kingdom's economic stagnation in the 1970s by drastically reducing government expenditure, cutting subsidies and social security benefits, and combating inflation. Her reform package included extensive privatization, even of key industries such as the national railways. In this way, Thatcher put an end to the Keynesian policies pursued by her predecessors, which had failed to solve the country's problems following the oil crisis and ended in spiraling inflation and national debt.

Experts in think tanks, universities, and international financial institutions had prepared this political paradigm shift for some time. An increasing number of economists at British, American, and, eventually, other Western universities held neoliberal views, and they did not confine them to academic discourse. Milton Friedman, one of the best-known proponents of the Chicago School, appeared in his own TV series in 1980 to convey his views to a mass audience. The first episode, entitled "The Power of the Market," clearly spelled out his message of faith in free, unfettered markets.[10] He coupled his economic doctrine with an ideological, libertarian critique of big government and the welfare state, which he demonized as an obstacle to economic activity and the cause of the day's crisis. A follow-up series was made in 1990 in a slightly different format. This time, prominent politicians and actors including Ronald Reagan, former US Secretary of State George Shultz, and Arnold Schwarzenegger moderated the programs, lending additional weight to the PBS series. Since the Eastern Bloc had recently collapsed, one episode was dedicated to the "Failure of Socialism."

Initially, neoliberalism and the teachings of the Chicago School resonated less in continental Europe. In France, the Socialists led by François Mitterrand won the 1981 general election and pursued an opposite course, increasing public expenditure and government intervention in an attempt to boost the economy after the second oil crisis. But inflation remained high, debts mounted, the economy stagnated, and the government was under constant pressure to devalue the French franc against the West German mark. Just two years later, Mitterrand was obliged to bow to the international capital markets and introduce a cost-cutting program in order to avert the further devaluation of the franc and an even higher rate of inflation.

Meanwhile, the social-democratic chancellor Helmut Schmidt was brought down by the burgeoning budget deficit and disagreements over how to overcome the deep recession caused by the second oil crisis. The new center-right government distanced itself from the Keynesian policies of the previous government. Christian Democratic chancellor Helmut Kohl announced a new economic policy, "away from more state to more market; away from collective burdens to more personal achievements; away from entrenched structures to more flexibility, individual initiative and competitiveness."[11] Germany's tradition of proportional representation and coalition governments prevented radical changes akin to those in the United States or Britain with their two party systems. But a pronounced paradigm shift nevertheless took place in German economic think tanks and universities. They now saw the strong state as a burden rather than a solution to the current economic problems. For the first time in postwar history, social expenditure was criticized and cut. When the Berlin Wall came down in 1989 and the course was set for the transformation of East Germany, hardly any Keynesians remained in Germany to support state interventionism or state ownership of industries.

As Geoff Eley has argued in his groundbreaking work on the European Left, the Social Democrats in all European countries adapted to neoliberal economic paradigms over the course of the eighties.[12] "The markets," which Friedman had still referred to in the singular, became a buzzword in the media and politics. Like a supreme, personalized, and yet anonymous authority, "the markets" have judged the economic power and viability of companies and even entire nations ever since. As the stock market crash in 2007 demonstrated, it remains unclear who exactly is passing judgment or who will take responsibility for errors.

The Chicago School wanted society and the economy to be propelled by the "hidden hand" of the market(s) and demonized the visible presence of the state. Friedman and other commentators railed against big government "standing on your shoes," as Arnold Schwarzenegger put it in the aforementioned TV show. And in some respects, Europe's new social movements and the up-and-coming "Green" parties voiced similar demands for less government control and more public participation in environmental protection, education, and many other fields. Still, the paradigm shift away from government intervention was less prominent in continental Europe than it was in the United Kingdom and the United States. In broad terms, the West reacted in one of two ways to the economic problems following the two oil crises and recessions of 1973–74 and 1980–81, either attacking the welfare state and its allocative functions (Thatcher and Reagan), or returning to more defensive, conservative politics (continental Western Europe). All of Europe's moderate political parties, from the Christian Democrats and other center-right parties who now assumed government (as in West Germany) to the left-leaning Social Democrats and Socialists who remained in power (as in France, Sweden, and Austria), tried to preserve the welfare state. In terms of growth rates or, perhaps more importantly, the discourse on economic policy, neoliberalism clearly triumphed over welfarism *within* the West. European policymakers enviously watched the United States emerging from the recession in the early eighties with greater economic growth than the core states of the European Community.[13] In fact, there were many different reasons for this. Reagan's policy of rearmament had the effect of an economic growth program (something that was theoretically anathema to his economic advisers); the "digital revolution" generated further growth. Great Britain profited from the oil boom in the North Sea, as well as London's status as a global finance center. The growth figures in the United States and the United Kingdom were also partly the result of statistical adjustment: from the basis of their earlier and deeper crises in the late 1970s, their recoveries appeared more rapid. The extent to which Reaganomics and Thatcherism were responsible for their countries' economic upturns can, then, be questioned. But they certainly placed increasing pressure on the welfare states of continental Europe to conform. These had been designed during the "*trente glorieuses*"; in times of rapidly rising unemployment and aging populations, it was becoming impossible to finance them. As a consequence, even confirmed Social Democrats and Socialists, including the later president of the European Commission, Jacques Delors, eventually adopted neoliberal ideas.

The Eastern Bloc, in contrast, seemed virtually immune to all the crises affecting the West in the early eighties. The developments that put an end to Fordism (the labor-intensive mass production of consumer goods) and full employment, along with all the problems this posed for social security systems, seemed to stop at the Iron Curtain.[14] The Soviet Union even indirectly profited from the two oil crises. These enabled it to demand higher prices for oil and gas from the West while cushioning the oil-price blow for its allies by supplying them cut-price energy.

But under the surface of apparent stability the problems were mounting. Hungary and Poland were not able to pay back their foreign debts from the 1970s. The GDR accumulated increasing debts in order to maintain its standard of living—the highest in the Eastern Bloc. Bulgaria accrued mounting foreign debt in the late eighties; the Soviet Union suffered from the rapid drop in oil and gas prices after 1982. The economic problems were reflected in the increasing divergence between the official and unofficial rates of exchange for foreign currencies described above.

Poland faced additional problems. The imposition of martial law and the suppression of the Solidarność movement plunged the country further into recession. Almost all basic foodstuffs were rationed; the black market boomed.[15] State repression and constant scarcity demotivated the workers. Aware that the People's Republic of Poland was on the verge of economic and political bankruptcy, the Polish government welcomed perestroika and the opportunity to concede greater freedoms, especially to farmers and smaller firms. In 1986 General Wojciech Jaruzelski announced an amnesty for political prisoners. One year later, the government entered into negotiations with the opposition, mediated by the Church. In 1988 additional economic reforms were introduced that further loosened the restrictions on private entrepreneurs, and the following year the controls on prices for agricultural products were lifted. These measures were groundbreaking for Eastern Europe.

Even further-reaching reforms were introduced in the communist countries of East Asia. As early as 1979, the party leadership in Vietnam had allowed farmers to sell some of their output privately. In 1986, in step with perestroika, it abolished the entire system of compulsory levies and state price regulation in agriculture. This bold move to accommodate the individual profit motive in what was then a key sector of the Vietnamese economy paid off. Agricultural production rose and Vietnam soon became a rice exporter. But the communists protected their positions of power at the same time. The land the farmers cultivated was only ceded to them as usufructuaries; they did not own it. Like China, then, Vietnam introduced market economy without privatization.

By contrast, Poland's reform program of 1989 focused on privatization. One reason for this was the country's high foreign debt—the Polish government needed the revenue from the sale of state industries and enterprises. Two groups of actors cooperated to design the reforms: foreign advisers from the IMF and other international institutions, who prescribed Poland a neoliberal austerity program, as they had previously the ailing countries of Latin America; and national experts who had worked their way up the government career ladder and now supported radical reforms. These experts did not look to the Western European model of the welfare state for inspiration, but to the policies of Margaret Thatcher and Ronald Reagan. In late 1988, the Polish weekly *Polityka* had already commented on the growing influence of "eastern Thatcherites."[16] These were on the rise because of growing discontent with Gorbachev's perestroika and its Eastern European variants. Hence domestic circumstances paved the way for 1989's radical reforms.

Similarly to Yugoslavia, Poland lurched toward hyperinflation. The cheap aluminum coins of the seventies were immobilized and ever more zeroes printed on Polish banknotes. International and Polish economic experts agreed that the only way to curb the price rise was to strictly limit government expenditure and money supply. Even wages were not safe. In 1988 industrial workers had successfully taken strike action to have their wages index-linked to the rate of inflation. While this boosted incomes, it also caused inflation to rise even further. As a consequence, wages and salaries were rigorously controlled and de facto reduced after 1989.

Reforms in Hungary were shaped by debates within the Communist Party. The Hungarian private sector was expanded during the eighties, as was the Polish. But Hungary's private enterprises did not have sufficient influence or scope to propel the economy. In 1987 the party abandoned its guarantee of employment for every adult citizen; the specter of unemployment loomed on the horizon. At the same time, Hungary opened its borders to foreign direct investments.

In the Soviet Union, too, the authorities were forced to admit that they could not simply grind on. Leonid Brezhnev's successor Yuri Andropov, a former head of the KGB, had been aware of the dismal state of the economy since the early eighties. In 1986, Andropov's protégé Mikhail Gorbachev proclaimed glasnost and perestroika (literally, "openness" and "restructuring"). He also introduced a different course in foreign policy. Recognizing the hopelessness of the Soviet intervention in Afghanistan, he tried to end the arms race in order to redirect more resources toward the economy.

Gorbachev hoped to save state socialism by reforming it. State enterprises were to retain some of their output to sell on their own initiative; kolkhoz farmers were encouraged to cultivate small plots of farmland independently; productivity was to be improved by raising workers' morale. These measures were less targeted than the reforms in China and Vietnam, and, thanks to glasnost, discussed more than they were actually implemented. Such a tentative approach to reforms and decentralizing the economy only served to aggravate the Soviet Union's problems. The individual republics drifted further apart and pursued their own increasingly nationally defined interests. Even glasnost had unintentional side effects. While the opportunity to articulate criticisms and discuss problems initially had a liberating effect, as long as it failed to alleviate the USSR's economic plight, it ultimately undermined the authority of the party.

In 1989, the disclosure of major crimes committed by the state under Stalinism shook the foundations of the ailing Soviet Union. The Politburo's admission of the existence of the Molotov-Ribbentrop Pact delegitimized Soviet rule in the Baltic states and gave the oppositions in Lithuania, Latvia, and Estonia a tremendous boost (see fig. 2.1). Civil rights activists started demanding independence for the Baltic republics. They, too, took advantage of contacts with exiles and other actors in the West. In the Caucasus, armed conflicts broke out between Armenians and Azerbaijani, forcing tens of thousands to flee their homes. The pogroms and unrest further undermined the legitimacy of the Soviet empire, which was proving incapable even of maintaining internal peace. In retrospect, the interethnic violence of the late eighties can be seen to have presaged the war in the former Yugoslavia and the Caucasus. Then, as later, conflicts flared up over the issue of whether to preserve the territory of the constituent republics or draw new, ethnic borders. Nationalism, then, was a crucial factor contributing to the breakup of the Soviet Union.[17] But it was bred on the ground of economic crisis.

Struggling enough with the economic problems in his own country, Gorbachev ceded the peripheral states of the Soviet Union greater freedoms, and encouraged the other Eastern Bloc

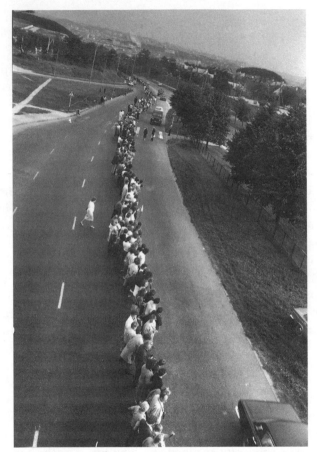

Fig. 2.1. On August 23, 1989, over a million people marked the fiftieth anniversary of the signing of the Molotov-Ribbentrop Pact by forming a human chain that stretched approximately four hundred miles, from Vilnius via Riga to Tallinn. Photo: ullstein bild / Juraitis.

countries to introduce reforms. But glasnost and perestroika created new difficulties without remedying the flaws of the existing system. Soviet experts and managers increasingly doubted the viability of—or possibility of reforming—"real existing socialism," a term that now inevitably carried a mocking overtone.

⬤At this point, several of the Eastern Bloc's later reform politicians finally rejected state socialism and embraced neoliberalism.

They included Václav Klaus, Leszek Balcerowicz, and Yegor Gaidar, all three of whom were state-employed experts working in official think tanks. Balcerowicz had even received a government scholarship to study in New York, where he became familiarized with the teachings of Milton Friedman. Having hitherto known only ineffective, spoon-feeding governments, these Eastern European economists were particularly drawn to the antistatism that is characteristic of neoliberalism.[18] Thus neoliberalism and the theories of the Chicago School were disseminated via various channels: first, encounters between individuals, especially economists (interpersonal cultural transfers); and second, the reception of various writings (intertextual transfers). Both channels of exchange with the West were, however, more restricted in the Soviet Union than in East Central Europe.

The manifest failure of the reform communists' efforts in the Soviet Union, Poland, and Hungary had repercussions in the West, too: Western variants of socialism lost their appeal. A number of comments and writings by prominent contemporaries such as US economic historian Robert Heilbroner testify to this. In early 1989, even before the Eastern Bloc crumbled, Heilbroner wrote in the *New Yorker* that "the contest between capitalism and socialism is over. Capitalism has won."[19] Milton Friedman took this up in the abovementioned TV series of 1990 and produced a sequence with the title "The Failure of Socialism."[20] It is interesting to note the choice of vocabulary: not communism—the United States' Cold War adversary—but socialism was seen to have failed. By this cipher, Friedman and other confirmed anticommunists conveyed their hostility toward the already much-reduced welfare state and liberal left in their own country. Friedman's TV program features a bizarre appearance by Ronald Reagan, who confused the Nobel Peace Prize with the Nobel Prize for Economics (the latter of which Friedman had indeed received) in his introduction declaring Friedman the recipient of the "Nobel Peace Prize in Economics."

While Heilbroner focused primarily on the past, the neoconservative Francis Fukuyama looked to the future. In his controversial theory of the "end of history," he claimed there was no longer any alternative to democracy and market economy, a view that liberal

sociologist Ralf Dahrendorf shared. The Western elites' entire political and ideological spectrum seemed to be made up of variants
of dissociation from socialism. Previously Heilbroner had viewed
economic history from a Marxist perspective. Clearly the failure
of state socialism had such a deep impact that it changed the nature of the Left in the West, too.

Yet even at this point, some Eastern European civil rights activists continued to propagate a Third Way, linking market economy with the positive achievements of state socialism in their
countries. Left-wing Western social democrats such as Egon Bahr
supported their views. But the economic collapse of the Eastern
Bloc and the de facto bankruptcy of Yugoslavia and its system
of self-administration precluded the combination of the two systems. Czechoslovakia was less encumbered with debts and so
could afford to postpone drastic reforms (which Friedman explicitly criticized in his TV series). But Yugoslavia, Poland, and
other debt-ridden countries had no other choice than to follow
the recipes of the Washington Consensus to secure the financial
support of the West. As attempts to reform socialism failed before the eyes of the world, its Western, welfare-state variant also
lost support and legitimacy. Even Sweden's Social Democrats,
who had run the country for many decades, were soon forced to
surrender power. After 1989, then, the traditional Left-Right political framework was fundamentally challenged in Eastern and
Western Europe alike.

The proponents of deregulated, free market economy seized the
opportunity these changes presented. The Washington Consensus established the hegemony of neoliberalism on a global level.
Here, too, it is important to note the subtle use of terminology.
Referring to the economic prescriptions it advanced as a "consensus" implied that alternatives were deviant. Thus the ground was
prepared in East and West for the revolutions of 1989–91 coming
to a neoliberal end. But neither the civil rights activists nor the
millions of people out on the streets foresaw this conclusion.

# 3

# The Revolutions of 1989–91

## Milestones of the Revolutions

The term "revolution" is commonly used to denote a great change, attended by mass mobilization and exuberance, that leaves a lasting imprint on the course of history. But in the fall of 1989, only a few demonstrators and dissidents dared to spell it out. Doing so would have put them at considerable personal risk and perhaps provoked a violent crackdown by the communist security forces. After decades of obligatory annual celebrations to commemorate the Bolshevik Revolution, the term had become tainted and overused. Indeed, revolution was still associated with mass violence, which conflicted with the opposition's strategy of nonviolent resistance. Moreover, for a long time, dissidents called for the reform of the existing system, not its abolition. They formulated their demands within the parameters of perestroika and its Eastern European variants. To a degree, then, describing the upheaval of 1989 as a revolution is anachronistic. Contemporaries did not refer to it as such until the communists were already losing their grip on power.[1] But then this term endowed the turmoil with meaning, and hope that communism in its gray form of "real existing socialism" was over. It signified that better times were ahead.

In the sense of Charles Tilly, Theda Skocpol, Hannah Arendt, and other older revolution theorists, the years between 1989 and 1991 certainly fit the definition of the term.[2] There was a prehistory and a classic causal precondition—the decay of the ancien régime—followed by a revolutionary process and completed by revolutionary results. The main questions in this chapter are then: What *kind* of revolution occurred at the end of the twentieth century and what impact did it have? Were the opportunities presented by the revolution adequately used? (This question is explored further toward the end of the book.) The young people, especially, out in the streets in the fall and winter of 1989 (among them the author of this book) were united by a sense of excitement and potential. But the period did not spawn a "generation of '89" similar to those from the historic years 1968 or 1848. So is there a lasting legacy of 1989, and if so, what would define it?

Before exploring these questions concerning the form, impact, and legacy of this most recent wave of revolutions, it seems appropriate to briefly survey the major events.[3] The key milestones, in chronological order, were: 1) the establishment of a "round table" in Poland in early 1989 and its resolutions to permit independent trade unions, hold elections in June, and introduce further economic reforms; 2) the Hungarian communists' reappraisal in the spring of 1989 of the failed revolution of 1956 and decision to allow a multiparty system, freedom of assembly, and other basic democratic rights; 3) the devastating defeat of the communists in Poland at the elections on 4 June 1989, on the same day as Chinese armed forces crushed the protests on Tiananmen Square in a countermodel of violent suppression; 4) the mass exodus of GDR citizens across the Hungarian border that summer, bringing down the Iron Curtain; 5) the popularity of the Monday Demonstrations in Leipzig and other East German cities, corroding the regime of the Socialist Unity Party (SED) and compelling it to open the Berlin Wall on November 9; 6) the breakdown of the communist regime in Bulgaria just one day later and the "Velvet Revolution" in Czechoslovakia in mid-November; 7) Moscow's confirmation of the existence of the Molotov-Ribbentrop Pact in December 1989, which opened the door to independence for the Baltic republics; and 8) the bloody final act in Romania, with the execution of dictator Nicolae Ceaușescu and his wife on December 25.

Media portrayals of the radical changes are often confined to the year 1989, but in fact there were further crucial developments in 1990 and 1991, including 9) election victories for the distinctly national parties in the constituent republics of Yugoslavia, presaging the final disintegration of the economically bankrupt state; 10) the end of the GDR by economic union with the FRG and the accession of the five East German states (the "*Fünf Neue Länder*") to the former West Germany; 11) the outbreak of armed conflict in Yugoslavia in summer 1991; 12) Lithuania, Latvia, and Estonia finally gaining independence following a coup d'état against Gorbachev that August; 13) the end of communism in its last bastion, Albania; and 14) the official breakup of the Soviet Union in December 1991. This staccato sequence of quantum leaps and jumps created a sense of time accelerating. Individual contemporaries could hardly grasp the ramifications of all the changes.

When the communist regimes collapsed, so did Europe's postwar order. The depth of the changes can only be understood from a long-term historical perspective. In 1991, Russia lost all the territories it had acquired since its imperial expansion westward in the seventeenth and eighteenth centuries: Ukraine on the left bank of the Dnieper (Treaty of Andruszowo, 1667), the Baltic states (Treaty of Nystad, 1721), Ukraine on the right bank of the Dnieper (first partition of Poland, 1772), and further Lithuanian and Polish territories (second and third partitions of Poland, 1793–95). The current conflict over Ukraine stems from Russia's ambition to at least partially reverse this loss of power and influence.

In a speech to the State Duma in 2005, Vladimir Putin described the disintegration of the Soviet Union as the "largest geopolitical catastrophe of the twentieth century." He went on to give a foretaste of his neoimperialist foreign policy in 2014 by declaring himself the protector of Russians living in neighboring states.[4] Yet one of the major accomplishments of the revolutions of 1989–91 had been Russia's (temporary) relaxation of efforts to be a rival superpower to the United States. President Boris Yeltsin realized that attempting to rule over neighboring nations and large parts of Europe and Central Asia was too costly for Russia and resulted in imperial overstretch. The Russian Soviet Federative Socialist Republic declared independence, spelling the definitive end of the Soviet Union. For the first time in its history, Moscow broke away from its own empire.

The geopolitical situation in Eastern Europe improved as a result. The region no longer formed a buffer zone between the West and the East, as it had in the interwar years and the first years after the Second World War. The Czech Republic, Poland, and Hungary joined NATO in 1999; Slovakia, Slovenia, Romania, Bulgaria, and the Baltic states—three former Soviet republics—followed in 2004. As the European Union and NATO expanded, most of the East Central and Southeast European states clearly aligned themselves with the West. When Romania and Bulgaria joined the European Union in 2007, it gained two more predominantly Orthodox Christian countries, after Greece. Commentators in Romania were inspired to speak of a "Europe from the Atlantic to the Black Sea." No other revolution in the history of Europe, other than those of 1789–94, had had such a deep impact on the political geography of the continent.

The collapse of the last European superpower and the multiethnic states Yugoslavia and Czechoslovakia heralded a new phase of nation-state building in Europe, the "third wave" following Italian unification and the Congress of Berlin in the nineteenth century (1859–78) and the period of reorganization after the end of the First World War. As previously, it triggered violence and even wars. The former Yugoslavia was engulfed by violence as Slobodan Milošević and the leaders of the Serbian minorities in Croatia and Bosnia tried to construct an ethnically defined Greater Serbia and refused to accept the preexisting borders of the constituent republics. In contrast, the former Soviet Union, with the exception of the Caucasus and small conflict zones such as Transnistria and the Fergana Valley in Central Asia, remained mostly peaceful—perhaps because Yugoslavia served as a warning example. Czechoslovakia, the last explicitly multinational state in Europe, also disintegrated without bloodshed. Nationalism was not the only reason for these states' collapse. Rifts appeared in Yugoslavia and Czechoslovakia over the course transformation should take, with proponents of gradual reforms fiercely opposing the supporters of radical changes.

The model of the monoethnic nation-state was more stringently followed in 1989 than after the First World War. Yet few borders were redrawn, unlike after 1918. The existing federal units of multinational states were largely retained. In the 1990s, some observers

**Map 1.** The new Europe.

extrapolated that the success of transformation was linked closely to levels of national homogeneity. According to Milada Vachudová and Timothy Snyder, this was the reason why the largely monoethnic countries Poland, the Czech Republic, and Hungary were pioneers of reforms.[5] Certainly, the Romanian and Serbian (post)communists exploited ethnic dividing lines to their political advantage. But the later development of Slovakia and Romania— countries with large Hungarian minorities—disprove the thesis. It is one of the negative aspects of transformation that the situation of the Roma people, however, remains desperate throughout Eastern Europe.

The "new Europe" consists predominantly of small or very small states. There is a rough balance of ten or twelve countries with populations of up to two million inhabitants (some not even as large as Connecticut or New Hampshire), between two and five million, and between five and ten million. Only eight countries have populations of over twenty million: Germany, France, Italy, Great Britain, Spain, Poland, Ukraine, and Russia. Jan Zielonka, a political scientist at Oxford, has proposed that the enlarged European Union is like a "neomedieval empire" with a federal structure held together by a weak central power, similar to the Holy Roman Empire, dissolved in 1806, or the Polish-Lithuanian Commonwealth, which ceased to exist in 1795.[6] Not only the extent, then, but also the quality of statehood in Europe has changed. Brussels has gained considerably more power by its active involvement in the transformation.

## Causes of the Revolutions

Is it possible to view all the turbulent events of the years 1989–91 in the same context and to explain them in one master narrative? Has enough time passed for the staccato sequence of radical changes listed above to be reassessed and evaluated? More than twenty-five years after a new order was established in Europe, contemporary historians should at least give it a try. Below, some existing explanations will be considered, and the proposed main temporal, spatial, and human factors analyzed. The question of "how" is just as important as that of "why." It is truly remarkable that the European revolutions of 1989 occurred largely without violence, by a process of negotiation. But despite the lack of bloodshed, the changes are not undisputed. The economic and social outcomes of the revolutionary changes, which eventually also affected Western Europe, remain politically contentious.

The simplest and most media-compatible explanation for the revolution was presented in 2009 at the events' twentieth-anniversary celebrations under the Brandenburg Gate, in the heart of united Germany. Artists had been commissioned to create a Berlin Wall of polystyrene blocks, which were knocked down in a chain reaction at the climax of the celebrations. This action symbolized the domino theory that one small revolutionary stone caused the next to topple and so on until the entire structure collapsed, leaving a (wall-)free, united Germany and Europe. It is true that the revolutions of 1989 interacted. Dissidents and civil rights activists across Eastern Europe were in contact with each other throughout the eighties. The state and party leaders of the individual Eastern Bloc countries were, of course, also in close contact. The fact that Europe's communist regimes collapsed in quick succession seems to confirm the domino theory. The sudden precipitation of events prevented the people in power from anticipating, and halting, their own fall and the end of the old order.

But there are drawbacks to the domino theory. For one thing, it blurs the differences between the power shifts in individual countries and local protest movements. In Hungary, change occurred relatively gradually, modulated by debates within the Hungarian Socialist Party, or MSZP, whose reformist wing came to predominate. In Poland, as mentioned above, direct negotiations took place between the government and the opposition. In Czechoslovakia and the GDR, the communists obstructed reforms for so long, even in defiance of Gorbachev, that by 1989 they had forfeited all room to maneuver.[7] In Romania, Bulgaria, and the successor states of the Soviet Union, communism ended under still different circumstances. The opposition in each of these countries was distinctively composed, took different action, and had varying levels of support within society. Another problem with the domino theory is that it suggests a linear sequence. But where in this line is the place for the largest, central "stone"—that is, the Soviet Union in the years 1989–91? The domino theory also paints a simplified picture of interplay between the revolutions. Unlike 1789–94 or 1848–49, there were no itinerant revolutionaries in 1989, moving from one hot spot to the next. But there were transnational electronic media. The protesters in Prague in November 1989, for example, knew from Radio Free Europe and other information channels that they faced the last hardliner regime in the region. This knowledge emboldened them and demoralized the security forces.

The domino theory does have a narrative advantage thanks to its strong, vivid imagery. In his book *We the People*, Oxford-based contemporary historian Timothy Garton Ash acts as narrator and observer, dashing from Warsaw to Budapest, Prague, and Berlin.[8] The reader experiences the end of each country's regime and the opposition's takeover as if watching the plot of a thriller unfolding on the big screen. Former Hungarian dissident György Dalos takes the same approach, dealing with each country in sequence, in his excellent analysis of the year 1989.[9]

Garton Ash's reportage-style account emphasizes the significance of mass mobilization. During the anniversary year 2009, when argument over the nature of the events reignited, he defended his view that the peoples of Eastern Europe made the revolution. Garton Ash is not alone in this opinion; Padraic Kenney also underlines the role of the opposition in *A Carnival of Revolution*.[10] Both historians attribute the peaceful revolution to the civil society formed by courageous dissidents in East Central Europe before the radical changes of 1989. Highlighting the role of the opposition in this way, there is a danger of heroizing dissidents such as Václav Havel and Lech Wałęsa. But unlike all good works of fiction, these books offer no villains. The old rulers barely feature in Garton Ash's narrative. On the rare occasions that the communists are mentioned, they appear as gray figures, paralyzed with indecision.

US historian Stephen Kotkin responded to Garton Ash's interpretation with a powerful polemic.[11] Arguing that "the opposition" was poorly rooted in society, Kotkin questioned whether it was appropriate to use the term at all, or whether it would be more apt to speak of isolated dissidents. According to him, the general public had been so disengaged in these countries that they formed "uncivil societies," making nonsense of the term revolution.[12] Poland (dealt with by Kotkin's coauthor, Jan Gross) was the only exception. Kotkin attributes the changeover primarily to Gorbachev's reform policy and its unintended effects. His explanation, then, falls within the tradition of Sovietology, focusing on Moscow and the Kremlin.

More recent historical research provides evidence to challenge Kotkin's thesis. Canadian historian James Krapfl has shown that social mobilization in Czechoslovakia encompassed the entire country. Large demonstrations were held in even the small district capitals, and did not stop until the leading figures of the old regime stepped down.[13] Demonstrations in the GDR were by no means confined to Leipzig and Berlin: they also took place in provincial towns such as Plauen. In the Baltic republics, virtually the entire non-Russian populace took part in protests from 1988 on. However, the Russian postwar immigrants, and the Polish minority in Lithuania, were ambivalent about the Estonians', Latvians', and Lithuanians' demands for autonomy and, later, independence. Hence, they tended to stay away from the demonstrations, which somewhat reduces the myth of the Poles' indomitable will for freedom. Mobilization was weaker in Gdańsk, Warsaw, Poznań, and other centers of Solidarność, especially in comparison to 1980–81. This was partly due to the fact that the opposition was now able to negotiate directly with the government. The Solidarność leaders took their demands straight to the Round Table, rendering public protests superfluous.

The Romanian secret service, Securitate, managed to suppress all mass demonstrations until December 1989. But the regime was crumbling on the periphery. In Timişoara the planned relocation of the dissident priest László Tőkés brought 100,000 students and workers out into the streets in protest. Unlike the leaders of other Eastern European regimes, Ceauşescu gave his forces a shoot-to-kill directive that claimed the lives of twenty-six people in Timişoara alone. The bloodshed fanned the flames of unrest. Within a few days the spark of revolution had reached Bucharest. The second and third ranks of the party assumed power and ordered the shooting of Nicolae and Elena Ceauşescu following a hasty trial before a military tribunal. The Romanian revolution can therefore also be considered an intraparty putsch.[14]

Mass mobilization was strongest in Yugoslavia. Demonstrations had been taking place since the mid-eighties, mostly for social and economic causes or the demands of individual factories. In 1989 Slobodan Milošević harnessed this tendency to kindle nationalist aspirations among Serbian society with a mass rally on the mythical *Kosovo Polje*. Beginning in 1991 he purposely incited violence against other nationalities and Serbian opponents.

By provoking a nationalist escalation, Milošević engineered the *de*mobilization of society.[15] When the War of Yugoslav Succession began, Serbian demands for more reforms and a change of government died away. The Serbian Socialist Party was able to stay in power longer than any other postcommunist party—until 2000, when the first "color revolution" took place in Eastern Europe; a term that should not be used uncritically.

Ⓢ A fourth and very important explanation can be found for Yugoslavia's collapse: the economic failure of state socialism.[16] As mentioned above, the two oil crises of 1973–74 and 1979–80 were more harmful for the West than for the Eastern Bloc. The Soviet Union actually benefited from the rising oil price. Exports of oil helped it to increase its foreign exchange revenue. In the West, the dual price shock and rising employment costs led to a boom in investment and technical innovation. The Eastern Bloc failed to keep pace and fell behind the West in terms of economic performance.[17] From 1983 on, moreover, the price of crude oil dropped as sharply as it had previously risen (from $66 to $20 per barrel). The Soviet Union struggled to raise the money to pay for its grain imports and staple goods. Ironically, by 1989, it was the center of the Red Empire that was in the worst shape: as Gerald Easter has shown, at over 10 percent of the GDP, the Soviet Union's budget deficit was higher than that of any other Eastern Bloc country. Inflation rose as it had previously in Poland and Yugoslavia. The USSR could no longer maintain the population's already low standard of living.[18] The most obvious symptom of the weakness of these planned economies was low productivity. In the late eighties, Eastern Bloc industries needed roughly five times as long as factories in Western Europe did to manufacture lower-quality refrigerators or cars (see fig. 3.1). Gorbachev and other reform communists recognized these problems and launched the politics of perestroika in response. But as Kotkin has convincingly shown, they had unprecedented and unexpected effects.

Findings of social and economic history can be fruitfully combined with inquiry into the history of everyday life. The communist countries' growing investment in mass consumption improved local living standards until the seventies. But it also raised

Fig. 3.1. An East German Trabant and a West German Opel Kadett coupé parked in front of an Intershop on one of the transit highways to West Berlin, 1984. Photo: ullstein bild / Günter Schneider.

expectations to a level that ultimately could not be sustained. The reality was constant scarcity and daily standing in line, which undermined the *contrat social* of the postwar era. The volatility of the situation was tangible in the protests in Poland of 1970, 1976, and 1980. Each of these demonstrations was triggered by government moves to raise the prices of basic foodstuffs. This made economic sense: subsidies overburdened the national budget; supply and demand were wildly disparate and compounded by low state purchase prices, which in turn fostered the black market. But industrial workers came out in protest because the price rises injured their "moral economy." They were under the impression that party members enjoyed vast (often overestimated) privileges. Partly in the light of events in Poland, East Germany did not attempt any comparable cuts but, like Bulgaria, opted to take on more foreign debt. The only party leader in Eastern Europe to force frugality upon his citizens was Nicolae Ceaușescu. To some extent, it was the Romanian dictator's rationing of heating fuel, electricity, and basic foodstuffs in the 1980s that earned him the hatred of his citizens. Eventually, he paid for his tyranny with his life.

An explanation based on economic and social history can also be useful for drawing comparisons between Eastern and Western Europe and countries within the Eastern Bloc.[19] System rivalry, among other things, spurred countries on both sides of the Iron Curtain to increase their social expenditure. This is especially true of West Germany, Austria, and Sweden, which had probably the highest welfare spending worldwide. Eventually, this caused similar problems of growing budget deficits and rising taxes in both the East and the West. By 1989, Thatcherism and Reaganomics had placed Western European countries under distinct pressure to reduce their welfare states. As a result, their appeal and model function diminished. The postcommunist countries, which could not have afforded such lavish welfare states in 1989 anyway, opted to take the neoliberal path.

The détente made it possible for citizens of the Eastern Bloc to compare their standard of living with that in Western countries. Thus they could see for themselves that the communist propaganda about the imperialist-capitalist West ruthlessly exploiting the downtrodden working classes was false. As the gulf between rich and poor grew in their own countries, Eastern Europeans increasingly looked to Western Europe for orientation. The state socialist regimes responded with propagandist campaigns promoting the values that they stood for, such as full employment, social security, and solidarity. As the revolutions of 1989 show, the public gave the communists little or no credit for their social policy achievements. Yet in the nineties, when demonstrations and strikes were called in protest against reforms, it was precisely these endangered values that the protesters invoked.

The complex field of mutual and retrospective perceptions touches on the influence of the media on the revolutions of 1989. Images of mass demonstrations, the Round Table in Poland and other oppositional successes inspired the populations in neighboring countries. Communication channels within the Eastern Bloc had already played a role during earlier crises of communism. The residents of Lviv in western Ukraine, for example, had received information about the Prague Spring and the Red Army's invasion of Czechoslovakia via Polish broadcasting.[20] Polish television and radio was an important factor contributing to western Ukraine's development into a stronghold of civic resistance in the Soviet Union. The town of L'viv even evolved its own hippie culture. In Poland, the cities along the Baltic coast were hubs of opposition, not least because they were the first to receive information from the West. The opposition was able to disseminate its views among the population using printing presses and typewriters smuggled from Sweden.

The media played an important role in other Eastern Bloc countries, too. Many journalists, newspapers, and radio broadcasters remained loyal to their regimes for several years, but swiftly changed sides in 1989. More than by sheer opportunism, they were motivated by a sense of professional ethics, which they retained despite all communist governments' demand, since Lenin's time, for *partiynost* (partisanship). Despite the ideological controls, Eastern European journalists aspired to inform their publics. Crude propaganda, such as appeared on the infamous *Black Channel* (*Der schwarze Kanal*) TV show broadcast in the GDR, was respected neither by journalists nor by the populace. As the reality of "real existing socialism" diverged ever more from its propagandist image, it became increasingly difficult to reconcile journalistic standards with the party line. Consequently, subversive resistance began to form long before any radical changes occurred. Cracks in the censorship first appeared due to glasnost and perestroika, then widened in 1989, until the dam of suppression finally burst during the revolutions.

The media in the GDR and the ČSSR contributed significantly to toppling their countries' regimes. Illegally filmed images of the Monday Demonstration in Leipzig on October 9 were smuggled to West Berlin. Subsequently broadcast by West German television, they exposed the scale of the protests and challenged the GDR regime in a decisive phase.[21] Following the quashing of a demonstration in Prague on November 17, there were radio reports claiming that security forces had killed a student. The news provoked outrage and fueled the protests against the government.

Later it transpired that the information had been no more than a rumor, but it was too late to contain the public's anger. Sometimes journalists played right into the opposition's hands, as when a Polish TV team filmed the violent suppression of workers' protests in Gdynia and Gdańsk in 1970 and 1981. Polish director Andrzej Wajda later incorporated these images into his film *Man of Iron* (*Człowiek z żelaza*), which was seen by a mass audience. These examples illustrate how the media not only relayed events but also shaped them.

Nationalism was a sixth factor, one that can be regarded as inherent in the system. The Eastern Bloc consisted of socialist nation-states, or federal states with nationally defined constituent republics. They were forced into line during the Stalinist era, but persisted in striving for autonomy from Moscow. The constellation in the Soviet Union was similar in some respects and different in others. Taking a *longue durée* perspective and following the model developed by Czech historian Miroslav Hroch, one can distinguish between three phases of nation-building here: In the 1920s, the Soviets sought to consolidate their legitimacy by a policy of "rooting" (*korenizacija*) that fostered nationally defined cultures, especially in Ukraine.[22] Stalin ended this first phase with the "Great Terror" of the thirties, targeting nationalist-minded cadres with repression and persecution. After his death, the various Soviet republics and their party apparatuses regained a degree of freedom.

Nationalist discourse continued to be censored, but positions in state administrations and industries were increasingly assigned to native cadres.[23] A creeping process of nationalization occurred that was barely registered by Western Sovietologists (phase 2). During glasnost, the various republics and nationalities openly voiced their often-cited "national interests." The intelligentsia in each group played a leading role in mobilizing the masses, mostly by invoking historical arguments (phase 3). As in the late years of the Tsarist Empire, nationally motivated debate and unrest did not reach the Russian heartland and Moscow until somewhat later. But when it did, it had a resounding impact.

The phase model can, of course, be extended to take further spatial and chronological coordinates into account. The first mass national protests were launched in the Baltic republics; mobilization was greater in western Ukraine than eastern Ukraine, where the predominantly rural population and industrial workers did not relate as strongly to a strictly national identity.[24] Nationalism did not, then, have an overwhelming, blanket appeal. But as in the nineteenth century, the ideology proved highly adaptable and transferable. Each Soviet state's nationalism reinforced that of the others, even on the margins of the Soviet empire. The Baltic states and Ukraine were emboldened by the former satellite states' achievement of complete sovereignty and the Red Army's retreat from Eastern Europe.[25] Their demands for independence, which had seemed completely unrealistic in the late eighties and were not supported by the West out of deference to Gorbachev, now gained real prospects of success.

The breakup of Yugoslavia is traditionally attributed to ethnic nationalism. But whether the ideological impetus came from a few influential politicians such as Slobodan Milošević, or was rooted in the population, continues to be debated.[26] The fact that it was difficult to recruit fighters at the start of the war in summer 1991 (especially in Serbia) seems to indicate popular detachment. But most commentators agree that the demise of the Yugoslav communist party left a political vacuum that was filled by nationalist politics. Elections in Slovenia, Croatia, and Bosnia and Herzegovina in 1991 resulted in victories for explicitly national parties. The constituent republics had drifted apart economically, politically, and culturally since Yugoslavia's federalization in 1974. Nationalism (in the constructivist sense of Benedict Anderson or Ernest Gellner) was therefore both a long- and a short-term factor contributing to the radical changes of 1989.

Problematically, these attempts to find explanations switch between places and periods, despite a dominant focus on the year 1989, and between structural factors and individual actors. Moreover, almost all of them view the events from the point of their conclusion—the collapse of the Eastern Bloc and state socialism. It is important to note that the oppositions in Eastern European countries in the eighties thought and operated within the parameters of their respective regimes. This was even the case in Poland.

Fig. 3.2. On February 6, 1989, representatives of the government, the opposition, and other interest groups began Round Table talks in Warsaw. Photo: picture alliance / ZB / Jens Wolf.

Here, the two sides met at the Round Table in spring 1989 to discuss reforms to state socialism and a division of power, not a regime change (see fig. 3.2). The opposition was represented once more by Solidarność, continuing a tradition started in 1980–81, when the trade union movement had rallied the support of some ten million activists. This was the largest twentieth-century mass movement in Europe, in relation to the country's total population. The sequence of events in Poland between two revolutions is loosely comparable to the Russian revolutions of 1905 and 1917.

Placing the focus on socioeconomic factors, a wider temporal horizon comes into view. It had been obvious that the planned economies were floundering since the late seventies, when Hungary and Poland had tried in vain to modernize by infusing them with Western capital and technology. Other countries' more or less drastic attempts at reforms, sometimes in combination with measures to decentralize the planned economy, sometimes as part of recentralizing policies, were no more effective. The economic crises became insurmountable when it came to paying off loans from the West. The Soviet Union, moreover, was badly hit by the drop in oil and gas prices. In view of this, the temporal horizon of any explanation should be extended well into the 1980s.

The "refrigerator theory"—arguing that the communists had merely frozen the nationalist conflicts, which began to "thaw" forty-five years after the Second World War—circulated for many years. This explanatory model, which informed the West's treatment of the crumbling Yugoslavia with disastrous consequences, does not stand up to scientific analysis. First, it overstates communism's ability to supplant other ideologies; second, it obscures the fact that renationalizing tendencies emerged long before 1989.

Czechoslovakia was federalized in 1969—the most fundamental change made in response to the Prague Spring in terms of domestic policy. Yugoslavia gained a new federal constitution in 1974, which sowed the seed of its later dissolution. Nationally motivated violence erupted in the Soviet Union in the late eighties; Armenians and Azerbaijani persecuted each other in their respective constituent republics, and conflicts also broke out in Central Asia. In Bulgaria, the government under Todor Shivkov repressed the Turkish minority; in consequence, some 320,000 of its members fled to Turkey. In some respects, this served as a blueprint for Slobodan Milošević. He counted on the West remaining similarly passive when confronted with the Albanians' persecution in Kosovo and, later, the conflicts in Croatia and Bosnia and Herzegovina. The fall of the Berlin Wall and the promise of German unification gave additional momentum to nationalist arguments. When the protesters in Leipzig and Berlin chanted "We are *one* people" (*Wir sind ein Volk*), it marked the first call for a change of state borders in Eastern Europe. German unification set an example for all other nations hoping to detach from Moscow or Belgrade.

Lastly, as Mary Elise Sarotte has suggested, an additional factor in every revolution was contingency and, in the case of the GDR, luck.[27] A fatal shot fired during a mass demonstration, an attack on a Red Army barracks, an earlier putsch in Moscow or other spontaneous action might have triggered a very different, more violent chain of events. Contingencies have always played an important role in the history of European revolutions. The same applies to the course of postrevolutionary transformation, which would certainly have been quite different if it had happened ten years earlier, when the economic mainstream was still influenced by Keynesian theory.

In summary, analysis shows that the 1980s was a key period with respect to all six causal factors of the revolution (the domino theory, mutual triggers, mass mobilization, economic decline, the media, nationalism). Though perhaps unsurprising, this assertion challenges the frequent portrayals of communism and state socialism as flawed systems that were destined to fail from the start, or were forced upon countries from without. Neither the former nor the latter is true. But as in previous revolutions, the weakness of the ancien régimes—in this case, most party leaders were literally very old—enabled the oppositions to consolidate their positions and create the "revolutionary situation" that has been stressed by Charles Tilly and other revolution theorists.[28] This situation arose, in turn, because most actors did not anticipate the approaching collapse of state socialism. If they had, the regimes would certainly have (re)acted differently.

## Centers and Agents of Revolution

All historic revolutions had a geographical center, from Paris in 1789 to St. Petersburg in 1917. Where did the revolutions of 1989–91 begin and who were the agents driving them? In a longer-term perspective, Gdańsk stands out as a significant hub. This is where the trade union movement Solidarność (Solidarity) was founded; it spread across Poland within a few months. Unlike in previous revolutions, then, resistance did not originate in the capital but in the provinces. The same was true in 1989 of the GDR (Leipzig), Romania (Timişoara) and, later, Ukraine (Lviv).

Earlier mass protests against communism had also taken place in regional centers: in Plzeň in 1953, in Poznań in 1956, in Gdynia in 1970, and in Gdańsk in 1980–81. In the second half of the eighties, Gorbachev gave the reformist governments in Hungary and Poland free rein to implement perestroika. At the same time, the communist party leaders of the GDR and the ČSSR, Erich Honecker and Gustav Husák, and other hardliners openly resisted reforms, deviating from Moscow in an opposite direction. In view of this long-term power shift from the center to the periphery, Moscow can hardly be regarded as the epicenter of the revolutions of 1989–91.

Nevertheless, Cold War history and literature on the collapse of communism and the Eastern Bloc tend to portray the Kremlin and Gorbachev as the originators of the changes. Despite the strong academic focus on Gorbachev, the last general secretary of the Communist Party of the Soviet Union (CPSU), information about his role remains limited.[29] More has been written about prominent opposition activists, especially Václav Havel, who was a noted dramatist and political philosopher.[30] Little is known about the mid-ranking party officials and second-string opposition who were not in the public gaze—the managers, industrial and agricultural workers, and other oppositional groups within society—or local centers of the revolution. James Krapfl is the only author to convey an impression of the broad mass of protesters in 1989, their ideals, and their rapid disappointment. His *Revolution with a Human Face* also marks the transition from "why" questions, or causal explanations for the revolutions of 1989–91, to "how" questions, inspired by considerations of cultural history. Krapfl's book inquires into the representations and interpretations of the revolution that shaped the further course of transformation.

The hermeneutic dilemma inherent in all the existing analyses is that their explanations are based largely on preexisting fields of inquiry. Anyone who focuses on Moscow—as most experts on Eastern Europe do, if only for linguistic reasons—will no doubt find the reasons for communism's collapse there. But shifting the focus to the smaller nations of Eastern Europe exclusively would be just as counterproductive. This is where the potential weakness of Timothy Garton Ash's explanatory model lies. His argument that civil society spurred the changes is tenable with respect to

Warsaw, Prague, and East Berlin but less so with respect to Moscow. The same in reverse is true of Kotkin's thesis.

The two lines of research can be combined by stressing the communicative links between Poland and the western parts of the Soviet Union. As recent studies on opposition networks around the Baltic Sea have shown, Baltic dissidents were well informed of the activities of Solidarność.[31] Polish underground publications reported on the mass demonstrations in Tallinn, Riga, and neighboring Vilnius. A number of GDR civil rights activists took Poland as their model, and Polish and Czech opposition members met in Krkonoše, the mountain range along their nations' shared border. These contacts broadened the horizons of civil rights activists. Moreover, the knowledge that they were not alone in their struggle had an important psychological effect.

The communication between the various opposition movements qualitatively changed their characters. This can be inferred from the images of history that were circulating in Eastern Europe in the late eighties. The dissidents (including a disproportionately high number of historians) had a common goal: to revise the official image of history, and especially to expose the truth about the Molotov-Ribbentrop Pact and Soviet terror against Poles, Baltic peoples, Ukrainians, and members of other nations. Thanks to their cross-border discussions, some of history's "blind corners," such as Katyn (where Stalin ordered the shooting of over 4,400 Polish officers), the gulags, the deportations to Siberia, and the Yalta Agreement, were researched and remembered in a broader, international context. United in their outrage at Stalinism and the major crimes committed in its name, the opposition activists initially neglected other conflictual issues, such as Polish-Lithuanian relations in the interwar period, the Polish-Ukrainian civil war of 1943–46, and the persecution of Jews by their compatriots. But by setting aside thorny bilateral issues, which the communists had actively misused in their propaganda, they prepared the ground for friendly relations among the Visegrad group, between Poland and Ukraine, and in a unified Germany, as well as for the revival of Jewish life. This contradicts the hitherto predominant image in historiography of a stereotypically nationalist Eastern Europe during the transformation era. This verdict only really holds for Yugoslavia, where the legacy of past conflicts, especially the persecution and mass killing of Serbs in 1941–44, was harnessed to fuel the war beginning in 1991. Remarkably, again, the impetus to reappraise Eastern Europe's history often came from provincial towns far from the capital cities, where there was less surveillance. This is a further indication that the revolutions of 1989–91 had multiple centers, and cannot be attributed to just a few "big men of history."

It is also worth looking beyond the borders of the Soviet empire. In the spring of 1989, tens of thousands of people were taking part in demonstrations in the center of the other communist superpower, China. While on June 4 the Poles were invited to freely elect a section of their parliament for the first time since 1947—resulting in a crushing defeat for the Polish United Workers' Party (*Polska Zjednoczona Partia Robotnicza*, PZPR)—the Chinese party leadership was using tanks and gunfire to clear Tiananmen Square of demonstrators.

The violent suppression of the protests in Beijing marked a victory for the hardliners over the reformers in the Chinese politburo. The military crackdown was also a reaction to the authorities' loss of control in the Soviet Union, which the Chinese leadership had closely observed. In spring 1989, there was growing unrest in the Baltic states, the Caucasus, and neighboring Central Asia. From a Chinese perspective, glasnost (openness) seemed the primary threat to stability. The Tiananmen Square massacre, then, is as much a part of the global history of the year 1989 as was the Washington Consensus.[32] The repercussions were perceptible in Europe: the party leaderships of the GDR and the ČSSR discussed the possibility of a "Chinese solution."[33] In the end, only Ceaușescu risked an escalation in December 1989, with disastrous consequences for himself and his wife.

The above events illustrate the internal dynamics of the revolutionary and postrevolutionary periods. With the wisdom of hindsight, the aging Eastern Bloc regimes seem predestined to fall. But the reform communists, especially, still believed that they could save state socialism. When Gorbachev introduced glasnost and perestroika, he did not foresee the consequences. Despite their conciliatory intentions, neither Gorbachev nor the reform communists in Poland and Hungary should be idealized. Poland's last communist government, under Mieczysław Rakowski, entered into negotiations with Solidarność on a political gamble. Rakowski, the former editor-in-chief of the weekly newspaper *Polityka*, presumed that once power had been divided, the public would blame the opposition for the country's economic plight. This is exactly what happened, and in 1990 the trade union that had become the ruling party was struggling to contain its internal disagreements. While Solidarność tried to implement reforms that were not in the interests of its own clientele, the reform communists in the opposition had a chance to regenerate and develop a new program and economic policy.

In the GDR and the ČSSR, the dynamics of the revolution cut the period of power-sharing short. The East German Socialist Unity Party (SED) and the Communist Party of Czechoslovakia (KPČ) had blocked reforms for so long that their legitimacy was rapidly waning. The mass protests in Leipzig, East Berlin, Prague, Bratislava, and many provincial towns marked a psychological watershed. The demonstrations showed that the public had lost its fear of the police and security forces. This dynamic was repeated in Romania, the Baltic states, and Georgia, and, following the attempted putsch of 1991, in Moscow. The tendency of revolutions to gather momentum has often been observed and incorporated into various revolution theories.[34] Yet it has been disputed whether the radical changes of 1989–91 can be included in the long tradition of modern revolutions—paradoxically because of the predominant lack of violence. The time is right, then, to update the established revolution theories in the light of the events of more than twenty-five years ago.

## The "Negotiated" Revolution

In Europe, the 1989 revolutions are often referred to as "peaceful." This attribute suggests a contrast with the bloody revolution of 1917. But the divisions and transfers of power of 1989–90 did not take place completely without violence. On October 3, the People's Police in Dresden attacked hundreds of protesters demanding the freedom to travel for all GDR citizens as trains carrying the embassy refugees from Prague passed the city.[35] In Leipzig and East Berlin, the police initially used water cannons, tear gas, and batons to control crowds of protesters. In Prague, police tried to suppress the protests by force until the evening of November 17. In Tbilisi, twenty protesters died when paratroopers were deployed against the Georgian opposition in April 1989. The attempted storming of the TV tower in Vilnius by task forces from the interior ministry claimed fourteen lives in January 1991. It is not known whether Gorbachev personally backed these violent measures. The orders were probably given by hardliners within the military and the KGB, who stood behind the putsch of August 1991. Their coup failed not least because the security forces refused to open fire on protesters outside the "White House" in Moscow, who had gathered to act as human shields around the Supreme Soviet of the RSFSR, the later Russian parliament.[36]

In summer 1991 parts of Yugoslavia were already in the grip of terrible violence. In Krajina and other Serbian minority settlement areas in Croatia, radical nationalists shot and killed Yugoslav citizens who defended the ideal of peaceful coexistence. They also attacked Croatian elites, and soon targeted civilians in order to stifle a guerrilla war. By late September the eastern Croatian town of Vukovar had been reduced to rubble. The term "ethnic cleansing" entered into common usage in international diplomatic circles. Yet despite the escalation in the former Yugoslavia, the over one thousand dead of December 1989 in Romania, and the flashpoints of fighting in the Soviet Union, the violence of 1989–91 remained minimal in comparison to the French and Russian Revolutions. There was no stormed Bastille, no Vendée (where tens of thousands of antirevolutionaries and nonparticipant farmers lost their lives in 1793–95), and no guillotine symbolizing a reign of revolutionary terror.

For the opposition, nonviolence was a way of contesting the superior power of the communist security services. For the regime, much had changed since Stalin's death. The end of Stalinism marked the end of mass terror and the gulag system. Of course, state repression did not stop in 1956—as the Warsaw Pact countries' invasion of Czechoslovakia, the violent suppression of the protests in Poland in 1970 and 1981, the killings of East German refugees at the Berlin Wall, and the persecution and exile of dissidents show. But violence was used selectively, in certain circumstances only. The history of state socialism, then, confirms the general trend toward less state violence in the twentieth century.[37]

The lack of bloodshed in the year 1989 was ultimately thanks to a rational choice made by governments. Had they given the order to crush the demonstrations in Leipzig, Prague, or Sofia by military force, they might have provoked civil war. In November 1989 the ČSSR, especially, was on the verge of disaster. The secretary of the municipal party committee in Prague, Miroslav Štěpán, was a ruthless hardliner and called for the deployment of armed forces. But his comrades in the Czech Communist Party politburo held him back for fear of the unpredictable outcome, and because the defense minister was not convinced that low-ranking soldiers would obey the order to shoot. The government's attempts to mobilize police units in rural areas for deployment in Prague were hindered by many of them breaking ranks—some buses headed for Prague simply turned back.[38] Similarly, the East German army (*Nationale Volksarmee*) and police (*Volksmiliz*) had considerable difficulties mobilizing additional security forces in October 1989.[39]

No doubt biographical factors also contributed to the general hesitance to use violence. The politburos in Prague and other Eastern Bloc capitals were dominated by old men who were less aggressive than their younger comrades, such as Štěpán, who was only forty-four at the time. Some members of the older generations had experienced Stalinist terror firsthand. In the light of these memories, and without backing from Moscow, they were reluctant to deploy armed forces and tanks.

Taking up negotiations and waiting for rifts within the opposition seemed the safer option. Some of the old elites, especially in the economic sector, hoped to be able to retain their positions in a more capitalist system. Such hopes contributed to the regimes' hesitance and, consequently, the largely peaceful handover of power. The exceptions were, as mentioned above, China, Serbia, and Romania. Here the old elites clung to power by force; in Romania the second string of communists around Ion Iliescu rose to do the same. Thus the violence factor in these revolutions had a reverse significance: in 1989, it did not propel the revolutions but worked against them.

Precisely because of this lack of bloodshed, the convention of referring to the turmoil of 1989 as "revolution" has been challenged. This is reflected in the vernaculars of Eastern Europe. East Germans tend to refer to the events as the "turnaround" (*Wende*), though the term was coined back in fall 1989 by SED party leader Egon Krenz in a bid to make any further changes seem unnecessary. In various Slavic languages the events are referred to as the "changeover" (*zmiany* in Polish, or alternatively *przełom*); in Czech and Slovakian they are also known as the "turnaround" (*převrat* and *prevrat*, respectively).

Following Charles Tilly's thesis, all three constitutive elements of a revolution—revolutionary situation, process, and outcome—were manifest in 1989–91.[40] According to Tilly, a revolutionary situation occurs when the old regime is weakened and disunited. The revolutionary process causes it to lose control incrementally and triggers the internal dynamic mentioned above. Revolutionary outcomes can affect various spheres and range from political regime-changes to social and economic transformations. With respect to the role of violence, however, Tilly remains equivocal. While identifying it as constitutive of revolutions, he offers no convincing explanation for the exception of 1989–91.

Regardless of how one defines revolutions, the general absence of violence is one of the abiding legacies of the years 1989–91. Both the opposition movements and, to a certain extent, the ruling communists relied largely on peaceful means. The opposition took the lead by opting for a strategy of nonviolence during its mass demonstrations. And the ancien régimes in Eastern Europe complied for want of convincing alternatives.

Nevertheless, the term "nonviolence" should not be used without question. If an event is nonviolent, the actors involved eschew a certain political instrument and confine themselves to peaceful means. This implies a passivity that was not the case. The participants in Round Table talks risked their reputations, overcame mental hurdles, and achieved important compromises, such as the power-sharing agreement "your president, our premier" (*wasz president—nasz premier*) in Poland. In this deal, the Polish opposition accepted General Jaruzelski, who had imposed martial law in 1981, as president on condition that one of its own leaders, Tadeusz Mazowiecki, was appointed prime minister. The sea change in Europe of 1989–91 is therefore best described as a "negotiated revolution," since it was based on a mutual willingness to negotiate. Polish sociologist Jadwiga Staniszkis anticipated this when she spoke of a "self-limiting revolution" in her 1982 study on Solidarność.[41] The self-limiting factors in 1989 included the willingness to share power and conduct talks to this end at a Round Table. In the GDR, the ČSSR, and Bulgaria, the exit criteria were different insofar as the opposition did not have as broad public support as in Poland. But these countries still had Round Tables, where free elections, the first economic reforms, and the change of system were negotiated.

Among earlier revolution theories, Hannah Arendt's concept of "constitutional revolution" is a useful reference point.[42] The revolutionaries of 1989 were concerned primarily with changing the political system to achieve democracy, freedom of opinion, and the rule of law. Similarly to the American revolutionaries of 1776, they did not strive to change society radically or impose a new social order. After the transition had been negotiated, then, the new political elites had no further need for revolutionary mass mobilization, and the phase of fraternization, celebration, and euphoria ended quite abruptly in winter 1990. (See also chapter 10 on the opportunities taken and missed in 1989.)

Negotiated solutions always involve compromise, which comes at a social and political cost. Around 1989, the nonviolent transfer of power made it easier for the old elites to retain their positions in the economy and society. Some communist functionaries participated in the formation of postcommunist parties. In Poland and Hungary, especially, many observers were angered that the old cadres had not been removed and condemned the Round Table talks. Populist right-wing parties such as the Hungarian Civic Alliance (Fidesz), led by Viktor Orbán, and the Kaczynski twins' Law and Justice Party (Prawo i Sprawiedliwość, or PiS) in Poland propagated the view that the events of 1989 were not even a disruption, let alone a revolution.[43] According to them, the negotiated solutions merely enabled the communists to prevail under new circumstances.

Even former civil rights activists began to dismiss the revolution as their influence dwindled after 1990. Western intellectuals criticized the right-wing, neoliberal outcomes of the revolutions. Veterans of the protests of 1968, in particular, expressed deep disappointment. Jürgen Habermas complained of a complete absence of innovative and forward-looking ideas in 1990. Jacques Rupnik, a renowned French expert on Eastern Europe, described 1989 as a negation of the awakening of 1968, which he in turn idealized.[44] Indeed, the outcomes of the revolution—cuts, growing social inequality, and, above all, greater disadvantages for women, who as a group were among the movement's losers—did not correspond with the goals of the left-wing or left-liberal activists of 1968. Neither did they answer the demands of the protesters on Prague's Wenceslas Square (*Václavské Náměstí*) or Berlin's Alexander Square (*Alexanderplatz*) in fall 1989. These protesters had presumed that the accomplishments of socialism, in which the large majority believed, would be retained when a democratic order was established.[45] Initially, socialism was discussed in positive terms, too, most notably by 1968 veteran Alexander Dubček in Prague. Though such opinions soon disappeared from public debate, they demonstrate that the radical reforms—though later embraced— were not a foregone conclusion. Other revolutionary concerns, such as humanity (*lidskost*, or *ľudskosť* in Slovakian) and liberty, were timeless values (and are therefore discussed in greater depth in the final chapter). The shallow dismissal of the revolutions and the ideals behind them by some German and French commentators reveals less about the revolutionary values than about their reception in the West.

To historians, meanwhile, the debates surrounding 1989 and criticisms of the revolution are of particular interest, as they contradict the one-sided success story. Berlin and Brussels may try to create a national and European identity on the basis of the myth of "peaceful revolution," but scholarly inquiry must go further. It has to consider the steep cuts in social expenditures, immense demographic problems, and other side effects of the radical changes. It must also ask whether these outcomes were the result of the actual revolutionary process or of the subsequent, top-down transformation. This question is addressed in the next chapter, on the first wave of neoliberalism in the early 1990s.

# 4

# Getting on the Neoliberal Bandwagon

## Milestones of the Transformation

In his reflections on the year 1989 and the concept of revolution, Polish-born sociologist Zygmunt Bauman stressed how different the dissidents and civil rights activists were from earlier revolutionaries.[1] He argued that the actors who came to power that year strove to build a new order with concrete visions in mind. In this way they differed from the Bolsheviks and the Jacobins, whose main motivation had been to eradicate their respective ancien régimes. What was the reason for this? Why were the new power elites and the protesters behind them so constructive? Was the latest wave of revolutions in modern European history less destructive because individual and collective experiences of late state socialism were less humiliating and traumatic than those of French absolutism or Russian Tsarism had been? Even those civil rights activists who had personally suffered before 1989 rarely condemned communist ideology or "real existing socialism" outright.

The constructive mood among the revolutionaries of 1989–91 was due, perhaps, to their social backgrounds. Václav Havel hailed from Prague's bourgeoisie; Marianne Birthler, like many East German dissidents, came from a middle-class background; Bronisław Geremek and Adam Michnik were members of the traditional intelligentsia; Lech Wałęsa came from the upper strata of the socialist working class. The goal these middle-class revolutionaries pursued was not wanton destruction but a civil society.

To place historical processes in discrete time frames, one needs to identify the end as well as the start of the historical period in question. Neither is clearly determinable in the case of postsocialist transformation; in fact, the changes to the political systems and the former planned economies continue to this day. Although democratic structures have been installed in most Eastern European countries (and dismantled again in Russia), the privatization of state enterprises, the restitution of private property, and other measures considered to be key elements of the economic reforms are far from complete. West Germany forms the only exception; here the Trust Fund privatization agency (*Treuhandgesellschaft*) was closed in 1994, and its last relic, the real estate company TLG-Immobilien GmbH, sold to US and German investors in 2012.

A number of earlier milestones could perhaps be regarded as endpoints of the transformation, or the period of accelerated political, economic, and social change. At the Copenhagen Summit in 2002, the European Union declared that the eight East Central European countries, Estonia, Lithuania, Latvia, Poland, Slovakia, Slovenia, the Czech Republic, and Hungary, had successfully completed, or were well on the way to completing, the transition to democracy and market economy. In 2004 the European Union was enlarged as planned; in 2007 Romania and Bulgaria acceded. But though each of these events marked a milestone, none of them can be regarded as the end of transformation.

The global crisis of 2008–9, by contrast, was a watershed. It has weakened the global hegemony of neoliberalism and particularly shaken Eastern Europe. Since then, academics and politicians in the East and West have begun to challenge welfare cutbacks, deregulation, privatization, and growing social inequality. The critics of neoliberalism and the Washington Consensus have also attacked the manner in which neoliberal policies were communicated.[2] Variants of Margaret Thatcher's slogan "There is no alternative" (abbreviated and parodied as TINA) had characterized the political discourse in Eastern Europe and Germany since the 1990s. Most recently, austerity programs in Southern and Eastern Europe were also presented to the public as necessary, unavoidable, and the only alternative. The equivalent German attribute, *alternativlos*, was used so often and obtrusively in reference to the German labor market reforms between 2001 and 2005 that the

German Language Society (*Gesellschaft für deutsche Sprache*) declared it the ugliest word of the year in 2010.[3] While the linguistic term can be rejected, the convictions and power structures behind it are not as easily dismissed. Reforms are still prescribed by politicians and experts who operate from the safety of their desks and permanent work contracts. The elites are hardly affected by liberalization, the sale of state enterprises, or social cuts. These apolitical and essentially antipolitical arguments are among the distinctive features of neoliberalism.

The Russian intervention in Crimea and Eastern Ukraine in 2014 could be regarded as a political endpoint of the transformation period. By annexing the Crimean Peninsula in blatant violation of international law, Vladimir Putin broke with a major consensus of the transformation period: to respect the postwar European borders and those of the former Soviet republics and successor states. The purposeful destabilization of Ukraine undermined one of the basic preconditions of transformation—that every country could shape its future in peace and largely autonomously. Russian neo-imperialism has repercussions far beyond Ukraine. It jeopardizes the peace dividends from the end of the Cold War that helped the former Eastern Bloc countries to evolve economically and politically. If one heeds Putin's repeated pledge since 2005 (since shortly after European Union expansion) to "protect" Russian minorities in neighboring countries, the Baltic states, especially, have cause to be concerned about their security. Few international observers noticed when, in 2011, Russia confronted Poland and Germany with the threat of stationing nuclear missiles in the exclave Kaliningrad. Russia's geopolitical ambitions—geopolitics is a central concept in Putin's foreign policy—have ended the period of peaceful transformation that began in 1989.

## The Bumpy Road of Reforms in Eastern Europe

Dividing history into discrete eras always carries the risk of overlooking disruptions within these periods. The road of reforms in Eastern Europe was not straight and smooth, but curvy and bumpy, especially in the mid-nineties. Rather than arising from the revolutionary changes, these bumps and interruptions were the unintended results of neoliberal policies. Poland, which had been one of the first countries to end state socialism, led the way again. High unemployment, widespread poverty, and frustration at the outcome of reforms convinced the majority of Polish voters to support the postcommunists (*Sojusz Lewicy Demokratycznej*, or Democratic Left Alliance) at the parliamentary elections in 1993.[4] The SLD formed the government, together with the Peasant Party (*Polskie Stronnictwo Ludowe*, or PSL), which had already existed prior to 1989 as a "bloc party." Hence the former comrades returned to power—in the heartland of anticommunist resistance, of all places. The Western media and governments were surprised and shocked about this caesura; our family friends in Kraków and Gdańsk were aghast. What had happened?

One reason for the reformers' defeat lay precisely in the neoliberal buzzword "shock therapy." Leszek Balcerowicz had avoided this term when propagating his plan to reform the Polish economy in 1989. But Western media promoted it as a neat formula to sum up the radical reform policies.[5] The Balcerowicz plan was basically to cause a big bang: If the pointless subsidies for foodstuffs, coal, rents, and many utility items were scrapped, the prices for all products decontrolled, the unprofitable large-scale enterprises privatized, and the borders opened to foreign businesses, after a short, painful period of adjustment, the Polish economy would reach an "equilibrium" and start to grow again. The equilibrium theory—the assumption that the markets will autonomously create a balance between supply and demand without state intervention—is one of the basic tenets of neoclassical economic theory. The Chicago School also relied on the rationality of market players. The concept of the "hidden hand" (which stemmed from Scottish Enlightenment thinker Adam Smith, one of the founders of modern liberalism) added a metaphysical dimension; the market was regarded as a last judgment over all goods that can be exchanged.

Unfortunately, the architects of the reforms misjudged the extent of the economic downturn when applying the recipes of the

**Map 2**. Central and Eastern Europe

Washington Consensus.[6] In Poland, the first country to introduce shock therapy, Finance Minister Leszek Balcerowicz expected the economy to shrink by around 5 percent and unemployment to rise moderately. In fact, the gross national product fell by 18 percent in the years 1990 and 1991, and industrial production dropped by almost a third. Inflation was not as easy to control as had been hoped, and capped wages (also intended to fight infla- tion) additionally dampened demand. Moreover, legions became unemployed: in 1992, 2.3 million Poles, or 13.5 percent of the adult working population, were without a job.[7]

Strangely, these disastrous figures did not move the new political elites to seriously doubt the recipes for reform. The entire former leadership of the Solidarność movement, including the former left-wing dissident Jacek Kuroń, the more liberal Adam Michnik, and the right-wing Gdańsk liberals, right up to Józef Tischner (a prominent priest and philosopher influenced by Catholic social teaching), continued to support Balcerowicz's ten-point plan. The reason is probably to be found in human psychology. The reforms were like a pool of cold water that everybody jumped into without knowing how to swim. Because gradualism had failed with perestroika, the "Third Way" had been discredited by Yugoslavia's disintegration, and the Western European welfare model was too expensive, the only life buoy floating in the pool was neoliberalism. The reformers saw no other choice than to cling to it.

Perhaps another reason why former Eastern Bloc countries embraced the reforms was that, in some respects, they echoed the communist rhetoric of the postwar period. In the early nineties, as previously under state socialism, people were told that sacrifices now would make way for a better future. The faith in progress and the effectiveness of the reforms from above were reminiscent of the communist era. Karol Modzelewski, one of the few intellectual Solidarność leaders to speak out against the radical reforms, remarked with some irony that the only thing that had changed in 1989 was the slogan—from "building socialism" to "building capitalism."[8] Even the two doctrines' position on the state is more similar than one might presume. Orthodox Marxists believed that during a transitional period to create a classless society the state was necessary but that it would become superfluous once communism was established. The neoliberals needed a strong central bank and other state institutions to implement reforms before the hidden hand of the market would start to regulate all aspects of the economy and society and the state could be reduced to a minimum.

Two years after adopting the Balcerowicz Plan, Poland's economy actually did begin to show signs of recovery. But the upswing came too late to convince the voters. A growing number among Polish society did not want any more shocks or therapy. Many supporters of Solidarność stayed at home during the parliamentary elections of 1993. The postcommunists, who could rely on old party structures and supporters, emerged as the victors. Following this bombshell in Poland, there were parliamentary elections in Hungary. Here the socialists gained an outright majority of parliamentary mandates in 1994. In East Germany the PDS (*Partei des demokratischen Sozialismus*, Party of Democratic Socialism), the successor party to the SED, gained four Berlin constituencies at the parliamentary elections and became established as a regional East German party. In 1995 the former communist youth functionary Aleksander Kwaśniewski consolidated the SLD's lead in Poland, defeating the former labor leader Lech Wałęsa at the presidential elections.

This postcommunist *turnaround*, which the term far more aptly describes than the upheavals of 1989, coincided with a shift in the constellation of international actors. While the IMF and the World Bank had initially been the predominant agents of reforms (the Balcerowicz Plan hinged on the approval of the former), the influence of the European Union now grew. This was due not least to the 1991 treaty of association binding the Visegrad group, and subsequently all Eastern European countries, to Brussels. The European Union focused on the "third dimension" of transformation—rebuilding state structures and strengthening the judiciary—as well as consolidating constitutional democracy and maintaining at least minimal social benefits. With the postcommunists in power, the welfare state was no longer considered obsolete, and the impoverishment of large sections of the population was more critically observed. The new Polish and Hungarian governments slowed down the privatization of major industrial combines and made job preservation a top priority.

Despite this attenuation of the neoliberal hegemony in Eastern Europe in the mid-nineties, the postcommunists did not attempt to turn the clock back. They held on to the principle of reforms and persisted with their political practice. There were internal and external issues behind this continuity. For one, the postcommunist governments could not afford to radically change course. Debt-ridden Hungary and Poland, especially, were dependent on the goodwill of Western financial institutions and investors. Second, the Polish and Hungarian postcommunists were left-wing in the same vein as New Labour in the United Kingdom. They knew how often state intervention had failed before 1989 and therefore tended to act with "the market" in mind. The party leaders in each country—veteran reform communists such as Gyula Horn and the former youth affairs functionary Kwaśniewski—had experienced the demise of state socialism and the dysfunctional nature of planned economies firsthand. They hoped for a return to power and full coffers for themselves, but without a reversion to the situation before 1989.

The postcommunists were also aware that they faced mistrust at home and abroad. To compensate, they tended to overconform to contemporary neoliberalism. Beards and turtleneck sweaters—the trademarks of opposition members who came to power in 1989— were banished to history. With his permanent solarium tan and gleaming white smile, Aleksander Kwaśniewski embodied Eastern European aspirations to westernize on a visual as well as a political level. Thus the Polish and Hungarian postcommunists contented themselves with moderating the force of neoliberalism and changing only the sequence of reforms, stabilizing state institutions and state industry before embarking on privatization.[9] The electorates' rejection of neoliberal reforms in most East Central European countries (with the temporary exception of the Czech Republic, where Václav Klaus remained in office until 1998, when he stepped down in the wake of the bank crisis) reveals much about the relationship between democracy and market economy, which was regarded as symbiotic in the West. It was only possible to introduce such radical reforms because these countries' democratic structures were still inchoate. The postcommunist societies were too busy mastering the everyday challenges of transformation to put up much resistance to radical reforms. In Poland, moreover, some leading advocates of the government's polices openly stated that democratic resistance could and should be disregarded. Adam Michnik put it bluntly in several editorials for the daily *Gazeta Wyborza* (the most successful quality newspaper of all postcommunist countries, which he had founded) when he wrote that the broad masses had little understanding of economic policy and that rapid and irreversible reforms were therefore the best recipe.[10] Many intellectuals from Solidarność circles shared Michnik's opinion. The tragedy of the trade union movement was that its brightest minds entered into government, where they co-operated on a program that could hardly be reconciled with the interests of their own clientele.[11]

In Russia in 1993, the Congress of People's Deputies refused to back the reforms, prompting President Boris Yeltsin to resort to alternative methods. He dissolved parliament and, when his opponents refused to yield, had armed forces open fire on the building. The outcome was 187 fatalities and permanent damage to Russia's fledgling democracy. In broad terms, then, the neo-liberal reforms in Eastern Europe were pushed through on the basis of deficient democracy—a scenario that in some respects was repeated in technocrat-ruled Greece and Italy during the initial phase of the euro crisis. The governments under Loukas Papadi-mos and Mario Monti were not elected but appointed in the wake of the crisis. These two former bankers tried to implement auster-ity measures and reforms without a democratic mandate. But they were both defeated by internal resistance—and Monti, finally, at the next parliamentary elections.

The former East Germany did not go through a political trans-formation crisis as did Poland, Hungary, and, somewhat later, the Czech Republic and Slovakia. Despite the election victories of the PDS, the West German elites and Chancellor Helmut Kohl had a firm grip on power. But the economic transformation crisis in the region was all the more dramatic on account of the measures introduced in 1990. Without any major declarations or ideological justifications—neither Kohl nor his finance minister Theo Waigel were Thatcherites or advocates of the Chicago School—the econ-omy of the GDR was exposed to the most radical shock therapy in postcommunist Europe.[12]

The first shock was the "economic union" of July 1990. Its extent can be better gauged by looking a little further back in

**Fig. 4.1.** A currency exchange office at Berlin's Zoo station on November 10, 1989. Photo: ullstein bild / Ritter.

economic history. In the 1980s, the GDR was only able to export at drastically reduced prices. The (strictly confidential) rate of exchange for one West German mark used for internal clearing by the Bank for Foreign Trade deteriorated from 2.50 East German marks in 1980 to 4.40 in 1988.[13] The black market rate was even worse, having leveled off at around 7:1 after the fall of the Iron Curtain but occasionally dipping considerably lower (see fig. 4.1).

Other East Central European currencies depreciated as well. The Czechoslovak crown fell below its previous black market price of fifteen koruny to one German mark. Whereas Václav Klaus let the currency float, Helmut Kohl decided on a political exchange rate. In spite of warnings by the West German Central Bank, which argued for an exchange rate of two East German marks to one West German mark, the currency union was enacted in summer 1990 at an exchange rate of 1:1 (the only exceptions being large savings deposits and company debts, where a rate of 1:2 or 1:3 applied). The upward revaluation meant that all wages, salaries, rents, and other cost factors were converted evenly.[14] Thus products from the GDR became four times more expensive than they had been in 1988.

The imbalance is even more staggering in relation to Czechoslovakia, which was about as wealthy and developed as the GDR. As mentioned above, the Czechoslovak crown was devalued to around one-third of the previous official exchange rate. Against the depreciated Czechoslovak currency, East German currency appreciation made goods from the former GDR around twelve times more expensive. It is no wonder that this imbalance caused huge economic problems for East German industry. In the rush to accomplish German unification, nobody looked beyond the borders of Germany; the currency union was administered and communicated like an internal affair.[15]

Why did Helmut Kohl opt for a currency union and reform under these conditions? Besides the pressure from East Germany, he was probably concerned about his success in the first nationwide elections in the fall of 1990. He also seems to have believed optimistically that East Germany could be westernized quickly. In his election campaign, Kohl promised a flourishing future of green pastures ("blühender Landschaften") which soon became a laughingstock. In the spring and summer of 1990, a third argument gained urgency: if incomes in the former GDR remained too low, ever more East Germans would leave for the West. Indeed, a saying went: "if the deutschmark comes, we'll stay; if it doesn't, we'll go away" ("kommt die DM bleiben wir, kommt sie nicht, geh'n wir zu ihr!"[16]). East Germans soon found that the mark came, but the jobs were gone.

The second shock for the GDR economy was German unification in October 1990, by which it also entered the European Community. The economy of the former GDR had no customs, tariffs, or other defenses against competition from the West. Unification brought it the most radical liberalization in the former Eastern Bloc. In spite of all the neoliberal rhetoric, neighboring Czechoslovakia proceeded with greater caution. Finance minister Václav Klaus took a gradual approach to decontrolling the prices for consumer goods, and liberalized foreign trade in several stages. This gave Czech companies the opportunity to adjust to European and global competition. Klaus also took care to accommodate the public. The property market remained strongly regulated, with capped rents and protection against eviction for long-term tenants. As rents remained relatively low, individuals could more easily weather a job loss or change of workplace or other negative outcome of the reforms.

The third peculiarity of East German transformation was its unusually fast and radical process of privatization. First, all large companies were transferred to the Treuhand (literally, trust fund) privatization agency. This colossus held over thirteen thousand companies, where more than four million people were employed.[17] The second step was the sale of these companies to domestic or foreign investors. But the oversupply of companies thus created was bound to cause a drastic drop in prices. When Treuhand proudly announced in 1994 that it had completed its task, it had incurred a loss of more than 250 billion marks rather than making the expected six hundred billion profits on privatization.[18] Neighboring Poland and Czechoslovakia again proceeded more carefully and kept some companies under state or mixed ownership and management for many years.

The threefold shock therapy in the former GDR caused industrial production to drop within a few years to a mere 27 percent of the rate in 1988.[19] No other country in Europe, aside from war-torn Bosnia and Herzegovina, experienced such a dramatic decline. Amid this historically unprecedented depression, newly founded businesses had difficulty getting off the ground, too. Unemployment rose in some regions to over 30 percent. Such disastrous economic conditions would have provoked mass protests and revolts in any other postcommunist country. But the GDR had ceased to exist, and within the enlarged Federal Republic, political stability was ensured. Moreover, the German government compensated the losers of transformation with early pension schemes and generous unemployment benefits. These payments have often blurred the fact that the transformation was originally designed along neoliberal lines. The economist Hans-Werner Sinn criticized the government's economic policy in the former GDR as tantamount to "insolvency with special social benefits" ("Konkursverwaltung mit Sozialplan").[20]

The East Germans responded once again by voting with their feet. In the first four years after unification alone, some 1.4 million East Germans migrated to the former West Germany. After this initial exodus, labor migration abated, only to increase again in the late nineties, reaching a new climax in 2001 when 230,000 East Germans migrated west.[21] The statistics on company formations, which are considered in greater depth below in the comparative chapter on Central and Eastern European cities, give an indication of how badly these people were missed. The number of migrants from East to West Germany between 1989 and 1993 roughly corresponded with the number of new enterprises founded in Czechoslovakia in the same period. Germany's economic policy after 1990 has often been justified with the claim that it was the only way to stop further migration from the GDR.[22] But this goal was evidently not achieved. The former GDR was drained.

For several years, the German government pursued policies that effected comprehensive changes in the East while causing minimal disruption in the former West Germany. Nevertheless, transfer payments to the former GDR (including pension, health, and unemployment benefits) knocked the national budget and social security system off-balance. The result was tax increases and a nationwide economic crisis. Complaints about the "reform gridlock" (*Reformstau*) under the last Kohl government (1994–98) signaled the arrival of semantic ripples from the postcommunist economic reforms in western Germany. The term was coined to criticize the fact that more and more reforms were becoming necessary, even in the former West Germany. After some initial hesitation, Kohl's successor, Gerhard Schröder (the self-proclaimed "reform chancellor"), took advantage of this drive for change to carry out some drastic social and labor market reforms between 2001 and 2005 (see chapter 9 on cotransformation).

Despite the neoliberal hegemony, the political practice of reform in Eastern Europe always diverged from the pure theory. This was due in part to the compromises that the reform politicians were forced to make. In Poland, no government could afford to ignore the concerns of trade union workers in the industrial region of Upper Silesia or the shipyard workers along the Baltic coast. The Polish government's policy on the national shipbuilding industry is a good example of pragmatism in practice. When it became clear in 1992 that the large shipyards along the Baltic coast could not survive independently, the state helped out by deferring social security contributions, cancelling tax debts, and arranging bank loans. In this way it hoped to make businesses fit for privatization rather than immediate sale or closing. The German Trust Fund privatization agency proceeded in a similar way in the former GDR. Such measures actually conflicted with the Balcerowicz Plan of 1989 but proved in retrospect to be useful and stabilizing. In view of this, in 1991 political scientist Adam Przeworski proposed that an optimal economic policy is, by necessity, inconsistent.[23]

The Polish postcommunists won the election of 1993 not least because they promised to take a careful approach to privatizing major businesses. By this time, the process of "small privatization" in craft and trade, the catering sector, and other consumer services had been largely accomplished in all countries of the Visegrad group (though it had proved more difficult in the former GDR in the face of West German competition). Where large businesses were concerned, the government assumed safeguards for investors and in many cases engineered privatization by giving banks company shares in place of loan repayments.[24] In this way, the state increasingly resumed an employer function. Privatization was not cancelled, just postponed to a time when a better price could be obtained.

Czech Prime Minister Václav Klaus also deviated from his neoliberal concepts, although he continued to defend them vigorously to the outside world. Czech national banks were required to shore up major industry so that unemployment remained low. However, many companies could not service the debts, and by 1996 several major Czech banks were on the verge of bankruptcy.[25] Czech journalists coined the term *tunelování* (literally, "tunneling") to describe the cause of their country's bank crisis. It evoked comical images of the managers of loss-making combines digging tunnels to the bank vaults to help themselves to the loot. In fact, the crisis was caused mainly by bankers giving loans without sufficient security, or on the basis of old-boy networks, thereby undermining their own institutions.

Privatization went hand in hand with corruption. Bribes and deceptions were employed when it came to rating businesses and selling business shares, and in everyday management. The most highly publicized case was that of Viktor Kožený, who purchased over a million privatization vouchers through his company "Harvard Capital & Consulting Investment a.s." (Its only tenuous link with Harvard was Kožený's bachelor's degree from the university.) Eventually, he absconded to the Bahamas with a fortune of some 200 million dollars. There he was safe from all the requests for extradition from the United States (due to further scandals involving privatization in Azerbaijan) and the Czech Republic. In a sense, Kožený is a postmodern equivalent of the famous English train robber Ronald Biggs. But his loot was worth several times more, and allowed him to indulge in a high-octane, luxury lifestyle.

The bank crisis in a country that was thought to be a paragon of market-based reforms highlights two endemic problems of transformation: protracted bankruptcies and corruption. To the bankers' and industrial managers' credit, the loans given to large-scale Czech industries secured tens of thousands of jobs that would have been lost if their audits had been more stringent. Thus the Czech Republic was spared the kind of mass unemployment that the former GDR and Poland suffered in the 1990s. However, as in the global crisis of 2008–9, the Czech banking and economic crisis of 1996 very soon turned into a national budget crisis, followed by a recession that affected the entire economy. Only a devaluation of the Czech crown and state guarantees for the banks eventually brought about a recovery. Foreign banks were the ones to benefit, as they acquired Czech banks at cut-rate prices.

In contrast to the Visegrad countries and the former GDR, Romania and Bulgaria hesitated to privatize major state enterprises. But they did not find a "third way" between capitalism and socialism, or any other coherent program. In both Romania and Bulgaria, the postcommunists won the first free elections in 1990. Unlike the SLD in Poland or the Hungarian socialists, then, they did not have any time in opposition to regenerate, develop new programs, or acquire expertise in the field of economic policy. Initially, the Bulgarian and Romanian postcommunists tried to keep domestic industries afloat with state subsidies. When the burden on the state budget became too great, they privatized the industries, mostly by means of so-called manager buyouts. This entailed farming out or auctioning off businesses to their own executives. The practice created warped incentives by making it worthwhile to intentionally mismanage or break up state enterprises in order to buy them cheaply. The bidding process, moreover, was frequently distorted by nepotism and bribery. In the end, the state attained much smaller revenues from privatization than projected, and industrial production dropped, causing tax revenues to fall again. Romania and Bulgaria responded by printing more money. By the late nineties, they were suffering another period of crippling inflation.

In Ukraine and Russia, too, transformation was attended by deep crises. At first the Russian government approached economic reform by a process of "voucher privatization"—that is, a broad dispersion of vouchers, or company shares, among the population (following the model developed by Václav Klaus). By neoliberal logic, this would create a society of shareholders and proprietors. But the postcommunist public viewed equity culture and stock exchange trading with skepticism. Indeed, many shares turned out to be worthless, and voucher privatization failed to catch on in Russia. So the government tried to sell large companies by auction but did so in the worst possible way: it handed the role of auctioneer to Russian banks. This privatization of the very process of privatization (officially via a program in which the state received loans for its company shares) marked a moment of glory for the oligarchs. In cooperation with the banks they owned, they intentionally depressed the prices of the companies earmarked for sale. Corruption was an essential prerequisite for participating in the privatization of major state enterprises in Russia.

One infamous example of how the state was cheated was the sale of the Yukos oil and gas group to the oligarch Mikhail Khodorkovsky. Having accumulated seed capital in the late eighties by importing Western products, he was appointed deputy minister for fuel and energy under Yeltsin. In this position, he acquired insider knowledge. Unsurprisingly, Yukos was eventually sold by a bank that Khodorkovsky controlled. The price at auction in 1995 for the company and all its oil and gas fields was approximately 350 million dollars. Two years later, its stock market value had risen to nine billion dollars.[26]

If the oligarchs had reinvested these huge profits in Russia, the damage to the state, society, and the national economy could have been contained. But they transferred much of their profit abroad. They did so for the kind of rational reasons that neoclassical economists and especially the Chicago School would certainly endorse. The oligarchs tended to control a certain market sector (thus there were nickel oligarchs, copper oligarchs, and the like as well as oil and gas oligarchs). Consequently, it was not necessarily profitable for them to invest further in Russia. Their trust in the Russian economy was limited—after all, they knew best how it was manipulated. By transferring capital to the West, they dispersed their assets and their risks, as any economic adviser would recommend. The semilegal and illegal practices of the oligarchs cannot, then, be solely attributed to post-Soviet cultural peculiarities.

There were other reasons why reforms did not work as planned in postcommunist Russia and Ukraine.[27] The oligarchs simply seized the opportunities that the economic reforms offered; they were pioneers of capitalism who successfully accumulated capital. These "new Russians" flaunted their recently acquired wealth at home and abroad, becoming conspicuous consumers of luxury goods in Paris, Vienna, Berlin, and London, and even buying prominent football clubs such as London's Chelsea FC. Supervisory bodies in the host countries could have investigated the origins of the invested funds, but none did. After all, the free movement of capital is one of the basic principles of neoliberalism. London, especially, and to a lesser extent, Vienna, thereby became accomplices to the oligarchs.

The main victim of this "raider capitalism" (рейдерство or *reiderstvo*) was the Russian state, which received only a fraction of the privatized companies' worth after their sale. As in southeastern Europe, the outcome was a drop in industrial production, gross domestic product (which was approximately 35 percent in Russia in the 1990s[28]), and tax revenues, forcing the state to increase its debt. Again, the banks "solved" this problem by throwing high-interest government bonds onto the market. The debt burden, growing budget deficit, and flight of capital eventually led to the ruble crisis of 1998. Russian and foreign investors unloaded their state bonds in a panic; the Russian Federation was pushed to the brink of economic collapse and national breakdown.

In comparison to Russia, Ukraine appeared relatively stable. As a former Central Committee member of the Ukrainian Communist Party and director of a mechanical engineering and missile factory, President Leonid Kuchma, elected in 1994, stood for continuity with the Soviet Union. But Ukraine was no better able to ensure basic provisions for the populace than was Russia. Many industrial enterprises went bankrupt; the subsequent shortfall in tax revenue rendered the state unable to pay regular salaries, wages, or pensions. People still went to work, though, because despite rationed gas and electricity, their offices and workplaces were at least heated. It was precisely during this depression period that I visited Ukraine for professional reasons. The place to see was the beautiful West Ukrainian town L'viv, which used to look a little like the black-and-white images of Prague that lured thousands of Americans to the "Wild East" in the early and mid-nineties. But while Prague blossomed, L'viv was forced to limit household electricity and running water to only a few hours in the morning and again in the evening. The decrepit waterworks system, which dated back to the Habsburg era but had been poorly maintained by the communists, could cope with no more.

Population statistics on L'viv show the demographic consequences of Ukraine's economic demise. The town's population shrank from 786,900 in 1989 to 639,000 in 2001, a reduction of almost one-fifth.[29] Some people returned to the villages they had come from in the postwar era. (The same trend has been observed in Greece over the last few years.) Since the late nineties, ever more Ukrainians have migrated to Italy, Spain, and Portugal, typically to try their luck in either the construction business or home health care, depending on their gender. Several million Ukrainians have sought work in Russia since the economy began to pick up there in 2000. But the trauma of the 1990s, a period of demise and adversity in Russia, is not forgotten. In 2002, Swedish economist Anders Åslund compared the Russian transformation crisis with the global economic crisis in the 1930s. He found that the drop in economic strength and standard of living was more drastic in Russia in the nineties than in the United States after 1929.[30]

## Neoliberalism's Inherent Problems

Why was the path to market economy—to use a buzzword of the nineties—so rough? Most transitology attributes the crises of the 1990s to insufficient, abortive, or half-hearted attempts at reforms—in a sense, then, to a lack of neoliberalism.[31] It is true that the drawn-out reforms in Romania, Bulgaria, and Ukraine had worse results than the shock therapy in the GDR and Poland, or its milder variants in the Czech Republic, Slovakia, and Hungary. But the other extreme—weakening and self-disempowering the state, as occurred in Russia under Boris Yeltsin—was equally fatal.

Even if privatization, the key element of reforms, had worked as the experts had intended, one inherent, systemic problem would have remained: an excess of state companies for sale. Even if there had been more Western investors, the oversupply was bound to cause a sudden drop in prices (here, one might even justifiably say "there was no alternative"), and the closure of tens of thousands of companies. Because there was a glut of state enterprises on offer, many were sold at dumping prices or with massive subsidies from the state. Western investors were able to cherry-pick state socialist assets. The mass-scale, rapid privatization of half a continent's state industries depressed "the market." It was no auspicious start for the fledgling market economies.

The excess of companies earmarked for privatization had a second, unintended result, which can be illustrated by the example of the automotive industry. Western groups such as Volkswagen and Renault took the opportunity to acquire companies like Škoda in the Czech Republic or Dacia in Romania. But one such takeover was enough to break into the postcommunist automobile market and export to Western Europe. With so many state companies on offer, a number of them, including FSO in Poland (where the Polonez was produced), ARO in Romania (an off-road vehicle manufacturer), and VAZ in Russia (Lada), failed to sell. These enterprises or parts of them were eventually privatized with great difficulty, but many other companies and works remained unsold. This could be regarded as a form of market adjustment, which the architects of privatization had taken into account and even welcomed. A less welcome side effect was that the millions of newly unemployed consumed far less. The impoverishment of large sections of society caused a downward spiral that also hampered many of the new businesses founded in the early nineties. A third problem of privatization was that Western investors were also concerned with eliminating potential rivals in order to dominate the market. For this reason, some of the companies which did not find international partners fared better than those which were sold right away, disproving all the prognoses of the early nineties. One example is the Polish shipbuilding industry in Gdynia, which experienced a positive boom in the late nineties and even expanded into the old EU countries. It was hit by bankruptcy in 2007, however, when the competition from China and South Korea grew too strong and the European Union refused the Polish government any further assistance.

China and Vietnam proceeded differently with their state industries. Both these countries kept existing combines under state control but left new industries to the private sector. Only an in-depth comparison of countries, branches, and companies could show which approach to transformation was more successful in the long term. The Polish shipyards were driven out of the market partly because the Chinese currency (yuan, officially renminbi) remained undervalued while the fully convertible Polish złoty appreciated against the dollar. Moreover, Polish workers demanded higher wages than their counterparts in China. Hence, other factors than gradualism versus shock therapy need to be taken into account. Nevertheless the early and radical liberalization in Poland had severe side effects and triggered a process of deindustrialization, which the West had been going through since the 1970s.

The historical comparison of different paths of transformation points to another factor: timing. This was a variable that was given little consideration in the Washington Consensus or by the individual national reform strategies. Whether Western investors could be found for postcommunist companies depended to a large degree on *when* reforms and privatization were concluded.

The countries of East Central Europe, where regime changes first took place, had a head start of two years on the former Soviet Union and its successor states. Southeastern Europe, where the postcommunists remained in power after the first free elections, also experienced economic reforms later. These countries were, moreover, disadvantaged by their fewer contacts with the West prior to 1989. Consequently, Western corporations which had already invested in Hungary, the Czech Republic, or Poland—geographic proximity to the European Union was another significant factor—had fewer incentives to take over or found additional factories in the Baltic states, Southeastern Europe, or the former Soviet Union. In general terms, this shows that neoliberal reforms could never be the ideal way for every postcommunist country, even if stringently implemented. Contingencies, which have been shown to affect every historical process, played an important part.

Paradoxically, timing disadvantages, and the emulation of the "reform pioneers," triggered a new dynamic toward a neoliberal order in the late nineties. The governments of the Baltic states, Slovakia, Romania, and other countries were sorely aware that the first window for entering the global markets had closed. These latecomers became all the more determined to jump on the neoliberal bandwagon, in order to claim their share of international investments. They attracted Western companies with even more radical reforms, and lower social security contributions and tax rates. The result was a second wave of neoliberalism. In turn, this competition (Mitchell Orenstein describes it as "competitive signaling")[32] put additional pressure on the pioneers and ultimately on the entire European Union. Some countries reacted by partially turning away from the neoliberal model, albeit on more political grounds. Examples are the special case of Belarus and in some respects the Russian Federation since President Vladimir Putin's second term in office.

A fourth problem inherent in the neoliberal order was the liberalization of foreign trade. Milton Friedman and a number of Eastern European experts argued that the domestic and foreign competition would drive state enterprise to modernize. But the formerly state-run industries were simply not able to compete, especially in consumer goods manufacturing, where there was much pent-up demand in the nineties and thus great potential for growth. When the import market was opened, the citizens of the former Eastern Bloc were keen to buy Western products. They had had enough of scratchy toilet paper, dreary suits, and unreliable washing machines and cars. Domestic industries would probably have been able to manufacture the desired products themselves in a few years, but the colorful consumer world of the West was initially far more attractive. In the former GDR, a pioneer of liberalization, this problem was especially pronounced. Eastern products were hard to sell in the early nineties. They did not gain greater consumer appeal until "*ostalgie*" (nostalgia for East Germany) evolved, endowing them with symbolic value. Again, Russia was an extreme case. Liberalization and the complete neglect of domestic agriculture and food manufacturing had absurd results. In the mid-nineties, the supermarkets of St. Petersburg and Moscow stocked almost exclusively imported foodstuffs. This placed a strain on the trade balance and further hampered the domestic consumer goods industry and agriculture.

A fifth problem was the routine approach to economic recipes. When introducing reforms, policymakers paid too little regard to the fact that each postcommunist country presented a different set of economic, social, and cultural circumstances (which are analyzed in greater depth in the section on human capital). However, in the course of the transformation crises, neoliberalism proved adaptable. Even convinced neoliberals such as Leszek Balcerowicz and Václav Klaus ultimately acted with pragmatism.

This raises the question of whether neoliberalism is a consistent ideology at all.[33] As discussed above, the neoliberal practice of the

1990s entailed a number of deviations and compromises, but the core remained the same throughout: privatization (especially, but not only, in the economic sphere) and faith in the efficiency and rationality of the market. Flexibility is one of the major strengths of the neoliberal order. Despite the transformation crises, market economies developed in all postcommunist countries—even in Belarus to a degree.

Contrary to the neoliberal condemnation of big government, the success of new market economies depended primarily on the conditions provided by the state and administrative reforms. Liberalization and deregulation, on the other hand, proved counterproductive time after time. This is illustrated by a historical comparison with the postwar era in Western Europe (or the Western-oriented countries of the Far East, such as Japan, South Korea, and Taiwan). The socioeconomic context in the Federal Republic of Germany and other Western European countries was more conducive to developing new industries and export markets. In relation to the countries' purchasing power, the deutschmark, French franc, Italian lira, and other currencies remained undervalued for many years; foreign trade was liberalized in stages. Thus market players could concentrate on the domestic market before starting to export.

Moreover, the currencies' exchange rates were fixed by the Bretton Woods system, and flows of international capital remained regulated. A flight of capital as occurred from post-Soviet Russia could not happen under these conditions. Had they prevailed in Russia, they would have forced the oligarchs to reinvest more of their profits at home.

But the postwar Western economic system had ceased to exist in 1973 (when the oil crisis broke out, by which time the Bretton Woods system had already collapsed). Two decades later, it could have provided retrospective inspiration at best. Since the failure of gradual reforms to socialism prior to 1989, there was no approved or even broadly debated countermodel on a global level. True, the reforms in Eastern Europe were moderated in the mid-nineties in response to the acute crises and problems. But the postcommunists and the Left in the West lacked the power and intellectual resources to develop a convincing alternative to the Washington Consensus.

China, where the economy remained much more tightly regulated, might have provided a countermodel. Here, market-based reforms were tried out on certain economic sectors or special zones (such as Shenzhen) before being applied to the entire country. In the nineties, however, the viability of the Chinese economic model was yet to be proven. Furthermore, China's gradual reform program was devised on the premise that the communists maintained their power monopoly. That would have been unacceptable in Europe, though Putin's advisors began to contemplate the Chinese model toward the end of his first term. They suggested that the Chinese combination of capitalism with an authoritarian regime might be better suited to Russia than attempting to apply neoliberal reforms.[34]

Although some policymakers in the nineties had fundamental misgivings about the neoliberal order, they rarely expressed them. Openly denouncing market failures or criticizing capitalism would have seemed iconoclastic then. On the contrary, key players such as Leszek Balcerowicz vigorously defended the shock therapy, albeit for surprisingly disparate reasons. While in 1989–90 Balcerowicz pleaded mainly economic reasons (that there had been no alternative), in his 1995 review of transformation he cited mainly political arguments. Above all, he argued that it was necessary to present the reform-averse populace with a fait accompli in order to implement the reforms.[35] In addition, shock therapy served to remove the "red barons" and weaken postcommunist networks. Perhaps Balcerowicz's inconsistencies were overlooked because the reforms were starting to take effect. Poland took the lead again, achieving economic growth in 1992, and slowly raising wages and salaries in the following years. Hungary and the Czech Republic also experienced recoveries, and the Baltic states began to prosper. (See fig. 4.2. For the sake of visual clarity, this shows a selection of, rather than all, postcommunist countries.)

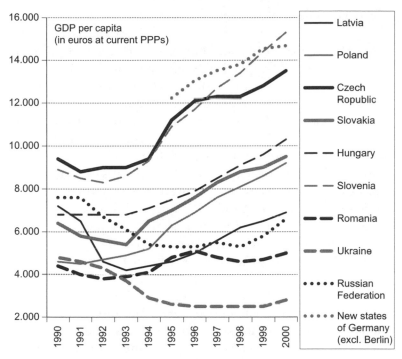

**Fig. 4.2**. Transformation crises and economic growth, 1992–2000. *Source*: WIIW Report 2012 (Table I/15).

Inviting prospects were painted, then, on a global level (by the IMF, the World Bank, the OECD, and other international organizations) and within the former Eastern Bloc. This dynamic explains the fact that all postcommunist countries in Europe applied similar economic recipes over the course of the 1990s, regardless of the sometimes-devastating transformation crises that arose. While variations were possible, from voucher privatization to manager buyouts and bidding processes, each had the same goal of privatization. Some countries hesitated initially to open their markets to Western imports, but eventually foreign trade was liberalized in all of them. Deregulation followed either from above, by reform legislation, or as the indirect consequence of weakened government.

## A Typology of Reform Outcomes

Although the triad of liberalization, deregulation, and privatization was universally applied, the outcomes in the 1990s varied greatly. Social sciences discuss this development under the topos "varieties of capitalism." While the term "capitalism" carries a critical undertone, the reference to its varieties suggests that no other order was considered viable, just different shadings of the same. This, too, was an indirect outcome of the global neoliberal hegemony established in 1989–90. Radical alternatives were supported at most by the politically marginalized, hidebound former communists in the Czech Republic, Ukraine, and Russia. In some respects, the "varieties of capitalism" research paradigm parallels the "multiple modernities" concept developed by sociologist Shmuel Eisenstadt in the 1960s. Interestingly, Eisenstadt rejuvenated his thesis almost four decades later, eliciting a strong response from the academic world.[36] In both periods of economic history, it was widely held that the contemporary economic and social changes could be controlled. In the sixties, the telos was modernity; in the nineties, capitalism. Looking at the postcommunist countries ten years after the first neoliberal reforms were introduced, it seems the changes were, in fact, rampant.

Research into the "varieties of capitalism" has increased so exponentially in recent years that it would be impossible to give a comprehensive overview of the existing literature. In general terms, it focuses on the relationship between the economy and the state, economic structures, and especially entrepreneurship. Occasionally the school of thought is criticized for underestimating the impact of political system change and noneconomic power relations on economic development. These criticisms will not be considered in depth here. In a historical perspective, it is remarkable that the "varieties of capitalism" paradigm conceives of the economic sphere in such autonomous terms. Yet it provides some good reference points for developing an economic-historical typology of transformation.

One useful example is a 2002 article by political scientist Lawrence King, contrasting Russia's patrimonial capitalism with

Poland's liberal capitalism.[37] King points out that market economy in Russia is organized along strictly hierarchical lines and rests predominantly on the exploitation and export of natural resources. At the time of writing, the oligarchs were at the height of their power. Although Vladimir Putin took steps against them a short time later, it did little to change the economy's hierarchical structure. Entrepreneurship in Poland, King argues, is much more varied and profits most from the export of semifinished goods such as machine parts and consumer items, many of which are finished in Germany to earn the "made in Germany" label. King also observes that the Polish economy is more open and shaped by foreign investors. This binary typology can, to a large extent, be applied to contrast all the countries of East Central Europe (including the Baltic states) with the post-Soviet countries.

In 2005, King and his coauthor Iván Szelényi extended this model to consider the differences between capitalism "from without" (as in East Central Europe), "from above" (as in the former Soviet Union), and "from below" (giving China as an example).[38] This second typology is based on considerations of management structure, the role of foreign capital, and power relations between the state and the economy. King and Szelényi, along with other social science scholars, investigated the strengths and weaknesses, and prospects for development, of each variant of capitalism. As denationalization is a central element and the ideologeme of neoliberalism, historians find the relationship between the state and the economy of primary interest. The economic reforms in all postcommunist countries aimed to reduce the state. Hence all sectors of the economy and eventually the social security system— core responsibilities of the state—were to be privatized.

The nature of the transformation of post-Soviet states depended, above all, on the relative weakness of the state and its bureaucracy. Russia, where privatization was privatized, is an extreme example. By 1995–96, the Russian oligarchs had become so powerful that they were able to plunder the state almost unchecked. Ailing President Yeltsin appeared to be a mere puppet of big business. The problem with oligarchic capitalism was that the "new Russians" generated very little growth or prosperity. Eventually the political system came to mirror the economic order; Russian democracy turned into an oligarchy. Developments in Southeastern Europe show certain similarities with those in Russia and Ukraine. But Romania and Bulgaria were encouraged to establish more constitutional structures to prepare for accession to the EU. The latter prospect, combined with the low cost of labor in those countries, attracted foreign investors.

Capitalism was more firmly rooted in East Central European society than in the former Soviet Union and southeastern Europe. This was due not only to the success of "small privatization" but also to the greater entrepreneurial activity of the newly emerged elites as well as the established middle class that had existed throughout state socialism. Here, then, a form of *middle-class capitalism*, or "capitalism from below," became established. This is illustrated by the fact that at least four million companies were formed in the Visegrad countries and the Baltic states between 1988 and 1993. These, in turn, generated further economic momentum.[39] In the nineties, this participation in capitalism was rarely discussed, despite its relevance to the popular contemporary maxim that democracies equaled markets.

The economies of East Central Europe were also propelled by foreign direct investments (FDI), as King and Szelényi have stressed. These could take the form of purely financial investments such as share-buying, or involvement as a dormant partner, or active influence on management. The more closely an investor is involved, the longer the FDI's lifespan tends to be. While a government bond or company share can be immediately unloaded and serve purely speculative purposes, the takeover of a company, construction of a new plant, or other costly measure usually indicates long-term interests. Iván Berend has further differentiated between "market oriented investments," which aim primarily to tap into new sales markets in the target countries, and "labor seeking investments," which are concerned mostly with exploiting cheap labor to manufacture products for export to Western Europe. Generally the type of foreign investment depends on the size of the country. While it serves the domestic market in larger economies such as Poland's, in smaller countries such as Slovakia the stress is usually on exports.

In the immediate aftermath of communism's collapse, Western players hesitated to invest in former Eastern Bloc countries, doubting that they would be able to simultaneously build up their economies, political systems, and governments. But with time, their confidence grew. From the mid-nineties on, a constant stream of foreign capital flowed from the old EU countries. In total, FDI in the period 1989–2004 in the Visegrad countries amounted to 146.5 billion US dollars (see figs. 4.3a and 4.3b).[40]

In relation to population numbers, the Czech Republic gained the largest volume of investments. Here, over $4,000 was invested per capita in contrast to around $1,500 in Poland. Millions of dollars in foreign direct investments also went to Russia. However, these consisted mostly of oligarchs' money that had previously

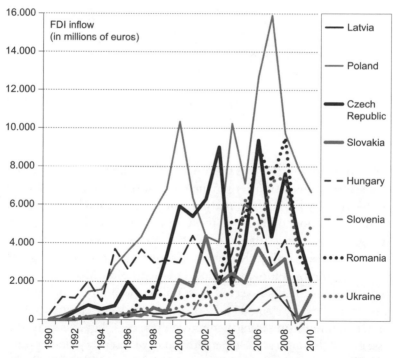

**Fig. 4.3a.** Direct investments (inflow) in the transformation states, 1990–2010.
*Source*: WIIW Report 2012 (Table I/2.8).

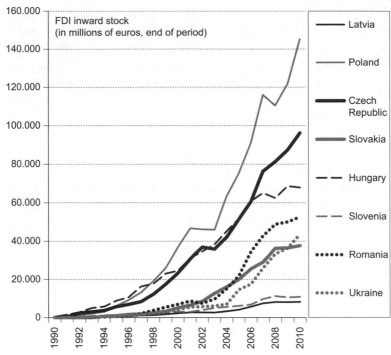

**Fig. 4.3b.** Direct investments (stock) in the transformation states, 1990–2010. *Source*: WIIW Report 2012 (Table I/2.9).

been laundered in the West. From 2004 on, the new EU member states also received transfer payments from Brussels. As these were not technically FDIs, their analysis will be saved for a later chapter.

The statehood of Poland, the Czech Republic, Slovakia, and Hungary was consolidated over the course of transformation.[41] These countries, unlike Russia or Ukraine, had the advantage of not being the breakdown products of an empire. Moreover, their middle-class capitalism served to stabilize the political order. The new managers and small- and medium-sized entrepreneurs had an active interest in strengthening democracy. Oligarchs played a lesser role, although some emerged and have recently gained political influence, especially in the Czech Republic and Slovakia. These countries' new governments and political systems stood the test of the transformation crises. While the ruble crisis brought Russia to the brink of collapse, the Czech government reacted swiftly and effectively to the bank crisis of 1996. Far from being a Czech peculiarity, the state's function as a savior in times of acute financial and speculative crisis is a permanent component of the neoliberal order.

Finally, to close this chapter, the significance of two main categories of history must be underlined: space and time. As discussed in chapter 2, the Visegrad group gained an early advantage by forging contacts with the West and familiarizing themselves with market economy during the period of détente. Consequently, its leading reform politicians had expert knowledge at their fingertips, which even the most ardent opponents of Leszek Balcerowicz and Václav Klaus do not dispute. Proximity to the West was another major advantage in the nineties: in a political respect, for export trade, and, not least, in the competition to win international investors.

The temporal factor—timing—was crucial in this competition. The East Central European pioneers of transformation attracted a great deal more foreign direct investments (per capita) than did the countries of Southeastern Europe and the former Soviet Union. Moreover, the foreign capital injected into East Central Europe was invested predominantly in long-term industrial projects (see chapter 7). The duration of communist rule is another important temporal factor. In a large part of the Soviet Union (but not the Baltic states or the Western territories annexed in 1945, including western Ukraine), communists had ruled for over three generations. The former intellectual elite, along with the executive and merchant classes and independent farmers, had been virtually annihilated during the Russian civil war and under Stalinist terror. Post-Soviet societies, then, had fewer surviving links with earlier free enterprise. By contrast, for East Germans, Czechs, Poles, Hungarians, residents of the Baltic nations, and western Ukrainians—people from all the areas that were annexed by the Soviet Union in 1945—entrepreneurial traditions were still within living memory, and business initiative remained a cultural value in their societies. Poland and Hungary, especially, had introduced reforms in the 1980s that opened up many more opportunities to evolve economically. Romanian society, meanwhile, had suffered such oppression under the neo-Stalinist Ceauşescu regime that its subsequent recovery from collective trauma left little strength and few resources to build market economy. These differences in duration and types of state socialist rule and the timing of reforms had a crucial influence on Eastern Europe's new economic and social orders.

Lastly, the time factor can be viewed in terms of the *longue durée* of economic and social structures. The forerunners among the postcommunist states had had well-developed economies before 1939. Saxony, Bohemia, and parts of Silesia were centers of industrialization in the nineteenth century.[42] Slovenia was the wealthiest constituent republic of Yugoslavia by far, with a gross national product just slightly lower than those of the southern EU countries Portugal or Greece. The more westerly countries of the former Eastern Bloc had generally better infrastructure, from road networks to hospitals and schools. This proved a considerable advantage for transformation and generating new wealth. In social sciences and history, the term "path dependence" is used to explain the endurance of political, economic, and social structures. In the nineties, historical paths of development in Eastern Europe and the former Russian Empire, which had converged under Soviet hegemony, came to diverge again, perhaps more than ever before.

However, national predispositions and path dependence should not be overstated. Large parts of Poland, for example, had been about as prosperous and developed as Soviet Ukraine or Lithuania in the 1980s. Poland's boom, in relation to its initial circumstances, was a positive surprise of the transformation period that demands closer investigation. This chapter has outlined mainly reform policies, viewing developments "from above." The following two chapters, which compare regions and cities, will take a more "bottom up" perspective and consider everyday life and experiences in postcommunist societies.

It is difficult to gauge the long-term effects of abiding structures and mentalities on political system change. Among the more westerly Eastern Bloc states, only Czechoslovakia had any enduring history of democracy. All its neighboring countries had become authoritarian states or dictatorships in the interwar period. But their lack of democratic traditions was compensated for by the creativity of their dissidents and reform elites. Polish historians and intellectuals constructed a democratic past for their country up to the early modern Noble Republic (which was indeed built on the political participation of a sizable nobility) or recalled the republic of the interwar period. The experience of democracy gained through the Solidarność movement, however, had a more profound influence on the political changes in Poland after 1989. In conclusion, it emerges that the postcommunist world was determined by a number of temporal vectors. Some stretched back to the nineteenth century and the age of continental empires (or even to early modern times and the feudal order). But the most important criteria were formed during late state socialism.

These reflections on temporal dimensions bring us back to the starting point of this chapter—periodization—and, by extension, the continuities and disruptions within transformation history. In specialist literature and, above all, in the world of politics, 1989 is often regarded as a kind of zero hour, and the transformation that followed as a continuum. But even the immediate aftermath in the 1990s was rife with changes and transformation crises. These cannot be precisely dated, as they were of varying intensity and duration. They occurred in the middle of the decade, affecting predominantly countries that had already introduced drastic reforms, and were one of the causes of the "postcommunist turnaround."

Poland was the only country of Eastern Europe to be spared a renewed economic slump in the nineties. Jeffrey Sachs has attributed this to the shock therapy and the policies of Leszek Balcerowicz.[43] But it could also be explained by the decision to moderate reforms and the (largely continuous) economic policy of the postcommunist government that came to power in 1993.

Moreover, Poland managed to avoid some of the mistakes its neighboring countries made. As the example of the shipyards in Szczecin and Gdynia shows, Polish management operated quite successfully under the direction of the state. Deferring privatization proved an advantage, especially in comparison to the former GDR. Here, privatization was such an imperative that the Treuhand agency was forced to throw all state enterprises onto the market or liquidate them before its closure in 1994. Adherence to the principle of returning communist-seized property rather than providing compensation ("Rückgabe vor Entschädigung") was symptomatic of Germany's passion for privatization. It prompted thousands of court cases and deterred many entrepreneurs from investing in land, real estate, or industrial plants because their future seemed too unpredictable. The Kohl government was at pains to help those who had suffered damages through communism, the majority of whom belonged to the pre–Iron Curtain, East German ruling class. But it was not concerned to the same degree with promoting future elites in the five new *Länder*.

The government of the Czech Republic took out cheap bank loans to cover state subsidies for large enterprises. The problem was, it had little control over the quasi-privatized businesses or the losses they incurred. Still, the Czech Republic managed to maintain relative stability and its middle-class structure. Hungary, however, was thrown severely off balance. While the West granted Poland a respite and even remitted a large part of its foreign debt in view of its strategic importance, Hungary had to continue paying interest on its loans. When the burden became too great, it devised the "Bokros package"—a neoliberal series of austerity measures named after then–Minister of Finance Lajos Bokros, appointed by the postcommunists. These measures had the effect of dragging approximately 30 percent of the Hungarian population under the official poverty line. Transfer payments from the West prevented the former East Germany from suffering the same turbulence as Poland or Hungary but could not kick-start its economy.

Yet the social problems in East Central Europe were slight in comparison to those in the former Soviet Union. In Russia and Ukraine, the economic crisis precipitated by the collapse of the old system was followed almost seamlessly by a transformation crisis after the first attempts at reforms. Russia's economy finally showed signs of minimal growth in 1997. But one year later, the ruble crisis caused a renewed crash. Many Russians lost their hard-earned savings as one bank after the next became insolvent. In 1991–94 Romania's rate of inflation rose to three figures, and in 1997 it was struck by another period of high inflation with over

150 percent currency devaluation; Bulgaria, meanwhile, went through a period of hyperinflation, with over 1,000 percent currency devaluation.[44] These developments in Southeastern Europe suggest that trying to avoid reforms was the worst alternative. But does this imply that radical reforms were the better—or only—way ahead? This question is hotly debated among economists and will be considered in the next chapter.

The transformation crises revealed how susceptible even the comparatively well-positioned postcommunist economies were to economic upheaval. Their fundamental weakness was acutely apparent again during the crisis of 2008–9.[45] The favorable global economic situation helped these countries to make relatively rapid recoveries from the crises of the nineties. With the economy booming in the United States and running steadily in Western Europe, businesses were seeking new export markets. In addition, domestic consumer demand began to pick up. Western European corporations discovered the advantages of Eastern European countries as manufacturing bases—namely, cheap labor and low prices—and the FDIs started rolling in. As shown in the section "Rich Cities, Poor Regions," only a fraction of these countries' population profited from the early upswing. But it allowed advocates to claim that the austerity measures were beginning to work, and that the situation would be far worse without radical reforms. This had profound consequences for those countries that had not yet jumped on the neoliberal bandwagon. The communicative dimension of neoliberalism came into effect. The negative repercussions of the reforms on society and the need for pragmatic adjustments were, to a large extent, glossed over. Policymakers focused entirely on growth statistics and a few macroeconomic indicators. Despite the enormous difficulties with which these countries put neoliberal doctrine into practice, the advantages outweighed the disadvantages in the international public's perception.

# 5

# Second-Wave Neoliberalism

## Neoliberalism at Full Speed

One decade after the breakdown of state socialism, the triad of privatization, liberalization, and deregulation had been implemented throughout Eastern Europe and in the post-Soviet states and was starting to affect Western Europe. Since neoliberalism was adopted and changed for the specific purposes of each country, the term "diffusion" is too simplistic. It is more useful to view this period in terms of "cultural transfers," and focus on the receiving more than the sending cultures. As in the years around 1989, the second surge of neoliberalism was propelled by the interaction of global and local players.

Among the former were institutions created in the early postwar years, such as the International Monetary Fund and the World Bank, which were still connected, at least indirectly, with national governments. Since the 1970s, economic policies had been influenced increasingly by a second group of global actors: private think tanks, consulting agencies, and media conglomerates. In the 1990s they invented a plethora of indices, the names of which speak volumes about the political and economic priorities of the time. In 1994, the British magazine the *Economist* came up with the "emerging markets index." The very title of this weekly column is remarkable, because it equates countries and their populaces with markets. The countries listed in it were not yet regarded as fully fledged market economies, but as "emerging" from obscurity into the light of Western modernity—the hidden telos of history. (The Western industrialized countries were listed and rated in a separate index.) In 1995 the conservative Heritage Foundation and the *Wall Street Journal* created the "Open Market Index." This was soon followed by the "Global Competitiveness Index," the "International Property Rights Index," and the "Ease of Doing Business Index." Karl Marx, whose legacy was virtually deleted in the 1990s—I remember how some of my fellow graduate students in Washington, D.C. protested against using Robert Tucker's *The Marx-Engels Reader* in 1992 because they regarded Marxism as failed—might have summed up all these statistics in one "Exploitation of the Working Class Index."

The thrust of these indices went beyond the Washington Consensus. This is especially visible in the field of privatization. In 1989 and the early nineties, privatization was still limited to state-owned enterprises; in the West it affected mainly the railways, postal service, and telephone companies. In the late nineties, discourse on privatization broadened to include key competences of the welfare state, such as pensions, health care, and education. Another recurrent focus of the indices and their guiding institutions was taxation and the introduction of flat tax systems. The general assumption was that lower taxes would generate growth and that the money spent by the rich would "trickle down" to the poor.

This chapter puts forward a different, sociohistorical explanation of how the postcommunist countries recovered from the deep recessions of the early nineties. It analyzes human capital and compares the resources of various postcommunist societies for coping with the daily challenges of transformation. One of the major results of the second wave of neoliberalism was growing social and regional divergence. But at least in East Central Europe, social inequality remained lower than in the United States—in contrast to the former Soviet Union. This was due to another international player, the European Union, which increasingly shaped transformation. Brussels' agenda was not strictly neoliberal, but focused on the reform of the state and the institutions that would guide transformation. Its transfer payments since EU enlargement were not entirely in line with neoliberalism and even alleviated some of its side effects. This thesis is supported by another guiding theme of this book: the deviations from and disruptions to neoliberalism, as well as its rise.

The aforementioned indices created the competitive atmosphere of a major international sports tournament. There were winners and losers, but everybody wanted to stand on the rostrum. Immediately after the fall of the Wall, Hungary and Czechoslovakia (and, after the latter's division, the Czech Republic) were applauded by various neoliberal indices, Western financial newspapers, and international investment agencies. In spite of its pioneering role in 1989, Poland was initially regarded with skepticism, mainly because of the power of the labor unions, its high proportion of agricultural workers (though the statistics were bloated due to the government's creation of a number of incentives for citizens to register officially as farmers), and the election victory of the postcommunists. But by the time Finance Minister Balcerowicz entered his second term in office, following the 1997 election victory of the post-Solidarność party AWS, Poland had also become a favorite of Western analysts. Slovakia under populist leader Vladimír Mečiar was the Cinderella of East Central Europe, but shed its dusty image and joined the other Visegrad countries once Mečiar was voted out of office. In the mid-nineties, the Baltic countries and especially Estonia started to climb the international rankings. The more open (that is, deregulated and liberalized) a country's market, the smaller its government and more advanced the privatization process, the further ahead the nation and its economy were considered to be. The mere act of listing these countries had a dynamic effect. Many Wall Street stockbrokers and hedge fund managers might otherwise not have known that Slovakia and Slovenia were two different countries, or where in the world Latvia and Lithuania were. It was not self-evident for financiers to turn their attentions to these countries. Global corporations such as Microsoft achieved a higher turnover in 2004 than their annual gross domestic products combined.[1] New York and London are more populous than all the Baltic republics put together. Their nomination on the emerging markets index signaled to international investors that they were potential targets. At the same time, an increasing number of specialized funds made it possible to invest in macroregions such as Eastern Europe as well as in individual countries.

Local stock markets were also evolving. In Warsaw, trading began at the reopened stock exchange (an outcome of the Round

Table talks) in April 1991 with five joint-stock companies and a daily turnover of the equivalent of $2,000. Twenty years later, the Warsaw stock exchange listed 426 companies, ran fifteen classified indices, and achieved an annual turnover of almost €85 million.[2] This exponential increase in the volume of sales affirmed the positive prognoses for Poland's economy. With its market of 38.6 million consumers—every citizen is a consumer under neoliberalism—Poland promised good business to investors.

Like shares in major companies, Eastern Europe had to be presented in a suitable light to make it attractive to investors. The reform countries did their best to convince the world of their neoliberal credentials. Leszek Balcerowicz's "shock therapy" and Václav Klaus' "market economy without attributes" were not only the products of personal convictions but also crafted to appeal to the international arena. Deviations from the standards set by the IMF and the World Bank—the Czechs' strict protection of tenants springs to mind—were glossed over.

About a decade after the end of state socialism, the countries of East Central Europe and the Baltic states were able to chalk up a number of key reform successes. Most of their large enterprises had been privatized, and their currencies were fully convertible. Capital moved freely; customs and trade barriers had been largely removed. In the late nineties, Western investors rewarded this "progress"—another recurrent term in contemporary media coverage and business journalism—by pouring more foreign capital into Eastern Europe each year. The region continued to entice investors with low labor costs and a "favorable economic climate." Indeed, in view of the dearth of domestic capital stock and still-large gap in productivity, it depended on an influx of foreign capital for its economic development.

## Flat Tax Systems and Populism

After the turn of the millennium, the race to win international investors and the debate on neoliberal reform led to a transnational discussion of flat tax rates. The Baltic states were the first to introduce an identical tax rate on all incomes, private and corporate.

Initially this was set at between 25 and 33 percent, varying from country to country. This was not far below the average level of taxation in the Western European welfare states.[3] The goal was a simplified tax system without scope for deductions or exemptions, to make it easier to collect tax. Other countries soon adopted, and radicalized, the flat tax arrangement. Russia, Ukraine, and Serbia set their rates of taxation at 13 or 14 percent, albeit with some exceptions.[4] Cultural factors were an additional motivation for these countries' policymakers. They had no illusions about the tax ethics of their citizens, especially the nouveau riche. But they hoped that if they set tax rates low, they might at least accept and pay them. In 2004, Slovakia followed suit with a flat tax rate of 19 percent for private and corporate income tax and value-added tax. Slovakia's tax reform caused a particular sensation as it coincided with the expansion of the European Union. Neoliberalism was no longer on the horizon; it had arrived in the EU.

The trend toward flat tax rates evolved in parallel with the aforementioned radicalization of privatization. In the early nineties, governments had privatized retail trade, the catering sector, and craft industries in the relatively quick and successful process of "small privatization." The sale of large enterprises proved far more difficult and resulted in losses, but it also progressed. By the mid-nineties, governments were selling companies responsible for public services and utilities such as postal and telephone services, power, and housing. A few years later, this trend reached Germany and eventually all of the core EU countries.

Around the turn of the millennium, privatization entered into a third stage, targeting key state responsibilities such as old-age pensions and health care. Again, the Baltic states blazed a trail. Hungary, Poland, Slovakia, and—somewhat half-heartedly—the now Social Democrat–ruled Czech Republic followed. While each country's welfare reforms differed in detail, the debates attending them were similar. Commentators criticized state pension and health care systems as antiquated, inefficient, and not viable in the long term, and commended the private sector alternatives as advanced, rational, and sustainable. This discourse was conducted in parallel to, and fuelled, the privatization process. Private pension funds and health-insurance schemes were promoted as a customized way of providing for one's old age, rather than paying into an anonymous social security system or ailing national budget. Private insurance schemes promised greater fairness by taking individual contributors' payments and risks into account when setting fees, rather than charging progressively, according to income. The fact that this was bound to cause redistribution from the bottom up ruffled few feathers. Some political parties—such as the German Christian Democrats in Leipzig in 2003, considered in chapter 9—even used it as an argument in favor of further welfare reforms. From a historian's viewpoint, this third stage of privatization is the most problematic. Indeed, it had unintended effects, and was reversed in most postcommunist countries after the crisis of 2008.

The redistributive effect was particularly pronounced, and welcomed, in countries that had adopted flat tax systems. Governments made good the losses incurred by tax increases—euphemistically referred to as fiscal simplification—in other areas. Slovakia, for instance, raised its value-added tax on foodstuffs and other staple goods to 19 percent, in line with income tax. The result: price increases of 5 percent and more and drastically reduced social benefits. The proportion of welfare spending in the gross domestic product dropped from 19.5 to 16 percent, almost the same level as in the Baltic states.[5] This hit the country's many Roma especially badly. In early 2004, they rioted for some days in eastern Slovakia, looting stores and attacking government institutions. But the protests were soon quashed. The Roma alone were held responsible for their problems.

Did these neoliberal measures have a macroeconomic effect? Foreign investment in Slovakia and the Baltic states increased markedly. Today Slovakia produces more cars per capita—in new factories—than any other country in the world. In Russia and Ukraine, by contrast, the flat tax system did not sustainably boost the economy or attract more investment. Countries that eschewed such tax reforms, such as Poland, experienced just as dynamic growth as Slovakia while developments in flat tax countries—Estonia and Lithuania, for example—diverged. Neither the results of these measures nor those of the shock therapy, then, point to a clear causal connection between certain fiscal and social policies and economic development.

The flat tax systems certainly had one effect: they raised international experts' and investors' awareness of these countries. Consequently, Estonia, Latvia, and Slovakia, to name a few, climbed the international rankings, and were even referred to as European "tiger economies" (together with the "Celtic tiger" on the Western fringe of the continent). With their high growth rates and low taxes and wages, the "Baltic tigers," "Slovak tiger," and "Slovenian tiger" (although Slovenia pursued a different macroeconomic policy) caused quite a stir. [6] Associating them with the growth economies of the Far East (the "East Asian tigers") was a promotional coup. Small Eastern European countries now appeared in the financial world's indices alongside South Korea and Taiwan, countries with far larger economies and populations.

Behind these positive headlines, social tensions were rising massively in all postcommunist countries. From the mid or late nineties, the rate of combines going bankrupt or laying off staff accelerated. Millions of people lost their jobs as one factory after the next closed down. The unemployed had few financial reserves to draw on; their savings had been largely devalued by high rates of inflation in 1989–90 or later. (The timing and rates of inflation varied from country to country; the former GDR and the Czech Republic were less severely affected.) Legions of pensioners were in need of assistance. There were very many potential recipients of social benefits—a factor only insufficiently considered by the architects of the shock therapy—but few potential contributors.

The imbalance was most pronounced in the Baltic countries, which had afforded minimal state pensions and social benefits from the outset. The ruling elites refused to raise welfare spending even when the economy had recovered, partly on account of the large national minorities in the region. Many losers of the reforms were resident Russians (some of whom were in fact Ukrainian or Belarus). The Baltic governments objected to supporting their countries' former occupiers with social benefits. After voting out the postcommunists in the mid-nineties, Romania and Bulgaria also introduced neoliberal reforms.

A side effect of these reforms was very low election turnouts in the postcommunist countries. In the early nineties and during the second wave of neoliberalism, many citizens evidently felt they had so little influence on politics that there was no point in voting. Deficient democracy and neoliberal reform policies were, then, mutually dependent.[7]

Under these conditions, a new political trend emerged: populism. The populists' simple strategy was to focus entirely on the nation, disregard the opinions of international investors, and, above all, promise the ethnically defined electorate protection against the rigors of transformation. They pledged to safeguard the populace from financial competition and criminality, and to protect their jobs and national values. Their allure tended to fade, however, once they were voted into government, and found themselves cooperating on unpopular reforms and forced to communicate with external actors. Due to the unpopularity of neoliberal reforms, governments were often voted out after just one term. The same has occurred in recent years to the reformers in Southern Europe. Despite vacillating voters, who caused the complete downfall of some ruling parties (one extreme example is the *Akcja Wyborcza Solidarność*, which emerged the clear victor in 1997 but failed to win any seats four years later), and the success of populist parties, the new EU member states are generally regarded as "consolidated democracies." (Hungary is a special case, considered below.)[8]

German transformation expert Wolfgang Merkel has stressed the contribution of longer-term factors, such as the stability of governmental structures and the high level of education among the population, to the success of reforms in postcommunist countries. His conclusion conflicts with the Chicago School's rejection of big government and the contempt for all legacies of state socialism that prevailed in the early nineties. After the fall of the Iron Curtain, virtually all forms of state interventionism were condemned as outdated. Yet some government investments turned out to be vital. One example is the postwar expansion of public education that had started earlier, and was more sweeping, in Eastern than in Western Europe.[9] Thus the state-socialist countries had accumulated a major resource that was useful for transformation: human capital.

## Human Capital

In this chapter, "human capital" denotes the individual and collective resources and abilities used to cope with the challenges presented by transformation.[10] These resources and abilities did not develop overnight or in 1989 but during, or even prior to, the era of state socialism. Human capital cannot be measured in the same way as the capital stock of a given country. Individual and collective education, expert knowledge, and qualifications cannot be converted into economic performance indicators. But cheap labor certainly attracted foreign investors. In the postcommunist countries, labor costs were only 7 percent of the EU average at the 1990 exchange rate (with the major exception of the GDR after economic union with the FRG).[11] News of a third factor, Eastern Europeans' work ethos, quickly got around investor circles.

Consider this "participating observation" of the early transformation years: Five years after the Volkswagen group took over the Czech automobile company Škoda, a group of German undergraduates and doctoral students linked to the social democratic Friedrich Ebert Foundation visited the company plant in Mladá Boleslav. The German visitors, along with the present author as their guide, expected the staff committees they had arranged to meet to complain about their low pay and bad working conditions. Indeed, Škoda then paid its skilled workers less than a third of the German wage (the equivalent of about $750 a month) and demanded longer hours without any extra pay. But contrary to the visitors' expectations, the apparently contented trade unionists did not want to bemoan their wages or exploitation but to present Škoda's latest model, a midrange car developed in part by their own engineers. They lovingly stroked the sample car's fender, proudly highlighting its merits and finally pointing out that their factory produced fewer rejects and maintained better discipline than the Volkswagen parent plant in Wolfsburg. (The Octavia model went on to become a bestseller as hoped.) With their presentation, the Škoda staff not only exemplified the popular myth of Czech *inženirství* (a nation of technicians and tinkerers) but also vindicated the new owners' clever concession of allowing the Czech plant to retain staff committees and strong trade unions.

Relations between Western investors and local employees were rarely as harmonious as they were at Škoda. But apparently here, at least, the workers and their representatives had adapted to the new system with ease. Under state socialism, factories such as Škoda had been notorious for producing goods of uneven quality and a high rate of rejects. Logistical problems arising from the planned economy were partly to blame. Manufacturers were often forced to improvise because certain parts were unavailable or deficient.[12] Work practices in state socialist enterprises were, moreover, rather loosely organized. It was normal procedure to take impromptu breaks (on top of the forced breaks while waiting for supplies or for material problems to be solved) and run a few errands during the working day. Yet within just five years, all trace of these habits had been erased.

Another example of human capital is the millions of self-employed who set up their own businesses. In Hungary and Poland, as mentioned above, this was possible years before the fall of the Iron Curtain. In Poland, communist party leader Edward Gierek gave the go-ahead in 1979 for the special Polonia enterprises, designed to attract investment from expat Poles or other Western shareholders and export to the West. Partners in these joint ventures enjoyed privileges such as permission to hold foreign currency accounts, and were subject to laxer import and export regulations. Looking back, these new entrepreneurs often stress the restrictions under which they worked, but their businesses were cradles of capitalism.[13] In 1988, the Polonia enterprises employed over eighty thousand people. They organized Poland's *komputeryzacja*, the import of more than one hundred thousand computers from the West, which were used to modernize the Polish economy from below.[14] The main difficulty was importing the devices, as memory chips were on the CoCom list of armament-relevant goods and their export to the Eastern Bloc was prohibited. To get around this problem, the computers were taken apart before being transported (for the most part, legally) across the borders, then reassembled in Poland. Polish traders also sold many products to consumers farther east. In 1986 the Soviet authorities registered eight hundred thousand visitors from Poland, most of whom were no doubt "commercial tourists." In 1989 the number of incoming travelers rose by 100 percent; the number of transit visas, which played an important role in long-distance trading, increased by 200 percent.[15]

As the Soviet Union collapsed, entrepreneurs such as Mikhail Khodorkovsky and Ukraine's future Prime Minister Yulia Timoshenko made fortunes dealing in computers and entertainment electronics. Trade in scarce products such as jeans, nylon pantyhose, Western cigarettes—the brands Marlboro and Kent were virtually currencies in their own right, ideal for mollifying customs officers and other state functionaries—whiskey, and cognac was equally lucrative. Oligarchs built their careers on a combination of business sense (knowing which products would reap the highest profits), contacts (how to get goods through customs and around police controls), insider knowledge (when to acquire companies earmarked for privatization with one's accumulated capital), and ruthlessness (when to bribe whom, or to offer other favors instead of cash bribes). The oligarchs' mostly semilegally or illegally acquired wealth was, then, also based on human capital. Neither this concept nor the abilities individuals acquired under state socialism should be viewed through rose-tinted spectacles. Even so, human capital is an important factor for explaining the fortunes of individuals, peer groups, and entire countries.

Poland, beginning in the postwar period, provides a good example. It was modernized in a far more piecemeal manner than were its socialist neighbors. Collectivization was aborted in 1956 in the face of resistance from the farming population; its agriculture remained compartmentalized and underproductive. Industrialization progressed more slowly than in the GDR, ČSSR, and Soviet Union. In contrast to its neighbors, Poland remained without a nuclear power plant, perhaps fortunately in view of the Chernobyl disaster. Neither did it build any substantial stretch of highway (the Autobahn in Silesia dated from the Nazi era), nor a single mile of subway track. The lack of economic modernization was one of the reasons why Poland remained distinctly poorer than the GDR and even comparably agrarian Slovakia, until 1989. But the resistance offered by farmers, workers, and intellectuals had also kept more market niches and entrepreneurial practices alive. As a consequence, Polish society was better prepared for the second, postindustrial wave of modernization. Within the Eastern Bloc, Poles were famous (or notorious, as will be seen in chapter 6) for their keen business acumen. Polish entrepreneurs displayed a sixth sense for gaps in the market.

An interesting illustration is provided by the Warsaw-based Eris cosmetic company. Just as Western shampoo or shower gel was de rigucur in prestigious communist households, today no sophisticated Polish bathroom is without a tub of Eris face cream. The company was founded at an inauspicious time, shortly after martial law was declared in 1981. Poland was deep in economic crisis. Even basic foodstuffs like sugar and flour were rationed; meat was rarely available.[16] But company founder Irena Eris sensed a demand for a little luxury amid all the hardship and misery. In 1983 she began producing semirich face and hand cream in an abandoned bakery near Warsaw. Gradually the business expanded. In 1989–90 the company set up its own distribution arm (the key to its continued success) and in 1995 extended its range to include exclusive, high-end cosmetics. Today the company employs some five hundred people and commands great respect.[17]

Scholars disagree over the extent to which the small-business owners of the eighties profited from the changed circumstances of the nineties. Many entrepreneurs were not able to withstand the competition they suddenly faced from the West (a problem that was especially severe in the former GDR, where the economy had been far more strictly controlled prior to 1989). And yet, the *Forbes* list of the hundred wealthiest Poles includes a number of former Polonia business-owners. With their greater freedoms and business experience, millions of Poles (including all the "commercial tourists," shopkeepers, tradesmen, and official Polonia entrepreneurs) were better prepared to deal with transformation than the average East German or Russian.

Due to the semilegal or illegal nature of many businesses, the contribution of private enterprise to the economic output of socialist Poland (or Hungary or any other Eastern Bloc country) is difficult to gauge. The Polish capital Warsaw, especially, spawned a class of self-employed in the late eighties, who emerged through the loopholes of the planned economy. These so-called *prywaciarze* (persons of independent means) made their money in the service sector, underground economy, and black market (see fig. 5.1).[18] Known in Polish and Russian by an almost identical, pejorative Anglicism, *biznesmeni*, they acquired their business skills some time before 1989.[19]

The same is true of the many executives of state industries who profited from manager buyouts during privatization. According to some estimates, at least half the new economic elite in Poland had held top positions in state industry prior to 1989.[20] In East Germany and the Czech Republic, many department heads (the buzzword "manager" and the hype surrounding them were characteristic features of the nineties) were able to retain their positions despite the radical break with the previous regime.[21] If they did not already have the necessary business skills, they rapidly acquired them after 1989. In the nineties, however, this continuity in the economy was hushed up. Governments and finance focused firmly on the new departures and, of course, the magic word: "reform."

Being ranked in the "emerging markets index" and referred to as "reform countries" by Western commentators considerably improved the postcommunist countries' external image. At home, too, neoliberal reform discourses boosted the confidence of many young people who profited from the new opportunities, found well-paid jobs with Western companies, worked their way up the domestic economy, or ventured into self-employment.

The spirit of capitalism was particularly vigorous in the Czech Republic, the postcommunist country with the highest proportion of self-employed people among the workforce in the early nineties.

Fig. 5.1. Polish *prywaciarze* at a market at Berlin's Reichpietschufer, February 22, 1989. Photo: DPA/Landov.

Two individual cases can help to illustrate the opportunities that arose through the new, neoliberal order. One friend of mine broke off his studies at the Prague conservatory due to the meager prospects of earning money by playing jazz, and to devote more time to selling musical instruments, his main source of income. In 1995 he established his own business, "Atelier Paganini," the Czech Republic's largest specialist dealer in old violins, cellos, and double basses. His primary customers now come from South Korea and China; the business started importing Far Eastern replicas of old instruments some years ago. Happy to show his newfound wealth, he drives to work in a top-range Audi. The second example is the son of my aforementioned great-uncle. With his family's financial and intellectual assets—his father had also been an engineer and an entrepreneur until the communist February Putsch of 1948—he set himself up in business. His company specialized in ventilation engineering and profited from the recent construction boom in Prague and its suburbs. But to outward appearances, this scion of an entrepreneurial family has remained as unassuming as ever. His interests do not lie in fast cars or expensive clothing. Though differing in their individuality, then, small entrepreneurs such as these became the backbone of the relatively successful East Central European economies.

In Southeastern Europe and the former Soviet Union, the element of nascent capitalism was much weaker. Only half as many, or even fewer, of these small-to-medium-sized business were established in Romania, Bulgaria, Russia, and Ukraine. Moreover, as long as these countries were unstable and had no prospect of joining the European Union, foreign investors had little confidence in them or their economies. They were left to their own devices, with meager social and cultural resources on which to draw. Once again, Poland provides a counterexample: despite its shaky economic foundations, it experienced a boom verging on an economic miracle, thanks to native entrepreneurship and massive external support. While the border between Germany and Poland still marked a prosperity divide in the nineties, two decades later the difference is barely perceptible. This was due not only to the Schengen Agreement enabling passport-free movement between many EU countries and the economic reforms introduced from above, but also to Polish society's human capital and the process of *transformation from below*.

## New Wealth

The result of this upswing was new wealth, generated under the steam of pent-up demand. Once postcommunist societies had overcome the poverty of the early transformation era, they eagerly indulged in any newly available products, from foodstuffs (every Pole over age forty remembers food stamps and the desperate hunt for meat in the eighties) to household appliances. Possession of a fully automatic washing machine, a telephone, and—the ultimate status symbol—a private automobile was a novelty for many. International investors calculated how many of these consumer items they would be able to sell in the former Eastern Bloc countries and invested accordingly. Export to Western Europe was also factored into investments in manufacturing, particularly in East Central Europe.

When European Union expansion was announced, the volume of investments shot up. In 2005, FDIs in the new member countries totaled seventy-seven billion dollars; by 2006 they had risen to 112 billion. Over these two years, almost twenty-nine billion dollars was invested in Poland—more than half the amount invested over the previous fifteen years.[22] In 2006 and 2007 Poland achieved an increase in gross domestic product of over 6 percent each year; unemployment dropped considerably. Overall, Poland's GDP and per capita purchasing power parity tripled in the twenty years from 1989 to 2009.[23] It would be no exaggeration, then, to speak of a Polish economic miracle, comparable to Germany's in the 1950s and '60s (qualified only by the facts that the boom in industry was much smaller and well-paid jobs are still hard to find). Having never plummeted to the same economic depths as other Eastern European countries, Hungary and the Czech and Slovak Republics did not see such dynamic growth. But in Slovakia the economy started to develop from 2001, peaking at over 10 percent in 2007. The populations of all the countries of East Central Europe got their shares of the growing cake; real incomes rose by 40 to 50 percent between 1999 and 2005.[24]

After the turn of the millennium, the Southeastern European and post-Soviet countries began to catch up. Foreign direct investments in Romania increased fourfold to over five billion euros from 2002 to 2004, and continued to rise in 2006 and 2008. The Baltic states recorded even greater increments; the volume of FDIs in Latvia increased sixfold between 2003 and 2007; ninefold in Lithuania. More foreign capital also flowed to Ukraine, though far less per capita than to Romania or other new EU member states. FDIs fueled Eastern European economies; Iván Berend has proposed that they were the principal growth engine. From 2001, the Baltic states' GDP grew annually by at least 6 percent; in 2006 they touched the 10 percent mark. Romania and Bulgaria had an upturn of between 4.2 and 7.5 percent. Russia achieved a record growth rate of 10 percent in 2000; Ukraine even reached 12.1 percent in 2004.[25]

When evaluating growth rates, it is important to take the poor initial state of the economy in the Baltic states, Southeastern Europe, and the former Soviet Union into account. After the long transformation crises of the nineties, these countries had plenty of catching up to do. The effect of FDIs should be interpreted with similar caution. For a while, as long as international investors followed their herd instincts, they fueled economic growth. Nobody wanted to miss out on getting a stake in Eastern Europe. In this respect, the conclusion that Andrei Shleifer and Daniel Treisman drew in their 2014 article for *Foreign Affairs*, that the postcommunist nations had caught up and developed into "normal" countries, would perhaps have been justified some ten years previously.[26] In 2005 and 2006, the prospects for the entire postcommunist world seemed bright, and were reflected in the local and global stock markets, which bounded from peak to peak.

Behind the scenes of rapid westernization, there were a number of important structural differences between various regions and countries of postcommunist Europe. In the reform-pioneering Visegrad countries, FDIs flowed predominantly into manufacturing. Foreign capital was used to upgrade existing factories or establish new firms to serve the domestic market and export to the EU. In the Baltic states, Croatia, Romania, Bulgaria, and Ukraine, the FDI were channeled primarily into the finance sector and from there to the real-estate industry.[27] These foreign direct investments did not necessarily signify actual economic activity; some were purely asset investments. Takeovers of privatized state enterprises also fell into two categories: nominal values in the account books, and actual investment in companies. The availability of venture capital and cheap loans caused demand, and prices, to rise. But incomes and securities for the loans did not keep pace, presaging the "Eastern Europe bubble," considered in chapter 7.

In general terms, countries with an advanced production capacity were at an advantage. Steelworks, modern car factories, and refineries require high investment and cannot be transferred easily to cheaper sites. Light industry, in contrast, can be relocated at any time, and is exposed to tighter international competition. A number of new light industry sites were established in the Baltic states and parts of Southeastern Europe. Nokia is a case in point. To reduce labor costs, in 2008 the company relocated its cellular phone production from the original site in Bochum, Germany, to a newly built factory in Romania. A few years later, it moved its production to Southeast Asia, as Romania not only proved to have difficulties with the logistics but had also become too expensive.

This case shows that economic growth in postcommunist countries hinged, to a large extent, on the supply of cheap labor. As soon as the skilled workers in Eastern Europe started demanding higher wages, investors lost the primary motive for manufacturing there. At the same time, budget dependence on FDIs gave the (mostly foreign) corporations more power than in Western Europe. Volkswagen Slovakia's announcement in January 2014 of a 4-percent wage cut fits this pattern.[28] When the Romanian government revealed plans in late 2013 to reorganize the tax system and raise corporate taxes, the Foreign Investors Council (an association of locally operating foreign corporations) threatened to leave the country.[29] The trade associations in the old EU countries would have exercised more diplomacy in the public eye. In nearby Austria, where average net incomes are triple those in Slovakia, the prospect of wage cuts would have unleashed storms of protest. But outside the Slovak capital Bratislava, unemployment is notoriously high. As in Poland, it only dipped below 10 percent at the end of the extended boom in 2008. Following the crisis, the unemployment rate in Slovakia rose again to over 14 percent; youth unemployment went up to 34 percent in 2012 (see figs. 5.2a and 5.2b).

Even after the wage cuts, automobile workers in Bratislava remain relatively privileged, earning about double the average

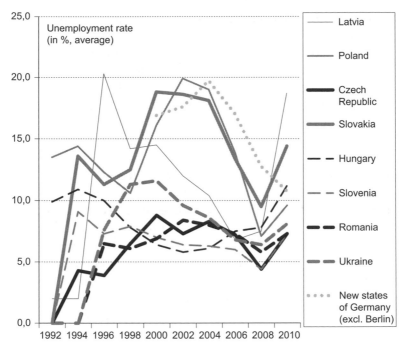

**Fig. 5.2a.** Unemployment in the transformation countries, 1992–2010 .
*Source*: WIIW Report 2012 (Table I/1.16).

monthly net wage of 600 euros.[30] Unlike Germany, Slovak industry did not conclude any nationwide collective wage agreements.
The result is a huge disparity of incomes in western and eastern
Slovakia. In the latter, average wages are estimated at about a
third of those in the metropolitan region of Bratislava.[31]

Regional divides exist in all the new EU member states. The
western parts of Poland, the Czech Republic, Hungary, Romania,
and Bulgaria are far more affluent than the eastern parts. A huge
gulf also emerged between the cities and the rural areas. This is
not immediately visible, as new roads have been built with EU
funding, and enormous shopping malls, containing the same
Western supermarkets, DIY markets, and home electronics stores,
have emerged on the outskirts of every medium-sized town. But
while the goods in the stores cost more or less the same as they

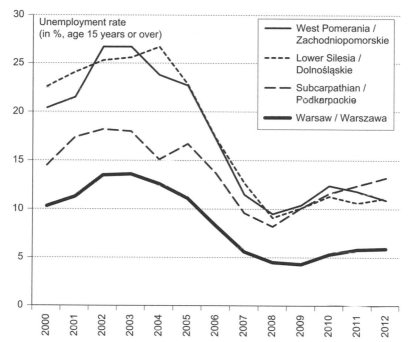

**Fig. 5.2b.** Unemployment in Poland, 2000–2012: Warsaw and selected voivodeships compared. *Source*: Eurostat regional statistics (table lfst_r_lfu3rt); Eurostat metropolitan statistics (Table met_lfu3rt).

do in the West, wages in the retail industry are a pittance. Most local residents cannot afford the goods on offer, or can buy only on credit. (See the section below on foreign currency loans.) The ostensibly greater prosperity is, then, a mere illusion.

In the face of such competition, starting a business or becoming self-employed is much harder today than it was in the nineties. The shopping malls at the city limits make ghost towns of the centers. While all Western countries are familiar with this problem, postcommunist countries are especially vulnerable. Beyond a few core growth areas (mostly the capital cities plus two or three regional centers), the kind of middle class has not been able to form that would patronize small boutiques, florists, health-food stores, art galleries, or other niche suppliers, or have the capital to start new businesses. Rapid westernization has eroded the social basis of capitalism and, indirectly, of democracy. There is new wealth in Eastern Europe, but it is unevenly distributed and distinctly fragile, as the crisis of 2008–9 showed.

## Rich Cities, Poor Regions

Eastern European backwardness is a stereotype that is still used by Western media and has formed the basis of academic inquiry for many years. How underdeveloped or poor is the former Eastern Bloc really, more than twenty-five years after the revolutions of 1989–91? The assumption of backwardness was a key point of departure for the communists' economic and social policy. Stalinist regimes aimed to catapult the predominantly agrarian societies into the modern age by swift industrialization.[32] At the same time, they hoped to produce politically loyal working classes by mass employment in large state industries. Steelworks were built in Eisenhüttenstadt (GDR), Nowa Huta (Poland), Košice (Slovakia), and Miskolc (Hungary), as were various mechanical engineering and chemical combines and other industrial sites. As a result of communist modernization, living standards in Eastern Europe rose. Planned economies, moreover, meant that wages, salaries, and the prices of consumer goods were fixed. Although the communists were not able to cancel out all regional differences, they succeeded in creating largely egalitarian societies.[33]

1989 brought about a quick—and lasting—change. The capital cities Prague, Warsaw, and Bratislava strove toward the imagined Western ideal. A few years after joining the EU, their economies had reached the average size within the Union. The western parts of Poland, the Czech and Slovak Republics, and Hungary also profited from the upswing. Numerous industrial plants were set up around Wrocław and Poznań in western Poland, Plzeň and Mlada Boleslav in Bohemia, the greater Bratislava area in Slovakia, and Győr and Sopron in Hungary. Unemployment in these places is relatively low on the EU scale; incomes are distinctly higher than the nationwide average.

The situation in the eastern parts of these countries is quite different. The regional GDP statistics compiled by Eurostat since 1995 show just how poor these predominantly agricultural regions are. In the rolling hills of the former Galicia and the even poorer regions on Poland's eastern periphery (such as Przemyśl in the southeast and Ełk in the northeast) the per capita GDP (ad justed to purchasing power parity) was only about 2,000 euros in 1995. It doubled before Poland joined the European Union and continued to rise robustly thereafter. Yet compared to Warsaw, the poor regions in the southeast and northeast of Poland stagnated; their GDP was only about a fifth of that in the capital in 2004.[34] As fig. 5.3 shows, regional disparity in Slovakia and Hungary was almost as large.[35]

Of course, statistics on GDP convey only a limited idea of a population's actual living standards. But other indicators confirm the findings they yield. Around 2005, unemployment in the eastern rural areas was up to five times higher than in the capital cities.[36] The quality of schools, libraries, medical care, and roads is still much lower than the respective nationwide averages.

East of the EU border, in Ukraine, the situation is even worse. The data collected by the state statistical office of Ukraine on the Carpathians and the former Galicia paint a bleak picture.[37] Transcarpathia, a region on the southern side of the Carpathian Mountains, was part of Czechoslovakia before 1945 and part of Hungary before 1920. According to the official government statistics provided by Ukrstat, in 2000 the residents of the Transcarpathian oblast (region or province) obtained a per capita GDP of the equivalent of 1,276 euros, or some 100 euros per month. The officially poorest oblast of Ukraine, Ternopil in Galicia, obtained only 1,216 euros. (All data on Ukraine are adjusted to purchasing power parity for this book; if they were not, they would be even lower.[38]) Glancing at just half the regional GDP in eastern Slovakia and southeastern Poland, this is striking evidence of how far behind its western neighbors Ukraine had fallen in its first decade of independence.

With incomes so low, emigration rates in western Ukraine are among the highest in all European regions, echoing the situation

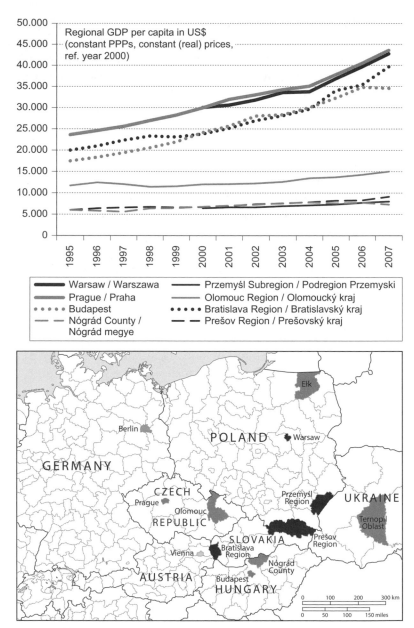

**Fig. 5.3.** Regional divergence within the transformation countries, 1995–2007.
*Source*: OECD Statistics (Regional Accounts TL3).

under Habsburg rule in the late nineteenth century. In some respects the region profits from its high rate of labor migration; many handsome family homes were built with money earned by Ukrainians working in the European Union or Russia. (Almost half Ukraine's migrant laborers work in Russia; most others in Italy, the Czech Republic, and Poland.) In 2011, such remittances amounted to seven billion dollars, or 4.3 percent of Ukraine's GDP, according to the Ukrainian National Bank. The total sum remitted is certainly greater and especially large in regions such as Transcarpathia and Ternopil.[39] It was hardly helpful, then, to present Ukraine with the choice between integration in the European Union or in Putin's Eurasian customs union in late 2013. The populace and the economy are dependent on money from both.

The wealth earned outside the region comes at a high personal cost. Many families have been split by the permanent absence of a parent working abroad. Unlike Poles and Slovaks, Ukrainian migrant laborers cannot easily travel home. Visas are required for EU countries; most Ukrainians are not employed as official guest workers (apart from the approximately 120,000 Ukrainians working in the Czech Republic) but earn their money clandestinely. The number of Ukrainian moonlighters in Poland alone is estimated to be 250,000 to 500,000.[40] Many are overqualified for the work they perform abroad: the women are mostly cleaners, chambermaids, or caregivers, even if they are university graduates; most men work in construction. Hourly wages of two to three euros are attractive enough compared to those at home.

In 2000, Ukraine began to recover from the depression of the nineties, as the regional statistics collated since then show. The GDP in the poorest regions had doubled by 2005 and continued to rise until the crisis struck in 2008–9. It is doubtful, however, whether this upswing reached the Galician villages and Carpathian valleys. Even today, most farmers own two or three cows, cultivate vegetables by subsistence farming, and forage for mushrooms and berries in the forests. Some wash their laundry in the nearest stream, offering the kind of pastoral scene one might find in a romantic nineteenth-century painting. There is hardly any traffic; the potholes prevent the few cars on the roads from driving any faster than about twenty miles per hour. But daily life for the rural population is far from romantic; their incomes are on a par with those in third-world countries, even if they live only 350 miles from Vienna.

Comparing Ukraine to developing countries, as Polish economist and entrepreneur Stanisław Szczepanowski did back in the late nineteenth century in his acclaimed study on "Galician misery" (*nędza galicyjska*[41]), is not such a far-fetched suggestion. Consider India's per capita GDP in 2005, adjusted to purchasing power parity, of 1,800 euros (at the exchange rate then amounting to around 2,220 US dollars). This is not that much lower than the 2,300 euros in Ternopil oblast. Morocco was better off, with an average of about 2,800 euros. In Turkey, which is commonly classified as an emerging country, the per capita GDP is about four times higher than in the poorest regions of western Ukraine and twice as high as the Ukrainian average.[42]

Scenes in the unspoiled Ukrainian Carpathians would fill any organic food enthusiast or hiking tourist with joy. But local farmers perform arduous, backbreaking work. Few are able to sell their products in the nearest town because of the poor state of the roads. Almost all the dairies and mills have closed. The residents of the Carpathians are in a similar situation to the Alpine farmers before the construction of the railroad. They have just enough to survive; some areas attract a little tourism. The main symbols of modernity are electricity—in between blackouts—TV sets, and the knowledge that more money can be earned abroad than at home. However, again similarly to India, other parts of Ukraine have relatively thriving IT and software industries.

The prosperity divide between the capital and rural regions is a problem in general in Eastern Europe. But regional disparities are particularly pronounced in Ukraine. Between 2000 and 2005, now considered a golden era in that country, the gap between Kyiv and the poorer regions widened to more than 6:1. The business elite in Kyiv, who learned to speak English, have mockingly dubbed the Carpathians "crapathians." The Russian nickname for poor peasants, "muzhik" (мужик), is even more contemptuous and recalls the social divisions a hundred years ago in Tsarist times. A zone of poverty has emerged stretching 250 miles from the north to the south, from the former Galicia to the northern periphery of the Danube plain, including the Carpathian Mountains, and more than seven hundred miles from the west to the southeast in Romania.

Poverty zones extending across several states are not confined to the east of Europe; they are on Berlin's doorstep. Broad areas on both sides of the Oder and Neisse rivers, which mark the border between Poland and Germany, are struggling with high unemployment and a lack of prospects. The endurance of feudal structures during communism is partly to blame. After World War II, the large Prussian estates were turned into agricultural cooperatives (LPG in German; PGR in Polish). Despite their intensified use of machinery and artificial fertilizers, they operated inefficiently. In the early nineties cooperatives on both sides of the German-Polish border declared bankruptcy by the score. The situation finally improved after the European Union enlarged; the GDP in the voivodeships (provinces) east of the Oder and Neisse grew by almost 50 percent between 2005 and 2008; unemployment fell, wages rose. Thus the westernmost regions of Poland leveled up with the easternmost German states, Brandenburg and Saxony. For some years now, real estate in the Szczecin and Gorzów areas, close to the border with Germany, has cost more than on the German side, where depopulation continues to be a problem.

This cross-border convergence is attended by a divergence between deprived and affluent regions in the former GDR. The greater Dresden area produces a roughly 50 percent higher GDP than the districts along the Oder and Neisse rivers. It has, then, reached the level of the old rust belt cities in the Ruhr valley of West Germany. Some districts in the Erzgebirge, the mountains separating East Germany from the Czech Republic, are also poor, though they are less than an hour's drive from Dresden or Leipzig.[43] At least these conurbations are relatively easy to reach. Commuting from eastern Poland to Warsaw or from eastern Slovakia to Bratislava every day is virtually impossible due to the long distances and bad state of the roads. To some extent, the regional differences in Poland, Slovakia, and Hungary have been absorbed into the nations' identities. No longer questioned, they shape internal perceptions and familiar stereotypes, such as the concept of "Polska B" to denote the underdeveloped eastern half of the country.

The question remains why the populations in the disadvantaged regions did not protest against such inequality. Perhaps it pales into insignificance in relation to other social divides that have emerged since the nineties, such as the gulf between the generations or between certain professional groups. Probably regional disparities have been overridden by more pressing concerns, such as the specter of unemployment, and the daily challenges of transformation. A third, laconic explanation might be that Galicia, eastern Slovakia, and Transcarpathia oblast are accustomed to deprivation. Having been extremely poor in the past, they possess knowledge, handed down over generations, of how to cope with poverty. The basic strategies are subsistence farming at home while the younger generation migrates long distances to work. To cite one example, according to a study by the Slovakian Academy of Sciences, sixteen thousand Slovak women worked in Austria as caregivers in 2009. The home care system in Vienna would collapse without this influx from the neighboring country.[44] These caregivers do not come from the nearby regions of western Slovakia—a short drive away—but from the remote east of the country.

Labor migration means that the more capable and mobile sections of society leave the country. The advantage of bolstered incomes is cancelled out, then, by the drain of human resources from the deprived regions. Traditional family values take on increased importance in this situation. In Poland, Slovakia, Hungary, and western Ukraine, it is common for more affluent family members to support close relatives. Younger relatives supplement the older generation's meager pensions; grandparents make sacrifices for their children and grandchildren. Consider the example of my longstanding research assistant in Frankfurt (Oder), who hails from one of Poland's poorest areas, and helped finance his younger sister's studies and contributed to the rent on his mother's apartment. Long-range labor migration and redistribution within families help to compensate for regional disparities. (The latter is also common in southern Europe—more on this in chapter 8.)

But many children grow up as semi-orphans, or are raised by their grandparents, because their parents work far away in the West and can come home only on weekends, or even less frequently. In Poland, a telling term has been coined for these children: *eurosieroty* (literally, "euro orphans"). The exodus of the working generation compounds the drop in the birthrate, placing the rural regions of the new EU member states in another predicament. For the first time since the population explosion in the nineteenth century, there are too few young people. The long-term impact of the twofold demographic decline—caused by labor migration and the falling birth rate—remains to be seen. It is clear, however, that it will be difficult to achieve economic growth with a declining population. This will inevitably affect investments and prospects for the future.

At first glance, the disparity between urban and rural areas seems reminiscent of earlier growth periods, such as industrialization in the nineteenth century. As early as the 1950s, future Nobel Prize winner Simon Kuznets showed that phases of intense development, such as industrialization, cause social inequality that generally abates when wealth increases.[45] But a number of factors peculiar to the neoliberal order of the transformation period continued to foster inequality. The demise of old industries that were built up under state socialism or prior to World War II impoverished many regions and, above all, medium- and small-sized towns with only one or two factories. The neglect of agriculture had even more severe consequences. Hundreds of counties and thousands of villages fell into deep decline. This was linked to the anticommunist revolutions. The "red barons" (the communist-appointed LPG chairpeople) held strong positions in many places. Breaking up the agricultural cooperatives and assigning the land to private owners was a way of bringing the revolution to rural areas. But the postcommunist administrations failed to provide the governance and investment necessary to help recover from a deep structural change of this kind. The simultaneous opening of the market to Western imports plunged local farmers and the dairies, slaughterhouses, grain mills, and sugar refineries that processed their products into ruin on a huge scale.[46] As a consequence, the still-operating farms had trouble finding purchasers.

The outcomes of this decline were already clearly visible in 1991. The former GDR and Poland were dotted with uncultivated fields; disused tractors and combine harvesters stood abandoned in machine halls. Many unwanted pieces of equipment were sold off at Warsaw's main bazaar at Dziesięciolecia Stadium, the Polish market in Berlin, or the Mexikoplatz flea market in Vienna. Iván Berend takes the agricultural crisis as cause for a fundamental critique of the denationalization of the early nineties, stating: "Most of the major mistakes were the consequence of the ideologically based, one-sided de-etatization, which fatally weakened state governance when it was badly needed in the difficult time of transformation. The blind belief—also ideologically based—in the automatism of market forces in countries where a full-fledged market was not yet in existence had similarly devastating consequences."[47]

Berend's criticism may seem harsh but there is evidence to support it. In late 1991, a full two years after the Balcerowicz Plan was launched, the Polish government founded a state agency for agricultural property (Agencja Własności Rolnej Skarbu Państwa) to coordinate the sale of land and farms. Inherent problems made privatization in agriculture even less destined for success than that in industry. Land prices crashed as cooperatives went bankrupt; any businesspeople with sufficient capital to invest had certainly not stayed in the country. The situation in the Czech Republic and Hungary was more stable, as most agricultural cooperatives were kept alive. But here, too, harvests and livestock dwindled.

Russia, meanwhile, proved that avoiding or delaying privatization was a no more viable solution, at least not if the borders were concurrently opened to import trade. The government waited until 2003 to regulate the ownership, sale, and resale of farmland. The beneficiaries were predominantly corporations, some of which cultivate several hundred thousand hectares today. But local farmers and rural workers continued to suffer from the reforms. They did not have the necessary capital, knowhow, or entrepreneurial spirit— hardly surprising, after centuries of serfdom and its continuation in the guise of the *kolkhoz* collective farms. Agriculture in Ukraine was at rock bottom, too; at one point, the former breadbasket of Europe imported more food than it exported.

With respect to the farming crisis, comparison with Vietnam is instructive. In terms of size and national homogeneity, Vietnam is comparable to Poland. A former close ally of the Soviet Union, Vietnam allowed its farmers to sell a proportion of their output privately in 1981. By 1986, under the Vietnamese variant of perestroika (*Đổi mới*) they no longer had to give any of their harvest to the government but could sell rice directly to consumers at the market price. However, the market freedoms here, as in China (where the pace and nature of reforms were similar), apply only to agricultural products, not the land, which is still formally owned by the state.[48] Neither did Vietnam (or China) link this gradual marketization with external trade liberalization. The state protected local producers against imports until the country was able to sell on the world markets. Today, agricultural exports contribute considerably to the nation's prosperity. The same policy could not have been applied in East Central Europe or the Soviet Union, because wheat cultivation and animal husbandry do not require the same conditions as the labor-intensive practice of rice farming, with two or three harvests annually. Nevertheless, comparison between Eastern Europe and the communist states of the Far East shows that agricultural decline was not inevitable. It resulted from a certain sequence of reforms.

Another factor contributing to the downturn of "Polska B" and similar regions was the breakdown of industry established under socialism. The collapse of the CMEA (Council for Mutual Economic Assistance, Eastern Europe's answer to the European Community) and the East's sales markets caused tremendous difficulties to all the countries of the former Eastern Bloc. Not only that, trade liberalization meant that they were suddenly confronted with competition from the West, unlike Western Europe in the postwar period or Vietnam and China in later years. Many industries went bankrupt; in the late nineties and at the start of the new millennium in particular, large combines that had not been able to make a profit or attract investors were forced to close. This wave of deindustrialization exacerbated the regional imbalance. In Poland and Slovakia it caused unemployment to rise to around 20 percent.[49]

Opening markets to import trade and investors is one of the key steps toward a neoliberal order. It invites foreign direct investments—another significant, though more positive factor contributing to regional disparities. Western corporations saw a potential sales market in the Eastern Bloc as early as the 1970s. On account of the low pay rates, German companies, in particular, also began manufacturing in the Eastern Bloc for export to the West.

When the Iron Curtain fell, many more opportunities for investment opened up. The postcommunist countries needed foreign capital, had a great deal of pent-up consumer demand, and promised low labor costs. Because they were competing with each other and on a global level for foreign capital, they did not impose any off-putting regulations on where to invest. Consequently, most FDIs were allocated to the capital cities or manufacturing bases close to what was then the eastern border of the EU, or the westernmost parts of the respective countries. The concentration of investments in a few locations was also an indirect result of enduring centralization, which stemmed from prewar times. Poland, Hungary, and other Eastern European countries had been more centralized than Germany or Austria even before World War II and continued to be so after 1989. The former GDR was an exception; it was pushed to the economic periphery by unification with West Germany. East Berlin, once the proud "capital of the GDR," lost its status as a political and economic center for East Germany. Local factors, considered in the next chapter, detracted further from Berlin's appeal as a business location in relation to Dresden, Leipzig, or Jena.

While villages sank into poverty, the international companies setting up in the large cities brought new opportunities for advancement and earning money. Western companies paid considerably higher wages than domestic enterprises; working for the state was the least lucrative option. This upset the social hierarchy in a way that echoed the situation under late state socialism, when taxi drivers, tourist guides, car mechanics, and other service providers who received payment or tips in Western currencies were often better off than doctors and professors. In the early nineties a similar scenario evolved: secretaries for Western firms could earn three to four times as much as the senior staff of domestic companies, and far more than public sector employees. The pay gaps encouraged corruption, which had already been on the rise in late state socialism. (On my many trips to Prague, I did not pay a single legal fine for speeding—the matter could always be resolved by inserting a small deutschmark note into one's passport before showing it to the police. Quite soon after the EU enlargement, this kind of petty corruption stopped.) The glamorous *biznesmeni* became a characteristic element of postcommunist society. Over the course of the nineties, the *menadżer*, as the top executive were now known in Polish, rose to the pinnacle of the social hierarchy.

These new professional fields and opportunities for advancement hardly existed in rural areas. Here, unemployment remained much higher than in the capital cities, making badly paid government jobs more attractive. There was no ambitious elite to stimulate consumption by patronizing new stores, eating out, or investing in new businesses. Shortly before the EU accession of Poland, Slovakia, and Hungary, driving out of Warsaw, Bratislava, or Budapest was like entering another world. In the GDR, too, unemployment in rural areas was especially high. Here, the number of people employed in agriculture fell within five years after the revolution from 850,000 to fewer than 165,000.[50] Belarusian writer Svetlana Alexeyevich, winner of the 2015 Nobel Prize, noted for her novels and short stories about postcommunism, interviewed a number of local residents for her book about life in the former Soviet Union. One interviewee in Russia put the situation here in a nutshell: "They should drive fifty kilometers out of Moscow . . . look at the houses, see how the people live there, how they get drunk on holidays . . . in the country there are hardly any men anymore. They've died out. Minds like horned cattle—drinking themselves to death. Till they drop."[51]

Another new term coined in Poland, "Polska dwóch prędkości" (literally, "Poland of two speeds"), describes the country in terms of the two predominant types of car driver. As the present author also observed from the comfort of a Swedish car's passenger seat in the nineties, one group of drivers sit in their *Maluch*s, the Polish-produced Fiat 126p, trundling along bumpy roads at a maximum of fifty-five miles an hour, the other in their Western sedans, cruising over the cracks at twice that speed.

It would be too short-sighted to regard the civil rights activists expelled to the opposition benches or the progressively disempowered industrial workers as the main losers of the revolutions of 1989–91. The worst-off were the rural populations, and especially agricultural workers. In view of these intranational divergences, how useful is it to view the postcommunist countries in terms of national units? Without wishing to call the concept of national economy into question, do not regional units of investigation say just as much about the course, and particularly the outcomes, of transformation as do the long rows of national statistics to be found in the specialist literature and various indices? One thing is certain: the term "Eastern Europe" can no longer be used to denote a relatively uniform area.

## The EU's Marshall Plan for the East

From the 1970s on, the European Community worked toward reducing regional imbalance. Regional policy gained further relevance when the EC enlarged southward in the eighties. Portugal, Greece, and parts of Spain were as economically underdeveloped, in comparison to the Benelux countries and Germany, as the new EU member states twenty years later. Thus the EC followed a two-track policy of investment in the peripheral regions of the South, providing its increasingly controversial agricultural subsidies on the one hand, and direct funding for infrastructure projects on the other. With a decades-long tradition of combating economic disparity, then, it is not surprising that Brussels was attuned to the problem of urban-rural divergence in Eastern Europe from an early stage. Eurostat, the Brussels statistical agency, began collating data on the regional development of postcommunist states associated with the European Union in 1995. They highlighted the growing divides within these countries, which the European Union consequently set out to target.

The first major aid program for Eastern Europe, PHARE (Poland and Hungary Aid for Economic Restructuring) was launched in 1989 and later extended to include Czechoslovakia and all other EU membership aspirants. At first, the program was primarily aimed at supporting administrative reforms and establishing the rule of law—much in this field still remains to be done in the former Soviet Union. PHARE was initially allocated an extremely modest budget of 8.9 billion euros for ten countries over a period of eight years (1990–98). In any event, not quite two-thirds of the funds were actually transferred. The frequent discrepancy between the amount approved and the amount actually spent continues to be a problem of EU funding, caused in part by the many bureaucratic obstacles imposed by Brussels.[52] In terms of volume, the aid program was far removed from a second Marshall Plan, contrary to claims to this effect by George Soros in 1989 and Jeffrey Sachs in 1992, perhaps in a bid to refute the theory that neoliberals were heartless. (For more than ten years since then, Sachs has turned his attention to fighting poverty around the globe.) A program of such dimensions would have cost some ten to fifteen billion dollars per year.

But after 1998, the European Union successively stepped up its aid. Brussels initiated a number of special programs: for rural development, transportation and infrastructure projects, adult education, and corporate loans. The stickers that appeared all over Poland bearing the motto "Finansowana przez Unię Europejską" ("financed by the European Union"), and twelve little stars against a blue background, inspired jokes about echoes of another gift-giving union, lost in 1991. But they were signs of Brussels' commitment, which in turn encouraged international corporations to allocate foreign direct investments.

Thrifty at first, the European Union spent abundantly later. Its budget for the first three years after enlargement (2004–6) included structural funds of 15.5 billion euros for the new member countries; more than half that amount was allocated to Poland, the largest and most populous new member. In addition, the European Union introduced subsidies for agriculture. Although only a quarter of the level in the old EU countries (more on this unequal treatment in chapter 10), they made a considerable difference in "Polska B" and comparable regions. Even higher transfer payments were paid out in the seven-year budget for the period 2007–13. Poland was allocated an additional 67 billion euros; by 2013 it had also received around 90 percent of the previously agreed funding.[53]

In concrete terms, Brussels spent at least €40 billion on Poland alone. Meanwhile, the influx of private capital amounted to about fifty billion euros between 2007 and 2013. But FDIs can be purely nominal values in a company's accounts, and not necessarily flow into the local economy at all.[54] Hence the EU's transfer payments appear all the more impressive, especially in relation to local prices and incomes. Divided by the population number, they totaled 1,000 euros per resident. Much can be achieved, especially in rural areas, with such amounts.

In contrast to the FDIs, a large proportion of the EU funding— two-thirds of which is earmarked for improving infrastructure and agriculture—flowed into less prosperous regions. The roads to eastern Poland have been improved (although, unfortunately, a large number of trees lining the avenues were felled collaterally); the market squares of most small towns have been renovated. Obvious signs of poverty have disappeared. The upturn in the rural regions has had a ripple effect on the entire economy. The EU commission estimates that "cohesion policies" boosted growth in Poland by 5.5 percent in the period 2007–13, and by as much as 8.5 percent in the Czech Republic and the Baltic states.[55]

In the meantime, the transfer payments made since EU enlargement have exceeded the volume of the Marshall Plan, by absolute numbers and in relation to the gross domestic product of the recipient countries. Overall, European integration and its attendant programs were a tremendous success. This is true even from the perspective of net contributors such as Germany, which was able to export more to the new member countries than it imports from them.[56] Despite the neoliberal rhetoric that characterized the *acquis communautaire* (the conditions fixed in 1993 for accession to the EU) and the Lisbon Agenda of the year 2000, the European Union served as an equalizing factor. Regions that achieve less than 75 percent of the EU average qualify for funding. Compared to the yardsticks applied for social benefits in Western welfare states, or official poverty thresholds, this seems quite egalitarian. The OECD defines individual poverty as an income of less than 50 percent of the average per capita income; most national statistics set the threshold at 60 percent. Since about 2005, EU investments in deprived regions have helped close the gulf between growth centers and regions such as "Polska B."

The upsurge in the eastern regions of the European Union is even more striking in comparison to the situation in Russia or Ukraine. Here, the villages still resemble those in the early nineties in Poland. Most are hard to reach because of the terrible state of the roads; there are no businesses where local products can be processed. Career prospects for young people are meager. The greater the contrast with Belarus, western Ukraine, and Russia, the more the residents of EU member countries feel they are living on the right side of the border. Many of the native nurses, chambermaids, and mechanics who left eastern Poland, Slovakia, or Hungary to work in the West have been replaced by workers from the neighboring non-EU countries. Funding from Brussels for agriculture and road improvement, as well as various smaller cultural projects (including heritage conservation and European cities of culture programs), helped the eastern regions of the new EU member states keep pace. The post-Soviet states, by contrast, seem to be out of bounds for the European Union (although that might change in Ukraine). Here, the difference between the cities and the rural areas remains striking.

The only postcommunist countries without stark urban-rural and east-west divides, even before the European Union started channeling aid into the region, were the Czech Republic and Slovenia. Some parts of the former have structural problems, such as the industrial regions in northern Bohemia and northern Moravia. Nevertheless, by the Gini coefficient (used to measure international income disparity by calculating the difference between various strata of society—that is, the rich and poor), the Czech Republic and Slovenia are as equitable as Sweden. The reason lies in privatization strategies as well as historical structures. In the nineties, the Czech Republic hesitated to sell its major enterprises to international investors, opting to distribute vouchers, or company share certificates, among the population first. Most of these were subsequently bought up by local banks and investment funds. Slovenia went one step further, allotting company shares to staff members, pension funds, and bankruptcy compensation funds in addition to distributing vouchers. This regionally and socially balanced approach was made possible by the fact that domestic investors financed economic restructuring. Economic growth or intense modernization, then, does not necessarily go hand in hand with increased social inequality. True, this occurred during industrialization in the nineteenth century and, as discussed above, in most postcommunist countries. But the outcome hinges on where the capital comes from and how it is channeled. Trade unions, which remained strong in both Slovenia and the Czech Republic, are also important for maintaining egalitarian societies.

One drawback of these national privatization and investment strategies was their susceptibility to insider deals and corruption. In the Czech Republic, an accumulation of nonperforming loans to large enterprises, often given as personal favors, caused the banking crisis of 1996. The government ultimately solved the problem by selling the banks, giving indemnity for their losses, and devaluing the Czech crown. Slovenia's problems after the crisis of 2008–9 are comparable. After independence, the government followed a predominantly national privatization strategy, prioritizing Slovenian investors. But the strategy was financed largely by cheap loans, and by the government giving bank guarantees in excess of its financial resources. As a result, many of these loans went bad, precipitating a severe banking and budgetary crisis. In contrast to the Czech Republic in the nineties, Slovenia, a member of the eurozone, was not able to devalue its currency, which prolonged the crisis. Besides these homemade difficulties arising from national privatization strategies, problems were caused by unfulfilled expectations and the herd instinct that continues to drive the world of international finance. Having been vaunted for years as a model transformation country, the flow of foreign capital to Slovenia virtually stopped after the crisis of 2008–9.

The geographical cluster of countries with more egalitarian societies (see fig. 5.4b)—the Czech Republic, Slovakia, Hungary, Slovenia, and neighboring Austria—points to a *longue durée* explanation rooted in the history of the region. The Austro-Hungarian Empire built a dense infrastructure of good roads and railways, public schools, and hospitals, and established a progressive social security system.[57] Thus the preconditions for development were better than in most of Poland (the former Russian partition) and Romania (with the exception of Transylvania). It is difficult to gauge the extent to which generations of welfare security have shaped contemporary attitudes, but the kind of deep social inequality that prevails in Russia and Ukraine would certainly be alien to Slovenian and Czech society. The same is true of Hungary and Slovakia, though these two countries are only equitable by the Gini coefficient, not in terms of regional wealth dispersion.

The above considerations negate one of the initial hypotheses on which this book was based—that the egalitarian social order in post-Habsburg Europe might be due to the relatively small size of these countries, especially compared to Poland. Looking at the Baltic states, however, it emerges that social equality is not a problem of scale: Estonia, Latvia, and Lithuania are characterized by even higher regional and social inequality than Poland (see fig. 5.4a).[58]

EU enlargement clamped the growing social and regional gaps. Until 2005, the Gini coefficient rose in all new EU states as a consequence of reform policies. Neoliberal reform packages such as Russia's in 1992–93, the Slovak flat tax rate, or the German labor market reforms during the second wave of neoliberalism, led to growing social inequality. In Russia, the Gini coefficient climbed from 23.8 in 1988 (approximately equivalent to Sweden's) to 37.1 in 1992, 46.2 in 1993, and 48.3 in 1998 (approaching the situation in Argentina).[59] A deep social divide also emerged in the Baltic states (almost on a par with the United States); Poland followed

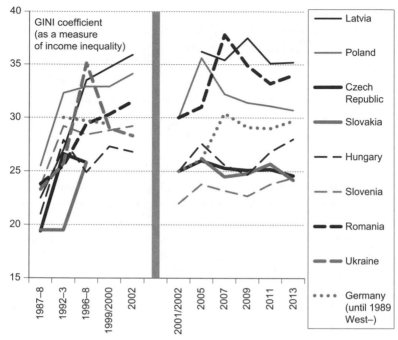

**Fig. 5.4a.** Social inequality in the transformation states, 1987–2013. *Source*: In the absence of a continuous database for the entire period, this diagram is a composite of two sources, the World Bank Data Catalog (until 2004) and Eurostat data (from 2004).

with a Gini coefficient of 35.6 in 2005. In Germany, too, social inequality increased: here, the Gini coefficient rose from 25 in 2001 to 30.4 in 2007. Although such changes are never monocausal, there is a clear connection with the Hartz social and labor market reforms (named after the Social Democrat and Volkswagen manager Peter Hartz) of the same period.

The case of Ukraine, however, shows that the Gini coefficient must be viewed with caution. In international statistics, Ukraine ranks as a relatively equitable country. But in fact, the wealthy elite is so small and the broad mass of the population so poor that the social divide is simply not captured by the quintile measurement commonly used for the Gini coefficient, which calculates an

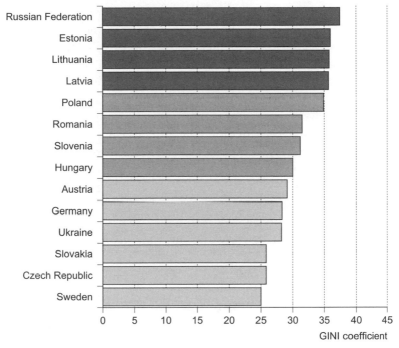

**Fig. 5.4b.** Social inequality in the transformation states, 2009. *Source*: United Nations Human Development Report 2009 (pp. 195–96).

average by certain threshold values and progresses in stages of 20 percent.

Without setting too great store by the Gini coefficient, then, it is useful for discerning broad trends. It highlights the stagnation of, or decrease in, social inequality in all countries about two or three years after European Union accession.[60] The crisis of 2008–9 temporarily interrupted this trend in some of these countries. Nevertheless, the EU transfer payments acted as a corrective antidote to the second wave of neoliberalism.

In the successor states of the Soviet Union, transformation had diametrically opposed results. The post-Soviet societies (with the exception of Belarus) are deeply divided. Largely impoverished populations face small elites of oligarchs, and in Russia, the so-called "new Russians" (новые русские). Long-term historical path dependencies are perhaps partly to blame. There were small upper classes and impoverished masses in today's Ukraine and Russia under the Tsarist Empire. But the main cause lay in the sequence of reforms. Under the influence of Western advisors, Russia began privatization before an institutional and constitutional framework was in place. As a result, the state was plundered, and a small class of oligarchs formed. Deindustrialization, wiping out countless workplaces, also had disastrous effects. Due to the lack of legal security and opportunity for export to the EU market, there was hardly any inflow of foreign capital other than the oligarchs' laundered money. As in the late nineteenth century, a small middle class formed in the big cities only; in rural areas, grinding poverty and, in some places, abject misery still prevails today.

The social divide is reflected in life expectancies. In the five-year period 1989–94, the average lifespan dropped in Russia by three years and remained low even after the country's economic recovery at the start of the new millennium. It increased slowly to reach an average of sixty-seven (almost twelve years less than in Germany and the United States) in 2006—the same level as in the late Soviet Union. Life expectancy in Russia is lower than that in Latin America and North Africa, and higher only than in South Asia and sub-Saharan Africa. It is no exaggeration, then, to say that the Russian and Ukrainian rural populations live in conditions akin to developing countries. Life expectancy in Poland, the Czech Republic, Hungary, and Estonia, by contrast, rose in the period 1989–2009 by five years or more; in Slovakia, by four, in Latvia, by three, and in Lithuania, by two (see fig. 5.5).[61] Because life expectancy reflects the quality of health systems from obstetrics to geriatrics, and of education from preschool to university, as well as labor market prospects, levels of social cohesion, and environmental factors, it is a broadly encompassing indicator.

Life expectancy in Ukraine did not nosedive in the nineties in the same way as in Russia. But here, too, the welfare state exists only on paper. Kyiv set up pension and unemployment insurance systems following the European model. (Neither of these

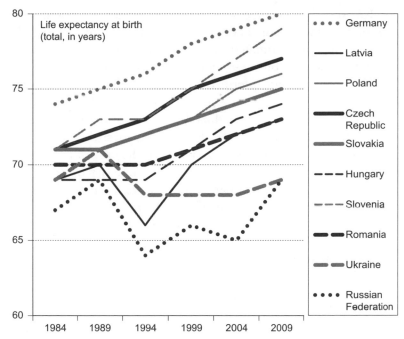

**Fig. 5.5.** Life expectancy in the transformation states, 1984–2009. *Source:* World Bank, Data Catalog ("Life Expectancy at Birth").

existed in the Soviet Union or other communist countries, where the state was supposed to take care of the sick and elderly; the lack of a universal social insurance system poses a major challenge to the Chinese government today.) However, the benefits they afford are just sufficient for the bare necessities—bread, potatoes, onions, and dairy products. Public hospitals still exist, but patients have to supply their own medication and syringes, and pay several hundred dollars for more complex treatments and surgery. Patients who cannot produce the money are only treated in emergencies. They depend entirely on the good natures of the doctors and the hopelessly underpaid nurses. While the poor in Ukraine are barely able to fend for themselves, eight Ukrainian oligarchs appeared on the *Forbes* World's Billionaires list in 2012.

How did they become so wealthy? Consider the example of one of Ukraine's most infamous oligarchs, Dmytro Firtash. He made his fortune, estimated in 2008 at five billion dollars,[62] with a strikingly simple business model: he positioned his company RosUkrEnergo as an intermediary between Russia's Gazprom and the Ukrainian gas monopolist Naftogaz, selling cut-price, state-subsidized Russian gas, directly or via subsidiaries, to industry and households in Ukraine. Firtash's business thrived—at the expense of the Ukrainian taxpayers. As in the case of prominent Russian oligarchs' dealings, the West became a party to these business practices: the company office was registered in Switzerland; the opulent headquarters of Firtash's holding company, DF Group, are in Vienna, Austria. No lesser institution than Cambridge University gratefully accepted the oligarch's support to launch a Ukrainian Studies program, complete with film festival and exhibitions. In Ukraine, Firtash channeled millions into cultural institutions (including the newly restored theaters in Chernivtsi and Kherson) and many festivals. As a result, he could be sure of being received in the West as a philanthropist rather than a tycoon of questionable repute—a *biznesmen*. In 2014, however, his fortunes suddenly turned. He was arrested by Austrian police at the request of the FBI on suspicion of bribery and leading a criminal organization. But so far he has seemed untouchable. The American extradition warrant was turned down by a Viennese court, and Firtash is still a political power broker in Kyiv.

How could transformation in the former Soviet Union and Ukraine lead to outcomes of this kind? From a neoliberal viewpoint, it was due to the lack of functioning markets, and could be remedied by pursuing deregulation and liberalization. The actual problem, however, was the weak state, which was and still is abused on all administrative levels. Top-level corruption has been mentioned above; consider the following example from the picturesque Carpathians (which look a lot like the Blue Ridge Mountains) in the southwest Ukraine. In the best hotel in the village of Slavs'ke, once among the Soviet Union's most prestigious ski resorts, a Ukrainian colleague of mine held international summer schools for historians from the post-Soviet states in the years 2011–13. Armed security guards, wearing the uniform of a Ministry of the Interior special unit, patrolled in front of the hotel. They checked every guest and visitor, presumably to prevent thefts from the hotel rooms or the fleet of SUVs, and to convey a sense of security to the hotel guests (mostly the oligarchs' senior staff members; the oligarchs themselves prefer to vacation along the Mediterranean). It was unclear whether the guards were still paid by the Ministry of the Interior or by the privatized hotel (which changed hands via a manager buyout). In either case, something was wrong.

Or take another example from the resort Slavs'ke: Prior to the 2012 European Soccer Championship, cohosted by Poland and Ukraine, a new soccer field was built on public land in the middle of the village in hopes that one of the national teams participating in the tournament would use it as a training base. The owners privatized the field and enclosed it with a fence. In keeping with the principles of "real existing capitalism," they charge to play on the well-kept pitch. As a result, it is usually abandoned, and has to be protected by "private" security guards. In this and the previous case, the root of the problem lies in the entanglement of state and private structures, and privatization at the public's expense. Despite obvious injustices such as these, there has been little public discussion of the economic reforms and privatization in Ukraine. A neoliberal order became established with minimal public debate about the course of the transformation.

The shock therapies in East Central Europe, in contrast, shook the public, provoked debate, and shaped election campaigns. Democratization led to gradualist modifications. Thanks to the consensus about maintaining at least a minimum of state welfare, social security systems were set up following the example of the old EU states, despite the second wave of neoliberalism after the turn of the new millennium, and despite the free-market speech acts by politicians such as Václav Klaus. Although welfare spending in East Central European countries is well below the average in the old EU states—in 2006, social security payments here made up 25.9 percent of the GDP; in the new member states, it was only 16.2 percent[63]—they at least afford some basic provisions and benefits. East Central Europe's social security systems would not have been set up without democratic mechanisms of control and correction. The successor states of the Soviet Union did not have these. Russia gained economic scope after the turn of the millennium thanks to higher oil and gas prices. But it was primarily the elites and the large cities that profited, whereas the rural population and the truly needy continue to live on the breadline. The lack of political participation is partly to blame. Since 2003, Putin has either brought Russia's oligarchs under state control or disempowered them. Mikhail Khodorkovsky's arrest marked a crucial turning point—he had been on the verge of floating his oil corporation Yukos on the New York Stock Exchange when the Russian government immobilized him. However, this partial retreat from neoliberal practices has done nothing to reduce either regional or social inequality. According to data collated in 2009, the Russian Gini coefficient remains over 40, primarily because of the huge gulf between the oligarchs and the new middle class in the big cities and the economic lowest fifth of society, especially the rural population.[64]

The oligarchic order is consistent with the neoliberal ideal insofar as it shapes the economy *and* the political system. But it conflicts with it by allowing politics to strongly influence the economy. Putin, moreover, halted deregulation and liberalization. But the privatization launched in the nineties was extended rather than reversed. The Russian blend of state capitalism, then, is a hybrid variant of neoliberalism within the framework of an authoritarian system.

Comparing transformation in East Central Europe and the post-Soviet states sheds light on the role of external agents. The successor states of the Soviet Union struggled to find their feet without any aid from Brussels, whereas the reforms in East Central Europe were supported by the EU's cooperation program. The prospect of accession stimulated domestic efforts to establish the rule of law as well as foreign investments; both tendencies increased from 2004. While FDIs created and compounded social and spatial disparity, the European Union helped compensate for social inequality in its new member countries. The question remains why Brussels did not pursue the same policy in crisis-torn Southern Europe after 2008.

Whatever the role of the EU, or the repercussions of the FDIs, the political elites retained their pre-1989 goal of catch-up modernization. Nevertheless, the continuities should not be overstressed. Stalinist modernization was based on the principle of autarchy and endogenous resources. After 1989, the IMF, the World Bank, and foreign corporations and the European Union stepped in. In Poland and Hungary, the transition from endogenous to exogenous modernization dated back to the period of détente, when they first opened to Western capital and technologies. The most problematic aspect of endogenous modernization is that it can lead societies' internal resources to become badly overstretched in pursuit of vague promises of future prosperity. The drawback of exogenous modernization is the economic dependency it creates. It can also activate cultural defense mechanisms, which can be articulated in quite harmless ways, such as revivals of traditional music ("Disco Polo," a blend of folksy songs, pounding rhythms, and Western disco music was one manifestation in Poland), or in more aggressive ways.[65]

There have also been strong political counterreactions. An amalgam of social inequality, badly paid and insecure jobs, the socialist heritage of collectivist thinking, and revamped nationalism creates a breeding ground for authoritarian right-wing parties. Viktor Orbán, Hungarian prime minister and Fidesz president, and Jarosław Kaczyński, Polish Law and Justice Party chairman and former prime minister (whose twin brother, then President Lech Kaczyński, died in an airplane crash on his way to visiting the site of the Katyn massacres in 2010), each operate on a political platform that combines social and nationalist populism with anti-European propaganda. Their parties' programs resemble a combination of right-wing US Republicanism and the collectivist heritage of state socialism. In the United States this strange blend would probably not threaten democracy, but in Eastern Europe it does. Both Orbán and Kaczyński have shown strong authoritarian tendencies and have cracked down on critical journalists and media. They have also made inroads into the independent judiciary. Such developments can also occur in established democracies—Silvio Berlusconi's monopolization of electronic media in Italy is one example. But the checks and balances of established democracy, and eventually electoral defeat, forced him to step down. It is uncertain whether political leaders such as Viktor Orbán or Jarosław Kaczyński would renounce power because of a negative ballot. Both did so after their first terms in office, but then turned out to be bad losers. Unable to admit to mistakes or accept democracy's right to change governments, they wove a fabric of conspiracy theories, criticized the West (often echoing Vladimir Putin), and attacked their adversaries in every possible way.

Since reelection, Orbán and Kaczyński have turned out to be even worse winners than losers. In recent years, Orbán has subordinated the constitutional court, infringed on the freedom of the press, and openly argued for an "illiberal" democracy. His government still suffers from rampant corruption, which the European Union and the United States have tried to counteract. But Orbán only responds to criticism from outside with even more nationalist propaganda. It is tragic indeed that Hungary, the country that opened the Iron Curtain, has evolved in this direction. In Poland, Kaczyński's PiS party has openly expressed admiration for Orbán, and tried to emulate his policies since its double election victory in 2015. The crisis of 2008–9 left a question mark behind the transformation economies; recent political tendencies have shown the 1989-created democracies to be precarious, too.

In view of this highly ambivalent picture more than twenty-five years after the revolutions of 1989, can a bottom line be drawn under the transformation period as a whole? As discussed above, it would be difficult to do so for East Central Europe alone, not to mention the rest of Eastern Europe. There are not only problems of scale to consider; that is, the nations' varying sizes. The inclusion in transformation surveys and emerging markets indices of small states such as Slovenia and Estonia alongside the two largest European territorial states, Russia and Ukraine, is due more to the legacy of the Cold War than to structural commonalities. Each of these countries had distinctive historical traditions before the communists seized power, and evolved along different paths under state socialism. In view of history, then, it is not surprising that the outcomes of transformation have been highly divergent.[66] In retrospect, the more pressing question seems to be why the

West expected all of these countries to become market economies and democracies.

Within the former Eastern Bloc, the contrast between the Visegrad countries and the successor states of the Soviet Union is most striking. A comparison of these two macroregions shows that the countries that cushioned society against the hardships of transformation rapidly returned to their 1989 levels of economic strength and prosperity. As early as 2001, the economists Michael Keane and Edward Prasad concluded from the example of Poland that an efficient (but not too costly) welfare state facilitated structural changes in the business sector and other market-oriented reforms.[67] Wherever a deep social divide emerged, it tended to hamper the economy. The reason is that a growing middle class propels the economy more significantly than do the small elites that exist in post-Soviet countries (oligarchs plus a small middle class dependent on them and the state apparatus). The Russian path also refutes the neoliberal trickle-down myth, which played a central role in legitimizing Reaganomics. In fact, the new wealth created by the Russian tycoons of capitalism trickled away, as did the wellsprings of economic recovery.

The history of the transformation period also disproves one of the central neoliberal theories: that higher social security spending curbs economic development. Although in comparison to the Baltic states, Southeastern Europe, and the former Soviet Union, the East Central European states and Slovenia expended relatively large sums on pensioners, the unemployed, and other people in need—according to Dieter Segert, the proportion of welfare spending in the 2006 GDPs of East Central Europe was between 18.1 percent (Poland) and 22.3 percent (Hungary)—they achieved high growth and greater prosperity in the twenty years following 1989.[68]

Until 2009, the Baltic states were often cited as evidence that an unfettered market economy generates even higher growth. (The proportion of social security spending in the GDP here was between 11 and 14.3 percent in 2006.) It should be noted, however, that the original motive for reducing the welfare state was political rather than financial—these governments did not want to support the déclassé resident Russians. This would explain why Lithuania, with its far smaller Russian minority, did not take as strictly neoliberal a course as Estonia and Latvia. Second, the pay-off was high emigration and demographic decline, which will be discussed in more detail in chapter 7. Third, the deceptively high growth rates after the turn of the millennium were largely based on venture capital, which disappeared in a flash in 2008–9.

At first glance, the example of Slovakia appears to better support the theory that less welfare (state) stimulates growth. But developments here since the 2006 election victory of the Left seem to point in another direction. The Slovak Social Democrats reversed some previous reforms (such as the comprehensive privatization of the healthcare and pension systems and part of the flat tax system) and moderated others. Like the postcommunist turnaround in Poland in the mid-nineties, these readjustments did not have any serious economic consequences. Slovakia's main problem is that its automotive industry is virtually a monoculture, and production continues to hinge on low wages. Yet Keane and Prasad's indirect warning should not be ignored: if social security spending becomes too costly, it can knock a country's budget and entire economy off balance, as the case of Hungary shows.

Societies can only be cushioned against the harsher effects of reforms and engender socially mobile middle classes where there is a functioning (constitutional) government. The European Union played a crucial role in establishing the rule of law in former Eastern Bloc countries. In the mid-nineties, it became the most important external transformative actor. Following EU enlargement, Brussels contributed significantly to preventing the social and regional divides in the new member states from widening further. One of the EU's often-cited founding principles was to promote peace after the devastation of two world wars. This mission was acknowledged with the Nobel Peace Prize in 2014. In the new member states, the European Union also carried out a prosperity mission to remedy some of the negative effects of neoliberalism. It would be wrong, however, to attribute the new member states' upsurge exclusively to external factors. As shown in this book's section on human capital, the crucial ingredients were social resources and "transformation from below." They are further investigated in the next chapter on metropolitan comparisons.

# 6

# Capital Cities Compared

## Chalk and Cheese? Or Why We Should Compare

Grayness was one of the main Western stereotypes of the Eastern Bloc. Indeed, the gerontocratic party leaders seemed to match the grayness of their countries. Smoke from factories, soot from coal ovens, exhaust from antiquated cars, and other environmental hazards rendered Eastern European cities gloomy and gray. In the fall and winter, Berlin (West along with East), Prague, Warsaw, and virtually every large communist city fell beneath a blanket of stifling smog. There were scant possibilities to brighten up the cities or even individual houses. Planned economy resulted in permanent scarcity. Building supplies and brightly colored paints were hard to come by, and there was not enough money to renovate the old apartment blocks anyway. The East also seemed gray because of its lack of consumer trappings. As supply was regulated by planned economy, there was no need for eye-catching window displays or flashing neon signs. The East German songwriter Wolf Biermann was exiled from the GDR in 1976 because of his critical lyrics and went to live in West Germany. Just after the fall of the Wall, he took up the stereotype of Eastern grayness and parodied it in his song "Berliner Liedchen": "The West is better / The West is brighter / And nicer and cuter / And richer and free . . . The East is grimmer / The East is grayer / Prospects are bleak / With more hardship ahead."[1]

On the "good side" of the Iron Curtain, West Berlin and the old Habsburg capital Vienna were also perceived as gray. Of course, comparisons always depend on the viewpoint of the observer.

Architecturally, Vienna resembled Prague and Budapest in many ways, and like Berlin, it still suffered from the aftereffects of the two world wars. The collapse of the Austro-Hungarian Empire caused the population of the Austrian capital to shrink from two million in 1913 to 1.5 million in the late 1980s. Berlin's population was reduced from 4.3 million in 1938 to 3.1 million in 1985 (almost 1.9 million in West Berlin and 1.2 million in East Berlin). A disproportionately large number of residents were elderly, as were the buildings. Because of World War II bomb damage and inner-city decay, many East Berliners moved to industrialized suburban developments, leaving large stretches of the traditional core empty and desolate. Ambitious new housing estates were built in West Berlin and Vienna, too; old stucco buildings and narrow lanes were not considered as desirable as they are today. In view of the cities' declining populations, their location near the Iron Curtain, and the loss of large parts of their former hinterlands, it did not seem worth investing in older districts. Apart from a few tourist areas, such as West Berlin's Kurfürstendamm and Vienna's old town, many streets were left unrenovated and appeared correspondingly gloomy.

Although "grayness" may inspire songwriters, it is not a suitable parameter for historical comparison. How could shades of gray be measured, and by means of which indicators?[2] The following comparison is chiefly concerned with the economic transformation of the cities examined. It will ask to what extent each city took advantage of the opportunities that arose when communism collapsed and Europe opened up. Zooming in on the capital cities can also help to shed light on the social effects of reforms, and how they affected the everyday lives and attitudes of the urban populations. Some of the aforementioned indicators will serve again as reference points, including gross domestic products, unemployment rates, average incomes, and home sizes. The main focus is on the *transformation from below*, which took place in the cities compared here in different ways. The sociohistorical analysis will be supplemented by observations in the field of cultural history and on changes to urban landscapes and topographies.

Before embarking on any scientific comparison, the question of whether the subjects are comparable at all must be addressed, or whether they are like the proverbial chalk and cheese. All the cities considered here were national capitals with over a million inhabitants. In Berlin's case, this status had a brief interruption: East Berlin had been the capital of the GDR, but it was not until June 1991 that the reunified city was made the capital of Germany, instead of the former West German capital Bonn, and once again played in the same league as Prague, Warsaw, Budapest, and Vienna—also Kyiv from 1991, and Bratislava from 1993.

The decades of separation by the Wall and West Berlin's special status may seem to challenge Berlin's suitability for comparison. Indeed, West Berlin did not experience any major changes to its political order or social elites, and retained its currency, the deutschmark. But the economic changes that occurred after 1990 in East and West Berlin showed a number of parallels. Industry in both parts of the city was rendered uncompetitive overnight: in East Berlin due to monetary union, in West Berlin because its subsidies were cut. A dual transformation took place, then, which is comparable to the economic development of the other Eastern European capitals.

This book is not intended as a study exclusively of the former Eastern Bloc. That would imply viewing recent European history through the lens of the Cold War, more than twenty-five years after it ended. To broaden the perspective, Vienna is included. Like Berlin, the former Habsburg capital was initially divided into four zones of occupation, which were abolished in the Austrian Independence Treaty of 1955. But Vienna remained locked in by communist states on two sides and could not evolve economically as it had in the past. However, serving as a western outpost had its advantages. Vienna and West Berlin continued to enjoy special attention and became hubs of East-West exchange.

## The Situation before 1989

Despite the aforementioned inhibiting factors—planned economy in the East and the peripheral location of Vienna and West

Berlin on the edge of the Western world, lacking their traditional hinterlands—all the cities compared here were privileged. Planned economies were centrally organized; the countries' notoriously scarce resources were allocated from the capitals—Warsaw, Prague, Budapest, and East Berlin. Austria, like Germany, is federally organized. But Vienna, often mocked within Austria as the "bloated city" ("Wasserkopf Wien"), profited from Austrian neutrality and its status as the capital and a federal state in its own right. In the postwar years, the United Nations and affiliated organizations such as the International Atomic Energy Agency (IAEA) and OPEC set up headquarters in Vienna. That was not possible in West Berlin because of the Cold War, but the western outpost was kept afloat by massive government subsidies, and thus got its share of West Germany's economic miracle.

East Berlin was given a modern face to show that the communists were keeping pace with the West. Special attention was paid to the buildings close to the Wall that were visible from West Berlin. They were freshly painted and renovated, though just one block behind them, the plaster was crumbling from the houses. The city center also bore the stamp of system rivalry. The Centrum Warenhaus department store on Alexanderplatz was designed as a counterpart to West Berlin's KaDeWe and offered a wider range of consumer goods than any other socialist store.

Other Eastern Bloc capitals also received preferential treatment, partly because many functionaries lived there. In Prague, oranges were available at Christmastime in the late eighties (at the black market rate, they were far cheaper than in Germany); East Berlin was a magnet for commercial tourists from all socialist "brother nations"; shelves in Warsaw stores were not as empty as they were in the Polish provinces. Moreover, at special stores in the capitals and large cities (Intershop in the GDR; Pewex and Baltona in Poland; Tuzex in the ČSSR; Beriozka in the USSR), Western products could be bought for foreign currencies. Shopping trips to the capital became a firm part of socialist consumer culture, as did trips from the capital to deliver provisions to the provinces. Financially, however, the capitals' inhabitants were not privileged. Wages and salaries were standardized and fixed nationwide; rents and prices for food and consumer items were regulated by the state. The result, to the bewilderment of tourists from the West, was prices such as 1.13 marks for a beer or 5.67 marks for a schnitzel in East Berlin.

The communists promised a classless society, and indeed, a leveling tendency arose from the rubble of World War II. The heavy bombing of Berlin, and the almost complete destruction of Warsaw, reduced or destroyed the property of industries, tradesmen, and homeowners. With Jews forced to emigrate or murdered, a large part of the urban elites were lost. In their efforts to create classless societies, communists allocated housing to laborers and members of the lower classes first, often expressly in middle-class districts. Similarly, Vienna's subsidized-housing program changed the city's social structure, building homes for blue-collar workers even in upper-class districts. Although the Wall placed West Berlin in an exceptional situation, here, too, there were no longer traditional working-class quarters or exclusive uptown areas. Furthermore, with the exception of West Berlin and, to some extent, Vienna, all the major cities attracted large-scale migration from rural areas. When economic reforms were introduced in 1989, the capital cities were therefore more homogenous than ever before in their histories.

The social cuts of 1989–90 hit postcommunist city dwellers harder than rural populations at first. Subsidies for staple goods were canceled and food prices decontrolled, resulting in sharply rising prices. Poland and Yugoslavia experienced hyperinflation with three-figure price increases; the situation in Bulgaria and the Soviet Union was only slightly better. In comparative terms, the inhabitants of Prague were best off, but even they faced price increases of over 50 percent for basic foodstuffs such as sugar.[3] In East Berlin, too, real incomes dwindled over the fall and winter of 1989. One indicator was the drop in the black market value of the East German mark—by early 1990 it had almost halved.

The advocates of the Washington Consensus had a standard recipe against high inflation, which the Americans and British also got to know in the early Reagan and Thatcher years: the central bank was to limit the amount of money while the government imposed austerity measures. A third element was added in the postcommunist countries: wages and salaries were frozen, or de facto lowered. In late 1989, as part of the Balcerowicz Plan, the Polish government introduced penalty taxes for "exaggerated" pay raises; Czechoslovakia followed suit in 1990. In addition, Poland, like Yugoslavia, stopped index-linking wages and other incomes to the rate of inflation.[4] In real terms, these two measures reduced the already low wages in Poland by almost half; in more affluent Czechoslovakia, by a sixth.[5] In other words, inflation was fought largely at the expense of workers and public servants. The GDR was an exception. Incomes there appreciated considerably in value due to currency union with the FRG in summer 1990.

One immediate consequence of the cutbacks was a drop in consumption. The storefront lines of waiting customers disappeared—few could afford to buy the goods on display. Official statistics show how dramatically incomes dropped in 1990. In the greater Warsaw area, the average monthly wage was 587,000 złotys. This sum would have been a small fortune a few years previously, but inflation had reduced the value to the equivalent of only sixty dollars by that point. Statistics for the Warsaw voivodeship (province) show that the population spent nearly half their per capita income on food. The residents of Warsaw, then, lived literally from hand to mouth.[6] Shampoo, detergent, cosmetics, clothing, and other basic consumer items became luxuries; the majority of the population could only dream of eating out or traveling on vacation. Citizens of Budapest and Prague were not exposed to such extreme vagaries, as inflation in Hungary and Czechoslovakia did not accelerate as rapidly as in Poland. But here, too, the equivalent of $100 ranked as a reasonable monthly wage. Unsurprisingly, then, Poles, Czechs, Slovaks, and Hungarians looked on with envy as GDR citizens collected their gift of 100 deutschmarks "welcome money" (*Begrüßungsgeld*) dished out by the West German government after the fall of the Wall.

In spring 1990, stores everywhere began to fill with previously scarce items. But now, particularly in Poland, the customers were missing. The new service sector, which had been supposed to propel the postcommunist economy, was struggling with low demand. The only thriving sector was the farmers' markets and open-air bazaars selling cheap homegrown produce, and kiosks offering a wide range of consumer goods within tiny spaces. In addition to food items, real ground coffee (not the adulterated, pre-1989 kind) and the type of Western products that had previously been sold at the state-run foreign currency stores—myriad cosmetics, shower gels, and shampoos—were available to be taken away in brightly colored plastic bags. The sanitary products were so much in demand and so costly that their proud owners displayed them conspicuously in their bathrooms. In Prague, the population had more fundamental needs: here, restaurants locked and chained their rolls of toilet paper to the holders to prevent guests from taking them.

For the first two or three years, the grayness of state socialism more or less persisted. The inhabitants of the capital cities grew initially poorer, not richer. Having a "big brother" in the West placed Berlin and the former GDR at a considerable advantage, while the other former Eastern Bloc countries were initially left to fend for themselves. Moreover, the political future of countries such as Poland remained uncertain for longer. The last soldiers of the defunct Red Army did not leave their East Central European headquarters in Lower Silesia until 1993. The Polish capital Warsaw had additional disadvantages to contend with. For one, infrastructure was weak; the city did not even have a subway. The hyperinflation of 1989–90 had obliterated nearly all monetary assets. However, Warsaw had a huge resource of human capital, including a rising class of self-employed craftsmen, service providers, and entrepreneurs, who had built up livelihoods under state socialism back in the 1980s.

## Transformation from Below

Two places symbolized the dawn of a new, capitalist era in post-communist cities in the early nineties: kiosks and bazaars. Kiosks had existed under state socialism, selling the same range of products as newsagents: newspapers, magazines, drinks, cigarettes, candy, tram tickets, and a few items of stationery. Following liberalization in 1988, more diversified kiosks emerged in Warsaw and other Polish cities—some for cakes and pastries, others for fruit and vegetables, cosmetics and sanitary products, or pantyhose and underwear. Some sold all the above at once. How the proprietors, many of them women, stored all their goods within a few square feet remains a mystery, yet in this way they made an independent living.

Open-air bazaars followed the reverse spatial principle of commercial sprawl. The Różycki bazaar, a well-known black market hub in Warsaw's Praga district on the eastern side of the Vistula River, spilled out over an ever-growing area. Similarly, the bazaar on Mexikoplatz in the central 2nd district of Vienna and the "Polish market" on Reichpietschufer in Berlin soon proliferated. Traveling traders set up stalls around Warsaw's Dziesięciolecia stadium, which had stood mostly empty since its construction for the communist International Youth Festival in 1955. During the nineties, an increasing number of anthropologists, ethnologists, sociologists and economists were drawn to study the vast bazaar at the stadium,[7] fascinated by the emergence of this site of burgeoning supply, as well as semilegal and illegal activities, including occasional shootings.

Initially, however, the largest bazaar in central Europe was not in Warsaw but at the aforementioned Reichpietschufer in Berlin, close to Potsdamer Platz and the western side of the Berlin Wall. Polish citizens, who made up the majority of the traders, could travel to West Berlin or Vienna without a visa. Here they purchased Western products of all kinds for resale at home at a high profit. As Polish historian Jerzy Kochanowski has shown, Warsaw thus evolved into a distribution center for the entire Eastern Bloc, or a "stronghold of speculation," as communist officialese labeled it.[8] Soviet customers played their part by paying for scarce goods such as jeans, nylon pantyhose, or Western electronic devices with barter objects such as gold, furs, or other valuables. GDR customs and border officers attempted to contain the export trade from West Berlin to Warsaw, frisking Polish travelers as stringently as the class enemy from the West. But when the Wall came down,

Fig. 6.1. Polish traders at Berlin's "Polish market" on Reichpietschufer, February 1989. Photo: ullstein bild / Günter Peters.

their zeal dwindled and cross-border trade became easier. According to official estimates, some eight thousand traders and many more customers attended Berlin's "Polish market" in winter 1989–90 (see fig. 6.1).[9] The Polish traders hoped to escape poverty in Poland; the Berliners came out of curiosity and to find a bargain, not least smuggled cigarettes.[10]

The label "Polish market" (*Polenmarkt*) signaled an operation of dubious repute. Old prejudices against Poles, vigorously propagated by the Nazis, still circulated in both parts of Berlin. The GDR regime had revived them in response to the emergence of Solidarność and "commercial tourists."[11] "Polish economy" became a dirty word again. Tasteless jokes were common, along the lines of "once it's plundered, it's in Poland . . ." ("Kaum gestohlen, schon in Polen . . ."). The presence of so many Poles in the city and the goings-on at the bazaar made Berlin's senators decidedly uneasy. The city government dispatched dozens of police officers, food hygiene inspectors, and customs investigators to crack down on the trade. A "Polish market work group" was set up, cooperating across several senate administrations, to organize checks on the bazaar at Reichpietschufer and the seizure of contraband. But no matter how closely the authorities monitored the traders, the latter were almost always one step ahead. Unauthorized stalls could be folded up and carried away in the blink of an eye. At the still existent intra-German border, the smugglers organized so-called "ant trade." The "ants" were a chain of contacts going back and forth across the border, carrying the largest permissible amount of cigarettes, liquor, and other customs-taxable goods each way. After a few fruitless attempts to contain the Polish market, it was banished to the less-central district of Wedding in 1993, and eventually closed down. The traders took their business to the border towns along the Oder and Neisse rivers, primarily Słubice, Gubin, and Zgorzelec. According to one estimate, this "small border trade" achieved a turnover of seven billion marks in 1996.[12] Just a fraction of that amount would certainly have helped Berlin's ailing economy.

While Berlin closed its Polish market, the Jarmark Europa bazaar at the Dziesięciolecia stadium flourished (see fig. 6.2). From 1990, and before EU enlargement, Warsaw had the locational advantage that neither Western Europeans nor their eastern neighbors, Russians, Ukrainians, and Belarusians, required visas to visit. The Polish capital was therefore an ideal meeting point between East and West. The stallholders at the stadium quickly converted their market stands into permanent, covered structures, creating a kind of strip mall. Jarmark Europa was essentially a vast, open-air shopping center. Unfortunately the fields surrounding

Fig. 6.2. The Jarmark Europa market in Warsaw in September 2007. Photo: Masti.

the stadium became trampled and strewn with cigarette butts and garbage, creating a layer of brown sludge that spread inexorably over visitors' shoes and trouser legs.

The bazaar offered counterfeit brand-name clothing, with and without the little crocodile, outerwear and underwear to fit all requirements, shoes, CDs and music cassettes (mostly pirated copies), cosmetics, over-the-counter drugs, water faucets, showerheads, tools, scrap iron (often sourced from the bankrupt agricultural cooperatives, no doubt), and contraband cigarettes—and, under the counter, firearms and other illegal items. Cheap clothes and shoes made up around a third of the market's turnover.[13] Occasionally, the police carried out raids and hounded rogue traders through the narrow galleries, but for the most part the city council seemed to have accepted the impossibility of controlling the bazaar.

Soon Jarmark Europa's trade, which reached a climax in 1996–97, extended across the entire country. Over half its turnover was achieved by supplying goods wholesale to smaller markets in Poland and the "Polish markets" along the German-Polish border. In 1997, some 8,500 people worked in Jarmark Europa; its external suppliers employed around 24,500. Around a quarter of a million jobs are estimated to have been created by the sixteen largest Polish open-air markets. But when the first modern shopping malls opened in the late nineties, the markets began to attract fewer shoppers and employ fewer people. Poles were growing more affluent and had less demand for cheap textiles. The ruble crisis in 1998 inhibited patrons from farther east. After the turn of the millennium, the Jarmark Europa bazaar never regained its former glory. It was finally closed to make way for the stadium's refurbishment in preparation for the 2012 European Soccer Championship. Nevertheless, Warsaw economist Marcin Peterlik has concluded that "the markets . . . were an important element in the evolution of private business and thus of the establishment of market economy."[14]

The markets in Vienna were never as large as Jarmark Europa, and usually open only on Saturdays. The largest was located on Mexikoplatz, stretching for a time to the adjacent Handelskai on the right bank of the Danube, where tourist coaches habitually parked. The street traders on Mexikoplatz (and at other Viennese flea markets, such as Naschmarkt) sold anything that might be converted into cash: dilapidated antiques and picture frames, crockery and glassware, battered musical instruments, discarded tools and scrap metal, huge piles of musty-smelling clothes from any era, and in some corners, agricultural produce direct from the farmers. The revenue from sales enabled the traders from Poland (who were the most numerous), Hungary, Slovakia, Romania, and the disintegrating state of Yugoslavia to finance their journeys and purchase Western products for sale at home, which was a way of escaping hyperinflation. At Mexikoplatz, too, not all transactions were entirely legal. The most lucrative scam was the sale of contraband cigarettes and liquor. In spring 1990, when the bazaar was at its zenith, the police arrested two hundred black-market traders during a major raid.[15] In one instance, Austrian customs officers, acting on a tip, uncoupled and searched a carriage of the express train from Warsaw. Hidden behind the carriage's side and ceiling panels they found not only fur caps, silver fox wraps, binoculars, cameras, household devices, and sports equipment, but also 360 cartons of cigarettes. (The customs officers reported 72,650 cigarettes to emphasize the enormity of the haul.) Goods weighing 4.2 tons were confiscated; the smugglers were forced to pay a thirty-thousand-schilling fine. The tabloid press devoted much coverage to such raids. Right-wing populist politician Jörg Haider seized on their allegations of criminal tendencies among Eastern Europeans to support his xenophobic 1990 election campaign. The Austrian government caved in to the pressure thus created and cancelled visa-free travel for Poles and Romanians in September that year.

The city of Vienna reacted with greater tolerance and laissez-faire, merely dispatching cleaning squads at the end of the day and collecting stallholder fees. In any case, beginning in the early nineties, the bazaar on Mexikoplatz steadily dwindled. The Polish tax on spirits had been raised, making liquor more expensive than in the West; prices for cigarettes leveled; supplies from Russia (presumably the source of the aforementioned furs) dried up; the demand for Eastern Bloc products and cheap paraphernalia was largely exhausted.

Due to the nature of the trade, the exact volume of sales achieved at Mexikoplatz is not known, but Vienna certainly profited from it. The traders often used their earnings to buy goods to export back home; some of them returned to the city later in other capacities. Retail trade in Vienna actively courted customers from the Eastern Bloc. In the shopping street Mariahilfer Strasse (popularly known at the time as *Magyarhilfer* Strasse in reference to the many Hungarians among the customers, taking advantage of the travel freedoms introduced in 1988), clockmakers, jewelers, and other stores displayed advertisements in Eastern European languages and Cyrillic script in their windows. Austrian banks offered anonymous accounts—a good hiding place for illicit earnings.

Though particularly visible, kiosks and bazaars were just one element of the transformation from below.[16] Small construction companies, handicraft firms, and services mushroomed in postcommunist cities, creating more new jobs than even the bazaars and far more than the state sector. But the open-air bazaars provide fascinating evidence of the diverging responses to the opportunities presented by transformation and, especially, borders opening. While Warsaw made the most of new economic activity, even at the expense of forfeiting bureaucratic control, reunified Berlin deemed itself above such trade.

These observations on the course of transformation from below can be supported by quantitative data. In Poland, 128,000 firms were established in the first five months of 1989 alone; in the ensuing four years, the number rose to 1.8 million.[17] Warsaw was at the epicenter of the boom. In 1991, over 40,000 "national economic units" (*podmioty gospodarki narodowej*) were registered here; in 1992, 65,000; in 1993, 132,000; in 1996, 205,000. Not all of them were companies within the meaning of most Western trade-and-industry laws, but certainly the large majority.[18] Figure 6.3 clearly shows the dynamic development of free enterprise in Warsaw.

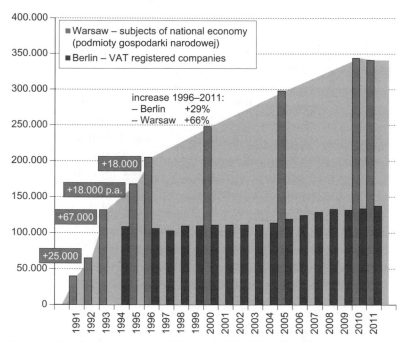

**Fig. 6.3.** New business boom in Warsaw and Berlin, 1991–2011. *Source*: *Rocznik Statystyczny Warszawy* (Warsaw Statistical Yearbook); Amt für Statistik Berlin-Brandenburg.

The powerful boom left its mark on the popular culture of the transformation era. In 1993, the weekly newspaper *Polityka* invited readers to submit literary texts on the subject of privatization. It received such an enthusiastic response that it was able to fill several pages with "privatization poetry." The compiled sonnets, rhymes, and limericks read like a satirical revue of the reforms and their social consequences.[19] Most of the poems are so context-specific that they defy translation, but at least one example must be given here: "A girl filled with desperation / resorted to privatization / But to her it was all the same / When it turned into a one-woman game" ("Jedna dziewczyna w wielkiej desperacji / Chciała się oddać prywatizacji / A że nie była to tęga głowa / Wyszła jej spólka jednoosobowa").[20] Indeed, many residents of Warsaw, Budapest, and Prague were not acting entirely voluntarily when they ventured into self-employment. The high number of newly founded businesses was linked to rising unemployment and dwindling incomes. Several participants in the *Polityka* poetry competition channeled criticisms of the economic and social changes into satirical, sometimes cynical texts. But most of the poems conveyed a sense of light-hearted, ultimately affirmative irony.

A similar upsurge started in Czechoslovakia in 1990. By summer 1992, 1.2 million private enterprises had been founded—even more, in relation to the total population of fifteen million, than in Poland. Hungary had seen the first signs of a business boom in the latter years of state socialism, and it continued at a steadier pace after 1989. A few years later, the Baltic states experienced an equally dynamic development. In Ukraine, small businesses began to emerge in the western regions, which had not become Soviet territories until 1944, and in the capital, Kyiv, but the rest of the country continued to languish for many years. This boom—at least four million new enterprises were founded by the mid-nineties in the Visegrad countries alone—provides evidence of the middle-class capitalism considered in the typology of reform outcomes below.

In comparison to Warsaw, Berlin fell distinctly behind. According to information from the regional statistical agency, 108,000 companies subject to turnover tax were registered in both parts of the city in 1994, dropping slightly by 1996. If one includes microenterprises that were not liable to pay turnover tax (as in the statistics on Warsaw), the numbers are slightly higher. Still, the trend was clear: after a short upswing in the years 1991 and 1992, the number of trade and business registrations stagnated at about forty thousand per year, while an increasing number of self-employed businesses closed down. Beginning in the mid-nineties a "phase of weakness" set in, as the Berlin Investment Bank (Investitionsbank Berlin) put it, during which there were almost as many cancellations as registrations.[21] At the same time, Warsaw's boom went from strength to strength; the number of companies in relation to the population was three or four times larger than that in Berlin.

In postcommunist Germany, many small-business owners who risked self-employment in the early nineties were among the losers of transformation.[22] The German government had opened up a new market for West German companies without sufficiently supporting the transformation from below. As a consequence, new small enterprises could not withstand the competition from the larger, established businesses from the West. In turn, the lack of entrepreneurial activity gave rise to the stereotype of the "*Jammerossi*," the apathetic, complaining East German. The nineties business boom in Berlin and East Germany, then, was weaker than in Poland, Czechoslovakia, Hungary, or the economically active Baltic states. Southeastern Europe and the successor states of the Soviet Union also saw fewer business-formings. In Bulgaria, for example, only 180,000 businesses were formed between 1989 and 1993. That number pales in comparison to the 1.8 million businesses formed in Poland (with a population nearly four times larger).[23]

## The New Business Boom

The transformation from below and the gradual influx of foreign direct investments launched a sustained upswing in all the capitals compared here, except Berlin. In 1995, Warsaw obtained a gross domestic product of 8,200 euros (converted on the basis of Eurostat and WIIW data) per capita, adjusted to purchasing power parity.[24] At 24,000 euros, Berlin's GDP was almost triple that amount. The difference in average incomes was even larger. According to the Warsaw statistical agency, the average wage in the Polish capital was a mere $160 per month in 1995 (converted from złotys at the contemporary exchange rate).[25] But this, at least, was two and a half times more than the average in 1991. Moreover, the official statistics do not include incomes generated by the gray economy, which played a substantial role in this period.

The upswing was tangible in everyday life. Privately run supermarkets opened on the main streets. There were more places to go in the evening than just the state restaurants and cafés, which closed at ten or eleven o'clock. Elegant boutiques appeared on Krakowskie Przedmieście, the boulevard connecting Warsaw's old town and the stock exchange. Two nightclubs that stayed open until well after midnight were launched close to the university. However, few Poles could afford to become patrons. A light meal and one or two drinks consumed the daily wage of a teacher or university lecturer. The proximity of enticing but costly new opportunities created powerful incentives to get started in business. Income trends in Prague were similar. Here, residents earned on average seven thousand euros per year in 1995; in Budapest, six thousand euros (each adjusted to purchasing power parity). The figures contradict the Hungarian elites' long-held belief that the country's "goulash communism" and early introduction of economic reforms placed it, or at least its capital, at the forefront of developments in Central Europe. But variations of one or two thousand euros were not particularly significant in the long run. More importantly, all three postcommunist capitals experienced upward trends.

Berlin had a huge head start on Warsaw and Prague, but began to suffer the effects of homegrown problems in the early nineties. Unemployment rose between 1989 and 1995 by more than two-thirds to 13.6 percent.[26] Despite the generous provision of early retirement, retraining, and job creation schemes, one in six adults was unemployed at the turn of the millennium. This problem was not specific to Berlin. Unemployment was a negative side effect

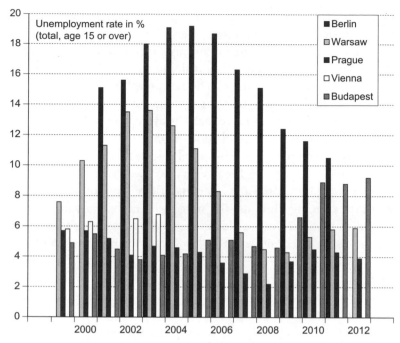

**Fig. 6.4.** Unemployment rates in East Central European cities, 1999–2012.
*Source*: Eurostat Metropolstatitistik (Tabelle met_lfu3rt).

of transformation that affected all of East Germany. Although the inhabitants of Warsaw, Prague, and Budapest obtained a smaller GDP than the average Berliner, and earned distinctly less, their job security was higher and their livelihoods less under threat (see fig. 6.4).

Vienna, the other Western metropolis next to the Iron Curtain, did not suffer such "shocks without therapy," as the later Polish Finance Minister Grzegorz Kołodko put it.[27] Market vagaries caused a slight rise in unemployment in Austria in the first half of the 1990s, after which it lingered at a low rate of 5 to 7 percent. Prague and Budapest boasted full employment, though not all reasons for this were positive. In all Eastern Bloc capitals except Berlin, housing was expensive and scarce. Few people from rural or old industrial regions could afford to move to the capital in search of better prospects. The rent for a two-room apartment on the free market in Warsaw or Prague consumed an average worker's monthly income.

While plenty of cheap housing was available in Berlin, the ailing economy deterred potential jobseekers. At the same time, few Berliners moved to the affluent south or west of Germany, as hundreds of thousands from Leipzig, Chemnitz, and Magdeburg had done—not even when unemployment reached 19 percent in 2005. Perhaps they were confident of Berlin's imminent recovery. Indeed, symbolic reunification projects such as the redevelopment of Potsdamer Platz, begun in 1993, nourished hopes of better times ahead.

But glimmers of light only appeared on the horizons of other capitals. Between 1995 and 2000, Warsaw's GDP, adjusted to purchasing power parity, rose from 8,200 to 13,800 euros—an increase of 68 percent. Prague's economic strength also grew robustly, from 7,000 to 11,900 euros (a gain of 70 percent); Budapest's per capita GDP increased from 6,000 to 10,000 euros (up by 67 percent). Of course, rising GDPs do not necessarily signify parallel improvements in living standards; these are better measured by the Human Development Index/HDI, but this is not recorded in the local or regional archives on the period in question. From 1995, wages and salaries actually increased more rapidly than the GDP—from an average equivalent of 160 dollars to 600 dollars per month in Warsaw.

However, averages are only meaningful to a limited degree. Teachers, most civil servants, and my university associates still earned no more than the equivalent of $200 to $350 in the mid-nineties. By contrast, any young person with an economics-related university degree and one or two foreign languages could take his or her pick of the best jobs and make three times as much. There were also many opportunities for those prepared to venture into self-employment. A culture of second and third jobs evolved. Many residents of Warsaw, Prague, and Budapest supplemented their incomes by moonlighting. But by the late nineties, the generation of 1989 had occupied the best positions and self-employment niches, and it became harder to find well-paid jobs.

Moreover, with the exception of Poland, there were serious economic upheavals in all postcommunist countries. In the Czech Republic, the bank crisis of 1996 brought the upswing to an abrupt end. However, the tourist boom in the capital, Prague, compensated for the crisis, and prompted the authorities to commission the large-scale renovation of the old town, creating many jobs. Hungary, in contrast, continued to struggle with its high foreign debt. In 1995, under pressure from the IMF and the World Bank, the postcommunist government adopted the aforementioned "Bokros package," an extensive austerity program that cut civil servants'—hardly extravagant—real income by over 5 percent. Economic growth dropped to 1.1 percent in 1996;[28] about 30 percent of the population fell below the poverty line. Although mostly rural and old industrial areas were affected, homeless beggars began to appear at store entrances in Budapest, too—a new and shocking phenomenon to postcommunist societies. Warsaw was spared an economic slump of the kind that Prague and Budapest suffered, but had higher unemployment (8.8 percent in 2000)[29] as the baby-boom generation born in the early eighties crowded the job market. This was a late repercussion of the curfew and the scarcity of contraception during the period of martial law in 1981–83.

Despite the general and specific problems besetting each of the former Eastern Bloc capitals, they all spawned urban middle classes over the nineties, whose living standards came close to those in the West. The wealthiest 20 percent of the population of Prague, for example, had an average annual income equivalent to 12,600 euros. With rents strictly regulated and food still much cheaper than in the West, this sum went a long way. The second-wealthiest fifth of the population, with annual incomes ranging between 8,500 and 12,600 euros, were also relatively comfortable.[30] But financial difficulties could arise if a major household appliance or car broke down. Hence the improvisational talent developed under socialism remained useful. Gasoline was very expensive; filling a car tank cost as much as several days' pay. For this reason, most vacations were spent in family cottages in the country, or camping, rather than in hotels abroad. A fifth of

Prague's population (no comparable data are available on Warsaw) had to make do with the equivalent of 300 euros per month. As prices for food and other staple goods were rising, they had just enough to survive from day to day.

Although the citizens of the former GDR and especially East Berlin were financially advantaged, rapidly rising unemployment made them deeply insecure. The proximity of affluent West Germans, who had been appointed to many senior positions in the East in order to westernize the former GDR, bred envy and inferiority complexes. The conflicts among Germans with different backgrounds found expression in stereotypical notions of "Wessis" (presumptuous colonizers from the West) and "Ossis" (whiners from the East). Interestingly, there was less antagonism  within reunified Berlin, perhaps because West Berliners were only slightly better off than East Berliners. Weathering economic crisis together seemed to foster social cohesion.

Though local balladeers continued to extol Vienna's tumble-down charm, in fact the city experienced a robust upswing. Between 1995 and 2005 the per capita GDP rose by almost 2 percent per year, in absolute numbers from 33,200 euros to 40,000 euros. What, then, sustained Vienna's blossoming? Economic historian Dieter Stiefel has calculated that the opening of the Eastern Bloc and trade with the postcommunist countries boosted Austria's economic growth by at least 0.5 percent annually from 1989.[31] And due to Vienna's geographical location and function as a center of trade and services, the city certainly profited more from the opening up of Europe than did the rest of Austria. As a result, banks, insurance companies, construction companies, retail trade, and tourism thrived. Austrian companies expanded, usually in two stages: first into former Habsburg territories, then into more remote Eastern European countries.

The former capital of the Austro-Hungarian Empire utilized Europe's opening in another way. According to the Viennese economic chamber, some three hundred Western companies chose Vienna as the location for their Central Eastern European offices.[32] At the same time, Eastern Europeans came to the city to purchase goods, open businesses, or settle permanently. Polish,

Ukrainian, Russian, Hungarian, Romanian, and various South Slavic languages are often spoken on the streets; some (though still too few) state schools provide classes in the above languages to native-speaker children. The influx of foreigners, including 35,000 Germans, caused the population to swell by 200,000 between 1998 and 2014 (from 1,541,000 to 1,741,000 inhabitants). These figures put a different complexion on the GDP figures. In the years of rapid population growth between 2000 and 2006, Vienna absorbed almost twenty thousand new residents annually while the per capita incomes continued to improve.[33] Vienna is poised to reach the same population density as it had in the late Habsburg Empire.

This business boom at the transition from the twentieth to the twenty-first century washed away Vienna's grayness, or displaced it to the poorer suburbs. The inner-city areas between the Ring Road and the Gürtel have been largely renovated, with mixed consequences. As in Prague and the fashionable districts of East Berlin, rents have risen, causing a separation of the urban rich and poor, both socially and geographically. But complaints about blanket gentrification seem exaggerated in view of Vienna's strict protection of tenants and the dispersion of subsidized housing in all districts of the city. Vienna's renaissance as a multinational service capital defies simplistic explanations claiming that radical reforms are the only key to economic success. Comparison with Berlin suggests that the reverse might be true, because Vienna resisted privatizing or deregulating its huge public sector.

The populations of Warsaw and Prague grew less rapidly; that of Budapest actually shrank, primarily on account of the difficult housing market and a delayed process of suburbanization. Many former residents of the capital moved out to the surrounding areas, where land was cheap, to build their dream homes in the country. The dream often ended in a nightmare of endless traffic jams for the commuter-belt residents. But the construction boom thus generated propelled economic growth in the postcommunist capitals to even greater heights per capita than Vienna's. As figure 6.5 shows, Warsaw's per capita GDP (all figures are adjusted to purchasing power parity and converted into euros) rose in

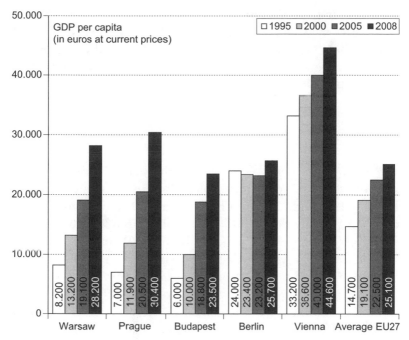

**Fig. 6.5.** Economic performance of compared capital cities, 1995–2008.
*Source*: Eurostat Regional Statistics (table nama_r_e3gdp).

the years 2000–2005 from 13,800 to 19,100—an increase of 38.4
percent. Prague recorded a 72 percent increase and Budapest a
mighty 88 percent.[34] The Ukrainian capital Kyiv experienced similar growth rates, though the upswing began some five years later.
Here, the per capita GDP almost tripled.[35]

Factors such as low starting points and the effect of foreign
direct investments on relatively small and centralist-governed
"emerging markets" must be taken into account when interpreting statistics on growth. Purchasing power adjustments must also
be approached with caution, as they are calculated on the basis
of national data, regardless of regional differences (between rural
areas, small, large, and capital cities), which can be substantial.
In a global perspective, it might even seem doubtful whether this
boom was anything out of the ordinary. Metropolitan growth is

a worldwide phenomenon. Viewed in this light, Warsaw, Prague, Budapest, Kyiv, and Vienna are just following a general trend.[36] Still, the fact remains that just two or three years after the revolution, a business boom started in Eastern European capitals that lasted until 2009 and even beyond.

## Poor Berlin

For many years, Berlin was the only city that failed to boom—a state of affairs that demands explanation. Its economy stagnated between 1995 and 2005. According to Eurostat data, Berlin's gross domestic product decreased in this decade from 24,000 to 23,200 euros per capita (see fig. 6.6).[37] Between 2001 and 2004, it even experienced negative growth of between 1 and 2 percent per year. Unemployment soared, despite extensive job creation schemes and early retirement programs, to 19.2 percent.[38] The effects of the seemingly endless transformation crisis could be felt on a number of levels. There was less rush-hour traffic; the newly built inner-city shopping malls were crowded during regular working hours and not at the end of the day; neo-Nazi attacks increased. The population figures reflected the economic trend, stagnating at around 3.4 million—in a city that had dreamt of growing to 5 million during its moment of hubris on becoming the capital of reunified Germany.

What were the reasons for Berlin's enduring crisis? The first and most important factor lay beyond the city's control. The double shock therapy—Germany's unique path of transformation—rendered industry in East Germany, and hence in East Berlin, uncompetitive overnight. Not one of East Berlin's large combines survived; West Berlin at least held on to its Siemens, BMW, and Schering works. The subsidies for the walled-in West of the city had not been as abruptly withdrawn as those for industry in East Berlin. West Berlin obviously had a stronger lobby in the German government than did the former capital of the GDR. The service sector fared a little better as real wages in East Germany appreciated in value following the currency union in 1990. This prevented consumption from tumbling in the same way as in Warsaw.

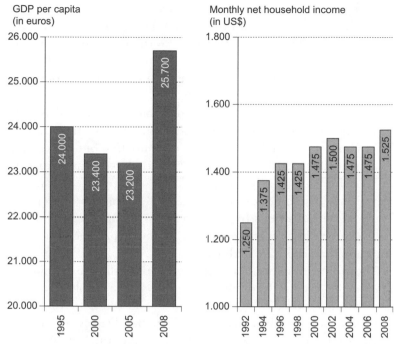

GDP per capita (in euros)

Monthly net household income (in US$)

**Fig. 6.6.** Poor Berlin 1992–2008. *Source*: Eurostat Regional Statistics (data for 2013): Amt für Statistik Berlin-Brandenburg.

However, the "transformation from below" in Berlin was far weaker than in the Polish, Czech, and Hungarian capitals. Taking the neoliberal view, this can be attributed in part to the generous social benefits afforded to compensate for the bulldozing of the former GDR's economy. Living on state unemployment support was possible in Berlin in the nineties, but not by any stretch in Warsaw, and difficult in Prague and Budapest. Some observers accused the citizens of the former GDR of lying back in the state's "safety hammock"—if such a thing ever existed anywhere in the world. But migration statistics tell a different story: around 1.4 million people left the former GDR for West Germany in the first four years after reunification alone.[39] This number of labor migrants corresponds almost exactly with the number of self-employed businesses founded in Czechoslovakia in the same period. (The latter country had a population of 15 million in 1990, only slightly smaller than the former GDR). One reason for the high rate of migration was that East Germans—unlike other former Eastern Bloc citizens—enjoyed unlimited freedom of settlement within the European Union including, of course, old West Germany, thanks to German unification.

In this way, the society of the former GDR was deprived of its most commercially active members. The outflow from East to West Germany abated a little in the mid-nineties, but peaked at a record 230,000 in 2001. East Berliners tended to commute to work in West Berlin rather than migrate to West Germany. Unemployment in the districts of the former East Berlin was soon lower than in the western districts. In summary, it seems that West Berliners had greater difficulty adapting to the new economic and social situation than did East Berliners.

The political constellation in reunified Berlin was similar to that in the Federal Republic of Germany as a whole. On local and national levels, Western elites ruled over the East. The grand coalition (between the conservative Christian Democrats and the Social Democrats) in power until 2001 failed to promote Berlin as a business location. Just one major company, Deutsche Bahn (the German railroads), transferred its headquarters to Berlin during the transformation period, and even this state enterprise threatened at one point to relocate to Hamburg due to various conflicts with the Berlin senate. No other large enterprise became established in the city. Schering AG, the only Berlin-based company quoted on DAX, the German stock index, disappeared after it was swallowed by a competitor. The Eastern European offices of international firms relocated to other places, such as Vienna and, more recently, Warsaw.[40]

Rather than making Berlin more attractive, the state-run regional bank Berliner Landesbank tried to play for much higher stakes. It speculated wildly with real estate, including tens of thousands of communist-built apartment blocks in East Germany. Its misdirected investments and inflated guarantees to investors resulted in multibillion-euro losses and toppled the grand coalition (which was run by exclusively West Berlin players) in

2001. Banking scandals and government bailouts at the taxpayers' expense were regular features of the postcommunist economy as much as of neoliberalism. The tragedy in the case of Berlin was that, in contrast to the "tunneling" that caused the Czech bank crisis, the squandered money did not flow into industry and thus help indirectly to save jobs. The astronomical sums lost by the Berliner Landesbank, estimated at up to 21.5 billion euros (or €6,000 per inhabitant), including all indemnities and guarantees, was channeled exclusively into speculative ventures.[41]

It was Berlin's citizens, especially those employed in the public sector, who bore the brunt. Berlin broke away from the German public sector employers' association and reduced its employees' and civil servants' salaries by up to 10 percent. In 2002, the financial situation was so dismal that the Berlin senate ordered several of the city's fountains and thousands of its streetlamps to be turned off and the sewers and street drains to be cleaned less regularly. On hot summer days, especially, the stench in some streets was a malodorous sign of the austerity measures. It was not the smell of a healthy investment climate.

There were cultural reasons, too, for the political failure to promote Berlin as a business location. Becoming the German capital went to the local government's head. Senators often spoke of being a "cosmopolitan city" (*Weltstadt*), "metropolis" (*Metropole*), and even "global city" (*Weltmetropole*)[42] during the city parliament's debates in the nineties. Exhibitions and marketing campaigns likened Berlin to Moscow, Paris, and New York. While commentators remarked on the rise of East German nostalgia (*Ostalgie*) and warned against idealizing the GDR, policymakers harked back eagerly to Berlin's *Gründerzeit* era of the late nineteenth century and 1920s modernism when it came to urban planning. Many new buildings in the old center, east of the Brandenburg Gate, quoted the aesthetic of these historical periods either in their proportions or their façades. The architectural legacy of the GDR, in contrast, was largely deleted in the government district.

A second local (and pan-German) problem was the public's negative perception of Eastern Europe. It resonated not only in the abbreviated history of Berlin's Polish market but also in attitudes to the largest group of immigrants arriving in the nineties: ethnic Germans, Russian Jews, and ethnic Russians from the former Soviet Union. True, a section of Berlin's elite was proud of the city's multicultural revival, as the active commemoration of the Russian exile culture of the twenties and the acclaim received by Russian migrant author Vladimir Kaminer show. But the prevalent view of Russian economic activity in Berlin was highly skeptical. The composite term *Russenmafia* put the prejudices in a nutshell.

Berliners showed a striking reluctance to accept migrants from the former Soviet Union as potential investors. It is, then, hardly surprising that Russians in Berlin, though hailing from a range of social backgrounds, tended to stick together in western Charlottenburg and the more affluent neighboring area, Grunewald. In contrast, the founders of the "Polish Losers Club" (Club der polnischen Versager) took premises in the central district of Mitte, using self-irony to promote it. The strategy worked so well that the club was soon being hyped in a wide range of blogs and among partygoers. Evidently foreigners were more favorably received if they acted like social and cultural underdogs.

Although there was no Vladimir Kaminer among them, Russians in Vienna were more easily accepted into the cultural and social life of the city. One distinctive feature of Viennese culture is the many balls that take place in the winter season in prestigious locations such as Hofburg Palace, the Musikverein concert hall, and the State Opera. Viennese Russians even have their own *russki bal*, which has been a firm fixture of the season for some years. Popular Russian singers and dancers are flown in from Moscow and St. Petersburg for the occasion, which is broadcast live on Russian television. In turn, Moscow started hosting an annual *venski bal* in 2003. A Vienna-based event agency now organizes Russian balls in cities across Europe, from Baden Baden to Biarritz—another example of economic opportunity arising from Eastern Europe's opening.

Berlin and Germany were reluctant to seize such opportunities, as shown in the alleged Ukrainian visa scandal. This was caused by the disclosure that, after the 1998 change of government, the German embassy in Kyiv had openhandedly issued visas to Ukrainians—as many as 300,000 in 2001. The German media used the news to inflate stories of immigration problems and other threats emanating from the East; the tabloid press ran hunts for Ukrainian "criminals" and illegal workers. But in terms of passengers, the number amounted to about two airplanes full, the night train from Kyiv and a few coaches, spread over a 365-day period. Nevertheless, the media campaign made waves. The scandal contributed to toppling the Social Democratic–Green government in 2005, after which the visa quota for Ukraine was reduced to around one hundred thousand per year. Other cities welcomed the extra trade with tourists from the East: Warsaw with its markets; Prague, which was especially popular with Russians and Ukrainians; and Vienna's retail stores on Mariahilfer and Kärntner Strasses. In the pre-Christmas period, especially, buses arrived in Vienna by the dozen from the former Soviet Union. Crucially, the Viennese had come to perceive Ukrainians and other Eastern European visitors as customers rather than intruders.

It is hard to estimate the amount of revenue this cost Berlin. It was certainly a lost opportunity and echoed the city's response to the bazaars of the nineties. To be sure, small-scale retail trade could not have brought about economic recovery. But it could have helped to alleviate Berlin's transformation crisis, which lasted from 1995 to 2005. When Mayor Klaus Wowereit famously declared that the city was "poor but sexy,"[43] he conveyed a sense that Berliners had resigned themselves to their economic plight.

Looking at Berlin in the lost decade between 1995 and 2005, it is clear that state-sponsored showcase projects, such as the reconstruction of the government district and Potsdamer Platz, did not generate enough growth or wealth to benefit the population at large. Becoming the capital of a major European nation-state brought some advantages, including transfer payments worth tens of billions, but no lasting economic upswing. Vienna, on the other hand, whose importance as a site of East-West mediation diminished with the end of the Cold War, benefited from its status as an international center of the service sector and its tradition as the capital of a multinational empire.

Despite the political and cultural factors that were peculiar to Berlin, the transformation crisis here followed the general pattern in East Germany. Most large industrial enterprises were forced to close; unemployment soared; the transformation from below was less dynamic than in the neighboring countries of East Central Europe. At first, the German government blamed the GDR and the legacy of state socialism for the economic problems. But the further the GDR slipped back into history, the less convincing this accusation seemed. In a historical perspective, the transformation crisis (which, despite some overlap, is distinguishable from the crisis following the collapse of state socialism) was caused by a contradictory combination of neoliberalism with a welfare state, or ordoliberalism. This socioeconomic program, named after the postwar journal *ORDO*, was practiced in the young FRG, and combined promarket liberalism with a regulatory welfare state. In Germany, this system is known as *soziale Marktwirtschaft*; that is, social market economy.

The rapid and ruthless opening of the GDR's economy as it joined the Federal Republic of Germany and the European Commission was, in effect, a particularly radical process of liberalization. Privatization, too, was carried out faster and more relentlessly in the GDR than in any other postcommunist country. As shown by the "return before compensate" (*Rückgabe vor Entschädigung*) principle applied to communist-expropriated property, private ownership came to be viewed as the apotheosis of the social order—this also tallied with the Washington Consensus and the doctrine of the Chicago School.

However, the economy of the former GDR was not deregulated but "reregulated." The five new German states were required to adopt the federal, West German administrative order, its complex social security system, employers' and employees' associations, collective wage agreements, extensive protection against unfair dismissal, and various other regulations. This extension of West Germany stabilized East Germany in many respects, especially politically. But the fact that West Germany was itself suffering a crisis was fatally overlooked. A number of problems that had loomed on the horizon since the 1980s were now coming to a head: the conundrum of financing the welfare state; the challenge of maintaining the pension system for an aging society; tackling, and not just administrating, unemployment; avoiding standstill caused by corporatist structures; and sustaining Germany's high rates of pay, relative to the rest of Europe. While wages were lower in the former GDR than in West Germany, they were still many times higher than in the neighboring Czech Republic or Poland. For this reason, East Germany had far less appeal as a business location than the other countries of East Central Europe.

In the 1990s, some political players suggested mitigating the path of rapid adjustment to West German systems by treating the former GDR, or certain regions of East Germany, as a special economic zone. But the proposal was rejected to avoid complications for the old federal states and with EU law. German politics did not want to encourage any intra-German system rivalry, which would have challenged the status quo in West Germany. Gradually, policymakers became convinced that comprehensive reforms were required not only in East Germany but in the entire country. These are considered in greater depth in the chapter on cotransformation.[44]

It remains to reiterate that the conservative-liberal coalition government led by Helmut Kohl tried to resolve the transformation crisis primarily with money. Around one trillion euros was pumped into East Germany by 2003, far more than the Marshall Plan had cost. By 2013, this amount had risen to between 1.6 and two trillion euros (varying according to the method of calculation applied).[45] Some of it was invested in new roads, railroad tracks, telephone lines, and businesses to be privatized, but about two-thirds was spent on social benefits. It would be an oversimplification to define German transformation in the nineties as purely neoliberal, although its origins and key elements were rooted in the ideology. Its social repercussions also deviated from the neoliberal reform pattern. Compared to Poland or the Czech Republic, the losers of transformation were compensated with generous social benefits.

But this strategy of social pacification did not coincide with a sufficient impetus to stimulate social and economic development. The self-employed, who contributed significantly to the upswing in Poland, the Czech Republic, Slovakia, and Hungary, were far

more likely to suffer income losses, bankruptcy, and downward social mobility in East Germany. They were up against the West German firms that capitalized most on German reunification. Many
of the younger and more enterprising East Germans migrated to
the West to escape the depression at home. "Poor Berlin," then,
was an indicator of problems affecting all of reunified Germany.

## Boomtown Warsaw

Contemporary Warsaw is a fascinating sight from afar. A high-
rise landscape of eighteen skyscrapers over 330 feet high has been
built around the city's central station and the Stalinist Palace of
Culture. Over a dozen more high-rise buildings are due to be built
or currently under construction. Such distinguished architects as
Daniel Libeskind, Zaha Hadid, Helmut Jahn, and Norman Foster are among the designers of contemporary Warsaw. One of the
most striking creations is the shopping mall known as Złote Tarasy
(Golden Terraces), a commercial and entertainment complex with
a spectacular glass roof resembling an Alpine ski slope with its
various bumps and dips. The very name Golden Terraces sums
up the gold-digging mood among international investors and
eager consumerism in Poland before the crisis of 2008–9. Immediately adjacent to the horizontally staggered terraces is the verti-
cally thrusting skyscraper known as the *Żagiel* (Sail), the façade of
which is punctuated by Libeskind's characteristic angular forms
and jagged-edged surfaces. This skyscraper was conceived primarily as an apartment building. In late 2013 the purchase price per
square meter was 65,000 złotys; the equivalent of about $17,000
for eleven square feet. Close by, the Hotel Intercontinental with
its triangular recess behind a fifteen-story-high leg is another symbol of postmodern architecture (and its dysfunctionality).

The skyscrapers surround Warsaw's Palace of Culture and Science (*Pałac Kultury i Nauki*), a "gift" from the Soviet Union in the
gingerbread style of the 1950s. After the regime change, the new
authorities were uncertain what to do with this 613-foot symbol
of Soviet hegemony. Some actors wanted it demolished or at least

scaled down, but in the end, the Warsaw city council found a more creative solution. They put a preservation order on the Palace and, in parallel, invited international investors to erect high-rise buildings all around the Płac Defilad, Europe's largest urban square, to overshadow it. The same solution of architectural relativization could have been applied to the GDR parliament building (*Palast der Republik*) in Berlin. But here, the federal government and the city chose to eradicate all remains of the previous regime.

Despite the many skyscrapers, Warsaw's city center does not feel like a US downtown where the lights go out after happy hour. The high-rise district around the Palace of Culture is a meeting place for a cross-section of the population, and buzzes with activity until well into the night. A number of arts venues are located here: the theaters Teatr Studio and Teatr Dramatyczny are housed in the Palace of Culture; the city's best known jazz club, Akwarium, can be found inside the Złote Tarasy. (The demolition of the jazz club's original premises, built in the elegant modernist idiom of the 1970s, was one of the biggest urban planning mistakes of the transformation era.) The remains of the bazaar economy can also be found here, represented by a few hundred kiosks clustered around the Palace of Culture, in defiance of the nearby shopping malls. Those who find the postcommunist, postmodern ambience of Płac Defilad not to their taste can amble along the traditional shopping street Krakowskie Przedmieście, rebuilt after the war, or stroll about the old town. The royal castle, reerected in 1974, is occasionally (and delusively) cited as a precedent for reconstructing the Berlin City Palace.

The construction boom has transformed not only Warsaw's city center but also the suburbs and the urban periphery.[46] Socialist housing was particularly cramped, and the city had great pent-up demand for improved accommodations. In the metropolitan comparison, Berliners live most comfortably, each with an average living space of 130 square feet as of 2012. The disparity in living space per person in East and West Berlin that existed in 1990 has since leveled. There are more single-person than family households in both East and West Berlin, and average households in both parts are two-person. Warsaw residents continue to live more modestly, with only 91 square feet per person, despite the construction boom that started in the mid-nineties.

Nevertheless, it is a huge leap from the situation under state socialism, when the people of Warsaw had to make do with fifty-five feet of living space per person.[47] The average number of occupants has changed, too. In the early nineties, an average household comprised more than three people sharing fewer than three rooms. Apartment sizes were standardized so that residents of middle-class districts lived in almost as cramped conditions as those in working-class areas. In all social strata, then, Warsaw residents were literally treading on each other's toes. In this situation, family life was a dominant factor, and the legendary *matka polska*, the Polish mother, consolidated her mythical importance. To escape the confinement and the constant contact, it was necessary to leave the house—a habit that has persisted to this day, and is one reason why central Warsaw streets are so lively at night.

Demand for living space has naturally risen. In the twenty years between 1992 and 2012, over 250,000 new apartments were built, almost exclusively privately financed and not state-subsidized. A divide has emerged between rich and poor that did not exist before 1989. While the poorer classes remain in their old homes, unable to afford newer or larger apartments, a considerable number of Warsaw's wealthier residents choose to live in gated communities. These have proliferated in the city: an author of the *Chasing Warsaw* anthology counted over 400 such estates,[48] with guards and porters to inspire a sense of security among residents. Demand for protected living environments arose in response to the rapid rise in criminality in the early nineties. The frequent burglaries left their mark on everyday life, even if one was not personally affected. High-sensitivity car alarms howled incessantly at night; residents barricaded themselves behind armored doors and elaborate locking systems, as many did in Prague and Budapest, too. In fact, crime in Warsaw has been decreasing for a number of years. But gated communities also fulfill a desire for social distinction and exclusivity, which the advertisements play on. Society's reception of them differs in each of the capital cities compared here. While plans for the first estate of this kind in the Friedrichshain district of Berlin unleashed a storm of outrage, the public in War-saw registered the phenomenon with indifference, or at most dis-cussed the merits and demerits of its aesthetics.

Signaling pockets of exclusivity, gated communities aggravate social tensions. In Warsaw, especially, rich and poor live close together. Warsaw has passed over the intermediary stages by which Western cities have become gentrified. The changes that have occurred in the Berlin districts of Mitte, Prenzlauer Berg, and Friedrichshain followed the pattern set by SoHo and Chelsea in New York City and large stretches of London, from Notting Hill to the East End: squatters move into derelict buildings and a semilegal club scene is established; the first galleries, small shops, and bars open; more upmarket restaurants, boutiques, and health food stores follow; finally, luxury refurbishments are carried out. In the fashionable districts of Warsaw, this process took place at high speed. In the formerly ill-reputed district of Praga, turf of the underclass and petty gangsters, alternative stores and bars have opened in parallel with expensive residential estates, next door to dilapidated buildings where the losers of transformation live.

The social divide is symbolized in consumer habits. The new middle class throngs the shopping malls, which boomed even more than private housing construction. According to city plan-ner Magdalena Staniszkis, shopping malls covering a total surface area of one million square yards have sprung up since the nine-ties. By contrast, the lower classes, who cannot afford brand-name clothing or 3D movies, make their purchases at bazaars or kiosks or in Biedronka discount supermarkets. Offering competitively low prices, these are similar to the supermarkets that have been proliferating for some years across southern Europe. (Biedronka belongs to a Portuguese supermarket chain.)

The construction boom that produced a glut of new shopping malls and apartment buildings helped fuel Warsaw's economy (see fig. 6.7). The per capita GDP rose between 2005 and the pre-crisis year 2008 by 47.6 percent to the equivalent of $28,200 (ad-justed to purchasing power parity). The city achieved the prover-bial Chinese growth rate of almost 12 percent annually. The rise in incomes was even more impressive: in 2005, the average monthly

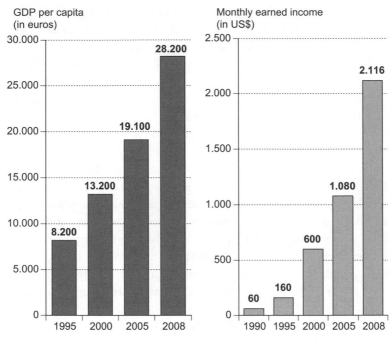

Fig. 6.7. Boomtown Warsaw: economic and income development. *Source*: Eurostat Regional Statistics (GDP); *Rocznik Statystyczny Warszawy* (Warsaw Statistical Yearbook) (Income).

gross income per capita in Warsaw was the equivalent of $1,080, in 2008, $2,116.[49]

Comparison with China is apt not least in view of the road traffic, which has reached Chinese dimensions. The jams on Warsaw's main thoroughfares and arterial highways started to appear in the mid-nineties due to a simple equation: From 1989 to 2008, the number of privately owned cars increased by over 100 percent (1989: 408,000; 2000: 604,000; 2005: 737,000; 2008: 943,000). With 551 cars per thousand inhabitants, the ratio in Warsaw is now the same or even higher than in many Western European cities. (Vienna, for instance, counted some 400 cars per 1,000 inhabitants in 2013.[50]) Add to these the many trucks, which multiplied even more between 1995 and 2005 than the new car registrations.[51]

The amount of light trucks, especially, reached record levels, signifying the importance of small traders and producers for the post-communist economy (and its traffic jams). The people of Warsaw respond to the constant congestion with calm resignation, no doubt in part because heavy traffic is considered an iconic element of modern city life. Berlin's "poor but sexy" slogan reflects the same tendency to identify with the less-agreeable aspects of urban life: if dark sides cannot be avoided, one might as well take pride in them.

Warsaw's traffic snarl is an inherent problem of the lack of urban planning and investment in infrastructure. It is symptomatic of the pitfalls of the neoliberal order that come to the fore in areas that defy privatization, such as local transport and traffic. The history of Warsaw's metro was due to begin in 1982, when it was resolved by the Polish council of ministers. The Soviet Union offered its assistance, which was certainly more welcome than Stalin's gift of the Palace of Culture. But not one foot of subway was ever built in the People's Republic of Poland. Though the first Russian metro carriages were delivered as promised, the country did not have sufficient funds to build subway lines. The story continued in a similar vein after 1989. Intermittent progress announcements were followed by extended delays. Finally, a few stations and a short subsection along the North-South route were opened in 1998. In 2001, the city announced an ambitious plan to complete at least two metro lines within two years.[52] But the goal of finishing in time for the European soccer championship in 2012 remained elusive; there was still no East-West route to take some of the load off the notoriously congested bridges over the Vistula.

Other areas of public infrastructure were also neglected. The number of child daycare centers almost halved over the course of the nineties while the number of children in daycare remained more or less constant. In short, there was a reduction in both the quantity and the quality of daycare.[53] Warsaw's public parks and open spaces became easy prey. Socialist Warsaw was designed to be a green city with expansive parks and swathes of undeveloped land leading to the center like verdant aisles, transmitting fresh air. It was badly needed: in fall and winter the exhaust fumes from the coal-run power station rested on the city like a gray-brown shroud. The air quality would have been worse still without all the green spaces. Today, what is left of them provides a valuable antidote to the burgeoning road traffic, now the city's severest environmental problem. Since 2000, Warsaw's parkland has shrunk by about 272 acres, and over 345 acres of open space has been developed.[54] In terms of surface area, that is the equivalent of the entire first district of Vienna. A number of shopping malls and gated communities have been built on former open spaces and marketed as greenfield developments. In the final analysis, the general public pays for this level of laissez faire, which adheres to the neoliberal logic of deregulation, liberalization, and privatization.

As well as revealing darker sides of transformation, a comparison of Berlin and Warsaw sheds light on the opportunities missed in the former city. While Warsaw gained a new face after 1989, the Berlin senate adopted a traditionalist, historicist policy. Guidelines for "critical reconstruction," designed to revitalize historical street layouts, stipulated a maximum height of seventy-two feet for façades, and building materials such as brick or concrete. It marked a nostalgic approach to urban development, based on the architecture of the late imperial period and the 1920s. Its chief proponent was the city's building commissioner, Hans Stimmann, who had led the acclaimed redevelopment of the old town of Lübeck (certainly one of North Germany's prettier towns). Stimmann was appointed building commissioner in Berlin in 1991 and later promoted to state secretary, unaffected by the change of government. His career is an illustration of the bon mot that bureaucrats rather than the elected representatives govern Germany. Because Stimmann disliked high-rise architecture, it was confined to the plans for Potsdamer Platz and Alexanderplatz, for which investors are still being sought.[55]

While Alexanderplatz looks much like it did in the GDR but with shinier facades, almost all traces of socialism's architectural legacy have been removed from the government district. Symbolic sites such as the Palace of the Republic and the State Council Building have vanished. The space left by the demolition of the Palace of the Republic in 2006–8 is currently being filled by a reconstruction of the city palace of the Hohenzollern dynasty, the postwar remains of which were razed by the communists under orders from leader Walter Ulbricht. Neither the act of getting even with the GDR nor the historicist style of architecture conveys any sense of new departure. The cityscape is again dominated by stone façades and head-high bossage that makes the individual appear as small as the political players of imperial Berlin intended. Though overpowered by its history, Berlin has become a magnet for young people from all over Europe.[56] They do not flock to the old city center at night but tend to gather in trendy districts such as Friedrichshain and Kreuzberg. In Warsaw, the reverse is the case. There, the city center is the main attraction.

Berlin's historicism not only characterizes its façades but also its residents' personal attitudes. The members of the educated classes—the predominant middle class group, as the city's business community is small—aspire to reside in large turn-of-the-twentieth-century apartments in peaceful neighborhoods. Senior positions in public administration or at state universities still have high social prestige attached. Warsaw, in contrast, is characterized by *biznesmeni* and tradesmen. In 2010 the number of national economic units (most of them companies) reached a new peak of 344,000. It subsequently dropped again for the first time since the late 1980s—perhaps an indication that the long boom is coming to an end. Warsaw residents aspire to own newly built, modestly sized apartments of less than two hundred square feet, which many finance by taking second and even third jobs. Holding down multiple positions is also the norm for many people in Prague, Budapest, Moscow, and Kyiv. There is, then, no reason to idealize the new business boom in the two decades after 1989. The upswing was propelled by hard, restless toil, bordering on self-exploitation. But the niches for small businesses and enterprising individuals that existed in the nineties are now disappearing. The retail and restaurant chains, franchises, and other forms of big capital concentration make it extremely difficult to establish independent companies.

The multiple-job culture contributes to Warsaw's high GDP and consolidates its position as the beating heart of Poland. The

drawback is that Warsaw has to pay over 80 percent of its tax revenue to the central government. That is bad for the local economy
and especially for the state of the metro, but good for the city's
self-image. While Berlin is dependent on equalization payments
from the more prosperous federal German states and the government, boomtown Warsaw helps the entire country progress.

## Metropolitan Convergence, or Why the East Looks like the West

Although the various capital cities took different paths of development, these have been leading in a common direction since
1989. Their convergence is due on the one hand to the sustained
rapid growth of Warsaw, Prague, and Budapest (and Kyiv, with
some delay), and to the transformation crisis in Berlin on the
other hand, which the city overcame after 2005. Following EU enlargement, the economic boom in Warsaw and Prague accelerated
further. Figure 6.8 gives a statistical overview of the period prior
to the crisis of 2008–9.

Kyiv's development can be variously interpreted. In the national currency hryvnia, the economic performance of the Ukrainian capital doubled between 2005 and 2008 (having tripled in
the period 2000–2005). But this increase in Kyiv's per capita
GDP, adjusted to purchasing power parity (which is always calculated on a national basis, disregarding local price differences) was
just 25 percent, similar to Budapest's.[57] Berlin's per capita GDP
grew in the same period from 23,400 to 25,700 euros, or by 10.8
percent. Although this marked a recovery from the long transformation crisis, the German capital was outpaced by Prague and
Warsaw in terms of per capita GDP by 2007.

Does this mean that the inhabitants of Warsaw and Prague are
now more affluent than the hypothetical average Berliner? Statistics cannot, of course, be left to speak for themselves. The figures
on GDP presented here (adjusted to purchasing power parity and
converted into euros) reveal nothing about the specific administrative and business environments in which they were collated.
Economic strength is far more concentrated in all former Eastern

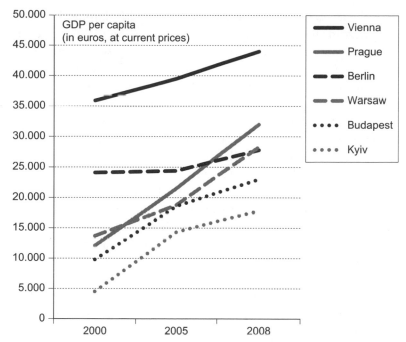

**Fig. 6.8.** Economic development of East Central European cities, 2000–2008. *Source*: Eurostat Regional Statistics; Статистичний збірник "Регіони України" (Statistical Anthology "Regions of Ukraine").

Bloc countries than in Germany or Austria. Most Polish, Czech, Hungarian, and Baltic company headquarters are in their respective capitals, where the profits boost the local GDP. Many German companies are based in Munich, Hamburg, or other regional centers. GDP is therefore more evenly distributed and mostly generated outside Berlin. The same is true of Austria, where a number of large companies are based outside Vienna.

Second, the figures on gross domestic product cannot be equated with actual incomes or living standards. In 2008, the average per capita household income in the metropolitan Prague region was 11,800 euros; in Berlin, by contrast, it was 18,000. Incomes in Warsaw were similar to Prague's; Budapest's were somewhat lower.[58] Hence, Berliners had almost 50 percent more disposable income than the average Prague or Warsaw household, despite the city's long transformation crisis. Unlike the figures on GDP, however, these statistics do not take purchasing power into account. Food and other staple goods were still cheaper in Warsaw and Prague than in Berlin in 2008; taxi journeys and metro tickets cost less than half. Privately leased apartments, on the other hand, were scarce and expensive. But Poles, Czechs, and Hungarians still pay similar rents, as they tend to live in smaller apartments. Overall, a convergence can be observed, which is astounding considering the disparity among these cities in 1989–90.

Even assuming that the inhabitants of Warsaw or Prague were somewhat poorer, or lived in more modest conditions, in some ways they were more privileged than Berliners. Prague had only 3.7 percent unemployment in 2009; unemployment in Warsaw dropped in the period 2005–9 from 11.1 to 4.3 percent. There was de facto full employment in both cities. Job prospects for young people, especially, were far better than in Berlin (or southern Europe).[59] In summary, Berliners had a higher standard of living (at least on average) but far fewer job opportunities.

High unemployment caused more Berliners to drift into poverty. By OECD criteria, which place the poverty threshold at half the average per capita income, 435,000 Berliners were classified as poor in 2002.[60] The recession of 2001–4 aggravated the situation. According to the benchmark usually applied in Germany—60 percent of the average income—almost one in five Berliners lived below the poverty line in 2005. The subsequent recovery reduced unemployment by a third but did not dent poverty levels. The "Hartz" reforms to the labor market had chiefly created more low-paid job opportunities (small grants for one-person firms, one-euro jobs, top-up benefits for the working poor).[61] The Warsaw statistical agency does not compile data on poverty rates (which is itself a political statement). But a survey of the wages paid in various Warsaw industries shows that employees in simple service occupations, especially, do not earn any disposable income.[62] Many compensate by moonlighting.

It is difficult to find a reasonable sideline in Berlin. However, in 2013, the Berlin state office for statistics announced proudly that the city had become one of the fastest growing locations in Germany, surpassing even Hamburg and Munich.[63] Indeed, Berlin has begun to see a business boom in recent years. This delayed upswing has reduced unemployment by almost half; the population has grown since 2011 by 40,000 annually.[64] Behind these statistics lies Berlin's peculiar situation. After years of recession (2001–4) and over a decade of stagnation, its economy was at a low point from which it was better poised to grow. Tourism, Berlin's most successful sector by far, boomed partly as a consequence of the long transformation crisis. This depressed property prices and rents in Berlin, offering ideal conditions for new hotels and restaurants and the city's famous club scene, and attracting gallery owners, artists, and players from other creative industries. All this contributed to Berlin's image as a cultural hub.

In 2005, the Social Democratic–Green government's labor market reforms launched a wave of business-forming that continues to this day.[65] But many self-employed owners of small businesses, prompted more by desperation than inspiration, were not included in the statistics on turnover-tax-paying businesses, and did not engender the kind of boomtime spirit of optimism that prevailed in Warsaw or Prague in the nineties. Since 2009, Berlin has profited from the euro crisis along with the rest of Germany. International and German investors looking for a safe haven for their money, out of the tax authorities' reach, have channeled huge sums into Berlin's property market. These property owners seem to be confident in the German capital's prospects. Positive predictions were also an important factor in the upswings in Warsaw, Prague, Budapest, and Vienna during the business boom of the late twentieth and early twenty-first centuries. The drawback for Berlin residents is rent increases—a trend that has already forced a number of gallery owners and club managers to close down.

A problem specifically affecting Berlin and Vienna is the large ratio of resident immigrants. In the districts of Berlin with a particularly high proportion of former "guest workers" (Wedding, Moabit, Neukölln, parts of Kreuzberg—all in West Berlin), unemployment and the number of welfare recipients are twice as high as the city average. Seen in this light, the actual losers of transformation are not East Berliners but the second and third-generation immigrants in West Berlin. All the capital cities, then, have a distinct but comparable underclass of transformation losers.

Vienna's far larger immigrant population—almost triple the size of Berlin's—is more socially mobile. According to official statistics, 49 percent of Viennese come from an immigrant background, and around a third were born abroad.[66] They are better-integrated into the majority society and the job market, partly on account of their numbers. A group this size cannot remain on the margins. Another factor is the city's low unemployment (which, however, has gone up in recent years) relative to Berlin. The better labor market enables even less-qualified immigrants to find a regular occupation and achieve upward social mobility. Moreover, the city's social democratic government has hitherto rejected most neoliberal reforms. As a result, there is no low-pay sector or significant group of working poor, as in London or New York.

Bratislava is smaller than the cities compared so far. Yet the Slovak capital experienced even more dynamic growth than Prague or Warsaw—per capita GDP tripled from 8,900 to 28,300 euros between 2000 and 2009.[67] According to a recent Eurostat survey on regional GDP in the European Union, the Bratislava area ranks fifth, after inner London, Luxemburg, Brussels, and Hamburg. With a GDP that is 186 percent higher than the EU average, it surpasses Paris, Stockholm, Groningen, Prague, Upper Bavaria, and Vienna.[68] The statistics are certainly somewhat distorted; for instance, centers such as Munich and Frankfurt are not considered in isolation but with larger regions, despite being more populous than Bratislava. Purchasing power is calculated according to national averages, not taking the higher prices in centers of growth into account. And the statistics do not say anything about urban household incomes. Bratislava would rank far lower in a rating of these, as much of its turnover is generated by foreign companies registered there; their profits boost the local GDP but end up in the company headquarters abroad. Nevertheless, the city undeniably profits from the presence of foreign business.

Vienna, less than forty miles from Bratislava, participates indirectly in the new prosperity in its neighborhood. In economic terms, the two cities are perfectly complementary: one is an international center for services and trade; the other, an attractive production site with many new factories, especially for vehicle construction. Berlin lacks a "hinterland" of this kind. Poznań and Wrocław, the two closest growth centers to the East, are both around 185 miles away. Admittedly, they have become much easier to reach since the expansion of the Schengen zone, and are closer to Berlin's Schönefeld airport than to Warsaw. Perhaps they can help Berlin evolve into a regional center. Moreover, Berlin can capitalize on its cultural appeal. Its nightlife is, after all, particularly popular among young Poles. But the urban-rural divide and the long distances between the three cities are continuing disadvantages. Despite the upturn since EU expansion, the western border regions of Poland and eastern Brandenburg, the state surrounding Berlin, remain poor and economically underdeveloped. Even if the European Union maintains its generous regional funding, it will take a long time to fill the empty spaces between the centers. Economist Paul Krugman has previously identified regional disparity as a fundamental hindrance to economic development.[69]

Budapest and Hungary face problems of a very specific nature. During the boom of 2000–2005, Budapest's economy grew faster than that of any other East Central European capital. At the same time, the Hungarian trade and budget deficit reached new peaks. In other words, the boom was financed largely on credit. For a few years, it was glossed over by the high level of foreign direct investments in Hungary. The banks issued substantial construction loans in the hope of high returns, and agreed to foreign currency loans in Swiss francs and other Western currencies, despite the exchange rate risks. Increasingly, Hungary's FDIs were channeled not into mid- or long-term projects such as building infrastructure or production sites but financing consumer loans. A housing construction boom resulted and the demand for consumer goods rose. But when the foreign capital stopped flowing in 2008, the credit-financed growth came to an abrupt halt. The Hungarian government was forced to introduce austerity measures (which the public had voted against in a referendum a short time previously). As a consequence, the recession during the crisis of 2008–9 was especially deep, unemployment spiraled, and the forint was devalued. Some other factors originating from the early transformation period also dampened Budapest's development in the last decade. To prevent long-term tenants from being ousted and protect residential areas from industrial exploitation, the first postcommunist government allowed tenants to buy their formerly subsidized apartments at low prices. In this way, the government led by József Antall (in power from 1990 to 1993) aimed to create a nation of homeowners in agreement with both neoliberal principles and the conservative Hungarian Democratic Forum. However, the new owners did not have the capital to pay for the eventual renovation of the stuccoed old buildings. For this reason, a number of streets in Budapest today look as gray and crumbling as so many did before 1989. The much-maligned socialist housing blocks made of precast concrete slabs are usually in better condition. They benefit particularly from the installation of more efficient heating systems, allowing residents to save on energy costs. Similarly, Prague's *Panelaky* (as these blocks are called, in reference to the concrete panels) do not have a bad reputation. Almost all the suburbs built during state socialism have been extended since 1990. In the meantime, Prague's city center—again similarly to Budapest and Warsaw—has transformed into a purely tourist and office area.

As the city centers have become increasingly commercialized, the suburbs have grown. The trend toward suburbanization that has shaped (and damaged) many Western cities was contained in the Eastern Bloc. In Berlin, the Wall prevented the city from proliferating; in Vienna, the long period of decline after the collapse of the Austro-Hungarian Empire inhibited urban sprawl. Today the smaller suburbs mean a higher quality of life. But a process of belated suburbanization has set in, as people realize their dreams of a family home with a garden. Following their Western counterparts, Eastern European cities are also displaying a tendency to separate the industrial from the residential. Many factories that were built near the central districts of East Berlin, Prague, Warsaw, and Budapest, often adjacent to residential buildings, have been closed. If investors can be found, the sites are redeveloped as housing estates or shopping centers. The speedy pace of urban development has resulted in new residential and commercial centers being built in the same neighborhoods as tumbledown tenements; upper- and lower-class districts are separated by only a few streets.

The new middle- and underclasses, especially in Warsaw, meet in supermarket parking lots. While the former load their cars with their purchases, the latter are glad to pick up the abandoned shopping carts or empty returnable bottles to claim the deposit. Social contrasts are even more striking in Kyiv, where some suburbs and inner-city areas with modern apartment buildings are hardly distinguishable from Western streets. A few blocks along and around a number of metro stations, however, the streets are populated by shabbily dressed street traders and down-at-heel grandmothers. The very goods on offer speak of poverty—anyone trying to sell a few bunches of spring onions or hand-picked flowers (a common sight in Warsaw's city center in the early nineties and later at Jarmark Europa) will make a few dollars a day at most.

Global statistics show that only a fifth of the populations of postcommunist countries profited from the economic reforms introduced since 1989, while around two-fifths grew poorer.[70] In the East Central European capitals compared here, the ratios are reversed. The upswings in Prague, Warsaw, Budapest, and Bratislava have led to the emergence of broad urban middle classes. Around half of these urban populations have achieved the same standard of living as the Western European middle classes. Whether this applies to Kyiv is questionable. The population of the Ukrainian capital has grown by around 200,000 since 2000. A large proportion of the influx is made up of immigrants from rural areas in search of better prospects; their poverty is obvious even in the capital. In East Central Europe, by contrast, the new affluence dominates the urban landscape. Indicators are the proliferation of private cars (which in the Czech Republic and Poland are not significantly smaller or older than those in the West), upmarket household appliances, Western retail chains, and lifestyle diseases such as obesity.

Behind this convergence, however, lie divergent developments. In 1989, Warsaw's unprecedented rise did not seem any more probable than reunified Berlin's ten-year stagnation and recession. The convergence was not planned—economic reforms in East Germany were designed to bring the region up to West German standards as swiftly as possible—but caused by Berlin's unintended downward adjustment. Vienna, Prague, Bratislava, and Warsaw experienced new-business booms, which continue to the present. The same finally began in Berlin some years ago. It is harder to draw conclusions about Budapest, where the impact of the crisis of 2008–9 has caused outcomes that can not yet be gauged. The new sheen of all these cities has banished the gray of the eighties, with which this comparison began, to their niches and peripheries. But as the saying goes, all that glitters is not gold. The gulf between rich and poor not only divides urban and rural populations but is also a very real factor in the social life of the capitals.

# 7

# The Great Recession

## 2008–9 and Its Consequences

### The End of Economic Convergence?

With rich and poor so closely juxtaposed, and different developments occurring in each European country and region, it is not easy to take stock of the outcome of neoliberal reforms. Any conclusions about transformation would depend upon the investigator's vantage point: the view from the panorama terrace of a newly built Warsaw skyscraper tells a very different story from the scene in the Carpathian Mountains, where the poverty of the peasants contrasts oddly with the natural beauty of the landscape. In addition to this urban-rural divide (which is also growing in Western Europe and the United States), distinct results of transformation can be observed in each country. Czechs or Slovaks have probably less cause to complain than Romanians or Ukrainians. But subjective perceptions do not necessarily correspond with the supposedly objective truth told by facts and figures.

The crisis of 2008–9 was not confined to Eastern Europe but gripped—and continues to grip—the southern EU states, too. *La crisi* is still omnipresent in Italy's public and political discourse, and indeed the great recession is far from over. Greece is suffering from an even worse depression, comparable to that in the United States in the 1930s. The German government, in contrast, is proud to have overcome the crisis at home very quickly, and has gained additional political clout as a result. The various causes, characteristics, and phases of the financial, budget, and economic crisis in the different countries are explored in greater depth below. For now, the imprecise term "crisis" will serve as an all-encompassing cipher.

As well as the spatial context, the point in time is highly relevant for any balance sheet of transformation. Until 2008, when the shock waves of the Wall Street crash reached Europe, all the postcommunist states had been booming. In the second transformation decade, the upturn was especially vigorous in the countries and regions that had been struggling to find their feet in the nineties. In 2004–5, several successor states of the Soviet Union achieved double-figure growth rates, including Estonia and Ukraine.[1] Romania and Bulgaria seemed to be echoing the developments in East Central Europe. Even the underdeveloped regions of eastern Poland and the other new EU member states profited from the boom. A stock-taking of economic transformation in early 2008, then, would have looked as rosy as Jeffrey Sachs's resumé of the shock therapy.

Before the crisis, economic forecasts were also optimistic—in fact, overoptimistic, in view of the floods of foreign capital that deluged most countries in Eastern Europe. Current account deficits grew as a result—for example, to over 22 percent of the GDP in Latvia in 2007 and 2008. In other words, within the space of two years, the country imported and consumed almost 50 percent more than it produced in terms of manufacturing and services. This huge imbalance could only be counterbalanced by a huge inflow of foreign capital. The volume of FDI tripled between 2005 and 2007, flowing primarily into the financial and real estate sectors. At this level, return expectations could never have been fulfilled, not even by a supposed "tiger" like Latvia. An Eastern European bubble emerged that was bound to burst, even without the global financial crisis in 2008.

A comparable situation arose in southern Europe, where the economies of Greece and Spain were in no condition to justify the loose approach to loan granting they took after the introduction of the euro. In both parts of Europe, vast amounts of money were pumped into consumption and real estate. Although the framework conditions were neoliberal, the result was a kind of "privatized Keynesianism," facilitated by cheap loans. The Czech

Republic, Poland, and Slovakia—the countries that political scientists Béla Greskovits and Dorothee Bohle identified as "embedded neoliberal systems"—exercised greater caution. Here, borrowing was somewhat curbed, and FDI inflows were used primarily in commerce and industry, not in finance.

Thanks to the buoyancy of their economies, FDI inflows, and transfer payments from Brussels, the new EU member states continued to catch up with the old EU countries (see fig. 7.1a). In the year before the crisis, the GDP (adjusted for purchasing power) of Slovenia and the Czech Republic was almost on a par with the EU average: the former's economic output reached 91 percent of this in 2008; the latter's, 81 percent. These two countries even overtook East Germany in 2006, casting a negative light on German transformation. Slovakia followed at a distance in 2008,

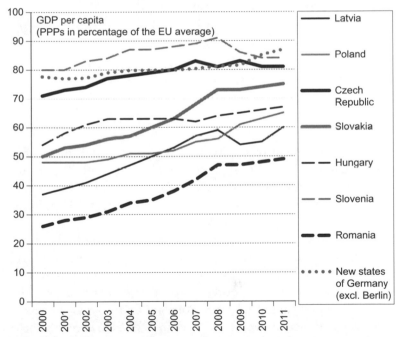

**Fig. 7.1a.** Catch-up processes of postcommunist countries, 2001–2012. *Source*: Eurostat, ongoing releases.

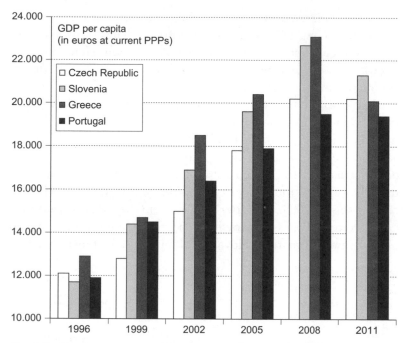

**Fig. 7.1b.** Catch-up processes of postcommunist countries with southern European Union countries, 1996–2011. *Source*: WIIW Report 2012 (Table I/1.5).

achieving 73 percent of the average per capita GDP in the European Union; the Baltic states notched up 69 and 59 percent; Hungary, 64, and Poland, 56 percent. Romania and Bulgaria were the laggards, with economic outputs of 47 percent and 44 percent, respectively, but they, too, quickly caught up.[2]

The countries in transition were soon hot on the heels of the southern EU countries (see fig. 7.1b). As early as 2002–3, Slovenia achieved the same per capita GDP (adjusted for purchasing power) as Portugal, the poorest old EU member country. The Czech Republic caught up with Portugal and East Germany in 2006, as mentioned above, and Greece in 2011.[3] However, the field was leveling for different reasons than before the crisis. Greece, like Berlin in relation to the other cities of East Central Europe (see chapter 6), was meeting upcoming nations—Slovenia and the Czech Republic were the economic trailblazers among the post-communist countries—on its way down. The readjustment was perhaps unsurprising, considering that the historical kingdom of Bohemia had been as economically advanced as its Western neighbors from the nineteenth century.[4] Moreover, the Czech Republic and Slovenia border on old EU countries, making them obvious choices in every respect for Western corporate investments.

Poland's advance, however, cannot be explained by historical traditions or an ideal geographical situation. Only its westernmost regions, such as Silesia and the area around Poznań, were close to Western markets. Yet this largest and most populous new EU member closed the gap between its GDP and the EU average by 10 percent in the first five years after EU expansion, achieving 61 percent of the EU economic output in 2009 (as opposed to 51 percent in 2004). By 2013, Poland's GDP had grown to two-thirds the EU average.[5] If the economies of the southerly EU countries continue to stagnate or shrink, and the Polish economy continues to grow apace, it is only a matter of time before Poland, too, catches up with the poorer EU member countries, and even closes in on Italy.[6] But historians usually refrain from making predictions, and rightly so, because there is always the possibility of political disruptions or other unforeseen problems. More important than statistics are the real prospects for the younger generation. Young Poles who have good qualifications, speak one or two foreign languages, and don't live in the wrong part of the country (Polska B) have good chances of finding a better-paid job than their contemporaries in Spain and Italy. (See the figures in chapter 8.) On the negative side, the tendency to work with "trash contracts" (śmieciówki)—that is, short-term employment arrangements—even in government, is growing in Poland, too.

The benchmark for prosperity in central Europe is Germany. Until 2004, the River Oder marked a distinct rich-poor divide. It ran along regions of Poland that bore the legacy of defunct agricultural cooperatives: high unemployment and weak infrastructure. But after EU expansion, conditions in Poland began to converge with those in the former GDR. As in the case of the

"Polish economic miracle," this was caused by mistakes made during East Germany's transformation. The statistics on economic convergence in East and West Germany attest to this. Despite all its economic problems, in the first years after reunification East Germany caught up with the West. But in the mid-nineties, its economy began to lag behind. In 1996, the five new German states (of the former GDR) achieved 62 percent of the West German GDP per capita, and lingered at that level until 2002. In later years, the East German GDP improved somewhat to reach 66 percent of West Germany's (see fig. 7.1c).

These ostensibly positive statistics leave a bitter aftertaste. They hint that East Germany has little chance of catching up with West Germany in the foreseeable future. Moreover, economic development in the new German states, as in all postcommunist countries, is regionally uneven. While growth centers such as Dresden,

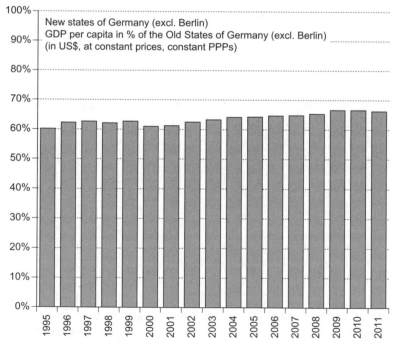

**Fig. 7.1c.** New German states against old German states by percentage.
*Source*: OECD Statistics (Regional Accounts TL3).

Leipzig, and Jena, and Berlin in recent years, are flourishing, rural regions and old industrial centers such as Lusatia have still not recovered from the shock therapy in the early nineties. Neither have the huge transfer payments to the former GDR helped these regions find their feet; they seem to challenge the entire premise of economic reform from above. The far speedier recoveries of the Czech and Slovak Republics and Poland point to the importance of transformation from below, from within society, which was obviously neglected in the former GDR.

Wide sections of the Polish population embraced self-employment, and this propelled the country's boom. According to UN statistics, in 1991 the annual German per capita GDP was the equivalent of $22,321 while the Polish GDP was $2,188—a difference of ten to one.[7] By 2009, Poland's GDP had grown to 50 percent of Germany's (see fig. 7.2).[8] Considering the economic

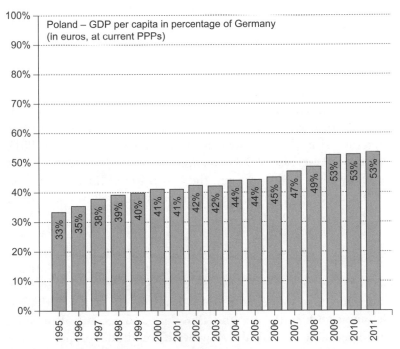

Fig. 7.2. Poland's economic catch-up process with Germany, 1995–2011. *Source*: WIIW Report 2012 (Table I/1.5).

gulf that existed twenty years previously, the Polish glass is more than half full.

The psychological effect of this economic convergence cannot be overstated. As affluence increases, ever more citizens of the new EU countries can afford to travel abroad, as the statistics on tourism show. Poles travelling to Germany today are not necessarily seasonal workers, cleaners, or bazaar traders, as many were in the early nineties, but increasingly tourists. Especially for the younger generation, the proverbial "return to Europe" is no mere empty phrase. Sharing in European prosperity has retrospectively legitimized the reforms since 1989 and EU accession in 2004.

The global finance, budget, and economic crisis brought the boom to an abrupt end. Double-figure growth rates were replaced by equally dramatic negative growth in 2009. The Baltic states, the staunchest followers of neoliberalism in the region, suffered the worst slump. Latvia had the most dramatic crash with a decrease of 17.7 percent, followed by Lithuania (-14.8) Ukraine (-14.8), Estonia (-14.1), Slovenia (-7.8), the Russian Federation (-7.8), Hungary (-6.8), and Romania (-6.6). Excepting Poland (and to some extent the Czech and Slovak Republics), all the former Eastern Bloc countries experienced deeper recessions than Germany and Austria (see fig. 7.3).[9]

While the German and Austrian economies soon recovered, even the new EU countries that chalked up high growth rates after the crisis (Estonia was the European frontrunner in 2011 with a GDP increase of 8.3 percent) did not return to 2008's levels for many years.[10] Slovenia and the Czech Republic, the erstwhile trailblazers among the new EU member states, fell into a second, prolonged recession in 2012.

The trend toward convergence has turned. Slovenia is once again as far removed from the average European Union GDP as it was in 2003; the Czech Republic has ceased to catch up. Intra-German convergence has also stopped since 2010 as the new German states take longer to recover from the crisis than old West Germany.[11] Only Poland and Slovakia, and recently Romania, have been able to defy the downward trend and propel growth rates beyond those before 2008. But even Poland has not been

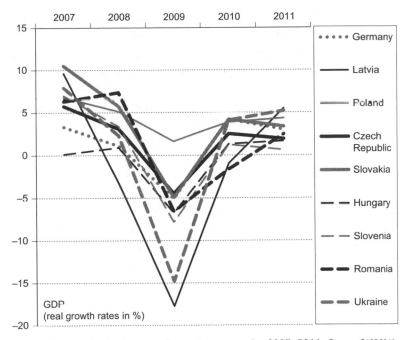

**Fig. 7.3.** Recession in the transformation countries 2007–2011. *Source*: WIIW Report 2012 (Table I/1.6).

able to close the gap on Germany and Austria any further since 2010. Not only that, but the national debt of Eastern European countries has risen so sharply that doubts about the sustainability of the economic miracle are beginning to grow, even in Warsaw.

## Variations of Crises

Why did the crisis hit almost all the new EU member countries and the successor states of the Soviet Union harder than Germany or Austria? Has the time come for a negative appraisal of the transformation and the neoliberal economic model?[12] To answer these questions, it will be useful to briefly review the effects of the global crisis of 2008–9. It began, as is well known, on Wall

Street in 2007, when the US real-estate bubble burst, and reached an initial climax with Lehman Brothers' bankruptcy in September 2008. In this first phase it was still a financial or stock market crisis. The shock waves rapidly reached the new EU member countries as Western investors withdrew capital to cover their losses at home. By late 2007, the Baltic countries had been thrust into the aforementioned recessions. (Already in 2008 Estonia had negative growth of 4.2 percent and Latvia of 3.3 percent.[13]) Hungary, Romania, Ukraine, and all the other countries that depended on foreign capital felt the immediate effects of the crisis. As tax revenues dropped and governments channeled funds into bailout programs for banks, the crash turned into a budget crisis. This second phase hit the postcommunist countries first and especially hard. In 2008 the International Monetary Fund and the European Union extended loans of tens of billions to avert an economic breakdown in the Baltic states, Hungary, and Ukraine, and in Romania in 2009.

In 2010 the shock waves reached the countries of Southern Europe, although except for Spain, these did not have property bubbles. Neither had southern European banks participated in US subprime speculation, unlike German financial institutions. But the Mediterranean EU countries were exceedingly vulnerable to crisis because they were deeply in debt. Meanwhile, the great recession further reduced national tax revenues and increased budget deficits across Europe. Investors withdrew from countries such as Greece and Italy, lacking the confidence that they would ever pay off their debts. The debt problem spiraled into the so-called euro crisis, which, however, did not have a direct impact on most postcommunist countries, since they had retained their national currencies. But they struggled with the problem of foreign currency loans, more on which below.

In a third phase, the budgetary crisis turned into an economic crisis. In 2009, all the old EU countries went through their deepest recessions of the entire postwar period. Some postcommunist countries suffered slumps almost as dramatic as in 1990 or 1991. Indeed, the decline deepened on a West-East scale, with the new EU member countries far harder hit than those in the old

European Union, Poland and the often overlooked Albania being the only exceptions. But Germany, too, was badly affected because of its reliance on exports. The entire financial, budget, and economic crisis of 2008–9 approached the dimensions of a great depression—but the political and economic elites were eager to avoid any associations with the crash of 1929. In fact, the GDP of some countries in the world, especially China, was still growing. In a global-historical perspective, then, the familiar eastern European pattern was repeated: the crisis hit those countries worst that had curtailed government intervention, liberalized markets, and given banks free rein to extend loans. Nonetheless, it is too simple to blame neoliberalism. A range of coinciding factors determined the course and duration of the great recession in postcommunist and southern Europe.

As Bohle and Greskovits have shown, the type of Foreign Direct Investments in the years preceding 2008 had a crucial influence on the course and consequences of the crisis. Wherever FDI flowed primarily into the financial and real estate sectors rather than manufacturing, international capital sources dried up or were withdrawn. This occurred in the Baltic states, Romania, Bulgaria, and Croatia. Their balance of payments was poor even before the crisis—that is, they imported and consumed far more goods and services from abroad than they exported. FDI in the Visegrad countries, in contrast, flowed predominantly into industry. They were able to increase their exports and stabilize their balance of payments, and were less dependent on international capital as a consequence.[14]

Hungary was the exception in this regional pattern. Similarly to the Czech Republic and Poland, its FDI inflow was favorably structured. But its high national debt made it nonetheless dependent on the influx of foreign capital, which stopped abruptly in 2008. In addition, it was the only country in the region to extend loans liberally in foreign currencies. This practice is considered in detail below as an illustration of the pitfalls of the neoliberal order. Slovenia, meanwhile, had its own specific set of problems. Privatization here was financed primarily by manager buyouts and generous loans from Slovenian banks. As in the Czech Republic before 1996, this investment strategy led to an accumulation of bad loans. With the onset of the crisis, the likelihood of their being paid off became utterly illusory. A banking crisis resulted, one with which Slovenia is still grappling. The problems in Russia and Ukraine were slightly different again. Russia suffered primarily from the drop in commodity prices, caused by international stock market speculation. Ukraine's import-export imbalance had been worsening since 2005. Like the Baltic states, its economic growth was financed on credit.

FDI inflow into Poland, the Czech Republic, and Slovakia was more favorably structured, and the governments here had tried to limit private consumer borrowing even before the crisis. These countries were affected worst by the unprecedented slump in exports and their dependence on the German economy. Germany, in turn, relied on the export markets that were now faltering. But major German banks had also actively gambled away hundreds of billions on the US property and subprime markets. The postcommunist world, where the credit sector was dominated by foreign banks, was largely innocent of this. Few of the new EU member countries had to pass "rescue packages" for banks as Germany and the United Kingdom did. However, this was small comfort in the heat of the crisis, when international investors were withdrawing as much capital as they could or refusing to lend any more to debt-ridden countries.

The only exception in this gloomy scenario was Poland. Although the Polish export market slumped, like the Czech and Slovak markets, Poland managed to compensate for its foreign trade losses by increasing government expenditure, devaluing the national currency (which is not possible in the eurozone), and using its human capital, analyzed in chapter 5. The severe recession in the United Kingdom and Ireland prompted at least three hundred thousand of the two million migrant workers who had left Poland since the nineties to return home with their savings.[15] This wave of remigration increased the population of Poland by at least 0.7 percent. The returnees invested their earnings in new livelihoods. In this way, they helped Poland achieve economic growth of 1.6 percent even in the crisis year 2009, compared to

−5.1 percent in Germany. In the midst of the crisis, then, Poland caught up economically with the West more rapidly than in all the previous twenty years. At the same time, the individual countries of East Central Europe diverged more than ever.

Expert analyses of the crisis must have sounded like gibberish to the citizens of postcommunist countries. In general, the language of crisis has fallen into two categories. While remaining firmly abstract when referring to the world of finance—consider the key phrase "systemically important" (often paraphrased in the United States as "too big to fail")—it becomes idiomatic when nations and societies are under discussion. The Baltic states and Greece were said to have "lived beyond their means" and would consequently have to "tighten their belts" (both favorite terms of the German chancellor Angela Merkel), as if it were a matter of losing a few surplus pounds. Staying with the body weight metaphor, the speculative capital that flowed into Europe until 2009 was like a bad diet. The financial equivalent of fast food, it provided instant satisfaction but generated a craving for foreign capital, which left states and economies with the long-term problem of high debts. The private consumers who succumbed to the credit frenzy and incurred debts to buy property or consumer goods are now feeling the effects.

## Predatory Lending in Central and Eastern Europe

One of the most difficult legacies of the pre-crisis period has been the many billions of foreign currency loans. Since these loans were highly speculative and given to borrowers with weak financial records, Joseph Stiglitz's term "predatory lending" seems just as appropriate for Eastern Europe as it is for the United States.[16] International banks and their national subsidiaries in the new EU member countries were keen to beef up the amount of lending. They did so by arranging loans for prospective homeowners and private consumers not in their national Eastern European currencies, but in euros, Swiss francs, or other foreign currencies. In this way, the debtors were told, they could take advantage of the lower interest rates in Western countries. But as the Hungarians, Poles, Latvians, or Ukrainians did not earn euros or Swiss francs, they paid off their loans in their respective national currencies. The benefit of low interest, then, was counterbalanced by the risk of currency fluctuation. Overall, foreign currency loans were more attractive for banks than for their clients: on top of the usual fees, the banks earned money on converting the currencies and could also add a substantial markup to the comparatively low interest rates in Switzerland, Germany, or wherever the bank was based.

If they had looked back to 1989–91, the citizens of the former Eastern Bloc might have remembered that exchange rates can fluctuate and even tumble. But since the turn of the century, Poles, Czechs, and Hungarians—and since the mid 2000s, Romanians, Bulgarians (who had experienced triple-figure inflation rates in the late nineties), and even Ukrainians—had known only stable or revaluated national currencies. The dollar, once the under-the-mattress reserve of the Eastern Bloc, was weakened. Between 2000 and 2008, it steadily lost value against the Polish złoty, Czech crown, and Hungarian forint. This state of affairs made foreign currency loans attractive in the first place—unlike in the nineties when the currencies of postcommunist countries were constantly depreciated in order to bolster exports and entice Western investors. At that time, purchasing power had been high in the former Eastern Bloc. Western tourists had been able to dine out for two or three dollars in the Czech and Slovak Republics (one of the reasons why thousands of young Americans went to live there, particularly in Prague). German and Austrian car drivers swarmed across the border to fill their tanks; the Viennese flocked to the coffeehouses of Bratislava, the Berliners to the Polish markets along the River Oder at the German-Polish border. Few local residents, however, could afford to travel abroad or buy Western products. But at least it was possible to get by on a monthly salary the equivalent of just a few hundred dollars.

From the year 2000, the situation reversed. Exchange rates changed in favor of the Eastern European currencies: wages and salaries rose, buoyed by these countries' continuing high purchasing power, and, crucially, they possessed the asset most treasured by the international stock markets: positive forecasts. EU accession was in the cards; by 2002 the treaties had been concluded, awaiting only ratification, and the postcommunist economies were expected to grow robustly. After accession, the optimism bubbled over into excitement, and some of the new EU members were vaunted as "tiger economies." The values of their currencies seemed to rise and rise, with only the Hungarian forint weakening for a spell in 2006, presaging the coming crisis. Banks granted ever more loans in foreign currencies,[17] running aggressive advertising campaigns to sell their new product. The Hungarian Raiffeisen Bank (a subsidiary of Austria's Raiffeisen Bank International) produced a particularly attention-grabbing TV commercial. In it, a Hungarian family is being advised about a loan at a bank. The father tries to report how much they earn a month but is repeatedly interrupted by the advisor, who says the amount is unimportant, puts her hands over her ears, and blurts "bababab" to drown him out. Finally, a sonorous, off-screen male voice assures the viewer that the property being purchased on credit is security enough.[18] The press occasionally ran cautionary articles, warning of the risks linked to exchange rate fluctuations. But hidden deep in the business sections or supplements, they had about as much impact as the small print in a sales contract.[19] The exchange rates and growth figures continued their upward trend; the entire transformation seemed to be a wonderful success story.

In fall 2008, the Eastern European bubble suddenly burst. The crisis, or to be precise, the drying-up and reversion of international capital flows, caused a dramatic drop in the values of Eastern European currencies. Within six months, a euro no longer cost 3.20 Polish złotys, but 4.90; the exchange rate for the Hungarian forint dropped from 1:230 to 1:300.[20] These currencies fared even worse against the Swiss franc, which benefited from its reputation as a safe haven as the euro crisis loomed. The value of the Swiss franc rose from around two złotys in summer 2008 to three in winter 2009; from 143 forints to 200 forints. Unfortunately, the majority of foreign currency loans—over 90 percent in Hungary—had been arranged in Swiss francs. In bread-and-butter terms, this meant that a Polish or Hungarian family who had borrowed 100,000 francs to buy a home suddenly faced a debt mountain one-and-a-half times as high as they had bargained for—in this case, 300,000 złotys rather than 200,000, or 200 million forints instead of 140 million (which would have grown to 240–50 million forints by 2011 as the franc continued to rise).

This problem was not confined to the new EU member states. Austrian banks had also offered loans in francs (and Japanese yen) on the domestic market. In 2010 there were an estimated 250,000 foreign currency debtors in Austria, with combined debts worth 35 billion euros,[21] or around 140,000 euros per debtor. Hungary and other postcommunist countries had their very own legacies of the neoliberal epoch to shoulder. According to the government in Budapest, around one million Hungarians had taken out loans in foreign currencies before the crisis.[22] In Romania and Ukraine, too, loans in foreign currencies had made up over 50 percent of total bank loans.[23] But Latvia, where Swedish banks had been particularly active, topped the charts. These countries' economies suffered the worst slumps, while countries that had attempted to partially regulate lending markets (including Poland and the Czech Republic) were less badly hit. The specific effects of crisis in any given country were not only linked to types of foreign direct investment, as Bohle and Greskovits found, but also to another (closely related) factor—the volume of foreign currency loans allocated.

Ideally, banks would have refused to conduct such predatory lending or at least warned their clients of the currency risks. But there was method behind the madness. Transformation discourse had led to an idolization of private property and inflated demand for it in the postcommunist markets. Banks addressed the demand by borrowing money from their countries' central banks, or on the international markets, to extend to their clients, adding on substantial markups. The postcommunist countries tend not to be tenants' markets, as in Germany and Austria, but owner markets. City rents were often higher there than in Berlin or Vienna, and property prices relatively low. One exception was the former GDR, where the major exodus of around two million people to West Germany by 2000 left plenty of accommodation available, even in Berlin for many years.

The revaluation of loans was catastrophic for borrowers, who faced paying higher rates for longer or losing their recently acquired property. The foreign currency loan fiasco had repercussions for Eastern European politics. Hungarian right-wing populist Viktor Orbán curried favor by pledging to tackle the electorate's unmanageable debts and put the international banks in their place. In September 2011 the Hungarian parliament enacted legislation providing for a sort of compulsory exchange: the foreign currency loans were to be converted into forints at an exchange rate determined by the government if the debtors paid off their loans.[24] Around a third managed to do so, logically enough, the better-off borrowers. The banks that stood to lose out were mainly Austrian; they responded with protests and lawsuits, but eventually caved in and wrote off part of the loans. Orbán was to some extent vindicated when the European Systemic Risk Board (EBRD) and the Austrian Financial Market Authority (FMA) expressed serious concerns about the foreign currency loans, with the latter declaring in late 2010 that they were "not suitable to be a mass product."[25] It was too late for the many debtors, who struggled for years to pay off their foreign currency loans. But their fate did not warrant any headlines, unlike the Greek and Italian national debt crises.

The belated attempts to regulate borrowing on a national and European level brought the phase of foreign currency loans for private consumers to an end. This episode illustrates how the boom in the postcommunist economies was fueled and inflated, creating bubbles that eventually burst. Once again, these countries were serving as sites of experimentation, no longer with government reform policies (as in the nineties) but with private investors' new business models. Riding the second wave of neoliberalism, international banks took advantage of the possibilities created by the deregulation of the international financial markets to devise and exploit a new product, foreign currency loans.

Reregulation took place in different spirits. While Western European governments and banking authorities confined themselves to issuing "recommendations" against foreign currency loans and largely echoed the language of finance, Hungarian prime minister

Viktor Orbán, especially, fashioned himself the champion of the ordinary folk and debtors. His ostensibly left-wing policies demonstrate how far the left-to-right political axis has dissolved: his nationalist rhetoric and political courting of the middle classes have more in common with the traditional mode of right-wing parties. By pointing the finger squarely at the foreign banks, he demonstrated an obvious bias; after all, the borrowers had accepted the risks in order to profit from lower interest rates. This shows that neoliberalism did not only cater to the business and finance sectors but, as in the United States, also had a popular dimension.

The neoliberal order was accepted from below, by society. After years of vague promises for the future by reform politicians and communists alike, Eastern Europeans seized the opportunity to fulfill their immediate wishes.

The swing of the pendulum from communism to consumerism changed popular perceptions of time. The focus shifted from working toward a better future for one's children, or waiting for reform promises to come true, to raising standards of living in the here and now. In broad terms, the younger generation has fewer children (in Poland, around half as many as in the early eighties), is more consumer-oriented, and lives more for the moment. Warsaw's high-rise landscape offers ample space for billboards. The constant exposure to advertising stimulates desire for things that not everybody can afford, if they are realistic about their income. The statistics on car registrations illustrate this. Many residents of Warsaw bought cars on credit. When the crisis hit in 2009, the number of cars registered in the city fell by over thirty thousand. Evidently cars were quickly offloaded in anticipation of the crisis,[26] which in fact did not hit Poland as badly as other countries. Another spontaneous reaction to the crisis (considered below) was labor migration.

## Political Reactions: Between Neoliberalism and Authoritarianism

The world of politics, in Eastern as in Western Europe, was initially taken up with responding in the short term to the various challenges of the great recession. In 2008–9, the postcommunist states had their hands full preventing the further decline of their currencies and economies (and, in some cases, national bankruptcy), and restoring the "markets' confidence." In a foretaste of things to come in Southern Europe, the IMF and the European Union helped Latvia, Hungary, Romania, and Ukraine with bailout programs. But these were subject to strict conditions, the social and economic consequences of which will be considered below. This neoliberal variant of crisis management was only one of many ways that countries dealt with economic turbulence. Which one they chose depended to a large degree on the course of transformation they had previously taken. Historians and social scientists speak of "path dependencies." But the deviations from the paths taken before 2008–9 are perhaps the more interesting phenomenon.

Bohle and Greskovits have traced three different transformation outcomes that shaped the crisis in each individual postcommunist country: first, a neoliberal order cushioned by welfare state provisions ("embedded neoliberal regimes"—in the Visegrad countries); second, unambiguously neoliberal regimes (in the Baltic states, Romania and Bulgaria); and third, a neocorporatist model (in Slovenia). The list can be extended by the addition of oligarchic-neoliberal systems (to be observed in the post-Soviet states, in a slightly different form in each). This typology is useful for explaining the different paths of transformation (see also "A Typology of Reform Outcomes" in chapter 4) and the trajectories of crisis in 2008–9. But it does not extend to the western neighbor states of the former Eastern Bloc or the European Union in general. Comparison with Germany, especially, is illuminating as it reveals a number of parallels with the Visegrad countries in terms of crisis development and government responses. Similarly, Slovenia does not stand alone with its neocorporatist order. Austria also has a distinctly corporatist character: membership in the chamber of commerce (*Wirtschaftskammer*) is more or less compulsory for all enterprises; trade unions and the chamber of labor (*Arbeiterkammer*) are strong as well, and there is a general tendency to seek political consensus.

Germany, Austria, Poland, and Slovakia tried to cushion the effect of recession on society by increasing government expenditure.

The German public spending program raised eyebrows and made headlines worldwide for schemes such as the car-scrapping premium (devised by the German government to encourage car owners to trade in their old models for new). But Poland pursued the most distinctly Keynesian policy. At a time when tax revenue was rapidly dwindling, the Polish government hazarded a budget deficit of over 7 percent to increase public spending. Slovakia left the neoliberal path it had started on ten years previously, abolishing the flat tax in 2012. The Czech Republic wavered between austerity measures and active crisis management, and fell back into recession in 2012. Logically enough, only relatively affluent countries with comparatively low debts could afford to introduce Keynesian countermeasures. Slovenia, with its neocorporatist model of government, responded to the crisis with no more effective measures than desperate attempts to shrug off international assistance and to overcome the banking crisis alone.

Alternatively, countries embraced neoliberalism even closer. The Baltic states, Romania, and Bulgaria resorted to drastic austerity measures to deal with the crisis. These involved slashing the salaries of government employees and their—already low—expenditure on basic social services. In this way, they passed along the cost of the crisis to the general public. But Romania and Latvia, certainly, had no other choice. Like Poland in 1989–90, they depended on Western loans, for which they had to fulfill the IMF's strict criteria. As a result of the austerity measures, unemployment soared (in Latvia, for instance, it more than tripled between 2007 and 2010 from 6.0 to 18.7 percent), masses were plunged into poverty, and many moved away, depleting the population. Latvia lost almost two hundred thousand inhabitants between 2009 and 2011, or 9 percent of its population;[27] Lithuania lost three hundred thousand; Romania, 2.4 million.[28] Population shrinkage is not attributable solely to migration. It can also be caused by rising mortality rates and other factors; the incidence of illness and suicide rose dramatically in the wake of the crisis. But at least two-thirds of those who disappeared from the population statistics were migrants. The crisis compounded the downward demographic trend that had begun in the nineties. Latvia has lost six hundred thousand of its previous 2.6 million inhabitants since independence; Romania, 4.2 million of 23.2 million. An analogous development can be observed in the Republic of Ireland, which also responded to the crisis with a draconian austerity program. Its rate of migration has tripled since 2004 to between 80,000 and 90,000 migrants annually. Unlike in Romania and Latvia, however, its population losses were to some extent compensated by immigration (partly from Romania).[29]

Shrinking populations find it harder to achieve even nominal economic growth. This in turn has repercussions on forecasts, stock markets, capital flows, and investments. Thousands of places have become ghost towns, with a few hundred residents where once a few thousand lived. The decline in populations is a longer-term process that cannot be attributed to one single factor or economic policy. Nonetheless, the sudden rise in migration in the years 2009–11 in precisely those countries that had pursued neoliberal policies before and after the crisis points to a direct link with the economic and social recipes prescribed by the IMF and the European Union.

A third mode of response to the crisis was basically muddling through without a clear concept. This applies to Ukraine, which was "rescued" from national bankruptcy with an IMF emergency program in 2009. This, like others, was motivated in part by the Fund's need to prevent losses for the Western banks and financial institutions that had invested large sums in the country; the combined western FDI in Ukraine amounted to over 36 billion euros in 2009, the bulk of which would have been lost if Ukraine had declared state bankruptcy.[30] As controversial as the rescue package was, it gave Ukraine a chance to weather the crisis. However, Ukrainian president Viktor Yushchenko's successor Viktor Yanukovych redirected the international aid into the pockets of his family members and allied oligarchs. Consequently, Ukraine's economic demise continued and the huge gulf between rich and poor widened. This was the deeper-rooted reason for the revolution against Ukraine's kleptocratic regime in winter 2013–14.

A fourth mode of response was making a rhetorical repudiation of the West while still trying to implement key elements of the neoliberal order. Russian president Vladimir Putin has taken this line since the start of his second term in office. In 2006 Putin set about ousting international corporations from Russia, including Shell and other Western energy groups. By revoking drilling licenses, bringing charges of pollution, and finally setting his tax police on them, he harassed the companies into selling their shares in Russian companies.[31] In one high-profile case, the American chairperson of a joint venture of BP and the Russian oil company TNK was subjected to summonses, police questioning, and home raids until he eventually escaped abroad in fear for his safety. (TNK "took over" BP's shares some years later.) The Russian government's ruthless conduct was a symptom of its determination to regain control of the key sector in the economy—gas and oil production. The Kremlin had begun silencing politically critical oligarchs in 2003. Putin also railed against the West in the international arena. At the Munich Security Conference in 2007, he gave an inflammatory speech challenging the hegemony and universality of Western values.[32] But Russia persisted in its efforts to join the World Trade Organization (succeeding in 2012), and welcomed Western investors into other sectors of the economy and the Moscow stock exchange.

The weakness of the state-capitalist system that Putin established lies in the primacy of government. Political scientist Neill Robinson has labeled it "political capitalism."[33] To do business in Russia, it is essential to have access to policymakers. This access is based on personal ties; it is not regulated or transparent. Opaque business connections are the tools of corruption, and making payments to elicit favors one of the methods. If the very system breeds corruption, it cannot be eliminated by raising state officials' salaries, which helped to significantly reduce corruption in the new EU states, or threatening them with draconian punishments.

Another problem endemic to state capitalism is a large rich-poor divide. Authoritarian systems are not answerable to the public in the same way as are democratic systems. To some extent, feedback from the public caused the countries in East Central Europe to moderate their neoliberal reform policies and devote more attention to achieving social equality. In contrast, authoritarian regimes

THE GREAT RECESSION | 231

can more easily ignore discontent among the population, because they do not depend on popular voting. Nevertheless, Vladimir Putin has increasingly pursued a populist line and tried to raise the standard of living of the Russian middle class. The communist regime in China has acted similarly. In this way, they have made state capitalism more globally competitive, at least against a West that is whittling away its social security systems. Thanks to high returns from its natural resource exports, Russia had the means to spend generously on active social policies until the conflict over Ukraine erupted and the West imposed sanctions.

At the moment it seems that aggressive nationalism and military intervention against Russia's neighbors is succeeding in raising Putin's popularity. China is also pursuing a policy of expansion in the South China Sea. From a historical viewpoint, aggressive foreign policy is nothing new for authoritarian regimes. It repeats a pattern known from the nineteenth century and the age of imperialism.

In parallel with attacking the West, Putin has sought to build an alliance to rival the European Union. In 2010–11, Russia founded the Eurasian Customs Union together with Belarus and Kazakhstan; in May 2014 the Eurasian Economic Union was formed. From a Russian viewpoint, the Union is not complete without Ukraine as a member. Russia would certainly gain from closer economic links with its southwestern neighbor. But the Ukrainian oligarchs do not intend to bow to Putin's political primacy. And the Ukrainian public does not wish to be dominated by its neo-imperialist neighbor, especially as Putin supported ousted president Viktor Yanukovych. The basic problem of Russian (and Chinese) state capitalism is that in contrast to the European Union it relies on the hegemony of *one* state. Nevertheless, the combination of capitalism and authoritarianism certainly has some appeal. Belarus and Kazakhstan voluntarily joined the Eurasian group because, unlike the EU, it is not concerned with their observance of human rights, and perhaps allows greater autonomy than Brussels would. Under Russia's umbrella, these countries can also avoid the economic regulation pursued by the European Union. International investors have returned to the Moscow stock exchange, notwithstanding governmental abuses of power like those in 2006 or the aggression in Ukraine. They may not be able to take over Russian corporations or exert much influence on Russian management, but they can expect high returns.

Since the great recession of 2008–9, the state capitalist system has also proven capable of an effective foreign trade policy. Recently, Russia concluded several business agreements with Hungary, including a treaty on the supply and construction of two new reactor blocks for the nuclear power station in Paks. Hungary will finance the plant, projected to cost around ten billion euros, through a loan from Russia, to be repaid over thirty years. The deal is a sign of the encroaching influence of Russian state capitalism on some eastern EU countries. It was a defeat for Western corporations such as Areva (France) and Westinghouse, which were outbid by the Russian Atomic Energy Agency Corporation (RosAtom). This is not a regular company, but a government authority controlling various companies, including a nuclear power plant construction firm.[34]

On a personal level, Putin no doubt found a sympathetic partner in Hungarian premier Orbán, with whom he shares a similar temperament and outlook. Both have displayed authoritarian tendencies—Orbán is sometimes nicknamed "little Putin"—and both favor the use of emotionally charged rhetoric, often referring to the greatness and suffering of their nations. Hungary lost two-thirds of its national territory under the Treaty of Trianon in 1920. Putin regards the disintegration of the Soviet Union as Russia's Trianon. Both politicians cultivate virile, masculine public images. But there the similarities end. As a member of NATO and the European Union, Hungary cannot attack a neighbor as Russia did Ukraine. Bound by the EU treaties, Orbán has less political latitude than Putin. Nonetheless, Hungary has undergone a remarkable transformation from model reform country—the Bokros package of 1995, the pension reforms of 1998, the complete opening of the economy and several other measures ticked all the IMF's boxes—to deviant. In response to the crisis of 2008–9 and the huge deficit in the national budget, Viktor Orbán has slackened the neoliberal order. He has nationalized the second-pillar compulsory private pension fund established in the late nineties. Ironically, he had introduced the scheme himself during his first premiership (1998–2002). By the time it was nationalized in 2010, Hungarian employees had invested the equivalent of over ten billion euros, which was then redirected into the national budget.

Ostensibly in order to consolidate the budget, Orbán introduced a number of special taxes on banks, energy companies, telecommunications groups, and international supermarket chains.[35] Using nationalist rhetoric, he accused foreign corporations of profiteering at Hungary's expense and causing many of the country's ills. Similarly, the aforementioned sanctions against the international banks that had provided foreign currency loans were both populist and popular. They were followed by laws against international service companies, landowners, and leaseholders. While EU regulations prevented the Hungarian government from legally exempting native companies or citizens, the laws were implemented in such a way that in practice they mostly were.

Hungary's economic nationalism is an indication that the Orbán government is not concerned merely with consolidating the budget but, like Russia, with reducing foreign involvement in the economy and renationalizing domestic profits. But Hungary cannot afford to go as far as harassing international investors. It has made several fiscal compromises, either at the European Union's insistence or in order to avoid completely alienating foreign banks. A flat tax rate of 16 percent was introduced in 2011 with an eye to satisfying international investors, echoing the policy of many postcommunist countries after the turn of the millennium. It remains to be seen whether this contradictory economic policy is viable in the long term—most economists doubt it.[36]

For some time, however, Hungary has been improving its trade and current account balances; the economy is growing again. As labor costs in China and other Asian countries rise, countries like Hungary may regain their appeal as production sites for European companies. Yet despite levying so many special taxes, the Hungarian government is still in deficit. Crucially, Orbán has neglected perhaps the most important resource in the neoliberal order—investors' confidence and positive forecasts. The younger generation, meanwhile, are voting with their feet. Since the out-break of the crisis, some two hundred thousand young people have left the country to work abroad.[37] Many of them are well-educated former residents of Budapest, who oppose Viktor Or-bán's policies. His combination of nationalism and populism is anathema to young, cosmopolitan Hungarians. However, the vot-ers gave Orbán a comfortable majority in the parliamentary and European elections of 2014. In this way they rewarded him for his clever harnessing of popular discontent with the neoliberal order and its acute side effects.[38] Recent developments in Poland after the election victory of the national conservative party PiS (Law and Justice Party) point in the same direction. The working poor, young people with trash contracts, and Polska B in particular voted for PiS, which has pledged to create a "fourth republic" of Poland (as distinct from the third republic created in 1989). These political reactions are probably the most dangerous legacy of the neoliberal transformation, and might cause further damage to the already weakened European Union.

# 8

# Southern Europe

## The New East?

### Crisis Commonalities between Southern and Eastern Europe

The crisis of 2008–9 marked a watershed for the southern EU countries, perhaps even more so than for Eastern Europe. Evaluating the recent upheavals in European history is no easy task for the contemporary historian, as many problems, such as the euro crisis, remain unresolved; they are uncompleted processes that elude appraisal. Looking ahead (which is not the historian's specialty), it is hard to predict whether the southern EU countries will manage to permanently exit from the crisis or whether they will slide ever further behind the rest of Europe.

This chapter will compare the two macrounits of Eastern Europe and Southern Europe as well as the individual countries and societies within them. Special attention will be paid to Italy and Poland, since they are economically the most important countries in both larger regions. (Greece received far more coverage in the international media due to its destructive potential for the euro but, with its horrendous national debt, structural problems, weak industry, and low tax revenue, it is an exceptional case.) Maintaining the focus on social history, the chapter will consider the crisis and attempts to overcome it "from below." One central argument proposed is that, while the older generation and pensioners bore the brunt of the neoliberal reform programs launched in Eastern Europe in 1989, the crisis in Southern Europe has been dealt with at the expense of the younger generations. This thesis sets the two time frames of the analysis: on the one hand, it will make a diachronic comparison of the period after 1989 and the period after 2008-9; on the other, it will compare contemporaneous reactions in various countries and societies to the recent crisis.

The focus on Italy also has practical reasons. (The other southern EU countries are considered mainly in comparative contexts.) As a historian, it is a boon to be able to read key sources in the original language. During a three-year stint at the European University Institute in Florence (a think tank and the only EU university) in 2007-10, I witnessed the outbreak of the financial, budget, and economic crisis firsthand and gained initial impressions of the deeper political and social causes.

In 2007, when almost all seemed to be well in Southern Europe, Italy was ruled by the former president of the European Commission, Romano Prodi, a social-democratic political realist. Since Prodi's arrival in office, Italy's national debt had been reduced and unemployment brought down lower than in Germany and most of the new EU countries. Italy's only major concern was slow economic growth—it had the lowest rate in Europe. Prices were remarkably high; filling a shopping cart at the supermarket cost around a fifth more than in Germany. Rent, telephone costs—in short, everyday life—was more expensive. Labor, on the other hand, was far cheaper. My wife and I advertised for a babysitter and were inundated with replies—from undergraduate and postgraduate students, even qualified educators, and many other working people who wanted or needed to supplement their incomes. We became acquainted with other downsides of life in Italy: sprawling suburbs of crumbling apartment blocks; the ubiquitous stifling traffic, squeezed onto congested roads; and the disturbing contrast of private wealth displayed alongside decaying schools and nurseries.

A year later, *la crisi* struck. Initially, Italy's economic slump was similar to Germany's, but in contrast to the Federal Republic, it precipitated a change of government. Silvio Berlusconi resumed power, less on account of his—rapidly dwindling—charisma than the decline of the Left in Italy and the lack of political alternatives. From the start of his third term in office, Berlusconi put more effort into evading prosecution for tax evasion and corruption than actively combating the crisis. In any case, with its high national debt, Italy did not have the means to launch a spending program like Germany's. But this did not prevent the country from paying into the European Union's joint emergency fund to come to Greece's aid. In 2010, the Italian government introduced its first austerity program in a bid to contain the euro crisis. The stability law (*legge di stabilità*) led to major cuts in education. Universities and schools were forced to slash four billion euros, or 8 percent of their total budget.[1] In spite of these cuts, concern over Italy's national debt, which already amounted to more than 100 percent of its GDP, sent the interest rates on government bonds soaring, and necessitated one austerity package after the next to deal with the additional costs. To make matters worse, the government could no longer pay its bills: its outstanding commercial debt rose to almost one hundred billion euros (in addition to the country's two-trillion-euro national debt) and caused an unprecedented wave of bankruptcies.[2]

*La crisi* gnawed at the Italian economy for over five years. Industrial production dropped by almost 25 percent; Italy experienced the longest recession since the Second World War. Though more protracted, Italy's decline was almost as dramatic as Poland's in 1990 or Czechoslovakia's in 1991, following the collapse of communism.[3] After 2008–9, Italy's per capita GDP fell by about 10 percent to the level it had been in the mid-nineties.

The central question this chapter asks is: Are the southern countries of the European Union taking the place of the East? Both these EU peripheries were especially badly hit by the crisis of 2008–9 and its aftereffects (with the aforementioned exception of Poland). The new EU member states were particularly vulnerable to the global financial crisis whereas the southern EU states struggled with the budget and euro crises. Despite these differences, the recession has in many respects had similar consequences: unemployment and poverty have increased, social inequality and other economic and social problems have dramatically worsened.

In view of these parallels, the chapter will begin by taking stock. It will compare durations and extents of the recession in the various regions and countries in question. Second, it will explore the political and social responses to the crisis, especially labor migration. A third topic of comparison will be international (stereotypical) perceptions of Eastern and Southern Europe. Without wishing to consolidate stereotypes, I cannot deny my personal impressions of the satellite towns surrounding Rome, Naples, Palermo, and Cagliari. Compared to the high-rise suburbs there, the prefabricated residential estates in the poorest regions of Poland seem cheerful and neat. The Mediterranean light dispels the gray, but illuminates a stark and disturbing contrast with the chic, affluent middle-class districts that exist in all the above cities (but not in those of eastern Poland, such as Białystok or Rzeszow).

Comparisons usually aim to identify differences and similarities, and to formulate generalizing and individualizing hypotheses. Below, I will endeavor to take comparison a step further by asking: Is there a connection between the economic development in the new EU countries and the situation in the crisis-torn countries of the EU's south? It is still too early to support this thesis with the findings of scholarly research into recent economic history.[4] Nevertheless, a number of indicators point to a connection between the economic gulf separating Germany and Southern Europe and the proliferation of economic interrelations within the expanded EU, and specifically between Germany and East Central Europe. This spread of economic ties is evidence of a process of "small-scale globalization."

Although almost all the new EU countries were plunged into a deeper recession than the fifteen original members, they recovered faster. Foreign investments soon began to flow again, albeit not as abundantly as before 2007—expectations had been revised from overoptimistic to more realistic. As figure 8.1 shows, from 2010, the countries of East Central Europe achieved higher growth rates than Italy and Greece. With labor costs and taxes still low, their prospects for further economic recovery are good. But their neoliberal orientation comes at a high social cost, and causes other difficulties for the erstwhile reform front-runners. In Slovenia and the Czech Republic, for instance, rising prices and salaries have necessitated a different economic strategy than in the nineties. These countries are caught in the "middle income trap"; it took

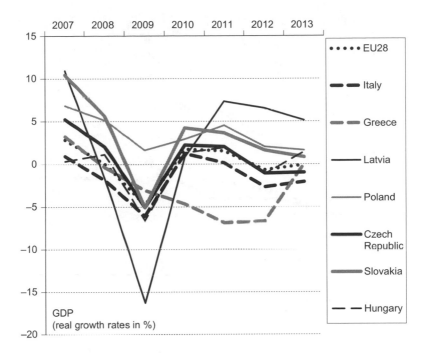

**Fig. 8.1.** Economic growth in Southern and East Central European EU states 2007–2013. *Source*: Eurostat Regionalstatistik (Tabelle tsdec100).

them many years to overcome the crisis. Slovenia also struggled with a homemade banking crisis. But it managed to recover without a eurozone rescue package and the social cuts this would have entailed.

The southern EU states have no such prospects of recovery. Greece has been in unparalleled economic distress since 2010. Its per capita GDP has fallen by over 30 percent in that time. The Greek crisis has proven far lengthier and more severe than the economic slump experienced by the Eastern European countries in the early nineties (see fig. 8.2). The recession in Italy has also lasted longer than that in Poland or the Czech Republic after 1989.

The decline in economic performance has further compounded the debt crisis. Italy's national debt rose to 134 percent of GDP in 2014, from 105 percent in 2005. Even Hungary, the most heavily

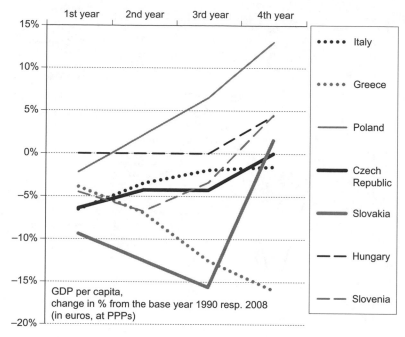

**Fig. 8.2.** Crisis trajectories: East Central Europe after 1990 and Greece/Italy after 2008. Source: WIIW Report 2012 (Table I/1.5); Eurostat, ongoing releases.

indebted new EU member country, is sitting comparatively pretty with a debt-to-GDP ratio of 78 percent.[5] It remains to be seen if Italy can escape this trap. In purely mathematical terms, it can succeed if the economy grows robustly and tax revenues increase. But exactly the reverse has been the case since the crisis of 2008–9: The austerity policy has slowed domestic demand—an inevitable state of affairs where the state accounts for over 50 percent of the GDP. While Germany and Austria have stabilized their economies by increasing exports, Italy has so far been beaten by the strong international—particularly German—competition.

Even before the crisis, Italy had been overtaken by Germany in a number of respects. It had failed to forge as many economic links and secure as many cost advantages in the new EU countries as German companies such as Volkswagen and Bosch. Back in the early nineties, Italian industry was a major investor in Eastern Europe. One example is Fiat in Poland; Italian banks and insurance companies such as Unicredit and Generali also expanded into the region. Small enterprises had ventured into Eastern Europe even earlier. One of the first private restaurants to open in Kraków was an Italian trattoria in 1991. The improvement in the quality of restaurants, cafés, and bakeries is one of the most remarkable achievements of transformation in all of Eastern Europe. Italian boutiques also flourished.

However, Italy's dynamic appearance on the "emerging markets" soon lost momentum. This is illustrated by statistics on the inflow of foreign direct investments. Italy usually ranks fourth or fifth among foreign countries investing in Eastern European states and the former Soviet Union (except in Poland), often behind its much smaller neighbor Austria. In some national statistics, Italy is not listed as an investor at all.[6] That does not imply that the Italian economy missed the boat on Eastern Europe. Italy is a leading investor in the Adriatic states of Albania, Montenegro, and Croatia (in Albania, after Greece; in Montenegro, after Russia). But these countries have profited least from the European boom of the last twenty-five years, and are small markets. In a sense, then, Italy's FDI flowed in the wrong direction. In total, between 70 and 90 percent of the FDI in the new EU countries came from the old member states of the European Union;[7] further proof of the process of "small-scale globalization."

Compared to Germany, the Italian (or French, for that matter) industries active in the rising economies of Eastern Europe have the distinct disadvantage of longer transport distances. While Volkswagen's Polish production sites are virtually on the company's doorstep, the distance between Tychy in southern Poland (the site of the largest and most modern Fiat plant) and the parent plant in Turin is considerable.

Initially, however, Germany's geographical proximity to Eastern Europe caused some difficulties. To take another example from the automobile industry, the new factories built by Volkswagen and its suppliers in Poland, the Czech Republic, Slovakia, and Hungary, cost at least one hundred thousand jobs at German production sites.[8] But in the long term, not only companies like Volkswagen but the entire German economy profited from industry's expansion into Eastern Europe. By taking advantage of cheaper manufacturing, turnovers were increased and profits swelled. This structural change took place at a time when economies worldwide were buoyant. Apart from the dip after 2001, the world economy boomed in the fifteen years between 1992 and 2007, bolstering the export-oriented German economy along with it. Since 2008, the global economy has not been robust enough to moderate the crisis in Italy in the same way—by compensating the lack of internal with greater external demand.

Moreover, Italy's industry centers on products that require little technological expertise to manufacture, such as textiles, shoes, and furniture. These can be more cheaply produced in Eastern or Southeastern Europe, or even more so in Asia. Intra-European and global competition has also placed considerable pressure on the other southern EU member countries. Portugal lost much of its textile production to Romania and Bulgaria even before the European Union expanded eastward.[9] This trend accelerated after the introduction of the euro, which pushed unit labor costs upward in Portugal and the other southern countries.

German trade unions confronted the cost problem head-on. Unemployment was relatively high in Germany around the turn of the millennium, and German workers were informed by their staff committees of how much less their Polish, Czech, or Hungarian colleagues earned. Consequently, they approached the employers' associations with the offer of dropping pay raise demands in exchange for job guarantees. In this way, a "social pact" was concluded, based on the kind of "old" corporatist structures that were widely condemned in the neoliberal epoch, and which made German industry more competitive than southern European or French industry. This can be regarded as a further example of cotransformation.

Another factor affecting location decisions is the educational background of the local population. In this respect, too, the southern European states have fallen behind. In the Program for International Student Assessment scheme of ranking national education systems, Italy is a clear laggard.[10] (The launch of PISA in 2000 created a new international market, where confidence in the—not necessarily market-oriented—education systems was influenced not least by when and how the participating countries adjusted to the competition. For this and other reasons, PISA warrants some healthy skepticism.) Moreover, Italy is dragging its feet in the digital revolution. In terms of internet expansion, it ranks third lowest in Europe, just ahead of Romania and Bulgaria.[11]

Italy's regression to a "low-tech" country (though this only really applies to the south; the northern Lombardy and Piedmont regions are economically advanced) is all the more striking in contrast with its position in the eighties. Italy was the fifth-strongest Western industrial economy, ranking only behind the United States, Japan, West Germany, and France. It was a strong contender on the electronics and computer market. The Piedmont-based typewriter manufacturer Olivetti produced several successful personal computers and—even more sensationally—a laptop as early as 1982–83. Olivetti held the second-highest market share, after IBM, in Europe.[12] (Some PCs were still made in Germany at the time, too.) In 1997, however, the company finally caved in to the fierce competition from the United States and Asia and discontinued its personal computer line. Olivetti's retreat from the computer market was, then, caused by the pressure of global competition rather than developments in Eastern Europe. Meanwhile, in other fields, such as vehicle construction, Italy struggled to keep pace with Germany and other parts of Europe.

As the economic gulf between Germany and Italy widens, the more the latter becomes a contender of the new EU member states. Labor costs in these countries are hard to beat, especially in Romania and Bulgaria. Devaluing the national currency to increase competitiveness is no longer an option for Italy since it adopted the euro. While the crisis-torn countries of Southern Europe are bound by the euro to Germany's financial and economic policies, the new EU states have become the extended workbench of German industry, enabling it to produce at low costs. This constellation has helped Germany to acquire a perhaps overwhelming level of economic power in Europe.

The euro crisis further compounded the economic imbalance. International investors turned away from Italy and its ailing public finances. At the height of the crisis in fall 2011, the interest rate spread between Italian and German government bonds, known in Italian as *lo spread*, rose to 5.74 percent.[13] Even at around 1 percent (the level at the time of writing in early 2015), for every billion-euro debt, Italy has to pay almost one hundred billion euros more in interest over a ten-year period than Germany. It is only thanks to the European Central Bank's decisive action that the interest rate spread was realigned to this level: the ECB first declared it would defend the euro at all costs, then directly intervened in "the market" by buying government bonds. Whether one regards the ECB's work as admirable or questionable, it is confined to the field of monetary policy and cannot stand in for a comprehensive European economic policy. Alone, Italy and the other Southern European EU states do not have the means to support their economies and halt the downward spiral of recent years. The more prosperous countries Germany, Poland, Slovakia, and, to some extent, the Czech Republic, have taken precisely this Keynesian course since 2009.

Though widely regarded by the Italian public as the spawn of neoliberalism, recent austerity programs differ from the reform programs of the nineties.[14] "Austerity" was only one of ten points on the Washington Consensus. Following neoliberal logic, it is just the start and should be followed by further reforms. Mario Monti's *governo tecnico* tried to introduce a number of deregulation, liberalization, and privatization projects but had to abandon them halfway. Italy and the other southern European EU countries cannot, then, be grouped together with the Baltic states as examples of continued neoliberalism. Italy's nonelected government of experts only went so far as to avert national bankruptcy and stabilize the budgetary situation.

Italy's total debt is considerably higher than that of the new EU countries, and has forced the government to repeatedly raise taxation levels. This in turn depresses demand and therefore growth. On paper, the realignment of the interest rate spread on government bonds makes Italy's capacity to service its national debt and overcome the worst economic crisis since 1945 more credible. But on the streets, many young unemployed seem to have given up all hope of finding a job. Unemployment among the young has risen to over 40 percent.[15] In 2014, 20 percent of fifteen-to-twenty-four-year-olds (some 1.3 million people) neither had a job nor attended school or college. They are the so-called NEET, "not engaged in education, employment, or training." While the younger generation has tremendous difficulties breaking into the employment market, more men and women over age fifty-five are employed in Italy than ever before. Since the outbreak of the crisis, employment in this age bracket has risen from 33 percent to over 40 percent.[16] No doubt propelled by sheer necessity, this trend compounds the asymmetry between young and old.

Italy's generational imbalance cannot be blamed on the neoliberal order. It has arisen from patriarchal structures in Italian society and, more concretely, the country's protection regulations for permanent staff. In 2015, Matteo Renzi's government at last relaxed Italy's employment protection amid fierce protests. It is cheaper and easier to fire a young employee, or decline to extend a short-term contract, than to lay off an older member of staff and have to pay a compensation settlement, or to answer to an industrial tribunal. This generational imbalance marks another difference from the Eastern European situation in the early nineties: in the latter region, workers over age forty and pensioners were the worst affected by mass unemployment and social security cuts.

The regional gap in Italy has also widened—in this case, similarly to Poland, Hungary, Slovakia, and the Baltic states in the nineties. In the period 2008–10 alone, Italian industries cut 532,000 jobs. This trend has continued to the present.[17] Over half these jobs were cut in southern Italy. Relative to the total number of people in employment, job losses in the *Mezzogiorno* were twice as high as in the north of Italy. More than that, the state has all but abandoned its regional policy to deal with the acute budget crisis. The tens of billions that Silvio Berlusconi pumped into the Italian structural fund for the South (*Fondo per le aree sottoutilizzate*, or *FAS*) since 2003, hoping to win voters in southern Italy, was largely consumed by immediate crisis management.

With fewer transfer payments arriving from Rome, the municipalities responsible for social expenditure are in turn forced to reduce their outgoings. In 2011–12, welfare benefits in southern Italy were 35 percent lower than in northern Italy.[18] Social expenditure in the *Mezzogiorno* is about the same as in Poland, and not too far removed from the neoliberal regimes in Romania and Latvia. In theory, the government in Rome could alleviate the problem by increasing transfers to the South. But the fact that its extensive regional aid of the postwar period came to nothing is no incentive to launch a new spending program.[19] The economy of southern Italy was in decline even before the crisis; long-term growth in the region had been around 0.5 percent lower than the Italian average since the mid-nineties. Southern Italy achieved a per capita GDP of around 79 percent of the EU average in 1995, falling to around 69 percent by 2007. (Overall, Italy's purchasing-power adjusted, per capita GDP was 104 percent of the EU average prior to the crisis.) By 2012, the *Mezzogiorno* had a smaller purchasing-power-adjusted GDP than Poland.[20] In view of these figures, the south of Italy has indeed shifted toward the East, insofar as this region can be regarded as an integral unit.

## Escape Route: Mass Migration

In 2015, European public debate was dominated by the Syrian refugee crisis and migration from the Middle East. A couple of years previously, labor migration had been a common reaction to the economic crisis in Eastern Europe. Masses left their homes in search of employment abroad. In a national perspective, this mitigated the impact of the economic downturn. Without mass migration, unemployment and social tensions would have taken on far more daunting dimensions. Relative to the total population, Romania, Latvia, and Lithuania had by far the highest rates of migration. Since these three countries further reduced their rudimentary welfare systems after 2009, the connection between welfare provisions and migration seems clear. By contrast, fewer citizens left Hungary and Slovenia, countries with much higher welfare expenditure, for Western Europe, although the impact the crisis was felt there, too.

Labor migration took place via contacts and networks that had existed before the crisis. But there was no long-established migration system analogous to the transatlantic emigration of Germans, Scandinavians, or Eastern European Jews in the nineteenth century. For political reasons, it was almost impossible to leave the Baltic states or Romania for the West before 1989. (Only members of the German minority were permitted to move to West Germany, and this on payment of a fee, not unlike a ransom.) East-West mobility from these countries and the entire eastern half of the continent is evidently a result of the neoliberal order. The first to migrate en masse were East Germans moving to West German states. They were followed beginning in the mid-nineties by around two million Poles heading west. Since the crisis of 2008–9, Romanians, Latvians, and Lithuanians have made up the largest groups of intra-European labor migrants.

In broad terms, these developments were the result of post-communist societies gradually acquiring the human capital to be able to deal with economic crises without relying on the welfare state. In a sense, these populations have been conditioned by neo-liberalism to be mobile and flexible, two key values of this ideology. Those who stay at home often try to survive in the traditional manner of subsistence farming—that is, with a few cows, a large vegetable garden, and occasional jobs.

In comparison to the new EU states, the Mediterranean societies of Europe are far less mobile. Today, the waves of guest workers arriving in Germany from these countries in the 1950s and '60s are a distant memory. Spain and Italy have themselves become major immigration destinations since the nineties. Unlike Latvia or Romania, they had not experienced a phase of mass migration before the crisis. Social and cultural norms also play a role. With greater affluence than the new EU states and better welfare provisions, Mediterranean countries provide relatively stable security nets. Spanish and Italian families have tried to additionally cushion the effects of the crisis by, for instance, letting their unemployed offspring live at home. Before the crisis, it was common for young people to find their first job in their parents' business or through family ties. Personal networks, then, take precedence over spatial mobility. Moreover child daycare is expensive and hard to find (at least in comparison with Germany, the Netherlands, or Scandinavia), and the state does not provide child allowance independent of income. These factors additionally increase young people's reliance on family networks, confirming dependencies that conflict with neoliberal principles.

The labor migrants from the new EU states, in contrast, act in accordance with the neoliberal system. This offers little security, but encourages and rewards mobility across the European Union with far higher wages in Western Europe. By deciding to migrate for work, the citizens of the new EU countries are making "rational choices"—another key term in the practice of and philosophy behind neoliberalism—and placing pragmatism over emotional ties. The majority would stay at home if wages there were higher and job prospects better. Surveys have shown that financial considerations are the main motivation for migrating, with most interviewees expressing the intention to return home after a few years. However, this emotional bond has a best-before date: if migrants start to feel they are better off abroad, they revise their plans to return.[21]

## Mental Maps of Europe

Public perception of Southern and Eastern Europe is a field in which many interesting differences and commonalities can once again be observed. In the postwar period, negative views of Mediterranean societies and cultures faded away north of the Alps.[22] The once-widespread derogatory stereotypes of Southern Europe had emerged around the same time as those of Eastern Europe. They were rooted in eighteenth-century, occidentalist, Enlightenment-based ideas of progress. Neoliberalism, with its orientation toward a specific model of historical development—in this case, liberal democracy combined with market economy—is also rooted in this tradition. In the light of their firm belief in progress, Enlightenment thinkers in the West began to reflect on the state of modernity, and contrast it against the supposed backwardness of some countries or wider regions of Europe. However, negative perceptions of Southern Europe have always been counterbalanced by Romantic admiration, as Goethe's *Italian Journey* or William Turner's paintings of Italy illustrate.

After the Second World War, views of Southern and Eastern Europe began to diverge. As Larry Wolff wrote in his important book *Inventing Eastern Europe* more than twenty years ago,[23] the West's existing negative stereotypes of Eastern Europe were reinforced during the Cold War era. The Soviet Union and the Eastern Bloc were perceived as threats. As a consequence, Russia's place in Europe and (the homemade construct of) Western civilization was called into question. Even countries like Czechoslovakia were seen to fall within Eastern Europe (and therefore the subdiscipline of Eastern European history), although historically the Kingdom of Bohemia had far more in common with Austria or Germany than with Russia. Of course, prejudices against Eastern Europeans did not disappear when the Eastern Bloc crumbled. On the contrary, they were initially reinforced, as the rash of Polish jokes in circulation in Germany indicated.

Southern European countries were more positively perceived in the West because they were on the right side of the Iron Curtain. Pre–Cold War prejudices against the region were no longer mobilized by other Western countries. In 1955, West Germany concluded its first recruitment agreement with Italy, inviting migrant labor. Agreements followed with Spain, Greece, Turkey, and even one socialist country, Yugoslavia. Labor migration, along with the burgeoning tourist industry, facilitated intersocial encounters. Initially, this spawned new conflicts and prejudices (as the pioneer generation of Italian guest workers experienced to their dismay), but eventually, the various Western European nations grew accustomed to each other. The process was aided by gradual economic convergence: Spain, Portugal, and Greece became more affluent after the European Community's expansion southward, like the countries of Eastern Europe in later years.

Since the crisis, this divergence has ended. The gulf between the South and the North (now including parts of the former East) of the "old" European Union has reemerged. Today "the South" is once again widely regarded as backward, poor, or reform-averse. The latter is an especially damning verdict in a neoliberal perspective. The pejorative acronym "PIIGS" was invented for the economically depressed Mediterranean EU countries. (The second "I" stood for Ireland, and was removed when that nation left the euro rescue plan.) In 2010, international investors and rating agencies employed PIGS to refer to Portugal, Italy, Greece, and Spain. Intentionally evoking disconcerting associations with the animal world, the acronym groups "the South" together as one large area, like the Eastern Bloc previously. Whether there is any factual basis for this blanket categorization is another matter. Even in terms of finance, the countries it referred to had disparate problems. Spain had exorbitantly high private household debt and a real-estate bubble; Italy's most pressing problem was government debt. While Spain's dependence on the construction sector puts a strain on the economy, Italy is struggling with a crisis in industry. As mentioned above, Greece is in many respects an exceptional case, and Portugal has different problems again. The latter was the only southern EU country to accept the reform program prescribed by the Troika (the trio made up of the EU Commission, the European Central Bank, and the IMF) largely without resistance.

Regardless of these differences, the countries labeled "PIGS" suddenly found themselves in one and the same semantic barnyard. Neither popularly perceived differences, especially between North and South, nor actual divergence are new to modern European history. But the decisive role of international actors (such as the authors of the acronyms) in creating a materialist mental map of Europe is new. As affluence has increased since 1989 in most of the new EU countries, and the South languishes under economic decline, a role reversal has taken place: The Mediterranean countries are now expected to make the kind of economic and cultural adjustments that were demanded of the EU candidate countries in the nineties. They are called on to rationalize their economies, be fiscally conservative, and, in principle, conform to a Protestant ethic. These demands point to an asymmetry of power extending beyond the sphere of economics.

The international response to Latvia's post-2008 crisis management program illustrates the role reversal that has taken place. In the wake of the crash, the Latvian government acted as if it had already introduced the euro by pursuing a policy of "inner devaluation" rather than devaluing the national currency, the lats (which would have caused higher inflation and debt revaluation). While stabilizing the lats, it cut government employees' salaries by an average 25 percent, slashed pensions and social security benefits, closed schools, and reduced hospital services to life-saving operations only. As a consequence of this unprecedented austerity program, economic output plummeted by almost 18 percent in 2009 alone and the population shrank by 9 percent by 2011.

From 2010, the GDP started to grow again—albeit from its drastically lowered level. In early 2013, the IMF president Christine Lagarde made an official visit to Riga to "celebrate Latvia's achievements," as she announced. Metaphorically patting herself and her organization on the back, she declared that the IMF was proud to have contributed to the Latvian "success story" with its rescue package. In late 2008 the monetary fund had granted assistance to the tune of $7.5 billion—an enormous sum for such a small country.[24] Her choice of terminology, evoking Hollywood-style rags-to-riches dreams, demonstrates neoliberalism's discursive power. The media sent news of the Latvian success story across the globe (as it had the Polish and Chilean success stories[25]), with coverage appearing in all the major German newspapers as well as the *New York Times* and the international business press. The German business daily *Handelsblatt* headed its article with a paraphrase of a GDR propaganda slogan about the Soviet Union: "Learning from Latvia Means Learning Victory" ("Von Lettland lernen, heißt siegen lernen," originally "Von der Sowjetunion lernen, heißt siegen lernen").[26] The unprecedented wave of emigrations in the wake of the crisis was not mentioned in any of the articles.

Latvia's economic triumph raised the international pressure on Greece to follow suit, as Christine Lagarde, among others, demanded. But a repetition of the Latvian scenario would have triggered the migration of a large section of the Greek population. If this occurred at the same rate as in Latvia since 2009, several hundred thousand Greeks would have to be absorbed into other EU countries. If the Italians and Spanish became as mobile as the Romanians, the handful of EU countries with robust economies would have to accommodate over three million Italian and two million Spanish jobseekers. These figures are, of course, hypothetical.[27] They are merely intended to illustrate the fact that a standard formula for dealing with crises in all countries alike is surely not a recipe for success.

The experts' praise of Eastern European reform countries and criticism of the southern EU member states, especially Greece, is symptomatic of a long-term shift in the mental map of Europe. The East-West axis is being replaced by a North-South divide, both in terms of how the European Union sees itself and how it is seen from outside. This reconfiguration was caused partly by the economic changes discussed above, but is also self-reinforcing. Cultural stereotypes have always influenced economic decisions. Foreign direct investments in Poland are increasing not least because the country is no longer perceived as part of backward Eastern Europe.

In summary, the countries of East Central Europe have managed to overcome a number of prejudices in the last twenty-five years. The best example is the change in meaning of the term "Polish economy." Once used by German nationalists as a byword for disorder, poverty, and backwardness, today it stands for prosperity based on initiative and industry. Southern Europe, in contrast, has returned to its starting point of around 1960, before the period of economic and social convergence that lasted three decades.[28]

The younger generation feels the decline the most. People under age thirty-five in Italy earned an average 540 euros taxable income per month in 2013.[29] Even if one does not factor in the unemployed in this age group, the work income of young Italians falls below the minimum social welfare payment in Germany or Austria, including housing allowance. And the cost of living is higher in Italy than in Germany. No comparable statistics on Poland were available at the time of writing, but Poles under thirty-five certainly earned more than 540 euros per month, adjusted to purchasing power; at least those living in growth centers such as

Warsaw, Poznań, or Wrocław. Italy's pitifully low wages and trend toward temporary employment contracts have forced even working members of the younger generation to live with their parents. Even a room in a shared apartment is too expensive for many. While a certain attitude of complacency among the *mammoni* (male adults living with their parents) might be a contributing factor, independent living is precluded by the financial circumstances. Interestingly, there is no female equivalent of *mammoni*, perhaps indicating that daughters show greater determination to leave home. High rents also inhibit mobility in Poland, Slovakia, and the other new EU countries (and increasingly in Germany), but more living space is available now than in the nineties due to the construction boom of the last twenty years.

Despite the crisis, plenty of Italian teenagers and twenty-somethings can be seen driving sports cars, wearing designer clothes, and carrying the latest iPhones. They seem exempt from austerity. Their elevated social status is not a result of their own hard work, or an indication of high qualifications. Wealth in Italy is usually inherited—the offspring of wealthy families can still live off the fat of the land. Social inequality is perpetuated by the Italian tax system: employment income is taxed moderately, as in Germany and Austria, consumer items at a much higher rate, but inheritance and wealth hardly at all (similar to the United States). In a parallel to the employment situation, those from secure backgrounds can expect to remain comfortable, and probably have more than enough to live on. Those from poorer backgrounds, who do not have a permanent employment contract or who move to another town to seek work, struggle to make ends meet.

The Italians speak of "not arriving at the end of the month" ("non arrivare a fine mese"). Surveys have shown that 30 percent of Italians do not earn enough to live on; 37 percent have to ask their parents for support; 14 percent turn to other relatives for help and 8 percent to friends. (Interviewees were able to give several answers.) Only 45 percent of Italians earn more than they spend and are able to save some money over the year.[30] The situation in Greece is even worse. There, a third of the population no longer has health insurance and ekes out a living on the poverty line.

These statistics show once again that the neoliberal order weakens the very social resources it depends upon. Lower incomes, rising unemployment, and reduced social benefits inhibit the mobility and flexibility of people in Southern Europe. At the same time, social, generational, and regional inequality has grown. The situation calls for a reform package extending beyond the ten points of the Washington Consensus or the current IMF programs. But so far none has been forthcoming. Italy's government of experts under Mario Monti (prime minister 2011–13) evidently realized that liberalization and deregulation could only cause superficial adjustments and would not solve any fundamental problems. (There was not much left to privatize as most state enterprises had already been sold.) The poor record of this proreform *governo tecnico* raises the question of whether European welfare states can be reformed at all when their troubles are as deep-rooted as Italy's. Perhaps gradual reforms are as difficult to accomplish in existing state systems as they were in the Eastern Bloc in the eighties.

Recent developments in Greece hint that this might be true. None of the three (socialist, technocrat, or conservative-led) governments in power between the outbreak of the crisis and the elections of January 2015 managed to convince the Greek public that the reforms were the right way to go. This is astounding considering that Greece's bloated apparatus of state was so inefficient it even failed to gather regular taxes. But all the governments were reluctant to introduce more fundamental reforms, as they would have hit their major clientele of civil servants. For this reason, they did not venture beyond austerity measures, which further depressed the already declining economy.

The Greek economy's sustained downward spiral unleashed a fatal political dynamic. Even the pre-2015 conservative government had shown a tendency to blame foreign creditors for the austerity choking the country. The left-wing populist Syriza party was even more inclined to mobilize images of bogeymen. It painted a picture of Angela Merkel, the European Union, and the IMF as a kind of demonic triumvirate, which it promised to fight by deflecting the austerity measures. The party's charismatic leader, Alexis Tsipras, won the elections of January 2015 on the back of this argument. Instead of forming a coalition with the moderate Socialists, Syriza joined forces with the right-wing populists, shifting the political contest even further into the populist corner. Negotiations with the international creditors were therefore ill-fated from the start. After months of wrangling, Syriza broke off negotiations in July 2015 and called a referendum on further reforms and "rescue packages." The populace unsurprisingly voted against them. But as banks closed and the Greek economy teetered on the brink of collapse, Athens was compelled to return to the negotiating table and ultimately accept even more drastic austerity measures and inroads into its national sovereignty. It is not, then, a very promising new start. The tax increases enacted in summer 2015 will further dampen economic growth. The fifty billion euros projected to be made by the Greek trust fund agency charged with selling the companies to be privatized is probably just a pipe-dream, if the history of the German Treuhand trust agency is anything to go by. After five years of economic depression, the mood among the population is at rock bottom. It is certainly not a good investment climate. But perhaps the statistical effect that has helped economies in the past will work again: having shrunk since 2010 by around 35 percent, at one point the Greek economy must surely rebound.

It is still too early to judge the Greek tragedy in a historical perspective. One day historians will analyze it as a case of failed modernization *within* the EU, as in all the years since it joined the European Community in 1981, Greece evidently failed to establish sustainable economic structures or a functioning apparatus of state. In the midterm, the tragedy was caused by the ineffectiveness of the old political elites and parties. A short-term reason for the continuing crisis was the combination of Syriza's hubris and inexperience with the lack of creativity shown by the international finance organizations and the European Union, along with its unofficial leader, Angela Merkel. Apart from proposing ever more austerity measures, Brussels and the IMF had few ideas or visions on how to strengthen the Greek economy. In the midst of the depression, purposeful investment (in, for instance, solar power) might have created hope and jobs.

Perhaps Greece would indeed benefit from a new start, like Eastern Europe after the revolutions of 1989. But Poland and the other former Eastern Bloc countries had the advantage that their old systems had become defunct. This made it possible to break up traditional structures and start afresh in many areas. One example is university education. Salaries at state universities and the Polish Academy of Sciences were so low in the early nineties that scholars were forced to find other sources of income. As a result, they founded private colleges, offered private courses of study, or became involved in extraoccupational courses offered at the university. Thanks to this burst of initiative twenty-five years ago, Warsaw today has a highly diverse and dynamic academic landscape.

Furthermore, the regime change prompted Poland's international creditors to make financial concessions. Poland had accumulated foreign debt worth 75.9 percent of the GDP by 1990. With only weak exports, it was incapable of paying it all back. In 1991, half of these debts were deferred or cancelled—for mostly political reasons. Poland was the key state in the Soviet Union's outer sphere of influence. The West could not allow the reforms there to fail, at least not on account of communist-era loans. Compared to Poland twenty-five years ago, the Southern European countries are even deeper in debt. Italy, a key state of the European Union, currently has debts worth over 130 percent of its GDP. Unlike Poland in the early nineties, only some 20 percent are foreign debts. Superficially this seems a relative advantage.[31] But Italy's large domestic debt is not any easier to relieve if prohibitive losses for domestic banks and government bond holders are to be avoided.

The comparison of debt levels raises the hypothetical question of how a country like Italy *might* develop if it followed the IMF's recommendations and passed an extensive neoliberal reform program. Italian companies might invest more in the domestic market again (unlike the postcommunist countries, Italy does not suffer from a shortage of capital). Foreign investors' interest might also be stimulated. Italy is a large market with an educated population and moderate labor costs. Investors would be delighted by the Italian work ethic: unlike in Germany or Austria, plumbers and car mechanics do not resolutely hang up their overalls on Friday afternoon not to return until Monday morning. The *bella figura* principle applies not only to clothing but also to personal conduct; appearing moody and uncooperative is unacceptable. The traditional principle of *volontà* readiness to help—is still an important factor in the national culture, and distinguishes Italy from the postcommunist fustiness that societies are still struggling to banish. In some respects, then, Italy is better poised to end the crisis than Eastern Europe was in the early nineties.

But even if Italy underwent a "mighty, magnificent modernization" as Poland did (in the words of the respected Catholic weekly *Tygodnik Powszechny*[32]), one may presume that only a few growth centers and social groups would benefit. Following the Eastern European pattern, the South and other regions plagued by weak infrastructure would hardly profit, or only in the very long term. The postcommunist countries enticed investors with sweeping tax exemptions. It would be difficult for a country such as Italy, which is shouldering a huge burden of public debt, to do the same.

Without inspired political and social vision, efforts to reform Italy according to neoliberal principles have had little impact. Although the technocratic government under Mario Monti managed to identify a number of shortcomings of the existing system—for instance, the taxi business is characterized by mediocre to bad service and high, seemingly arbitrary prices, another problem familiar to the United States—and convey the necessity of emergency measures, it failed to create any promising prospects for the future. Perhaps the reform politicians' arguments would have been more convincing if they had been more radical. In 2013, the IMF published a paper advancing the idea of a 10 percent property tax to deal with the debt crisis. The proposal sparked a debate in Germany.[33] But in Italy, the same discussion was soon stifled. Liberals and Social Democrats did not want to risk antagonizing a large part of society and their own voters. The status quo may be unjust and even untenable in the long term but the social majority is still comfortable with it.

In contrast, reform politicians in Eastern Europe twenty-five years ago addressed publics who were aware of the pitfalls and dysfunctionality of the old systems. In addition, they identified three important goals to work toward: the introduction of market economy (amid fierce debates over which variation); the consolidation of democracy, despite a popular lack of identification with the new system and reluctance to participate in elections; and accession to the European Union. The conditions for generating wealth were good: they had human capital and international support, the global economy was growing, and peace prevailed. These conditions cannot be created artificially more than twenty-five years later. The crisis-torn countries in the South of the European Union are already integrated into Europe and democratically governed and have market economies. The South is, then, not the new East, even though it is increasingly perceived as such.

# 9

# Cotransformation

## The Case of Germany

Transformation studies have tended to deal with Eastern Europe as if it were a box, with fixed boundaries drawn during the Cold War. The West was present in this box, but only as a model of development and superior advisor for reforms. Transfers in the reverse direction, by contrast, and the question of whether and how changes in the postcommunist world influenced the West, have rarely been addressed. In the period after 1989, the winners of the Cold War felt so smugly superior (evident in book titles such as *The West and the Rest*) that learning from the East would have appeared sacrilegious.

Studying the European and global feedback effects of transformation also poses some serious hermeneutic problems: Although similar phenomena can be observed in Western as in Eastern Europe (such as neoliberal reform debates), direct causal connections cannot necessarily be inferred. Moreover, certain changes in Western Europe might be due to stimulation by an external, global source, such as the Washington Consensus. The distinction must also be made between loose connections, correlations (causal connections), and interdependence (necessary and mutual connections). The term "cotransformation," then, is not advanced as a simple explanation but to signify links between the contemporary history of Eastern and Western Europe (and maybe extending to North America). It does so under the premise that "East" and "West" are not inflexible units and that the states and societies within these wider areas have diversified both in relation to each other and internally.

The cotransformation is especially intriguing in Germany. A number of towns in East Germany have become so prosperous and picture-perfect that they have prompted some observers (especially in the now run-down former industrial heartland of West Germany) to question the sense of the billions in transfer payments for East Germany. Poverty is not restricted to the East anymore; West Germany now has its own Rust Belt that looks almost as depressed as the former GDR in the 1990s. In short, the West has become partially like the East, and the East has become like the West. Overall, the countries lining the former Iron Curtain have undergone the most striking changes in the last twenty-five years. Is this due to the proximity to the formerly opposing Bloc countries—combined, in Germany, with unification in 1990? Have the reforms in Eastern Europe placed Sweden, Germany, and Austria under greater pressure to adjust to neoliberal economic and social policies?

These questions have methodological implications. Historical research into cultural transfers has now found plenty of examples to refute the earlier notion that systems, models, or ideas spread more or less unchanged from country to country.[1] Neoliberalism is one example of a school of thought that ever more countries adapted rather than faithfully and rigidly adopted.[2] Neoliberal "speech acts" played a crucial role in spreading neoliberal ideas. In public, and especially on the international stage, politicians such as Václav Klaus portrayed themselves as radical market liberals.[3] But the content of their acts varied depending on whether they were addressing national or international publics, and did not always reflect the policies they actually pursued. This underlines the need to integrate a more data-based social history with a more discursive cultural history approach.

The following section will start by analyzing the reception and discussion of the course and outcomes of postcommunist transformation by the public in the West, and especially in Germany. On the basis of its findings, it will go on to ask whether the reforms in East Central Europe and East Germany in particular contributed to the cotransformation of (former) West Germany. Three topics from recent German history will be spotlighted: the social and labor market reforms of 2001–5, the debate on "civil society," and the role of politicians who come from the GDR, but have made their career in the transformed Germany. *Time*'s 2015 Person of the Year, Angela Merkel, is among them.

## Social and Labor Market Reforms in Germany

In the first years after unification, influences from East Germany were simply not welcome in the former West Germany. A number of former GDR dissidents called for amendments to Germany's constitution in order to carry over some elements of the democratic revolution to the West. But German chancellor Helmut Kohl, acting the Cold War victor, refused such demands point-blank. Still, the mood in Bonn was less triumphant than that in the United States, where Ronald Reagan, George H. W. Bush, and prominent intellectuals such as Milton Friedman and Francis Fukuyama consigned socialism to the scrap heap of history. The Kohl government simply would not be told how to shape the constitution, or the future of the country, by civil rights activists who had been campaigning for a "third way" between capitalism and socialism, or for a reformed and independent GDR, just one year previously. Consequently, unification was legally accomplished by the "accession" of the five "new German states," pursuant to article 23 of (West) Germany's basic law, rather than by drawing up a new constitution "on completion of unity"[4] as had been envisioned under article 146. Furthermore, the (West) German government did not want any changes made in the economic sphere. The tradition of collective bargaining agreements, the strong position of the banks as shareholders in industry, and other elements of Rhineland capitalism were retained. In political and legal terms, German unification was the *extension* of the "old" Federal Republic of (West) Germany.

Expectations at first were that the former GDR would be quickly hauled up to the level of prosperous West Germany. This goal legitimized transfer payments of billions to the five new German states. But following a brief postunification boom, from which

West German industry profited most, the first serious problems began to surface. Instead of the projected privatization revenues of six hundred billion German marks, the Treuhand trust agency incurred a loss of over 250 billion marks (amounting to around fifteen thousand marks per GDR citizen, or almost ten thousand US dollars at the time).[5]

Unemployment in the former GDR soared, placing a huge financial strain on the German labor office. The federal pension fund was also stretched to its limits by the many new clients in East Germany, and proliferation of early retirement programs. The public health insurance system struggled with the lack of contributions from the new German states and was obliged to regularly transfer funds to East Germany.[6] Modernizing the former GDR's decaying infrastructure devoured countless additional funds. In overall terms, then, the "Reconstruction East" (*Aufbau Ost*) program—which some observers have more aptly paraphrased as "Deconstruction East" (*Abbau Ost*)—and its social and political consequences created large deficits in the welfare state and national budget (see fig. 9.1).

Despite the country's many fundamental problems, Helmut Kohl won the parliamentary elections of 1994. The electorate was not only rewarding Kohl for unification, but also responding to his party's "red socks" campaign, which played on Cold War fears and warned of the dangers posed by a left-wing alliance. It was a genuinely conservative election campaign, promising to continue "Reconstruction East" in the five new German states and preserve the status quo in West Germany. The difficulties caused by transformation were thus duly externalized. The problems *in* East Germany were presented as problems *of* East Germany. They were personified by the metaphorical *Jammerossi*, the passive, complaining East German, who calls out for help from the West because he does not know how to help himself.

The mood turned in Kohl's last years as chancellor. The problems in the former GDR had grown so acute that they were starting to hurt the west of the country, too. Doubts began to arise about the superiority of the West German system. Economists criticized government regulation of the economy, the close ties

**Fig. 9.1.** A faded sign in Magdeburg, April 2004. Photo: DPA/Landov.

between German industry and banks, and the country's high public expenditure. The employment offices could not cope with the level of unemployment in East Germany; social security contributions were steadily raised. Eventually, Chancellor Kohl's government faced accusations of a "reform gridlock." The language of transformation, with its fixation on reforms, had reached the former West Germany.

Kohl's main contender, the Social Democrat Gerhard Schröder, won the elections of 1998. It was clearly time for a change—like his role model Konrad Adenauer, Helmut Kohl had missed the right moment to step down—and Schröder's promise of a "new center" (*Neue Mitte*)[7] proved popular. Inspired by Tony Blair and "New Labour" in the United Kingdom, and in some respects Bill Clinton in the United States, it marked the first time in Germany that the old right-left political axis was sent spinning. This move of the Left to the center was a scenario familiar from Eastern Europe. The Polish, Hungarian, and Czech Social Democrats had achieved landslide election victories between 1993 and 1998 by distancing themselves from classically left-wing ideas. Schröder in turn declared he intended "not to do everything differently, but a lot better" and styled himself a man of action, who would combat unemployment with an "alliance for jobs."[8]

In its first year in office, however, the SPD-Green coalition government was preoccupied with internal problems. A sudden rift with Oskar Lafontaine, a prominent representative of the SPD's left wing, stunned the party. A short time later, it suffered an unexpected election defeat in the politically significant state of Hessen, where the Christian Democratic Union (CDU) had successfully waged a dirty campaign against dual citizenship—a symbol of the ongoing dispute over German national identity. In summer 1999, the government sustained a blow from abroad when the *Economist* described Germany as the "sick man of the euro" and listed the reasons for the country's economic stagnation.[9] This indirect comparison with the Ottoman Empire, which had been considered the "sick man of Europe" one hundred years earlier, ignited a widespread debate in Germany, which Schröder—the "media chancellor"—observed with vigilance. He subsequently charged his minister of employment and social affairs, Walter Riester, with reforming the German pension system. Riester, a high-ranking representative of the trade unions, was a clever choice: he had the best credentials for convincing workers of the need for social cuts (analogous to the popular, down-to-earth Solidarność activist Jacek Kuroń, who defended neoliberal reform policies in the same position in Poland). The pension system was in most urgent need of reform as the above-mentioned transfer payments to the former GDR had plunged it deep into the red.

The central element of the pension reform of 2000–2001 was the introduction of a capital-based pension scheme (dubbed the *Riester-Rente*) to supplement the government's pay-as-you-go pensions, which were set to be reduced beginning in 2011.[10] Pension cuts were part of the package. This unleashed a wave of protests, with trade unions and opposition politicians lambasting the government. The protests touched a weak spot of almost all neoliberal reforms: they went hand-in-hand with social cuts despite their claim of making existing systems more efficient and therefore affordable.

The transfer payments to East Germany were not the only grounds for the pension reform. In 1997, the contribution rate for state pensions had risen to over 20 percent, costing both employees and employers (who each paid half) additional billions. And the international hegemony of neoliberalism was at its zenith. The "new economy" boasted high growth rates, and stock prices climbed to record highs (though the attack on the World Trade Center soon brought the boom to an abrupt end). The time seemed ripe for a capital-based pension scheme in which contributions were invested on the stock exchange. (In the United States, where private pension schemes are common, the pitfalls of the system became painfully apparent after the stock market crash of 2008—many pensions were drastically reduced.) The insurance companies, which stood to make billions out of such a scheme, naturally promoted the idea.[11] Their arguments were supported by contemporary doubts that the pay-as-you-go model, in which beneficiaries are paid out of the contemporary contribution pool, would stretch far enough. The latter system conflicted with neoliberalism's principle of private ownership. Capital-based pensions, like life insurance plans, give contributors the sense of saving individually for their old age, but they are vulnerable to stock market fluctuations, not to mention crashes. And of course, having a contribution account at an insurance company is not the same as having private assets or a savings account.

As well as responding to global trends, policymakers in Germany and Sweden also took developments in Eastern Europe into account when debating the privatization of old age provision, hitherto a key responsibility of the welfare state. Most postcommunist countries had introduced privately financed components to their pension systems in the late nineties. The first to do so had been Latvia, which passed legislation on capital-based pensions in 1995, in response to the deep economic crisis following independence. Unemployment was so high that there was only one contributor to every one-and-a-half pensioners. To prevent pension contributions and tax subsidies from going through the roof, Latvia also raised the age of retirement.[12] This measure encountered the greatest resistance (as it did in Germany some years later). Few Latvians could afford to pay into a private insurance scheme and many did not know what to make of the pension fund. Yet despite the protests and various hitches delaying its introduction, after a few years the reform was generally deemed a success.

An interesting aspect of the Latvian case is its close connection with the Swedish pension reform, the foundations of which were laid by the parliament in Stockholm in 1994.[13] Swedish economists were very active in the Baltic states, where they advised neoliberal reforms. In the late nineties, however, the dynamic reversed. The system changes in Latvia and Estonia showed Sweden's reformers that they were on the right path. Developments converged in 1998, when Sweden and Estonia simultaneously introduced a "three-pillar system" (the word "pillar" suggesting unshakeable stability) to play a key role in privately financed old-age provision. A short time later, Poland followed suit.

A dazzling impression of the brave new world of private pensions is conveyed by the Estonian pension scheme's slickly designed website, which is also accessible in English and Russian.[14] At the push of a button, potential pensioners can check how meager their state pensions will be. (As in many Western European industrial nations, these are derived from two sources: a contribution-based fund and tax subsidies.) By far the largest link in the header leads to the Baltic stock exchange index, Nasdaq QMX—a name that calls to mind high-octane business and the riches of Manhattan. A click on this link reveals flashing charts and examples of stocks one could invest in. This site makes German or French pension scheme information look as dry as dust.

In relation to these trends in East Central Europe, as well as on a global level, Germany was a latecomer to pension reform and privatization. But supposed backwardness can sometimes be an advantage. When the Wall Street stock market crashed in 2008, dragging the retirement funds of millions of Americans with it, German pensioners were able to observe from a safe distance. Being more closely linked to wages and salaries, their pensions were not as vulnerable to stock-market vagaries (though Americans are currently enjoying rising stock market prices again).

After the pension system, Germany reformed its labor market in 2003–5. The reforms (formally divided into four legislative packages, known as "Hartz I–IV") were modeled on Blairite policies and involved even deeper cuts in the welfare state and social security system. Prior to the reform, most benefits had been calculated according to the amount of contributions previously paid into the social security systems. Contributors had a legal claim to these payments. For twelve months, unemployed people received at least 60 percent of their previous net wage (68 percent until 1982; 63 percent until 1993). This initial phase of unemployment benefit was known as *Arbeitslosengeld*. Subsequently, beneficiaries were entitled to a reduced payment (*Arbeitslosenhilfe*), also aligned to their previous labor income, for an indefinite period. By today's standards, social benefits in Germany were generous.

The Hartz reforms de facto abolished *Arbeitslosenhilfe* and replaced it with *Arbeitslosengeld II*. Rather than relating to previous wages, payments under this system (technically termed *Lohnersatzleistung*— "wage-replacement benefits") were calculated according to the claimants' current situations, incomes, and assets. Municipal social assistance was traditionally allocated in a similar way, to satisfy the beneficiaries' most basic needs. Now skilled workers, craftspeople, and many others who had fallen into long-term unemployment had to prove how poor they were in order to claim state benefits. It was a humiliating experience that conflicted with the popular understanding of the welfare state. (*Sozialstaat*, as the welfare state is known in German, has deeper implications than the English equivalent, including a social claim to a caring government, and acts as a point of identification among the public.) *Arbeitslosengeld II*, better known in Germany as "Hartz IV," is only paid to those who have used up their savings (down to a minimal personal allowance). It is possible, then, for individuals who paid social security contributions for several decades before becoming unemployed to be refused benefits because they still possess some personal assets. Unemployment thus became synonymous with deprivation. Affecting over four million people (plus their dependent family members) in the years 1997–99 and 2002–6, it was a problem confronting a substantial part of German society.

The basic premise of these reforms was that the prospect of losing all one's assets would motivate the unemployed to become more active and flexible. Tony Blair's slogan "welfare to work" put the principle in a nutshell.[15] The carrot-and-stick approach (promoted in Germany as *Fördern und Fordern*—support and demand, or give and take) was designed with a new idea of man (and woman) in mind. Citizens were expected to be autonomous subjects who took active control of their lives. By this logic, their freedom—a key concept in reform legislation—was coupled with an obligation to assume responsibility for themselves and the general good. In keeping with this conception, it was presumed that the unemployed would make *rational choices* in favor of badly paid jobs over the Hartz IV rate of benefits (€331 per month in East Germany or €345 in West Germany in 2004). In fact, unemployment was to be completely banished. In the new parlance, people were either employed or "jobseekers" (*Arbeitssuchende*).[16] One aspect the policymakers forgot to consider was the number among the population, including single mothers and those caring for sick relatives, who were not in any position to act as *homo economicus*.

The stringency with which Hartz IV was applied elicited furious criticisms and protests. Under the previous unemployment regulations, it had been relatively easy to turn down a position on grounds of overqualification or unreasonable distance. But the new legislation demanded that jobseekers accept whatever the employment agency offered them, even if it was a "one-euro job." Officially termed *Arbeitsgelegenheit mit Mehraufwandsentschädigung* (literally, "work opportunities with additional expenses compensation"), these were mostly community services that beneficiaries performed for one euro per hour in addition to their Hartz IV income. Soon, legions of frustrated one-euro jobbers were trailing through the parks of Berlin, collecting litter and the city's notorious piles of dog dirt. Anyone who refused to report for duty or attend training courses as instructed risked immediate cuts in their benefits. Another highly unpopular innovation was the deduction of spouses' earnings from calculations of potential beneficiaries' "need." Couples tried to circumvent this by sham separations, but faced the possibility of a visit from an inspector, checking for two toothbrushes in the bathroom or other evidence of cohabitation. It was a paradoxical situation: individuals were treated as subordinates, subjected to authoritarian monitoring, at the same time as being encouraged to be free and flexible citizens and take control of their destinies. In the former GDR, especially, the chances of finding new employment were exceedingly slim, with thirty-six jobseekers contending for each vacancy around the time that Hartz IV was introduced. Residents of Leipzig even revived the revolutionary tradition of Monday Demonstrations, much to the chagrin of Chancellor Schröder, who condemned it as an abuse of history (see fig. 9.2).

The Hartz laws also included provisions facilitating the founding of *Ich-AG* (the equivalent of "Me, Inc."), a program to smooth

**Fig. 9.2.** Mass protests against Hartz IV in Leipzig, August 16, 2004. Photo: ullstein bild / snapshot photography / Tobias Selliger.

the path to self-employment (at the cost of inferior social security), and the creation of a low-wage sector (*Niedriglohnsektor*). The relatively high wages in Germany were seen to have become a deterrent to industry. In transformation-era Berlin this problem was evident in many of the city's major construction sites. The government district and the new Potsdamer Platz (an area where the Berlin Wall had degraded the city in the worst possible way), for instance, were built largely by foreign subcontractors. Often the architects and the site managers were the only German-speakers. The many British, Italian, or Portuguese construction workers were obviously prepared to work for lower pay than the locals. But it was the "cheap competition" from Eastern Europe that featured most prominently in public debates.

The low-pay sector created by the Hartz reforms worked on the principle that the state added to (*aufstocken*) benefits under Hartz IV for recipients who pursued a regular occupation (and who were consequently known as *Aufstocker*). Internationally, demands had long been voiced for a "negative income tax" whereby governments would raise the income of the working poor by providing tax subsidies. One of the most prominent supporters of a state-subsidized low-pay sector was Milton Friedman—surprisingly, as the state bureaucracy it required contradicted the neoliberal goal of minimizing government. In the 1980s, several US Rust Belt states had conducted trials of the low-pay sector model on the initiative of the Chicago School.[17] But every one of the trials was aborted when it emerged that employers stopped creating regular jobs in these circumstances, and that the unemployed who were now earning again frequently contented themselves with their topped-up incomes instead of looking for new and better jobs. These unintended side effects apparently did not deter Germany's reformers. Why not? One answer lies in German society's traditional confidence in a strong state, which, paradoxically, was needed to push through neoliberal reforms. Another answer can be found in Eastern Europe: while currency union caused wages and salaries in the former GDR to rise several times higher than those in neighboring Poland and the Czech Republic, Hartz IV lowered them back to the same level. Admittedly, this comparison is somewhat imbalanced, as Hartz IV beneficiaries could apply for a number of additional subsidies, such as accommodation allowance. Few received the minimum rate only, but up to a maximum of €651 for single people and €1,251 for families[18]. However, the topping-up system made cheaper German labor available, and reduced the incentives for German companies to employ Eastern Europeans (something already subject to a number of restrictions under the treaties regulating EU expansion, more on which in chapter 10) or relocate production to Eastern Europe. In summary, after upward alignment—the strategy in 1990—had failed, Germany tried downward alignment by means of the labor market reforms and the establishment of a low-pay sector.

The reality of the postcommunist world had caught up with unified Germany. It hit the former GDR especially hard, bringing social cuts and high unemployment. This is reflected in the statistics on social inequality, which grew considerably after the introduction of reforms. The Gini index, cited above in chapter 5, rose from 25 in 2001—roughly comparable to Scandinavian welfare states—to 30.4 in 2007, exceeding Slovakia and Hungary. Bear in mind, however, that the standard of living in Germany was still far higher. Poverty in rich industrial countries is always relativized by local wealth.

Officially, average incomes in Germany's eastern neighbor countries did not influence Hartz IV rates. But it was certainly no coincidence that the largest labor market reform in Germany was introduced almost simultaneously with European Union enlargement (which took place on May 1, 2004, but had been resolved at the Copenhagen summit in late 2002). When the SPD-Green government implemented its reforms, it was known that the citizens of the new EU member states would be entitled to settle in Germany by 2011 at the latest (after completion of the seven-year interim period). After the Hartz IV reforms, Germany's eastern neighbors no longer had a competitive advantage in terms of labor costs, at least not over the 1.3 million working poor topping up their benefits.[19] The "cheap competition" (*Billigkonkurrenz*), a derogatory stereotype used to describe employees from Eastern Europe, could now be found within the country.

An inherent problem seems to have been thereby overlooked: When individuals can be employed so cheaply, there is little incentive to create regular, better-paid positions or to adhere to collective bargaining agreements. Entire branches of industry have become Hartz IV sectors. One example is the call center business, into which the state paid 36 million euros in wage subsidies in 2013.[20] Another problem is temporary work: A number of firms no longer supplement their own workforce if their commissions increase but turn to temporary employment agencies. They operate on the principle of maximum flexibility and minimum pay, combined with agency charges. Here, too, a kind of downward alignment has taken place. Short-term employment contracts are now the norm in Poland, in turn rendering temporary employment agencies superfluous.

Comparison with Eastern Europe reveals another commonality between the SPD-Green social reforms in Germany and the neoliberal reforms that were implemented in the early nineties in Poland and the Czech Republic: the manner in which they were communicated by politics. Gerhard Schröder presented his "Agenda 2010" using an apodictic rhetoric, never failing to point out that the reforms were either "necessary," "unavoidable," "inescapable," or "the only alternative"—period. His reputation for blocking any further discussion earned him the nickname of the "that's that chancellor" (*Basta-Kanzler*). It is hardly likely that Schröder, a former radical and leader of the SPD youth organization, copied his rhetoric from the similarly unequivocal Margaret Thatcher.[21] He was more inspired by Tony Blair, who often pursued as hard a line as Thatcher, but cloaked it in affability. A second element of SPD-Green rhetoric was the use of progress-related terms such as "modern age," "modernization," "innovation," "new departure," and the all-important "future." These terms implied that the opponents of reforms (again, as in the early nineties in East Central Europe) were fusty, blockheaded reactionaries. The dialectical construct of old versus new, nostalgic versus progressive, was one of the key mechanisms of neoliberal reform discourse.

## The Civil Society Debate

Around the time the German reforms were implemented, "civil society" was a buzzword and a fashionable topic of debate. It is especially relevant here because it also relates to east-west transfers. Eastern European dissidents relied on emancipative societies offering nonviolent, organized resistance, to oppose the repressive states they inhabited and overcome dictatorships. Their approach echoed earlier concepts such as nineteenth-century Poland's *praca organiczna* (literally "organic work"), by which Polish society aimed to assert itself against the partition powers Prussia, Russia, and Austria. In the 1980s, the goal of a civil society that practiced resistance was actually realized in Poland through the Solidarność movement. When martial law was imposed and leading trade unionists imprisoned, the Solidarność cells in industry survived. The oppositional press went underground; lecturers organized a "flying university" (*uniwersytet latający*). When the communist regimes were toppled, the notion of active civil society seemed vindicated.[22]

But in 1990 the civil rights movements splintered into many different factions, and the public soon had more pressing concerns than attending demonstrations. The countries in transition received democratic constitutions. But low election turnouts, the electoral success of political unknowns such as the Polish-Canadian millionaire Stanisław Tymiński—who gained 3.8 million votes in the Polish presidential elections of 1990, relegating Prime Minister Tadeusz Mazowiecki to third place—and the public's unease with democracy and its institutions (shown by opinion polls) were all signs that the new order was built on shaky ground. There was still some way to go to reach the goal of a politically active society, building democracy from below.

Eastern European intellectuals including Adam Michnik in Poland, György Konrad in Hungary, and Jiří Gruša in the Czech Republic, continued to propagate the ideal of civil society during the nineties. They were frequent guests in Germany, where they contributed to many discussions. Further west, in the United

274 | CHAPTER 9

States, a parallel debate was being conducted about the relationship between the state and society. In 1995, political scientist Robert Putnam published the essay "Bowling Alone." It lamented the rise of social isolation and the demise of community involvement in the USA.[23] The remedy Putnam proposed was to create more grassroots initiatives and associations to build up the necessary social capital for a functioning democracy. Politically, the author sympathized with the Republicans. Like them, he idealized small-town America and local community life, but was skeptical of "big government." The myth of big government was one of the most successful ideological constructs of neoliberalism. While it has a long prehistory in American libertarian thinking, its popularity grew in the 1980s until it eventually became a rallying cry of the Tea Party movement.

In Western Europe, Liberals, Social Democrats, and Green parties also advocated public initiative and an active civil society. The spectrum of proponents thus ranged from conservative Americans in the United States to mostly anti-American Greens in Europe. The leftist civil rights movement, inspired by Michel Foucault and Antonio Gramsci, regarded government as a repressive apparatus. The East German and Czech ecological movements, important centers of opposition in the eighties, were similarly critical of state power. The common ground thus shared by such a surprisingly broad spectrum was a desire for more public participation to strengthen democracy from below.

Germany was particularly receptive to calls for a more active civil society because of the strain on the welfare state after unification. Indeed, the concept seemed to suggest solutions for so many of the political and social problems of the late nineties. At the same time, it was vague enough to be interpreted in a range of political lights. The ruling Social Democrats mobilized it for their purposes and organized a number of congresses under the banner of activating civil society. Party committees debated it. The German Green Party embraced it. By the time sociologist Ulrich Beck, best known for his concept of reflexive modernity, warned against its becoming misappropriated by party politics it was already too late. Gerhard Schröder's manifesto for a civil society (which he tautologically termed *zivile Bürgergesellschaft—zivil* and *bürgerlich* both meaning civil)[24] marked the pinnacle of this trend in 2000. In the United Kingdom, Tony Blair's advisor and intellectual mentor Anthony Giddens also promoted the idea of civil society. From the loose jumble of notions associated with it, Blair and Schröder selected as the prime element the principle of reducing the state.

British and American skepticism about the state was echoed in Poland. In a country with a long history of foreign rule, Polish society traditionally viewed government with mistrust. These attitudes were in turn similar to views in Italy, where the state (especially the tax authorities and the Guardia di Finanza) is widely perceived as hostile, or at any rate a troublesome money-grabber. According to Putnam, southern Italy's economy and society are weaker than those of the north precisely because of the lack of public involvement and low confidence in the state, plus a shortage of social capital.[25] With almost eschatological assurance, experts and policymakers advanced the idea that activating civil society would solve a range of political and social problems. Moreover, the philosophical aspect of their arguments assured them the intellectual high ground, which the SPD in Germany was keen to take.

But none of this helped in the face of mass protests, which Chancellor Schröder unleashed with Agenda 2010. After a series of regional election losses and a defeat in the traditional SPD stronghold North-Rhine Westphalia, Schröder decided to take full risk and call new elections. The subsequent election campaign reflected the predominance of neoliberal reform discourse. Promoting his Agenda 2010, Schröder promised that the painful cuts it entailed would eventually bring improvement. Indeed, the first signs of economic recovery were already beginning to show. Opposition leader Angela Merkel advocated an even more radical program of reforms, devised by the Christian Democrats at the party conference in Leipzig in 2003. She announced the "largest and most extensive reform package . . . for a long time" and the dawn of a "second era of enterprise-founding" in Germany.

Merkel defended social security cuts, accusing "work-shy" recipients of "welfare abuse," and called for even more radical changes to the welfare state. She envisioned a "premium-based model" for the health insurance system, where everybody would pay a flat rate of two hundred euros instead of the progressive, income-based contributions. This poll tax for health care, she claimed, would have both economic and social advantages; the increase in "personal responsibility and personal provision" purportedly reflected the "free side of social security."[26] The Christian Democratic Union further stepped up its neoliberal rhetoric after the party conference in Leipzig. In 2004, Friedrich Merz, then deputy speaker of the CDU in parliament, suggested reducing the number of tax brackets to three and lowering the top tax rate to 36 percent. Although the proposed reforms were still far removed from the flat tax rates of the Baltic states and Slovakia, they would have marked a drastic change for Germany. To implement them, Merkel had chosen constitutional law expert and former constitutional court judge Paul Kirchhof. The prospective finance minister was not a party stalwart, but a technocrat. This made him vulnerable to attack, as Chancellor Schröder realized. The chancellor did not miss the opportunity to portray Kirchhof as an out-of-touch academic and the CDU reform program as a threat to society.

Angela Merkel's neoliberal election program almost ended in fiasco. The expected landslide victory for the Christian Democrats shrank on election night to a marginal lead of only a few tenths of a percent over the SPD. It was the CDU's worst election result since the war. Merkel had to abandon the idea of forming a coalition with the liberal FDP, which would have agreed to a flat tax system, and enter into a Grand Coalition with the SPD instead. In the run-up to the elections, the parties had competed to present the most radical reform program. But afterward, a different dynamic set in. The two major parties now tried to emphasize their caring sides. It could then be argued that neoliberalism had passed its peak before the crisis of 2008–9. Nonetheless, Germany continued to debate the flat tax, and retained the Hartz IV laws.

Reform discourses in Eastern Europe had an observable impact on Germany, not to mention on a global level. But pension reform and flat tax systems were two subjects on which opinions markedly shifted. Without going into the technicalities in depth, these two fields are examined below for evidence of east-west transfers.

German debates about the welfare state since the late nineties revealed a striking trend: growing doubt about the existing system and interest in international developments. In 1998, the influential conservative newspaper *Frankfurter Allgemeine Zeitung* published a lengthy article on capital-based pension systems in Latin America and Eastern Europe. It cited OECD expert Monika Queisser, who extolled the virtues of capital-based old-age provision—that is, supposed greater security and larger returns. Six months later, the weekly news magazine *Der Spiegel* ran an alarmist article on the impending "bankruptcy" of the existing pension system. Poland was mentioned for having introduced a third, privately financed "pillar" in its own system.[27] The magazine drew much of its information from an article in a specialist periodical on pension reforms in East Central Europe. In this way, the Baltic and Polish models entered into German specialist discourse, and later politics.[28] However, the importance of Eastern European models should not be overstressed. German policymakers and their advisors had examined the Swedish and American pension systems far more closely. Nevertheless, around the turn of the millennium there was a noticeable shift in focus among experts and in the media toward the "reform countries."

In the debate that was sparked about the flat tax some years later, the wind definitely blew from the east. The Baltic states and Slovakia garnered more attention than almost ever before; the conservative press in Germany praised their reformers' courage and vision.[29] Yet the prehistory and inherent conflicts of the reforms were largely overlooked. Latvian social policy only makes sense in the light of the economic slump the country experienced after independence. Poland reformed its tax system because unemployment rose to almost 20 percent in the late nineties; there were far too many pensioners for the younger generations to support with their social security contributions. While some international analysts took these background factors into account,[30] most commentators were concerned primarily with presenting foreign models as foils for the debates in their own country. They picked and mixed examples from abroad to serve as justification for neoliberal reforms at home. This discursive form of globalization has hitherto received little attention, perhaps because it is conceived as being driven mostly by finance and commerce.[31]

Lastly, it remains to add that most Eastern European countries overturned their pension reforms after the crisis of 2008–9. Hungary took the most radical action, in 2010 forcibly nationalizing the private pension fund it had introduced twelve years before (in order to plug the crisis-torn hole in the national budget, as discussed in chapter 8). In 2013, Poland confiscated Polish government bonds held in the private pension fund. This partial nationalization was to some extent motivated by budgetary considerations. It brought down the national debt in relation to GDP by several percentage points.[32] But it also allowed the government in Warsaw to redress high administration charges and low profit participation (of insurance companies including Allianz, Aviva, AXA, and Generali). In the course of this reform of a reform, Poland transformed the compulsory pension contributions into voluntary provision—analogous to the *Riester-Rente* pension scheme in Germany. Eastern Europe's flat-tax systems also came under pressure, and were abolished or relaxed in the Slovak and Czech Republics.

In recent years, the equitable distribution of tax burdens has been hotly debated in all Western countries. Unlike in the nineties and during the second wave of neoliberalism, the most pressing concern is no longer how to lower tax rates but how to maintain the welfare state, or at least some kind of basic government provision. Apple, Google, Amazon, Starbucks, and other hitherto privileged companies can no longer blithely use all the tricks in the book to evade taxation. Under pressure from the media and the public, some companies have even volunteered to pay slightly higher taxes. The trend toward reducing government is over. The introduction in the United States of the Affordable Care Act (Obamacare), albeit based largely on private insurance companies, is another indication of this.

Neoliberalism seems to have passed its peak in Eastern Europe, too, as pension schemes are revised and tax policies changed.

Taxpayers are happy to no longer have to contribute to the profits of international insurance companies. But as governments reassume greater responsibility, the onus is on them to do the math and provide for future pensioners. Will they manage? The latest pension reform in Germany does not give cause for optimism. In early 2014, the German government came up with a €6.5 billion "mothers' pension scheme" (*Mütterrente*) to benefit mothers of children born before 1992. This clear prioritization of the older generations at the expense of the young is further evidence of the short-term time frames in which democratically elected politicians operate—in parliamentary terms, not generations. If the new Polish government elected in the fall of 2015 fulfills its pledge to lower the pension age, the younger generation there will also be overburdened.

The German Social Democrats reworked their country's pension reform in 2014 without any direct external impetus. They interpreted their—rather meager—election result as a mandate to perform an about-face, in order to correct past injustices (some of which SPD Chancellor Schröder had been responsible for). They no longer heeded the warnings of economists or experts, whether German or international. This was indeed a turnaround from the SPD-Green government's pension and labor market reforms of 2001–5, which were introduced on the grounds that Germany had become uncompetitive and that other countries had evidently found better solutions for their problems. The semantics of these discourses are a sign that Germany, too, went through a process of *catch-up modernization*, motivated by a sense of having fallen behind as a country. It was a new experience for it to be measured not only against the West but in some respects also against the reform-hungry East.

## The Politicians Who Came in from the East

Initially, there was a distinct power asymmetry between East and West Germany, which later became blurred. After the fall of the Berlin Wall, it was clear at every encounter between the bulky, towering Helmut Kohl and the short, slight Lothar de Maizière (the last premier of the GDR) which of the two had the last word. Because German unification de facto entailed the extension of West Germany, "the East" (as the former GDR was commonly known) became defunct, and served at most as a negative point of reference. The unequal relationship between the two parts of Germany gave rise to stereotypical perceptions of those who inhabited them. In the eastern part, there were *Ossis*, perceived mainly as sad, dejected figures, not the courageous protesters or revolutionaries of fall 1989. In the other part, there were *Wessis*, the embodiment of overbearing, know-it-all boastfulness, who were fickle and untrustworthy.

The frustration and mutual recriminations rapidly intensified from 1990, fueled to a large extent by resentment of the financial cost of unification, which the population gradually came to notice. In spring 1991, the German government raised the statutory unemployment insurance contribution by 2.5 percent. Exactly one year after currency union, it introduced a "solidarity tax" on income (the *Solidaritätszuschlag*, commonly known as the *Soli*), along with a corporate income tax and other new taxes. In this way, German taxpayers cofinanced German unity. Many West Germans were under the impression that only they were paying the *soli* for East Germany. But the tax was of course levied in all German states, including the five new ones. In a sense, then, East Germans were required to show solidarity with themselves.

In early 1994, social security costs increased again when pension contributions were raised by 1.7 percent. As the West German media pointed out, around one hundred billion marks flowed from West Germany to East Germany each year. Resentment grew among the West German population, less on account of the sums transferred, which remained rather abstract in the popular perception, than the sense that the payments were for nothing, and that the supposed recipients lacked gratitude.

In this context, the stereotypes of the *Jammerossi* and the *Besserwessi* crystallized in the late nineties (see fig. 9.3). Such antagonisms may appear ridiculous today, but they were the source of serious dispute at the time. The conservative coalition party CSU

**Fig. 9.3.** "Stop whining, people will think you're an Ossi!" *Jammerossi* caricature by Reiner Schwalme, 1990.

threatened to stop transfer payments to the former GDR if so much of the East German population continued to vote PDS, the socialist successor party. Former German Chancellor Helmut Schmidt reprimanded the East Germans for their querulous behavior in an interview with *Der Spiegel*. Succumbing to a brief fit of rage, he said their "constant moaning . . . makes me vomit," and pointed out that women in East Germany received higher pensions on average than West German females.[33] This was because women's employment had been higher in the GDR, which Schmidt and his interviewer refrained from mentioning, no doubt to avoid addressing the thorny issue of gender inequality.

In 1998's election campaign, Gerhard Schröder pledged to make the reconstruction of East Germany his personal priority. In the summers of 2000 and 2001, he spent several weeks touring the new German states, talking to the locals about their concerns. As someone who had known hard times as a child, Schröder was probably an empathetic listener. He praised the East Germans' lifetime achievements and tried to exude a sense of optimism. But his own administration's Hartz laws put a particularly tight squeeze on East Germany, where a much larger proportion of the total population was affected than in West Germany. On the other hand, ever since the collapse of communism East Germany had had far fewer regular jobs ensuring full entitlement to unemployment benefits. Therefore the changes resulting from the Hartz laws were not as unsettling in the East as they were in the West. In effect, a fledgling low-pay sector also existed there previously, as standard wage rates were rarely paid in a number of branches of the economy. As the labor market reforms brought conditions in West Germany into line with those in the East, earlier preconceptions gradually started to dissolve.

Paradoxically, the growing gap between rich and poor thus helped the two parts of Germany to grow together and to approach the politically desired "inner unity." As Hartz IV and the fate of the unemployed affected the entire country, the differences between East and West faded into the background. One might say that the reforms did more to equalize Ossis and Wessis than did the welfare payments of the nineties. It was now clear that East Germans were not just staying at home and waiting for benefits from the West. The over two million East-West migrants and the four hundred thousand commuters (in 2000) were living proof of that. Gradually, prejudices were replaced by respect. This was evident, for instance, in the fact that the "Ossi" tag was increasingly dropped in favor of the more neutral *Ostdeutsche* ("East Germans").

Angela Merkel's election to the post of CDU chairperson also altered intra-German stereotypes, and balanced the power asymmetry between West and East. Merkel was the first woman and the first East German to become chairperson of a large political party. But she did not shout it from the rooftops. Merkel proceeded like most other migrants to the West and aimed to fit in by acting inconspicuously. In 2002, East German sociologist Wolfgang Engler published the insightful book *Die Ostdeutschen als Avantgarde*.[34] It paints the scenario of a postindustrial society that runs out of work, making reference to the East Germans' creative approach to coping with job insecurity and short-term contracts. Gerhard Schröder, meanwhile, had a more traditional working society in mind when, in a speech given in 2004, he described the East Germans as "willing to work and flexible" and commended their "tremendous achievements" since unification.[35]

Some of the East German elites took up this thread to weave their own neoliberal discourse. For instance, when Chancellor Schröder visited a successfully modernized former collectivized farm in the East German state of Brandenburg, the manager defiantly announced that "nobody in the West can tell us our people are not flexible or mobile."[36] The prime minister of Brandenburg, Matthias Platzeck, who later rose to become SPD chairperson, tried in a similar way to build the East Germans' confidence. He maintained that the East Germans had "overcome tremendous upheavals in the last two decades. [They had] worked longer than others and travelled longer distances to find work—not because they are better people, but because the circumstances forced them to."[37] Whenever the East Germans' adaptability and willingness to work was stressed, the West Germans were effectively called on to do likewise and accept reforms and social cuts. Cotransformation, then, took place on a discursive and social policy level, and was rooted in the transformation crisis that affected East Germany before the rest of the country.

Angela Merkel, the future first female chancellor, refrained from public reevaluations of her fellow East Germans. But she knew from personal experience what it was like to go through the upheavals of 1989 and the ensuing transformation. She had been working as a chemist at the Academy of Sciences of the GDR before the revolution. State-related institutions such as this were particularly vulnerable to dismissals and restructuring, partly for political reasons and partly because their research departments became superfluous. Under these circumstances, it was a smart move to look for a different job. In late 1989, Merkel took on a post as system administrator for the oppositional party Demokratischer Aufbruch, initially on a voluntary basis—that is to say, in a civil society context—later rising to executive. The party disintegrated after its chairman became embroiled in a Stasi (communist secret service) scandal in spring 1990. Nevertheless, Merkel secured a position as deputy spokesperson for the last GDR government, thus entering the public relations sector. A short time later, she joined the CDU, was voted into the Bundestag, and rose to become a minister in Helmut Kohl's government. Merkel's professional trajectory from chemist to system administrator, public relations woman, and politician was propelled by flexibility and mobility. Thus she was able to support the CDU's reform program of 2003 with convictions drawn from her own experiences. However, the party's near-defeat at the parliamentary elections of 2005 showed that the majority of voters were not convinced. So Merkel once again demonstrated flexibility and softened some details of the neoliberal reform program. Basically, however, she continued Schröder's political course, and did not revoke any laws that had already been enacted.

Although Angela Merkel's motivation toward reform distinctly flagged after the near-defeat of 2005 and subsequent social policy rivalry with the SPD, it has not completely dissipated. She continues to support further reforms in the crisis-torn countries of southern Europe. Germany's state president Joachim Gauck, elected in 2012, was at least as deeply affected by the transformation era as was Chancellor Merkel, and also adheres to a liberal concept of freedom (not, in this case, neoliberal, but the much older idea of political liberalism). Raised in the East German city of Rostock, the former Lutheran pastor advocates personal autonomy within society. He believes that citizens have a responsibility to themselves and the general public, and should not abuse the solidarity of society or the welfare state. Normative, anthropological principles such as these, as well as the financial "necessity" of economizing, were key values advocated by Gauck and Merkel, and shaped Germany's political landscape.

The neoliberal reduction of freedom to an economic principle cannot be easily imposed from without on established democracies, as the cases of Italy and the other southern European EU countries have shown. The reform recipes prescribed to the South follow the trends of the nineties and the German welfare state reforms of 2001–5. Their uppermost goal is to economize by reducing budget deficits and limiting government intervention. Second, they aim to reform their labor markets by relaxing employment protection and cutting unemployment benefits, and thus create incentives for jobseekers. The programs assigned to Greece, especially, reveal many parallels with the reforms of the nineties. For instance, measures to reduce staff in public service were previously introduced in the former GDR. Those affected were given one year's notice to look for another job. But while this measure affected hundreds of thousands in the five new German states, a mere thirty thousand civil servants have hitherto been hit in Greece, and the populist left-wing ruling party hoped to revoke even these dismissals. In the summer of 2015, the international creditors and the European Union compelled Greece to establish a Greek trust fund agency to privatize state enterprises. Recalling the Treuhand in name, the Greek trust fund will, one hopes, not make losses as huge as those of the East German privatization agency. The creation of special economic zones was also discussed (as it had been for the former GDR, but never realized to avoid creating stiffer competition for the rest of Germany[38]).

Getting, and keeping, the IMF on board was certainly a smart move by Angela Merkel. It improved the reform programs' prospects of success in southern Europe, since the monetary fund not only provides financial backing but also lends the neoliberal demands more weight. Without this external support, it would be hard to implement the reforms inside the European Union or the eurozone. Hence the rhetoric with which Merkel and the Troika presented them: every cut was declared to be "necessary" and "without alternative." In view of the southern European countries' high national debts and structural problems, perhaps it was even true.

In the more recent past, however, an alternative *has* emerged: to support the new EU member countries, Brussels devised a cohesion fund and other measures based on Keynesian principles. As shown above, this second Marshall Plan worked best in East

Central Europe. (Its success in Romania and Bulgaria is questionable, as both countries absorbed only a small part of the EU funds.) Social and spatial inequality steadily decreased until the crisis of 2008–9; even the regions on the eastern periphery of the European Union profited from the general upward trend.

Yet no comparable program has been introduced in the southern EU, where the focus has remained on austerity. Why is this? Programs for investment in solar energy, for instance, spring to mind as an obvious solution. (Consider Israel's example, where solar-powered hot water storage tanks have been installed on most roofs as a way of reducing dependency on gas imports.) But the European Union has had its fingers burned. It transferred assistance to the tune of hundreds of billions to Greece, Spain, Portugal, and southern Italy in the eighties and nineties. It is reluctant to launch renewed expenditure programs in the South since these earlier funds did not have the desired effect.[39] Furthermore, its substantial support for its new member countries in East Central and Southeastern Europe was not unconditional. The recipient countries were required to "do their homework" in return (to use the somewhat patriarchal parlance now also used on southern Europe)—to order their national budgets, restructure their finances, strengthen the rule of law, and implement administrative reforms.

When it came to exporting the reform agenda, Merkel was able to proceed without answering to an electorate, unlike in domestic politics. Perhaps this explains why she did not introduce further socials cuts in Germany while demanding extensive reforms of other European countries. But the success of the Syriza party in Greece, Beppe Grillo's Cinque Stelle in Italy, and most recently the Podemos party in Spain shows that this hard line can backfire. In all of these countries, left-wing populists gained widespread support by portraying Merkel, the European Union, and the international finance organizations as bogeymen who were entirely to blame for their countries' economic and social woes. These movements, and the right-wing populists who are more successful in northern Europe (and more dangerous on account of their xenophobic tendencies), can only be debunked if the dialectic between technocracy and populism is broken. The traditional parties must recast the term "reform" in a positive light and use it to develop visions for the future. But the future lies, above all, with the younger generation and its prospects. And these were far more promising after 1989 than at the end of the period considered here.

# 10

# The Roads Not Taken

## Mass Participation in Revolution

The great European revolutions have signposted the political land-scape of the continent in the nineteenth and twentieth centuries: 1789, 1848, and 1917 were pivotal, symbolic years. Conservatives, liberals, and leftists all formed their political identities around their standpoint on the respective revolutions. But the changes of 1989–91 do not raise any such passions. All political camps gener-ally approve of the toppling of communist regimes and the fall of the Berlin Wall, except perhaps the unreformed communists who can still be found in the Czech Republic, Russia, and Ukraine. This shallow consensus about 1989 has caused the values behind the revolution to fade from memory, or to become reduced to the rallying cry of "freedom." This last, possibly somewhat melan-cholic, chapter therefore explores why the revolutions of 1989 left the societies west of the Iron Curtain so unmoved. It inquires into the values the revolutionary actors fought for (focusing specifi-cally on Prague and the former Czechoslovakia), and how these values were received by Western European observers. It also asks how Western societies responded to the changes and challenges in Central and Eastern Europe. This question has gained new rel-evance through the revolution in Kyiv in 2014. In many ways, this most recent revolution in European history resembled the events in 1989. But again it is doubtful whether the West has realized the implications and reacted adequately.

The public in Western Europe experienced the revolutions as a media event, filtered through their TVs. That is true even of West

Berliners, who bided their time while the East Berliners stormed the Wall. Only a relatively small group of students, teenagers and residents neighboring the Wall actually celebrated the historic moment with the East Germans. The Viennese certainly stayed at home, although the borders with Hungary and Slovakia were only an hour's drive away. Apart from a few journalists, foreign visitors were rare in Prague in November 1989. It was, then, literally a one-sided revolution, which took place on the eastern side of the Iron Curtain.

There were reasonable explanations for the Western Europeans' reserve. Travel restrictions on the Eastern Bloc countries were still in force; even visitors from the immediate vicinity of the Iron Curtain would have needed visas, and to go through border controls and other inconveniences, to reach the hotspots of the revolution. The uncertain outcome of the protests also deterred Western Europeans from making the trip to Leipzig, East Berlin, Prague, or Bratislava. But so did the wall in their minds. Despite the increasing contact that the policy of détente had facilitated, Western and Eastern European societies had grown apart. The older generations still recalled old animosities, bred by the traumatic experiences of the Second World War and the early postwar period. People on the west side of the border with the GDR, and of the various Bavarian and Austrian regions adjoining the ČSSR, lived with their backs to the Iron Curtain. As the prosperity gap grew in the 1970s and '80s, they gained a sense of material distinction which reinforced the geographical separation. They now regarded the citizens of Eastern Bloc countries, including the relatively affluent East Germans, as poor neighbors. Sometimes this inspired solidarity. West Germans sent tens of thousands of food parcels to Poland when martial law was proclaimed in 1981. But on the whole, the saturated societies of Western Europe had accommodated to the Cold War constellation, perhaps even more so than the Americans, whose president ordered in 1987 in his famous Berlin speech, "Mr. Gorbachev, tear down this wall," and who flocked to Prague in their thousands in the early nineties.

Although there were valid reasons, then, for Western Europeans' failure to participate in the revolutions of 1989, in retrospect it seems like a missed opportunity. This is especially true of those segments of society that were very much inclined to become mobilized for other causes. In the 1980s, hundreds of thousands took part in demonstrations against nuclear power plants and the deployment of new NATO missiles in Western Europe. Yet in 1989, when Eastern Europeans took to the streets to end Soviet hegemony and communism, the peace protesters and environmental activists stayed at home. Today, a similar scenario is repeated with respect to the Russian intervention in Ukraine—in any case, no major demonstrations against it have yet been seen outside Russian embassies.

Perhaps revolutionary internationalism has always been a utopian ideal rather than a concrete practice. Yet there are examples of cross-border participation in contemporary history. Thousands of young Poles traveled to Ukraine in 2004 to take part in the Orange Revolution and join the protests in Lviv and Kyiv. The Polish daily *Gazeta Wyborcza* even published a special edition for its eastern neighbor. Polish empathy with Ukraine is rooted in the countries' historical ties and common experiences of the years 1989–91. It is hard to gauge whether Poland's solidarity influenced the course of events. But the knowledge that they were not alone in their struggle was certainly an important psychological support for the Ukrainian protesters. In view of this, Austria and Germany have shown shamefully scant solidarity with the democratic revolution in Ukraine. Their eastern neighbors were much more internationalist in the stormy fall and winter of 1989. In their revolutionary enthusiasm, Czechs and Slovaks even tried to mobilize their Western neighbors. In early December the Slovak civil forum (*Verejnost' proti násiliu*, literally "public against violence") organized a cross-border protest march from Bratislava to Hainburg in Austria, across the Danube.[1] The destination of the march was no coincidence: in 1984 it had been the scene of demonstrations involving tens of thousands of Austrians protesting against plans to build a giant Austrian-Slovakian-Hungarian hydroelectric plant.

Czech environmentalists had also protested against the feared damage to the unique Danube flood plain, and risked reprisals to forge contacts with the Austrian and German environmental movements. At the demonstration in Hainburg, the spokesperson of the Slovak civil forum gave a euphoric speech that ended with the words "Hello Europe." This was no mere greeting but a statement of intent, underlining the fact that Slovaks (and Czechs) belonged to this—normatively perceived—Europe, too.

To follow up, Czech civil rights activists organized various smaller actions along the Czechoslovak-Austrian border. Some sailed on large rafts along the Danube, singing and celebrating. The residents of the Moravian border town Břeclav organized a five-mile-long human chain to the nearest Austrian village. For a while, this spontaneous form of international understanding worked well. The Austrians welcomed their eastern neighbors with wine, sausages, coffee, and cakes. As in Berlin in 1989, there was a brief moment of unity.

But the internationalism of the Czech civil forum (*Občanské Forum*, or OH) and its Slovak equivalent did not last. It petered out as the cold weather set in and revolutionary activists became generally demobilized. When the last communist Czechoslovak government stepped down and Václav Havel was elected president (unanimously, by the federal parliament, as if the old communist ballot rules still applied), the opposition saw its primary goals achieved. By the time parliamentary elections were held in June 1990 (following those in March 1990 in the GDR), mass protests were no longer needed—insofar as one accepted the parameters of parliamentary democracy. In fact, the power play between parties and political organizations in the run-up to the elections had contributed to demobilizing the public. The situation confounded many Czechoslovaks, as it did the GDR citizens who had valued the sense of political and social unity that characterized the mass protests of fall 1989. The pluralization of political life may have been a sign of greater democracy, but its party political ramifications were not well received by the public.

This was evident in the low election turnouts. In Poland and Hungary, less than two-thirds of those eligible to vote took part in the first free elections; not even half participated in the Polish local elections of May 1990. The sudden redundancy of revolutionary activity went hand in hand with rapid transitions to parliamentary systems of government dominated by party politics. Their precipitate birth left the fledgling democracies decidedly anemic.

Societies and politics were further fragmented by nations reckoning up with their communist past.[2] In winter 1989–90, tens of thousands of Czechoslovaks took to the streets in protest against the continuing presence of communist functionaries in local administrations, the media, and industry. But the disclosure of ever more information on citizens' past activities as informers, including leading dissidents, soon diverted attention from other issues. An analogous situation arose in the former GDR. Here, even the first democratically elected premier, Lothar de Maizière, was suspected of Stasi collaboration. In the consequent atmosphere of general mistrust, demands were voiced for a renewed, more thorough "cleansing" of public life and administration. (There was less concern about the economy.) This created a rift in the former opposition, as one side called for the removal or punishment of all security service informers while the other warned against embarking on a witch-hunt. The social and economic cuts introduced in the spring and summer of 1990 swept away any remainder of the euphoria of fall and winter and finally replaced it with widespread disenchantment.

Left-wing West Germans and their intellectual mentors regarded the revolution with skepticism from the start. German sociologist Jürgen Habermas described it as "rectifying" (based on the slightly different German term *nachholend*).[3] He thus implied that it marked a departure from the wrong track of communism and a return to the right path of development toward Western modernity. As if wishing to externalize the antiutopian aspect of this evaluation, in fall 1989, Habermas attacked the revolution's "total lack of ideas that are either innovative or oriented towards the future."[4] He particularly disapproved of the fact that what had started as a political revolution had turned into a national movement in the GDR. The slogan "We are one people" ("Wir sind ein Volk"), which echoed with increasing intensity across Leipzig and East Berlin from November 1989 (and modified the earlier slogan of "We are *the* people"—"Wir sind das Volk") conflicted with Habermas's typically left-wing West German antinationalist sensibilities. So did the "return to old, national symbols" he observed in the other Eastern Bloc countries.[5] Indeed, the GDR's imminent unification with the FRG was set to conclude the political development of the first successful German revolution. Given the asymmetry of power between the two Germanies, it could only end in political alignment or, as Habermas would have it, rectification. It should be noted, however, that this was more in the interests of West German politics than of East German civil rights activists. All demands from East Germany to amend the constitution in the light of unification and introduce more elements of direct democracy or enshrine more basic social rights were quashed by the conservative government in Bonn.

Were the West German and Western European Left any more open-minded? Habermas at least took the revolutions of 1989 as an opportunity for a critical appraisal of his own political environment. He found the Left to be overly preoccupied with statism and smugly self-satisfied about the "welfare compromise." The remedy he proposed was to consolidate the "autonomous public sphere," a domain he conceived in sectoral terms, along the lines of a civil society falling between public and private life. The civil rights activists of East Central Europe held similar views, but Habermas acknowledged them in neither his German nor his English text on the revolution (at least not by name or in literature references). The only Eastern European he mentioned was Alexander Dubček, whose demand for a Third Way Habermas regarded as unrealistic. Despite being skeptical of statism, Habermas called for the state to rein in the market. Meanwhile, the reform programs introduced by Leszek Balcerowicz and Václav Klaus were establishing precisely the reverse conditions.

British contemporary historian Timothy Garton Ash had witnessed the turmoil in Warsaw, Prague, and Berlin with his own eyes. Politically, he is harder to pin down than Habermas but it would surely be fair to describe him as a left-wing liberal. In his book *We The People*, published shortly after the revolution, he expressed sincere admiration for the Eastern European civil rights activists. But over the course of the year 1990, his tone changed. He began to develop a far more critical view of figures such as

Lech Wałęsa and Václav Havel—the former on account of his political vacillation and the latter because of his moralizing.[6] He articulated his criticisms in publications, including an essay for the
journal *Transit. Europäische Revue*. This periodical was founded in
1990, partly in response to the opening of Eastern Europe, at the
Vienna Institute for Human Sciences (*Institut für die Wissenschaften
vom Menschen*, IWM), and will serve here as a rich source for a case
study and spot checks on the West's reception of the revolution.
Its editor, the Polish philosopher-in-exile Krzysztof Michalski,
invited a broad spectrum of authors to contribute to the first edition. From Left to Right, all political leanings were represented,
and supplemented by articles by respected Eastern European
dissidents.

Garton Ash was personally acquainted with prominent civil
rights activists in Poland, Czechoslovakia, and the GDR. But in
his *Transit* essay he cited only a few press articles and an interview
that Václav Havel had given *The Times* of London. He refrained from
examining the ideals of 1989, concentrating instead on the birth
pangs of the new democracies in East Central Europe. He issued
an explicit warning against the "risk of over-democratization" and
gave pragmatic advice on how to deal with the contemporary challenges. In his view, the most promising approach was to adopt the
German model of parliamentary democracy, and he called on the
government in Bonn to become actively involved in the former
Eastern Bloc. Though this may have been good advice, and at-
tests to his cosmopolitanism, Garton Ash's adherence to Western
conceptions for interpreting the changes in Eastern Europe is jar-
ring. His essay makes no mention of the democratic groundwork
performed by the Solidarność movement or the long tradition of
Czech democratic thought, which was an important influence on
Havel. Instead, Garton Ash warned against too much democracy.

The liberal, Oxford-based sociologist Ralf Dahrendorf also
took the role of a political-realist advisor in an essay in the same
edition of *Transit*. Dahrendorf praised the reformers' courage but
argued that social cuts and wage limitations, even a "deep valley
of tears," were inevitable.[7] Similarly to Garton Ash, he mentioned
various dissidents and politicians from postcommunist countries,

and was evidently most impressed by Leszek Balcerowicz. His deepest concern was the dilemma he feared the new democracies faced: predicting that a boom analogous to that in Western Europe after 1945 would not occur for several years, he warned that the unavoidable social cuts and resultant frustration could pose a threat to the young democracies. Alternatively, pursuing democracy could jeopardize the necessary reforms. Perhaps it was the latter scenario that prompted Dahrendorf to refer to the modernizing dictatorships of East Asia as external examples. Japan, South Korea, and Taiwan, he pointed out, generated wealth before introducing democracy in the first postwar decades. He rejected the use of the term "revolution" in the context of 1989. In his view of history, revolutions always caused more harm than good, especially on an economic level. To him, 1989 was, instead, a "transition" to a liberal democracy and market economy, which he hoped the West would assist, as actively and sympathetically as possible.

Dahrendorf echoed Habermas's call for the consolidation of civil society, which he saw as a "great project"—"the best of the modern age."[8] But while Habermas argued for "reining in" the market and Garton Ash avoided questions of economic policy, Dahrendorf supported radical liberalization. To him, it was a sign of dissociation from "illiberal regimes." He also referred admiringly to Friedrich von Hayek, one of the founding fathers of neoliberalism.

The essay by François Furet in the same issue of *Transit* stands for the conservative reception of the revolution. Furet started by tracing a long critical arc from "the fading star of October" (meaning the Russian Revolution of 1917), which, he proposed, had allowed "the star of 1789 to shine again."[9] At the same time, he relativized the significance of the French Revolution and criticized the way it was carried out. Furet condemned the Jacobins (thus continuing a long tradition of French conservative thought) and claimed that human rights were the only enduring achievement of 1789. Consequently, he argued that the revolutionary idea should be distinguished from the democratic idea. To Furet, the radical changes of 1989 confirmed the persistence of "capitalism and democracy" as the "key elements of modernity." Hence the subtitle of his essay was "Return Ticket". In principle, his line of argument echoed Francis Fukuyama's thesis of the end of history. But Furet was so preoccupied with France's reception of the revolution that his essay reads over long stretches like a French soliloquy. Only one page of the entire text was devoted to Eastern Europe. Here, Furet declared democracy and capitalism to be an "inseparable couple" but simultaneously distanced himself from the Polish and Hungarian "cult of free enterprise."[10] Eastern Europeans, to summarize his point of view, should embrace capitalism, but not too much.

These articles by German, British, and French authors are some examples of the 1989 revolution's reception among Western European intellectuals. Yet the essay by Habermas and the articles in *Transit*—founded by a Polish exile—can also be regarded as evidence of *non*-reception. Habermas and Furet repeated arguments they had previously advanced elsewhere (Furet in a text to mark the two hundredth anniversary of the French Revolution, Habermas in his writings as a pioneer of German social democracy), and were not prepared to explore the values behind the revolution in any depth. At least Dahrendorf and Garton Ash considered the changes in East Central Europe in some detail. But none of the authors analyzed the revolutionary demands and ideals of winter 1989–90. They did not even refer to the articles by Eastern European civil rights activists in the same edition of the journal. None of them raised the question of what the West might be able to learn or adopt from Eastern Europe. Instead, they offered paternalistic advice on how to develop the former Eastern Bloc countries. This is not really surprising; it reflected the contemporary asymmetry of power in Europe. In a sense, these Western European thinkers were continuing the tradition of Enlightenment thought. Since the late eighteenth century, most renowned men of letters have adhered to an occidentalist perspective, considering the East only in the case of ideational or military conflict. It remained thus in the years around 1989, despite the opportunity for more intensive intellectual exchange. But what values were the civil rights activists and millions of protesters actually going out in the streets for in 1989? In the GDR, national demands (for German unity) very quickly obscured other revolutionary goals. For this reason, the section below will focus on Czechoslovakia, which was effectively a laboratory for political and social values and utopias, at least until the local elections of fall 1990.

## The Values of 1989

Perhaps the most important element of the Velvet Revolution was the experience of community, and the most vital value the sense of solidarity among the protesters. On November 17, the police tried one last time to suppress the demonstrations by brute force. Several hundred protesters, mostly students, were badly beaten up. The police aggression violated a fundamental social value—that guardians should protect, not attack, their charges. Over the following days, tens of thousands of demonstrators returned to Wenceslas Square (*Václavské náměstí*). Soon the center of Prague became too small for the throng. Consequently, the opposition started holding rallies on the *Letná*, a large parade ground and park close to Prague Castle. On November 25, at least half a million people were gathered there. The next day, a Sunday, another 250,000 protesters appeared.[11] At that time, the capital of Czechoslovakia had a population of around 1.2 million. That weekend, more than half the population of Prague turned out to support "the revolution," as people were hesitantly starting to call it.

The demonstrations were attended by a highly heterogeneous cross-section of society, from all classes and age groups. They brought together individuals and groups who would otherwise probably never have met. In contrast to the French and Russian Revolutions, the Velvet Revolution mobilized the entire country within a few weeks. Similarly to the GDR, even residents of small towns and villages took to the streets by the tens of thousands to demand the end of the old regime.

The crowds developed common rituals, such as shaking bunches of keys (to symbolize funeral bells ringing out the demise of communism), singing songs, performing jumps in unison against the cold, and, in December, shouting the political rallying cry "*Havel na Hrad*" ("Havel to the castle"), demanding Václav Havel as president. He, more than any other person, reflected the mood of solidarity in his speeches. He addressed the protesters as "friends," and used other terms that underlined the sense of community, such as "unity," "fraternity," "solidarity," even "love." This heartfelt exuberance, the Romantic phase of the revolution, could obviously not last forever. Nevertheless, it would be wrong to understate the emotional aspect and common experience of revolution, to which Hannah Arendt refers in her writings.

Humanity (in Czech, *lidskost*; in Slovak, *l'udskost*; sometimes also *humanita*) was one of the key concepts of the revolution. The importance of this elusive notion can only be fully grasped against the background of the inhuman regime of the Czechoslovak Communist Party. The communists had reduced the country's citizens to mere cogs in the system. But the tables turned. The revolutionaries demanded the protection of human dignity (in Polish, *godność*) and respectful, friendly relations based on a sense of solidarity—in short, human compassion. In winter 2013–14, such demands were revived in Ukraine when the protesters on Kyiv's Maidan spoke of a "revolution of human dignity" (in transcribed Ukrainian, *revolutsiya gidnosti*—the close relation to the Polish language, especially the word *godność*, is evident).

Is the concept of humanity, which was endowed with such significance by the historical context, still relevant? To philosophers and scholars of the history of thought, it certainly is. *Lidskost* has a long and interesting prehistory, starting with the humanist pedagogue and theologist Comenius (in Czech, Jan Amos Komenský) and stretching to Jan Patočka, Václav Havel's philosophical mentor, and other Czechoslovak dissidents.[12] More than twenty-five years after the revolution, is there not a lack of *lidskost*, of humanity, all over Central Europe, and even the West in general? Some of the social cuts in East Central Europe and the labor market reforms in Germany certainly contradicted key values that the demonstrators of 1989 stood for. German welfare recipients, for instance, especially those who survive on the minimum Hartz IV payments, are too often treated with contempt. Derided as *Hartzer*, they are socially branded in everyday language. No wonder, then, that so many welfare recipients suffer from a lack of self-respect. Such moral considerations may appear old-fashioned today, but many dissidents and above all Václav Havel dwelled upon them in their speeches and writings of 1989–90.[13] They also wrestled with the problem of personally leading a "life in truth" while 1.5 million Communist Party members (almost 10 percent of the population) and large parts of society had complacently accepted the *contrat social*—more mass consumption in exchange for political compliance. Yet already in 1990, the dissidents' claim to the "truth" and the moral high ground had begun to grate on the public. Civil rights activists in other Eastern Bloc countries experienced similar disapproval.

Arguing implicitly from a postmodern Western standpoint, where there are no absolute truths or certainties, Timothy Garton Ash also criticized Havel's moralizing and questioned whether it was possible at all to rise above the murky terrain of everyday party politics.[14] His doubts were eventually vindicated. In the long term, Havel was not able to remain aloof from the petty intrigues of Czech party politics, and increasingly clashed with Václav Klaus, the finance minister in the first postcommunist government and later premier. Havel inevitably had to take a stand on the latter's radical reform program, with which he partly disagreed, and several other questions of daily politics. When the civil rights activists lost out at the parliamentary elections of 1992 (the Civic Party, *Občanské Hnuti*, led by Jiří Dienstbier, did not even clear the 5-percent threshold), Havel found himself necessarily drawn in, ultimately becoming a political party in his own right.

As they debated the shape of the democratic future, the protesters of fall and winter 1989–90 considered not only the political system but also the economy, the education system, and other institutions.[15] By demanding the democratization of all these fields, they were in line with many '68ers and West German chancellor Willy Brandt, who in 1969 had called on the country to "dare to have more democracy" ("mehr Demokratie wagen"). Self-administrative socialism, which the Solidarność movement had incorporated in its program of 1980–81, was initially considered as well. But the severe crisis and de facto national bankruptcy of

Yugoslavia in 1989 put paid to this idea. West Germany's model of trade union representation in the management of large companies (known as *Mitbestimmung*, that is, employees' participation in decision-making) would have also interested the activists, had they known about it. But the German government under Helmut Kohl preferred to keep this achievement of the trade unions quiet. Eventually, privatizing state enterprises took precedence over democratizing the economy in Czechoslovakia and all post-communist countries. The intended university reform became bogged down in endless discussions and debates; in other words, in the murky terrain of democratic practice.

Moreover, the economic troubles of the years 1990–91 created singularly unfavorable conditions for reflecting on the best democratic form and practice. The collapse of the Council for Mutual Economic Assistance, and thus of the region's most important export markets, the need for fundamental economic restructuring, and the growing deficits of many major industries and national budgets demanded quick decisions of the respective national governments. They did not have scope for theorizing or conducting political experiments. In the mid-term, then, democracy's idealization during fall and winter 1989 had negative repercussions. The practice of electioneering and parliamentary power-plays revealed sides to democracy that the public had not reckoned with. This engendered disenchantment and cynicism.

The conflict between functional and normative approaches also gave rise to misunderstandings in post-1989 discussions of Europe. Despite the frequent complaints of "Euro-fatigue," the member countries of the European Community took its existence largely for granted. On the whole, they viewed European integration as a (technocratic) process. But east of the Iron Curtain, Europe was defined in idealized terms as a community of values. Expectations of it were consequently high. During the 1990s, these were encoded in the often-invoked idea of a "return to Europe" (*návrat do Evropy*).[16] By this, Havel and other Eastern European intellectuals implied more than one-sidedly adjusting to Western European ways. The Czech "poet-president" envisioned a normatively defined, postimperial Europe, shaped by democracy and freedom, in which the "small" nations would have their place. (The fact that the European Union actually made this possible, before and after expansion, is one of its major achievements). This conception of Europe was influenced by Tomáš Garrigue Masaryk (1850–1937), the founder and "philosopher-president" of interwar Czechoslovakia, who had propagated the idea of the Czechs as a historically democratic nation. By "návrat," Havel meant a return to these philosophical traditions, among other things. When Eastern European countries recalled their national histories, they emphasized their sovereignty as well as supported their candidacy for European Union membership. They saw Europe as an association of fatherlands. This may have seemed nationalist and hidebound to Western proponents of a supranational state, but it complied with the structure and concept of the European Commission before the Maastricht Treaty.

Perhaps the opportunity was missed to discuss the goals and limits of European integration more openly before the enlargement of the Union. In 2005, just one year after the inclusion of ten new member states, France and the Netherlands voted against a European Constitution in public referendums. Like most votes on Europe, it was influenced significantly by the situations in domestic politics. The French public used the ballot to put the increasingly unpopular president Jacques Chirac in his place. But in the paternalistic terms the European Union tended to use on its eastern "candidate countries," one might say that the French and Dutch populations were "not yet ready" for EU expansion. The outcome of the constitution referendums might well have been different if politics and the public had embraced the debate about values that had blossomed in 1989–90 rather than persisting with a process-based conception of Europe.

Another controversial issue, especially in Poland, was the question of the European Union's Christian identity. Regarding European integration predominantly as a process, Westerners considered the continent's cultural or religious definition a secondary concern. Debating the matter from a normative point of view, the same question was bound to play an important role in Central and Eastern Europe. Opinions diverge even in Poland, where there is a strong, often overlooked anticlerical tendency. This is partly a reaction to the utopia of a re-Christianized Europe that emerged in the eighties, under the influence of Pope John Paul II, and can be regarded as another legacy of 1989.[17]

A further central value motivating the revolutions was freedom. Initially the focus was on freedom *from* something—from Soviet domination, from the communists, from censorship, and from persecution, oppression, and paternalism in various other areas of life. British philosopher Isaiah Berlin differentiates between these "negative" freedoms, which are stressed in classic liberalism, and "positive" freedoms *to do* something.[18] The latter dimension had less relevance during the revolutions and in the first years thereafter. Postcommunist societies were preoccupied with freeing themselves from communism and its legacies, especially reckoning up with the leaders of the ancien régime and secret police informers. Insofar as one adheres to Isaiah Berlin's conceptual differentiation (a philosophical appraisal of which would go beyond the scope of this book), transformation was attended by a partial *loss* of positive freedom for the postcommunist societies. Indeed, this is a general problem of the new, neoliberal order. Since the crisis of 2008–9, rising unemployment has reduced the numbers of those who enjoy the freedom to pursue their personal goals, even in Western Europe.

The crisis in agriculture and old industry, mass unemployment, the social decline of minorities such as the Roma, and other new inequalities left only a minority in the postcommunist societies able to take advantage of the newly won freedoms. The situation could perhaps have been remedied by observing an ethic of freedom, as the Canadian philosopher and communitarian Charles Taylor proposed.[19] In the mid-nineties, Taylor fundamentally criticized the liberal idea of freedom and outlined the risks of giving absolute precedence to free self-determination and individualism. Drawing partly on discussions with former dissidents at the IWM in Vienna, Taylor stressed the need for more community spirit and solidarity. Thus he echoed the protesters of 1989. They, too, thought largely in communitarian terms, though they did not usually refer directly to the concept. But it was demonstrated by the ubiquity of words such as "humanity" and "solidarity" in their flyers, pamphlets, and writings of the winter season 1989–90.[20]

In the postrevolutionary transformation era, consideration of the ethical and social implications of freedom largely died away. The normative exuberance of the revolution in postcommunist societies was replaced by a decidedly antiutopian mood. Furthermore, the hegemony of neoliberalism marginalized all other ideas and ideologies. As early as 1990, the principle of freedom became concentrated on the economy. The aforementioned TV series presented by Milton Friedman, the aptly titled *Free to Choose*, was an important mouthpiece. The third episode, devoted to "Freedom and Prosperity," discussed the end of communism briefly but paid far more attention to the liberation of the markets from government restrictions. In this way, Friedman set out his desired sequence of freedoms: after gaining political freedom, nations should lose no time in establishing free market economies—only then would there be complete freedom. Appearing every inch the benevolent and wise old uncle from America, Friedman explained to the poor deprived Eastern Europeans how to tackle reforms. His choice of terminology was remarkable: in speaking of an "unlimited" and "pure" market economy, he suggested that all other variations were impure. No mention was made of the civil rights activists such as Václav Havel and Lech Wałęsa, who had actually fought for their countries' freedom. But Czech finance minister Václav Klaus was invited to appear, and portrayed as a courageous reformer. In an appropriately real socialist setting, he treated Friedman and his wife, Rose, to coffee and cakes while reiterating the program's message: only free market economy has any future; political freedom must be followed up by the removal of economic constraints.

Once the concept of freedom had been appropriated by economics, it gradually disappeared from public debate. Politicians such as Klaus continued to propagate freedom for the economy in their speeches, especially to international investors. Some years later Friedman awarded Klaus membership in the Mont Pèlerin Society, where neoliberal thought had originated in the postwar period. But to the national public, the record was beginning to sound scratched. Indeed, neoliberalism's reliance on rationality is probably a major hindrance to its broad public acceptance. The arguments in favor of free market economy might have convinced in theory—Leszek Balcerowicz's analyses and reform plans are still compelling to read, whether one agrees with them or not—but they had little emotional appeal. The party conferences of the Civic Democratic Party (*Občanská demokratická strana*, or ODS), founded by Klaus, did not muster much enthusiasm even among attendees. (In the mid-nineties the ODS was the strongest neoliberal-oriented political movement in East Central Europe, and probably in Europe as a whole.) There were no pamphlets, chants, or demonstrations calling for free market economy. Prominent figures such as Leszek Balcerowicz in Poland and Yegor Gaidar in Russia exuded the aura of technocrats and business managers; they did not have or want any more charisma.[21]

The political-economic concept of freedom was reiterated at the celebrations marking the twentieth anniversary of the revolution in 2009. The German government thanked all those who had played a part in emancipating Germany and Europe and praised the progress of reforms. But German president Joachim Gauck's speeches emphasizing the value of freedom were unemotionally received, hinting that this rhetoric had already passed into contemporary history. The freedom gained in 1989 is now largely taken for granted in the EU. Perhaps the case of Ukraine will reignite the debate in the coming years. Its outcome will depend upon which concept of freedom is adopted: the comprehensive, ethically grounded variety of the revolution era or the reduced, economic one of the nineties.

One aspect of freedom was completely overlooked in 1989: women's rights. Although women certainly took part in the demonstrations just as men did, they did not voice gender-specific demands. This was due in part to the fact that, on paper, men and women were equal under state socialism. In practice, however, women shouldered greater burdens than men, not only going to work but also running the households and looking after the children. Their most pressing need at that time was a fairer distribution of responsibilities within the family. In the nineties, however, women were also worse hit by economic reforms than were men. They were affected by dismissals and restructuring in major industries disproportionately often (for instance, when service-oriented departments such as cafeterias were outsourced). Moreover, the new system drastically reduced state childcare and brought a shift in ideals, back toward a traditional conception of gender roles. Vladimir Putin's offensive machismo is one example of this shift. In fact, it provides the foundation for his domestic and foreign policy. In Poland, the influential position of the church led to the criminalization of abortion. Such developments in the gender field seem to corroborate Jacques Rupnik's thesis that the radical changes of 1989—or their outcomes in the nineties—marked a sort of "anti-'68."[22]

Yet there are glimmers of light on this horizon. For instance, in Poland the gap between men's and women's average incomes is small in relation to that in other countries. The country ranks fifth in OECD statistics on the male-female pay gap, well ahead of Germany and Austria, where it is twice as large (at over 15 percent).[23] Long before Angela Merkel became German chancellor, Poland had a female prime minister (Hanna Suchocka in 1992–93) and a female president of the national bank (Hanna Gronkiewicz-Waltz 1992–2000), and has more women in leading positions in business and university education than most Western countries. However, this can not be attributed entirely to the revolution. It owes more to the social and cultural dynamic of transformation.

Postrevolutionary disenchantment has clouded the public's memory of the values of the 1989 revolution. This is particularly evident in conversation with intellectuals and former politicians who played leading roles. Many now perceive the postrevolutionary "Realpolitik" as an inevitable and ultimately positive development, having paved the way for new affluence and European integration. But this political-realist reception of the revolution might in turn lose currency. Canadian historian James Krapfl, for one, has hinted at this in his empathetic analysis of revolutionary writings and culture in Czechoslovakia. Krapfl shows that the values of the Velvet Revolution still hold relevance, though primarily on the periphery of or outside Europe. A few years ago, for instance, some five thousand intellectuals and opposition activists in China signed the manifesto "Charter 08," calling for the democratization of China, an end to one-party rule, and, not least, greater social equality.[24] The Ukrainian revolution has also revitalized some of the values of 1989, which is why it is so despised by the former KGB functionary Vladimir Putin.

## Birth Pangs of United Europe

When East Germans stormed the Berlin Wall in a state of euphoria, many West Germans, too, shed tears of joy. For some, it marked the reunion of families who had been divided by the Iron Curtain. But after a time, as ever more East Germans flocked across the border, West Germans began to look askance at the new arrivals. This is illustrated by the popular use of the patronizing label "Ossi." It took another twenty years for West Germans to refer more respectfully to East Germans as such. But the difficulties the two Germanies experienced in growing together were nothing compared to the birth pangs of the newly united Europe. These were especially perceptible in Germany's relation to Poland. While the citizens of the GDR could count on a degree of national solidarity from the old Federal Republic of Germany, and indeed received it on a material level, the Poles were stigmatized by their poverty and the long history of anti-Polish prejudice in Germany. Despite the official eulogies on Poland's role in ending communism, social encounters in the first years after the revolution tended to compound the mutual sense of alienation.

This can be traced most clearly in Berlin and Vienna. As discussed above, tens of thousands of Poles took advantage of the open borders to trade at Berlin's "Polish market" or Vienna's Mexikoplatz market. In this way they hoped to supplement their incomes and acquire foreign currencies, to protect their meager assets from hyperinflation. The influx of Poles was not well received in the West. In one article, the German news magazine *Der Spiegel* reported "growing aggression" and the increasing use of "insults such as 'Polack vermin'" (*Polacken-Pack*). Yet in the leading paragraph, the finger was pointed firmly at the Poles. It read: "Polish black-market traders, smugglers and shoplifters in West Berlin fuel hostility toward foreigners among local residents."[25] In summer 1990, there were rising demands to close Germany's eastern borders and introduce a visa requirement for the citizens of former Eastern Bloc countries. The German government did not take up the idea, since it could not deny Czechs and Poles the same right to travel freely that the East Germans had fought for just six months previously. However, it established certain requirements for Poles wishing to enter Germany. They needed a written invitation, cash assets of at least fifty deutschmarks (a lot of money in Poland at the time), and proof of health insurance. The passports of any Poles caught conducting illegal activities, such as illicit street-trading or undeclared work, were marked with the dreaded stamp that barred them from entering Germany for several years. But it was possible to get around this by reporting one's passport as stolen and organizing a new one—at the market in Warsaw's Dziesięciolecia stadium if not through the official channels.

The Austrian government took far more drastic action. In September 1990, it overturned its agreements with Poland and Romania on visa-free travel, thus ending its traditional role as an asylum and transit country for refugees from Eastern Europe. Surveys showed that 80 percent of Austrians took a negative view of the growing number of Eastern Europeans in the country since the opening of the borders: 30 percent thought it was "bad," 50 percent that it was "a bit annoying sometimes."[26] The leader of the right-wing populist Austrian Freedom Party (FPÖ), Jörg Haider, harnessed this mood for his party's first blatantly xenophobic election campaign. Even the Social Democratic Party of Austria (SPÖ) espoused populism to a degree. It was the SPÖ parliamentary party leader in the National Assembly who had proposed the visa requirement for Poles. The city of Vienna, however, showed greater tolerance and continued to allow the large bazaar to be held on Mexikoplatz.

In April 1991, Europe took a huge leap toward opening borders and allowing freedom of movement. The six countries that then made up the Schengen zone (Germany, France, Italy, Belgium, the Netherlands, and Luxemburg) and Poland concluded agreements on visa-free travel. But like the association agreements of later that year, they were confined to the Visegrad states. It was not until the Soviet Union had completely disintegrated and war broke out in the former Yugoslavia that Western Europe considered opening to other countries in Eastern Europe. Encouraged by the United States, NATO pushed ahead in this respect. But it is a far more complicated matter to enlarge an economic, juridical, and, to some extent, political union than a military alliance. There were also social implications, such as the fear of labor competition. To the German public, the closer the accession of East Central and Southeastern European countries loomed, the scarier EU expansion seemed.

One indication of Germany's trepidation is the discourse about EU enlargement of the late nineties, which was characterized by terms such as "streams of people," "flooding," "inundation," "dam bursting," and "dam building." It was as if the unpredictable force of the two rivers separating Germany and Poland, the Oder and the Neisse, were under discussion. Although a flood catastrophe did indeed occur in 2002, the point at issue was actually the influx of labor from Eastern Europe. In the end, far fewer people immigrated than predicted.[27] Moreover, Germany had experience as an immigration country: in 1989, 377,000 "late repatriates" (people of German descent) moved to Germany, followed by another 397,000 in 1990. But with unemployment at a record level of over four million in the late nineties, the alarm bells started ringing. (This was a contrast to 2015, when over a million refugees from the Middle East arrived in Germany. The climate was much more positive, also because of the good shape of the German economy.)

Indeed, there was a dual competition: from the new arrivals on the home labor market as well as from the outsourced production of industrial goods in Eastern Europe. The label *Billigkonkurrenz* (literally "cheap competition") gained currency, expressing condescension toward the less affluent Eastern Europeans. At the traditionally rustic Ash Wednesday convention of the CSU (the long-time governing party in Bavaria), the state premier Edmund

Stoiber drummed up populist resistance against labor migration. He calculated the ridiculously low wages that Eastern European workers earned (Poles: 5.50 marks per hour; Bulgarians: 1.40 marks—in comparison to the 48 marks he claimed German skilled workers earned), and predicted mass immigration to the German labor market.[28] Trade unions and various professional associations echoed his concerns. A favorite phrase that Roland Issen, then chairperson of the white-collar trade union DAG, repeated on a number of occasions between 1995 and 2001 was: "We can't just open the floodgates."[29]

That is how a lot of East Germans felt when the European Union was extended by ten new member countries on May 1, 2004. It was a day of celebration in Poland. There were festivities across the country, including in Słubice, a small Polish town at the German border. The East German city of Frankfurt an der Oder is virtually within spitting distance, on the other side of the river. Corks were popping and fireworks exploding all night in Słubice. In Frankfurt, meanwhile, the quiet was broken only by some official fireworks. Germans were in no mood to celebrate now that they faced dual competition on the labor market—from companies relocating *to* the East (on account of the cheap labor) and from the (mostly overestimated) influx of labor migrants *from* the East.

The next day, the differences on either side of the border continued. Słubice's party guests wanted to take taxis to the station at Frankfurt an der Oder, which is much closer than the nearest Polish railway station. But the many Polish taxis available were not authorized to drive across to Germany and there were no taxis waiting at the border in Frankfurt. The Brandenburgers were obviously not so desperate to make money—partly because the unemployed in East Germany still received generous welfare benefits in comparison to those in Poland or the Czech Republic, although this soon changed with the introduction of the Hartz IV laws. Joy and fear, active industry and passive expectancy, were separated by only 170 yards—the length of the bridge spanning the Oder River.

A different kind of skepticism about Eastern Europe was expressed by the liberal-left-wing and conservative German elites alike. They envisioned a Carolingian version of Europe, as it had once been founded by Charlemagne. Consequently they feared that EU expansion might jeopardize integration as it stretched the union to encompass twenty-five member states.

With hindsight these fears can be regarded as the birth pangs of united Europe. But they were so acute at the time that they had an impact on the accession treaties. The new member states were included in the union on condition that their citizens did not settle or work in the old EU countries until a maximum period of seven years had elapsed. Only Sweden, Ireland, and the United Kingdom opened their labor markets immediately, which allowed them to welcome the best qualified labor migrants. This is now one of the complaints of the British nationalist party UKIP, along with some Conservatives, who are not only against Brussels but, like all populist groupings, also in favor of protecting the native population against labor market competition. On the continent, meanwhile, a little neoliberal loophole existed for entrepreneurial migrants: registering businesses was relatively easy for citizens from other EU countries, which is what thousands of Poles did. In addition, Germany's proximity to Poland gave rise to another, less permanent pattern of labor migration. On Sunday evenings, the trains across the border to Berlin were packed with middle-aged Polish women traveling to work as home helpers, cleaners, and nurses in Germany. Some of them even formed impromptu firms to share clients and alternate working hours, thus ensuring the uninterrupted provision of their services. In order to save on rent and bring more money home, two or three women often shared a single one-room apartment during the week.

Thus the labor market restrictions inscribed in the enlargement treaties were not as effective as intended. Nor did they serve to reassure the German population. Their fears were temporarily pushed into the background, but resurfaced when Romania and Bulgaria acceded to the European Union in 2007 and were nourished by tabloid journalists and right-wing politicians, who painted a menacing picture of cheap competition and mass immigration. The aforementioned Edmund Stoiber even proposed cancelling the EU membership of both countries.[30] In 2010–11 and 2013–14, shortly before the end of the seven-year limitation period for citizens of the new EU countries, similar horror scenarios were predicted again. This time, xenophobic fears were not articulated in blanket rejections of immigration but in preconceptions about what the new arrivals would do in Germany. The CSU declared its intention to take action against "social fraudsters from Eastern Europe."[31] Thus the immigrants were accused en masse of wanting to scrounge social benefits. In fact, in relation to the proportion of the population they make up, fewer Romanians and Bulgarians claim benefits than do German nationals. In Vienna, too, immigrants tend to line up in front of certain gas stations or supermarkets offering their labor rather than ask for help through the official channels. Bavarian companies, especially, need skilled workers and apprentices and often recruit them directly from Romania. Was it really necessary to humiliate these people by accusing them of mass-scale "social fraud"? Germany showed some remorse for its discursive aberrations when it declared the German equivalent of the term, *Sozialbetrug*, the ugliest word of the year 2013. But it was too late for those who were already stigmatized.

Similar debates sparked in France a few years later. Here, the *plombier polonais* eventually came to embody the rival Eastern European worker. In fact the stereotype of the Polish plumber became so ubiquitous that it was harnessed for election campaigns and the referendum over the EU constitution. The debate took a surprising turn, however, when the Polish tourist office retaliated with a humorous poster inviting French visitors to Poland. It showed a sexy-looking plumber with the caption "I'm staying in Poland. Come over here" (see fig. 10.1).[32]

Meanwhile, in Berlin, the flow of migration had reversed. Many Poles who had come to Germany to live or work, or for other reasons, moved back to their native country. Skilled workers still earned less in Poland than in Germany but the wage differences to Berlin and Brandenburg, where many branches paid lower than the agreed standard wage, were shrinking. In addition, there were more job vacancies in Poznań and Wrocław. If one factored in living costs and property prices, it paid off to move back.

These debates on immigration can be regarded as the birth pangs of 2004's new Europe. Western Europe proved itself remarkably

Fig. 10.1. The "Polish plumber": humorous riposte by the Polish tourist office, 2005. Courtesy Office National Polonais de Tourisme, Paris.

fearful and inhospitable. In essence, this can be attributed to three factors: its lack of participation in the revolutions of 1989, its fear of competition on the labor market, and its reluctance to share its wealth. These factors are, in turn, linked to the characters of German and European unification in 1990 and 2004, respectively: both events marked extensions of the West, or the existing Western systems. Citizens of West Germany and Western Europe were led to believe that they would remain more or less unaffected. But they sensed that changes were in the air. Openly facing integration as a change affecting everyone—and holding opportunities for all—would have been more honest and certainly more helpful.

Another troublesome aspect was the inequitable treatment of the new EU states by the older member countries. As mentioned above, accession was linked to restrictions on the former's freedom of movement. The EU candidates in turn negotiated restrictions on the purchase of land in their countries by foreign investors. It was a bad compromise for both sides. Farming subsidies were another point of issue. The European Union had missed the chance to reform these comprehensively prior to 2004 (prevented above all by the French farmers' lobby). Hence the large subsidies for Western Europe were retained and only a fraction paid to the new member countries. No doubt this was an economically reasonable move. Higher payments for the new members would have probably led to rising inflation and other unintended effects. But the inequity left a bitter aftertaste.

Bristling at the asymmetry of power between Western and Eastern Europe, the EU candidate countries sided with the USA over the Iraq war rather than with Jacques Chirac and Gerhard Schröder. The French president told the Eastern European countries awaiting accession that by supporting George W. Bush they had "missed a great opportunity to keep their mouths shut."[33] These, too, were birth pangs that have now abated. The invasion of Iraq and the country's occupation proved to be an ill-fated adventure. Moreover, the United States went back on its promise to overturn the strict visa regulations for its ally Poland. Feeling treated like a second-class country, Poland moved closer to Brussels and its European partners. In addition, the extensive aid programs instituted after EU accession helped to calm the waves of 2003–4.

However, since the crisis, new lines of conflict have emerged, especially between the North and the South. Many Southern Europeans hold Brussels responsible for the austerity gripping their home countries. As discussed above, the European Union is not an agent of neoliberalism and has actually alleviated social hardship and regional inequality in the new member states. But the austerity policies introduced in the wake of 2008–9 were propagated by the Troika, which includes two European institutions. They have severely damaged the EU's reputation and contributed to the landslide victories of left- and right-wing populist parties at the European elections of 2014.

The same scenario was repeated at the Greek parliamentary elections of January 2015. The left-wing populist Syriza party won the elections on the strength of its pledges to break the Troika's power, end the austerity policy, and restore the dignity of the Greek nation. But these promises did not help the country escape the debt trap, and the Greek government under Alexis Tsipras was forced to go back on some of them, including raising the minimum wage and reinstating civil servants whose jobs had been cut. It remains to be seen whether the Greek Left, political home of many former communists, will act as pragmatically as the Polish SLD or the Hungarian socialists in the mid-nineties. It seems doubtful, as Syriza is different in a number of ways. For one, it cultivates a marked machismo (with a first cabinet devoid of women), and it has entered into a coalition with the right-wing populists (shifting the political competition further into the radical populist corner). Not only that, in the nineties a certain amount of faith in the blessings of capitalism still prevailed, and confidence that social cuts and economic reforms would one day pay off. This faith has dissipated as a consequence of the ongoing crisis since 2008–9.

It is important to remember that the power of populist parties such as Syriza is dependent on the increasing influence of technocrats, and vice versa. Whenever the antipolitical argument that "there is no alternative" to one or other reform is asserted (which has been a key part of the neoliberal repertoire since the eighties), it prompts antipolitical reactions such as populism. Unfortunately for the EU, the line of conflict has shifted since the crisis of 2008 to mark Brussels as the aggressor. Populists locate their technocrat enemies in the EU administration, and claim to defend their respective nations against its insidious attacks. With this rallying cry, they win support regardless of their political leaning. Whether they are labeled left- or right-wing is insignificant. The main distinction between the two is that right-wing populists are not only against the European Union, the IMF, and the Troika, but also against foreigners, migrants, and minorities. This is not a birth pang of the united Europe but a structural problem of European politics.

## The Conflict over Ukraine

The new member states have made an important contribution to EU policy by championing their eastern neighbors. Poland was foremost in advocating a policy of openness to further "accession candidates" in the east. But a major opportunity to take an active role in Eastern Europe—the "Orange Revolution" in the Ukraine in 2004—arose at a bad time. Though not, in fact, revolutionary, the turmoil of that year did bring about a change of government, increased respect for the basic rules of democracy, freedom of the press, and more cultural pluralism. The demonstrators in Kyiv regarded this as a move closer to the European Union. Ukraine signaled its intention to take the Polish path and not follow Russia, where Vladimir Putin was cementing his autocratic power. Moreover, Putin's attempt to intervene directly in Ukrainian politics—then still by peaceful means, taking part in the election campaign and supporting the presidential candidate Viktor Yanukovych—was not well received.

In February 2005, the new, democratically elected president, Viktor Yushchenko, came knocking at the European Union's door. It could have been an opportunity to intensify European cooperation with Ukraine, but the EU commission decided on a "bilateral action plan" with Ukraine, explicitly without prospects of accession. The only, vague, decision made was to earmark the year 2007 as a possible date for an association agreement.[34] This contrasted starkly with EU policy toward the states of East Central Europe fifteen years previously. The association agreements with Hungary, Czechoslovakia, and Poland had been signed, sealed, and delivered just two years after the revolutions of 1989, even though the circumstances had by no means been more favorable: in late 1991, Russian troops were stationed in Poland, the region was still in the grip of economic crisis, and it was uncertain whether all the associated countries would ever become stable democracies.

Why did the European Union keep democratic Ukraine at arm's length? For one, Brussels had its hands full with the recently accomplished expansion of the Union, the impending accession of Romania and Bulgaria and the project of a European constitution. On a more fundamental level, the mental map of the old European Union was hard to shake off: From Brussels' or Berlin's point of view, Ukraine was a country far away in deepest Eastern Europe. The attitudes of the German elites (or at least the Social Democrats) were illustrated by former German chancellor

Helmut Schmidt in a book he published in 2000, claiming that over the course of several centuries, Russians, Ukrainians, and Belarusians had "undergone a cultural development that was only related to each other," and could therefore be regarded as belonging to a "Russian cultural sphere." Schmidt was apparently unaware of Ukraine's many hundreds of years as part of Poland (Moscow ruled over a large part of the country for less than two centuries—125 or 146 years depending on the region), the church union of Lublin (by which a part of the Orthodox church submitted to the Vatican in 1596; the Greek Catholic church in today's West Ukraine became a kind of national church in the nineteenth century), and other Western aspects of Ukrainian history.[35] But some German academics and even experts on Eastern European history were no better informed.[36]

In principle, Yushchenko could have looked on the back of any euro bill to visualize Ukraine's prospects of integration in the EU. The map depicted there shows the Canary Islands, the Azores, and even France's overseas territories, but to the east, Europe fades out along a line running from Kherson near the Crimean Peninsula to Cherkassy, Smolensk in Russia, and up to the Arctic Ocean. Ukraine had no place in Europe, at least not on the eurozone's banknotes, where it was cut through the middle. In the knowledge of the events of 2014, this depiction seems like an ominous, self-fulfilling prophecy. (The more recent-issue 5-, 10-, and 20-euro banknotes show a map shifted around 125 miles to the East. This includes Crimea and areas north of the Sea of Asov.)

Undaunted, Yushchenko headed for Berlin after talks with the EU commission. In March 2005, he was invited to address the Bundestag, a rare honor for a foreign head of state. However, his reception in the German parliament was cool. The Bundestag president, Wolfgang Thierse, greeted Yushchenko awkwardly, announcing that "Ukrainians are *just as* welcome in Germany as all other guests." As a former civil rights activist, he might have taken the opportunity, after the Orange Revolution and Ukraine's move toward the West, to declare the official Ukrainian visitor *especially* welcome.[37] Only two members of parliament had taken the trouble to wear an orange scarf or show some other symbolic gesture of solidarity. The applause after Yushchenko's speech was lukewarm, especially in comparison to the hearty reception he received in Poland.

Chancellor Schröder approached the visitor with chilly reserve (a faux pas by Ukrainian standards of hospitality, which often involve guests being clapped on the arms and shoulders or hugged) and grumpily broke off their joint press conference after only a few questions. The entire visit was clearly overshadowed by the "visa affair." Yushchenko was not even able to negotiate any substantially easier travel conditions for Ukrainian students or similar minor concession. His return almost empty-handed marked a missed opportunity for Brussels and Berlin and weakened his position in domestic politics. In Kyiv, as the economy slowed, Yushchenko's leadership was challenged by his power-hungry rival, Prime Minister Yulia Tymoshenko. These two former leaders of the 2004 revolt also argued over Tymoshenko's erratic economic policy. The oligarchs' influence remained unchallenged; the Ukrainian parliament became better known for brawls than debates. These domestic problems were another reason why the European Union did not seize the moment of the Orange Revolution to develop relations with Ukraine.

Moreover, the European Union was suffering from "enlargement fatigue." Brussels almost instinctively rejected all further overtures by non-EU states. Turkey, even more than Ukraine, was disappointed on this count. The two countries were frequently mentioned in one breath. As an alternative to full membership (and explicitly not as an interim stage), Brussels introduced the EU Neighborhood Policy in 2003.[38] This concept, revised in 2006, applied to *all* the European Union's eastern and southern neighbors apart from Russia. Suddenly Ukraine found itself in the same boat as Lebanon, Jordan, Egypt, and a dozen other North African and post-Soviet countries (Belarus, Moldavia, and Russia also border on the EU). Furthermore, the EU Neighborhood Policy was based on a twofold misconception. For one, Brussels overestimated its allure, especially to Ukraine, whose economy was still closely linked to Russia's; and second, it underestimated Moscow's resistance. While bilateral talks between Brussels and

Kyiv were deadlocked, Moscow was gradually consolidating its power over the post-Soviet sphere, helped by the German chancellor Gerhard Schröder. Germany and Russia cooperated on the North Stream gas pipeline under the Baltic Sea, strengthening their bilateral relations at the expense of the transit countries lying between them.

The clash between Yushchenko and Tymoshenko enabled Yanukovych—the ballot rigger of 2004—to return to power in 2010. Having won the presidential elections with a comfortable lead over Tymoshenko, he took corruption to new extremes. Within a few years, Yanukovych's family rose to become one of the wealthiest clans in Ukraine. The country was not able to recover from the economic crisis of 2009 due to the drop in the price of steel (one of its chief export products), a lack of investment in industry and agriculture, and the ubiquitous corruption. Moreover, Ukraine was one of the countries where banks had freely arranged foreign currency loans and still struggled with inherited liabilities. Due to the financial crisis in 2008, the IMF granted Ukraine (and the banks which had loaned too much money in the country) a rescue package of 16.5 billion US dollars. Though this had been arranged with the last Yushchenko government, it benefited Viktor Yanukovych, who thus entered his presidency in 2010 with some start capital. It soon disappeared into the pockets of the presidential family and its allied oligarchs.

Despite the clearly negative developments in Ukraine, including the imprisonment of Yulia Tymoshenko, the European Union pressed forward with its association agreement with Ukraine. It did not want to lose out to Vladimir Putin, who had founded the Eurasian Customs Union in 2011 as an alternative alliance to the EU. In fact, Ukraine was reluctant to submit further to Russian hegemony by joining the customs union. Negotiations with the European Union continued until, in 2012, the association agreement was ready to be signed. Its conclusion was only slowed by concerns over Tymoshenko, who portrayed herself as a victim of political persecution, and casting too positive a light on Viktor Yanukovych.

By 2014, the economy's continuing decline had plunged Ukraine into a truly revolutionary situation, in contrast to 2004.

Fig. 10.2. Thousands protesting on Kyiv's Maidan against the Viktor Yanukovych administration, December 22, 2013. Photo: picture alliance / ZB / Konstantin Chernichkin.

President Yanukovych's refusal to sign the association agreement with the European Union was the final straw that triggered mass protests. As soon as news of his refusal broke, tens of thousands flocked to the Maidan in Kyiv. At this stage, they were mostly students, who objected to the ongoing corruption and cronyism and widespread deprivation. Yanukovych probably hoped the demonstrations would peter out after a few weeks due to the cold weather. But in the night of November 30 to December 1, 2013, he made the mistake of deploying Berkut units—the special police force within the Ministry of Internal Affairs. As in Prague in 1989, the Ukrainian public refused to stand by passively as their fellow citizens were abused by security forces. The day after the Berkut crackdown, about half a million people swarmed to what was now dubbed the "Euromaidan," continuing the protests for weeks and months (see fig. 10.2).

In mid-January, the government tried to subdue the rebellion by means of new legislation. The parliament hurriedly enacted a tighter ban on demonstrations, anti-NGO laws (following the Russian model), and restrictions on freedom of expression and the press.

This catapulted the conflict into a sphere far beyond disagreement over the European Union or economic policy. It presented the Ukrainian public with a choice between two options: living with a Belarusian-style dictatorship or toppling Yanukovych. For this reason, this second phase of the revolution mobilized many family men and women (including a number of my own acquaintance), academics, small business owners, and white-collar workers to join the protests. Many of them had personally borne the brunt of corruption and cronyism and wanted a better future for their children.

Yanukovych's restriction of civil rights and simultaneous refusal to enter into serious negotiations with the opposition exacerbated the tensions. One group of protesters, the so-called "*pravii sektor*" ("right-wing sector") tried to storm the parliament building. The government responded with more violence: Berkut units kidnapped and abused protesters; the first four fatalities occurred, one of whom was a fellow lecturer at the Ukrainian Academy of Sciences in Lviv. This escalation destroyed almost all hopes of a compromise between the government and the opposition. In mid-February, the revolution entered into its third phase. Berkut units and snipers positioned on the roofs surrounding the Maidan opened fire on protesters. Between February 18 and 20, at least one hundred people were killed. The mass murder fanned the flames of protest; the government lost control over the center of Kyiv.

Seeing his power rapidly eroding, Yanukovych clutched at a different straw. On February 21, through the mediation of the Polish and German foreign ministers and in the presence of a Russian government representative, he signed an agreement to hold elections and renounce some of his presidential powers. But by this point, the revolution had gained such momentum—fuelled by the violence and killings—that no compromise could last. The protesters demanded that Yanukovych be brought to justice; the president fled to East Ukraine and via Crimea to Russia. He was declared deposed by the Ukrainian parliament on February 22.

The Ukrainian opposition prevailed in this latest revolution in European history—vilified in Russia as a putsch—mainly because of its greater capacity to mobilize. Yanukovych had several thousand Berkut men behind him but, at the crucial moment, was not able to convince the military and police to conduct an inevitably bloody campaign in the center of Kyiv. The opposition, meanwhile, developed a bottom-up strategy. The constant presence of demonstrators on the Euromaidan was ensured by a regular changeover of personnel, akin to shift-working. Ad hoc committees set up in the capital and in Central and Western Ukraine organized the complex logistics of the operation. These committees raised funds to pay for food, clothing, and emergency medical care. With Berkut forces abducting, torturing and, in some cases, murdering injured demonstrators, the latter was a particularly urgent problem.

Russia villainized the Maidan protesters from the outset as nationalists and fascists. Certainly, the "right-wing sector" was a prominent element on the Kyiv barricades. They shot back when security forces opened fire on protesters. But the political base of the right-wing sector, the Svoboda (literally "freedom") Party, founded in 2004, advocated no more radical policies than the Lega Nord in Italy or Marine Le Pen in France. And its following was a fraction of the size of the latter two. Its presidential candidate Oleh Tiahnybok gained a mere 1.2 percent of the vote at the election on May 25, 2014.[39] Insofar as Svoboda politicians participate in government at all (they have seats in Lviv and some West Ukrainian local parliaments), they have so far pursued a pragmatic course.

Another tendency Ukraine is repeatedly accused of is antisemitism. In a historical perspective, it was indeed rife here. While the Svoboda Party venerates the ultra-nationalist and fascist Stepan Bandera (1909–59) and the anti-Soviet resistance fighters of the 1940s, it tends to ignore the issue of antisemitism, as it does the Holocaust and Ukrainian collaboration with the Nazis. As yet, no xenophobic acts of violence similar to those in Germany in the nineties, claiming the lives of over one hundred non-Germans, have been committed in Svoboda's stronghold,

West Ukraine. The Jewish community in L'viv leads a peaceful existence; the synagogue does not have to be guarded round the clock, as in Berlin or Paris. In March 2014, a series of attacks on synagogues and cemeteries occurred. But these were confined to the southern and eastern areas of Ukraine that had slipped out of state control. In early March, the chairperson of the association of Jewish communities and organizations in Ukraine, Josef Zisels, and the Orthodox and Liberal chief rabbis defended Ukraine against Russian accusations of nationalism and fascism. In an open letter to Vladimir Putin, they declared that Ukrainian Jews felt neither threatened nor discriminated against.[40]

Yet Russia used propaganda against Ukrainian fascists, Bandera supporters, and antisemites to prepare the ground for the invasion of Crimea and rally support for the so-called separatists in East Ukraine. President Yanukovych's toppling proved to be a Pyrrhus victory for the opposition. Although a new government had been installed in the capital, it by no means controlled the entire country. Vladimir Putin immediately took advantage of the power vacuum in eastern and southern Ukraine. Just a few days after Yanukovych's removal from office, Russian security forces infiltrated Crimea, where they started organizing demonstrations against the new government in Kyiv and occupied the regional parliament. On February 27, 2014, a vote on Crimean independence was staged, and Russia was called on to "protect [Crimea] against violent Ukrainian nationalists and extremists." Putin then gave the official order for the Russian army to march in. Wasting no time, the new rulers held a referendum two weeks later (on March 16), promptly linking the issue of Crimean independence with the question of annexation to the Russian Federation. Of course the West protested against this blatant violation of international law, but Putin was determined to impress public opinion in Russia, where many still resented the fact that Crimea had become part of independent Ukraine in 1991.

Investigations by the Russian newspaper *Novaya Gazeta*, partly based on an internal strategic document, revealed that the invasion of Crimea and destabilization of Eastern Ukraine had been planned since early February.[41] The Russian government persistently denied any involvement of Russian soldiers or secret service agents, but later blew its own cover by awarding medals to several "heroes" of the Crimean invasion. Moreover, Igor Girkin (better known by his martial pseudonym "Strelkov," meaning "rifleman" or "shooter"), an officer of the Russian secret service involved in the invasion and occupation of the industrial town Sloviansk, gave away more than intended on several occasions. Announcing his appointment as defense minister of the "People's Republic of Donetsk" and boasting about his military successes, Strelkov disclosed key details of Russia's involvement.

Despite these blunders in the propaganda war over Ukraine, Russia prevailed on a number of points. In early 2014, Western media ran extensive coverage of the alleged threat posed by "fascists" in Kyiv, and also adopted other terms coined by the Kremlin. In the first half of 2014, there was much talk of the "Ukraine crisis" or the "Ukraine conflict," as if it were primarily an internal dispute between Western and Eastern Ukraine. In fact, the only part to break away from centrally governed Ukraine was Donbas, where the Yanukovych clan power base was located—not even the predominantly Russian-speaking regions Charkiv or Dnipropetrovsk followed suit, indicating that it was not, as some have claimed, an "ethnic" conflict.[42] The "separatists" are still referred to as such, although it would be more accurate to speak of "interventionists," as their leaders are mostly Russian nationals and intelligence officials. Contemporary history has not yet come up with a word for these actors in the new, hybrid warfare. The Ukrainian government's reference to "terrorists" is clumsy and misleading.

For the first time since the Yugoslav Wars of 1991–95, the Russian annexation of Crimea has drawn a contested territory on the map of Europe. Indeed, a number of structural similarities can be observed in the two conflicts. Like Putin today, Slobodan Milošević strove to extend his political hegemony to the surrounding countries. As long as these neighbors (in the case of the former Yugoslavia, the newly independent constituent republics) submit to the neoimperial center, the existing borders are respected. Belarus and Kazakhstan have allied with Moscow, but are not secure in their sovereignty—nobody knows how far their mighty neighbor is prepared to go. If a state tries to withdraw from the Kremlin's (or Belgrade's) hegemony, its minorities are mobilized. Putin made a rhetorical announcement to this effect in a parliamentary address as early as 2005. Speaking before the Duma, he described the demise of the Soviet Union as the greatest geopolitical disaster of the twentieth century and asserted his role as protector of the "Russian citizens" living abroad.[43] In this speech, which apparently only a few experts on Russia took seriously enough to read, Putin envisioned a Russian nation extending far beyond the borders of the Russian Federation. He has referred to this enlarged sphere for some years as the "Russian world."

A further parallel between Russia and Serbia lies in the role of the church. The Russian Orthodox Church explicitly supports expansionist nationalism, as the Belgrade Patriarchate did in the nineties. Both countries are home to far more radical nationalists than Putin or Milošević, respectively. Events in Serbia have shown that once public opinion has been whipped up by nationalist propaganda, it is difficult to calm. Alongside these commonalities, however, there are also differences. Milošević and his regional allies did not have the necessary resources at their disposal to gain control of the renegade republics, which were supported, moreover, by influential actors in the West. The Russian Federation, in contrast, is absolutely dominant in the post-Soviet sphere. No one country is in a position to stand up to it alone. After all, it is hard to confront a nuclear power by military means. And evidently Russia is needed to resolve international conflicts ranging from the nuclear arms deal with Iran to ending (or at least containing) the war in Syria.

At home, Putin can tap into Cold War–based Russian fears of the West, and particularly NATO, at any time. Although the North Atlantic defense alliance explicitly rejected the idea of including Georgia or Ukraine as new members since the Russian-Georgian conflict over South Ossetia in 2008, the implicit offer of alliance through neutralization still served to tread on Russian toes. In addition, the region's move toward the European Union in 2013 was perceived as a threat in Russia. Putin's emphasis on geopolitics is a message to the national public as well as the international community. It drew the focus away from pressing domestic problems, especially the ailing economy and the endemic corruption. On an international level, it has caused Western politicians to think more in terms of spheres of influence, too.

But the conflict over Ukraine cannot be won with political arguments alone. It can only be resolved if the Maidan protests and the overthrow of Viktor Yanukovych are understood as a genuine revolution. Eastern Europe has experienced several counter-revolutionary interventions in the past, such as 1792–94 and 1830–31 in Poland, 1849 in Hungary, and 1863 in Poland and parts of today's Ukraine, each with a negative outcome. The difference now is that Russia has no allies in the West and although Ukraine is weak, it is not powerless. After the presidential election of May 2014, the whole country (apart from the occupied areas) was organized enough to hold regular parliamentary elections by October the same year.

The annexation of Crimea and destabilization of Eastern Ukraine have nevertheless severely undermined the revolution. The protesters in Kyiv wanted to end oligarchic domination and kleptocracy. Similarly to Prague's Wenceslas Square in 1989, the Euromaidan was a forum for egalitarian ideas and utopias.[44] Participants were determined not to repeat the mistakes of 2004 by allowing the revolution to be reduced to a mere change of government. But the Russian intervention prompted the Ukrainian administration to enter into a compromise with the old elites. Nationally known oligarchs were installed as governors in Donetsk and Luhansk, in the hope that they would be able to keep control over the contested regions.[45] Kyiv also depends on regional oligarchs in Dnipropetrovsk and other areas in the East and the South. Owning chocolate factories, a shipyard, machinery construction plants and a number of media companies, the newly elected president Petro Poroshenko also belongs to the caste of oligarchs. The parliament in Kyiv continues to be dominated by stakeholders in large conglomerates. Indeed, the scenario increasingly resembles that in 2004, when new oligarchs simply replaced the old ones or the latter quickly changed sides.[46] Perhaps Ukraine will be bereft of its revolution for the second time in recent history.

The first time, its own elites were to blame; in 2014, Russian intervention was an additional factor.

At least the West has pledged substantial support to the new government in Kyiv. Funds from the IMF, the United States, and the European Union have already been made available. Nevertheless, the economic challenges are enormous and, in some respects, unprecedented. After the Orange Revolution, Ukrainian politics focused on the country's postcommunist transformation, liberalizing foreign trade and the domestic economy—as in every Western country, telephone companies have mushroomed in Ukraine—deregulation (which occurred predominantly on paper while the economy is de facto controlled by monopolists), and privatization (which took place in the manner of a final sale, with even school and childcare properties being sold off). The standard recipe for transformation, then, has already been applied, with the familiar outcome.

In order to overcome its economic plight in the long term, Ukraine needs to undergo a postoligarchic transformation. This would entail reducing the importance of often illegally acquired private property, breaking up monopolies, and establishing government structures to serve more than the interests of the oligarchs. The rule of law must be consolidated and a "transformation from below" made possible. If Ukraine manages to develop its economy, the European Union should not rule out giving it full membership; if it persists in doing so, as it did with its failed neighborhood policy, Ukraine will remain trapped in a buffer zone—"intermediate Europe"—akin to the countries of East Central Europe between the First and Second World Wars. Ukraine and the entire post-Soviet sphere can be stabilized only if actors in Berlin, Brussels, and Washington, as well as in Kyiv, reassess the reasons for the missed opportunities since 1989.

The conflict over Ukraine has shown that one of the key requirements for the post-1989 order in Europe was peace, based on secure borders. Precisely this precondition was missing in the Caucasus and the former Yugoslavia in the early nineties. The outcome for the economies of these countries was devastating. Since 2008, when Russia invaded the South Ossetia region of Georgia,

Moscow's neoimperialist policy has threatened the stability of the post-Soviet world. Until the conflict over Ukraine sparked, peace in Europe was more or less taken for granted. But European history has shown that it is not a given. In the postwar era, the European Union acted as a force for peace in Eastern as in Western Europe, and must continue to do so. Countries' prospect of EU membership was made conditional upon factors such as the protection of national minorities. Minority rights were strengthened in consequence, which in turn served to defuse a number of entrenched ethno-political conflicts during the nineties. Historically contested regions such as Upper Silesia, southern Slovakia, and Transylvania have stopped making negative headlines. The minorities came to accept their status which, in some respects, they even profit from.

One conclusion to be drawn from the conflict over Ukraine is that Vladimir Putin perceives the European Union as a rival in a global contest with the West rather than as a peaceful giant. This situation cannot be altered as long as one player regards world politics as a zero-sum game, where one side can only profit if the other loses. The European Union is therefore bound to accept Russia's challenge to stand up for the security of its member states (especially those threatened by Moscow's "protection" of Russian minorities), pool its resources, and support Ukraine—probably without Crimea, which appears to be permanently lost—as it did Poland after 1989.

What kind of support should the European Union provide? The experiences of the nineties have shown that the most crucial factor in stabilizing countries is the consolidation of state structures by means of rapid administrative reforms toward more autonomy for regions and municipalities. Structural changes of this kind made Poland's economic miracle possible. As paradoxical as it may seem, neoliberalism is dependent on regulating governments.[47] In addition, prosperity can only be increased if countries strengthen their human capital by investing in disadvantaged strata and regions. Wherever a deep social divide emerged in the nineties, economic development was slower in the mid- and long-terms (see chapter 5). Evidently, broad middle classes are more effective economic motors than are small elites such as the post-Soviet oligarchs. The former found more businesses, invest more, and consume more.

Whether neoliberalism fosters such broad middle classes is questionable. The shock therapy in Poland led to impoverishment and the decline of the educated middle class that had formed under state socialism. By neoliberal logic, the radical reforms were unavoidable and generated the forces that stimulated the later upswing. This was the argument put forward by Andrei Shleifer and Daniel Treisman in an article published in *Foreign Affairs* in the fall of 2014. But in fact it is highly questionable whether a direct causal link between specific economic policy stimuli and economic performance actually existed.[48] Certainly, Poland's shock therapy was effective in some areas, such as lowering inflation (which can be credited to Leszek Balcerowicz). But the success of the "transformation from below" and the entrepreneurial boom in Poland and the other Visegrad countries were made possible by social resources and human capital developed over a long period.

If Ukraine is to become a functioning market economy, it must give priority to strengthening such resources. Some examples are already emerging: The Carpathian village of Slavs'ke is home to a prettily situated private guest house. An exact replica of an Austrian mountain lodge, it is aptly named Alpiiskii Dvir (Alpine Manor). The proprietor acquired her startup capital by working in Polish-Ukrainian markets and bazaars in the nineties, until she had enough to build her first guest apartment and eventually an entire guest house. Her example cannot be transferred to an entire industrial belt, and far less so a country. But perhaps it could serve as a pointer that Western aid should be directed as much at such businesswomen as at banks and financial institutions.

The revolution of 2014 demonstrated the power of Ukrainian society and the supreme importance of transformation from below. The constant presence of protesters on the Maidan, the transport of supplies despite the traffic blockade between Western Ukraine and the capital, the provision of food and medical care to demonstrators—all of these were organized with great skill by civil society organizations. Taking these as indicators of economic creativity and performance, Ukraine's future is surely not as bleak as it might currently appear.

The many comparisons here of the situation in Ukraine with Poland in the early nineties are not intended to suggest that the same economic recipes can be applied today in Kyiv as were applied twenty-five years ago in Poland. Subjecting a country where much of the population already lives on the breadline to shock therapy might provoke another social revolt. Simply jumping on the neoliberal bandwagon is not, then, an easy option for Ukraine. The external preconditions are not in place, nor are the internal prerequisites fulfilled—above all a functioning state and a minimum level of prosperity. According to the World Bank, the Ukrainian GDP dropped by 6.8 percent in 2014 due to the war, and continued falling even more in 2015.[49] New programs must first be devised to stabilize the country's economy and society.

## Europe after Neoliberalism

In recent years, the authoritarian turn in Eastern Europe and the plight of the southern EU countries has prompted growing demands for new, post-neoliberal concepts.[50] The horrendously high rate of youth unemployment is only one factor in a fundamental social imbalance that affects even those who have been lucky enough to find a job. Most young people have short-term contracts, and their terms and conditions are as bad as their wages. With an average taxable income of 540 euros, very few Italians under age thirty-five today are paying substantial social security contributions. Poverty will therefore be passed on from today's youth to the middle-aged generation and the pensioners of the future. The Germans living off Hartz IV benefits face a similar problem. If the Italian economy continues its current downward trend, the welfare state as it now exists, with a pension and health insurance system, will not be sustainable.

As Western Europe's cotransformation since the nineties has shown, the states and societies of Europe operate as communicating channels. Changes on one part of the continent cannot take place without affecting the rest. Sooner or later the social hardship in southern Europe will have an impact on the wealthier EU countries, whether in the form of increasing wage pressure or labor migration. This admittedly pessimistic scenario is based on the premise that falling wages and reductions in welfare benefits will hit one country after the next.

Germany is a case in recent European history of this scenario's becoming reality, at least in part. The failure of a quick westernization of the former GDR and economic competition from Eastern Europe plunged the German economy and welfare state into deep crisis in the nineties. Eventually, the decline was halted by a downward adjustment of social standards. The welfare state reforms of 2001–5, initiated by the Social Democrats and the Greens, brought dramatic, controversial changes. Nevertheless, this path of development was evidently more successful than the ones taken by Italy or France—two countries with conservatively structured societies, which have compounded their seemingly endless crises by allowing their national debts to rise and losing economic competetiveness. Yet southern Europe's plight since 2009 was also caused by a downward adjustment. Wages in Italy, Spain, and Portugal have come under pressure because the goods traditionally produced in these countries can be more cheaply manufactured in the new EU countries or outside Europe.

Lastly, countries have faced strong pressure to conform in the sphere of economic policy. It is virtually impossible for any individual nation to resist the combined demands of all the major international financial organizations to initiate neoliberal-style reforms. The transnational character and discursive hegemony of neoliberalism ensured the resounding impact of the Chicago School doctrines. How they were adapted locally depended upon the individual countries' perceived need for reforms, and the extent to which they relied on international loans or aid. A third contingent factor was acute economic crisis. But rather than being externally driven, this is on the whole a systemic problem.

Neoliberal mechanisms and European history since the 1980s can be summarized best in metaphorical terms. This movement was like a shiny express train that promised to take passengers to an enticing destination—of growth and prosperity. At one point, all the countries of Europe wanted to get on board; none could resist its allure. Moreover, it seemed to be the only train to the future after the end of system rivalry between East and West. The first passengers to board were Poland, Czechoslovakia, Hungary, and one formerly known as the GDR. Sometimes the passengers felt nauseated because of the high speeds at which they were travelling and the reform-remedies they were forced to take, but by the mid-nineties they were starting to feel a little better. The conductor and the waiters in the dining car (the international financial organizations) proudly announced that the shock therapy was working. Whether this was actually true is disputable, but the signs were right: growth curves, foreign direct investments, and other coefficients—the neoliberal order was distinctly statistic-fixated—pointed upward.

For this reason, other countries that had previously missed the train due to revolution, independence occurring later, post-communists remaining in power, or other factors now wanted to get on board, too. Some of these passengers—namely the Baltic states, Slovakia, and, a little later, Romania and Bulgaria—tried to catch up with the frontrunners by implementing even more radical reforms (see chapter 5 on the second wave of neoliberalism). This, too, caused pain and sickness, but turned the postcommunist countries into "emerging markets" and some of them even into "tiger economies." Germany, which was still clinging to the running board, did not want to remain the sick man of Europe, so it entered the neoliberal train as well.

The passengers met several times a day in the dining car. There was no choice on the menu; the one, standard meal was served by Western waiters (the IMF, the World Bank, the OECD, and a number of private think tanks). The appetizer was a dish called "austerity." The travelers did not always want to eat the meal and certainly not to swallow all of it, but they sensed the power of the waiters, who could collect old debts at any time and who seemed to have a monopoly on economic wisdom. The waiter from Brussels was rather popular, as he served hors d'oeuvres (such as the aid program PHARE, see chapter 5) and promised many passengers that he would always serve them if they fulfilled the right requirements. The dining car was a great place to give speeches about reforms. The representatives of the "small nations" liked to be seen as model passengers, and spoke of a market economy "without attributes." Meanwhile, the waiters repeated their mantra of "privatization, liberalization, deregulation" like a mealtime prayer.

Other guests in the dining car were gentlemen in business suits (fund managers, bankers, and CEOs of various companies). They were looking for opportunities to lighten their heavy wallets, but not by making gifts—they tended to hide the fact that they sought high returns and profits. The men in suits were especially inclined toward passengers who demanded freedom for the economy, and rewarded them for their boldness. Even the poorest fellow travelers benefited from their generosity. They were given FDI, a kind of magic potion that, unfortunately, can be addictive. The businessmen said the train had to go faster. At their behest it accelerated so much that the railway switches and alternative tracks became a blur. Due to the extreme speed, the train overheated. Passengers started removing their outer clothing (the rather flimsy welfare state), encouraged by the waiters, who said they would travel even faster if lightly dressed. This prompted the passengers to remove ever more clothes. One of them, a former KGB spy named Vladimir Vladimirovych, protested against the waiters' opinions and left the train. Since then he has tried to get another train, named state capitalism, on track. At first, the others did not take him very seriously. But that changed when he started trying to drag his neighbors by force onto his train, which now bears the insignia "Eurasian Economic Union."

Despite these disruptions and intermittent crises, the neoliberal train sped so fast that one could no longer see the people driving it. Looking very closely, it was just possible to discern that they were also wearing business suits. They thought they were acting very rationally, but suddenly, in 2008, panic broke out, first in the locomotive and then in the passenger cars. The train almost came off the rails but, screeching loudly, came to a standstill just in time. Yet despite having narrowly avoided a disaster, it did not change tracks.

On the contrary, new passengers now boarded (the Southern European EU states) because nobody would lend them any more money for the station restaurant where they liked to dine, unfortunately on credit. The men in business suits started to act quite differently. For a while, they refused to hand out FDI, but persistently inquired about ratings and told the Southern European passengers that they should tighten their belts.

The constant diet of lean meals and bitter pills soured the mood in the train. Prior to 2008, all the passengers had believed they were heading for a rosy future. But now most of the travelers were becoming anxious or even furious. Some suddenly felt very cold, especially those who had ostentatiously stripped down to almost nothing. The German and Polish passengers and a few others noticed this and decided to take the Keynesian menu, which they found warming and wholesome.

But the German passenger, a very powerful woman who some thought was the new engine driver, refused to pay or even jointly manage the debts of other passengers (for instance, with the help of euro-bonds). On the contrary, she told the Southern European passengers to follow the example of the Eastern Europeans on board, who had swallowed the most pills and become quite thin. For the time being, all the passengers of Europe are still on board the same train. But whether this remains so is anybody's guess. Perhaps they are only sticking together because they know that similar trains in other parts of the world, like China, are traveling even faster, paradoxically driven by men who still call themselves communists.

Before setting aside the train metaphor, one question must be asked: Are there any signs that it might change track in the future? To assess the situation, the global context must be taken into account. This has changed considerably since 2008–9. The incumbent US president has given the country its first general health insurance system in history. Thus Washington has moved closer toward the European welfare state model. It did so not for purely altruistic reasons but partly on economic grounds. The predominantly privately financed American health system was far too costly, precisely because of its social selectivity. One can also observe a corrective tendency in the Chinese communists' policies. The upswing of the last three decades has split Chinese society into a small upper class, an urban middle class, disenfranchised migrant workers, and the undeveloped rural population. These divides—Chinese society is far more unequal than that in the United States or even Russia—generate social tensions, protest, and violence. In 2012 the authorities registered some 180,000 strikes and unofficial protest actions.[51] The population resorts to these methods because it does not have recourse to the kind of democratic institutions where compromises and solutions could be negotiated. Without renouncing its power monopoly, the communist party tries to ease tensions by encouraging consumerism and pursuing a more active social policy. For some years, it has created the scope for wage raises and mass consumption, and attempted to build a welfare state with a pension and health insurance system. But this more socially equitable version of state capitalism can work only if the economy generates enough growth. In recent years, Chinese growth has considerably slowed, while private, commercial, and public debt has sharply risen. The future of this model is therefore open.

In the Russian variant of state capitalism, economic growth is impeded by a lack of social underpinning. Private enterprise is poorly developed; Russia lives primarily off the revenue from its oil and gas exports. Up to 2014, these were sufficient to place Russia on an equal footing with the economically ailing West, but since 2015 oil prices have plummeted. The Eurasian economic union might seem like a poor copy of the Council for Mutual Economic Assistance, but it is nevertheless an alternative to the European Union for Eastern European countries seeking integration. The Eurasian union appeals more to autocrats, not least because of its looser approach to human rights, democratic participation, and supranational governance.

Both the Chinese and Russian variants of state capitalism are full of contradictions. But their blend of authoritarian regimes with partially free market economies (less so in Russia than in China) has nevertheless come to pose a serious economic and political challenge to the West. Viktor Orbán, an obvious admirer, has steered Hungary in this direction since the crisis. In a sense, then, system rivalry is an issue within the European Union; state capitalism, like neoliberalism some fifteen years ago, is not only looming on the horizon but has already arrived in the EU.

To deal with these external and, to some degree, internal challenges, the European Union needs to be as united as possible. But in fact the economic policies of the old and new EU member states are disuniting. Some postcommunist countries have further slashed their social benefits in response to the great recession of 2008–9, thus continuing along a neoliberal path of development. To some extent, this has been facilitated by labor migration, which has eased the pressure on these countries. Meanwhile, the southern European states are more hesitant to initiate reforms. Yet they do not have the means to counter the crisis with expenditure programs. Austerity policies may have helped lower the deficits in these countries' national budgets—Greece and Italy achieved a so-called primary surplus before paying interest on their old national debts for certain budgetary years—but they have paid a high social and economic price. Politically, the European Union carries the cost of being held responsible for neoliberal policies, even though it does not pursue them consistently.

In general, neoliberalism is not to be equated with uninspired austerity policies. "Austerity" was only one of ten points in the Washington Consensus. If a government is serious about obeying neoliberal doctrine, it should follow up austerity with further reforms, such as privatizing state enterprises and liberalizing the labor market. Since the failure of Italy's technocratic government under Mario Monti, the current premier, Matteo Renzi, has attempted to do this. His plans to deregulate certain sectors and relax employee protection, and the Italian Social Democrats' (*Partito Democratico*) move toward the political center, are reminiscent of the German reforms instituted by the Social Democrat–Green government in 2001–5, and of New Labour in the United Kingdom. Like then–German chancellor Gerhard Schröder, Renzi does not want to jeopardize his reform policies by adhering to a rigid austerity policy. He has therefore taken a loose approach to the Maastricht deficit limit of 3 percent of GDP for new debts. However, Renzi is facing problems that Schröder did not have:

the global economic context is considerably less favorable, and internally, confidence in the ability of reforms to generate prosperity has faded. But the consequences could be fatal if the reforms fail, ranging from Italy becoming ungovernable to the collapse of the eurozone. Therefore the current Italian government deserves as much attention and support as the countries of Eastern Europe previously received, maybe even including experts from these countries. If the reforms take effect, the result would be a revitalized Italian state, sharing in the relative vigor of regions such as Renzi's home, Tuscany.

Germany has been working toward a consolidated welfare state for some years. The growing tax revenues achieved by the various government coalitions under Angela Merkel have been used not to relieve taxpayers, as they were under the Social Democrat–Green government, but to achieve a balanced budget and finance social expenditure. Germany's eastern neighbor states are basically pursuing a similar budget policy. Economizing is no longer their top priority; they are building up their welfare states rather than stripping them down.

The about-face over welfare state reforms illustrates this particularly clearly. Beginning in the mid-nineties, European governments, first in the east, then in the west, tended increasingly to hand pension and health insurance systems to the private sector. This marked a new dimension of privatization, as it no longer affected only the economy or previously state-run enterprises such as postal services or railways, but also core areas of the welfare state. After the crisis, this trend was finally stopped and in some cases even reversed. Private old-age provision was either assumed completely by the state (as in Hungary, for the aforementioned dubious reasons) or greatly restricted (as in Poland and Slovakia, partly because of the high administrative costs incurred by the insurance companies). The pay-as-you-go system, based on social and generational solidarity, was thus revived. This had an impact on societies' values as well as their politics. It challenged the simple dichotomy between state-run (bad) and private, or privatized (good), which shaped the neoliberal epoch. The European model of the welfare state is no longer considered obsolete. It has a future again.

However, this orientation toward social market economy (or, alternatively, ordoliberalism) is not a universal phenomenon. While the German government is consolidating the welfare state internally, it is prescribing a debilitating austerity policy to southern Europe. Cost-cutting programs may be unavoidable once a certain level of debt has been reached, but these are rarely attended by the necessary measures to improve prospects for the underprivileged classes, especially the younger generation. As long as the focus remains fixed on fiscal policy and austerity, Angela Merkel will be perceived as an advocate of asocial rather than a social market economy. This inevitably causes tensions in the European Union and rising support for populist parties, a development that was evident at the European elections of 2014. One can resign oneself to the fact that the societies of the European Union are growing further apart (also as a result of the refugee crisis that broke out in 2015) or one can hope for better times ahead. But before the continent's future is left to "the markets," the wealthier countries of Europe should conduct an open political debate about the potential consequences, such as mass labor migration or the further weakening of the European Union. The history of Europe in the past three decades has furnished ample evidence of the vulnerability and volatility of the order created in 1989.

# ACKNOWLEDGMENTS

I would like to dedicate this book to my friends in central and eastern Europe, whose sincerity, hospitality, and joie de vivre made an enduring impression on me. I am particularly grateful to Mirek and my unforgettable uncle Ludvík in Prague, Ingo, Frank, and Thea in Berlin, Włodek in Warsaw, and Markian in L'viv. The experience of 1989 and the "wild '90s" in Czechoslovakia, East Germany, Poland, and Ukraine changed my life and motivated me to become a historian. Going further back, I owe a lot to my parents' spirit of adventure and their frequent trips to the Eastern Bloc when few people from the West went there.

The academic starting point for this book was a conference on the consequences of 1989 for Europe, which took place at the European University Institute in Florence in 2008. I would like to thank the EUI and its then-president, Yves Meny, and the director of the Academic Service, Andreas Frijdal, for their generous support.

I am grateful to all the colleagues and institutions who gave me the opportunity to discuss parts of the manuscript, including János Kovács (IWM in Vienna), Ulf Brunnbauer (IOS Regensburg), Sven Reichardt (Constance University), Oliver Loew (German Institute for Polish Studies, Darmstadt), Harold James (Princeton University), Elisabeth Hagen, Leon Podkaminer and Roman Römisch (Vienna Institute for International Economic Studies), Uwe Müller (GWZO Leipzig), and Ostap Sereda for inviting me to several of his ReSET summer and winter schools in Ukraine.

I have been asked why I switched back to social history, and took on economic history, for this book. This decision was influenced by Jürgen Kocka, the founder of the Center for Comparative History of Europe in Berlin. He has been a great inspiration, especially in the field of social history. Klaus Zernack, my Ph.D. advisor, has been a model of incisive thinking and showed me how histories of various nations and regions can be intertwined. Andrzej Kamiński, my early mentor at Georgetown University, encouraged me to think outside the box and question conventional wisdoms.

Other institutions and academics in the United States have also provided inspiration. I would particularly like to thank Charles Maier and Grzegorz Ekiert for our stimulating discussions and allowing me to present key ideas of the book at the Harvard University Center for European Studies. Mitchell Orenstein (University of Pennsylvania) has been an invaluable partner in conversation and debate for more than two decades. I am very grateful to Larry Wolff (New York University) for his innovative ideas about the geography of Europe and the asymmetry of power connected to it, and for moral and intellectual support on various occasions. Norman Naimark (Stanford University) has been a reliable source of information about Eastern Europe. In a way, this is an "American book," as it was during my two years as a Fulbright scholar and then a postdoctoral fellow in the United States that I learned the importance of telling a story in academic history writing. Last but not least I would like to thank my three reviewers for their useful and valuable comments. The review process organized by Princeton University Press was exceedingly quick and competent. I have followed their excellent recommendations as far as possible, especially to add more points about German transformation history. Any remaining imprecision and errors are my responsibility.

I have also benefited from the tremendous knowledge and excellent advice of Włodzimierz Borodziej (Warsaw University), Dorothee Bohle (CEU Budapest), Piotr Filipkowski (IFIS Warsaw), Mária Hidvégi (Constance University), Jaroslav Hrytsak (Iwan Franko University, L'viv), Jerzy Kochanowski (Warsaw University), Michal Kopeček (Prague and Jena University), Tomasz Królik (Warsaw), Thomas Lindenberger (ZZF Potsdam), Fredrik Löjdquist (Swedish Embassy, Vienna), Christian Ronacher (Erste Bank, Austria), Kiran Klaus Patel (Maastricht University), Michal Pullmann (Charles University, Prague), Joachim von Puttkamer (Jena University), Dieter Segert and Tatjana Thelen (Vienna University), Viktoria Sereda (Iwan Franko University, L'viv), Ostap

Sereda (Ukrainian Academy of Sciences, Ľviv), and Hans-Jürgen Wagener (Frankfurt an der Oder). I would also like to thank Iwona Kochanowska of the Polityka archive and Anna Lenartowicz of the statistical agency of the city of Warsaw for their kind assistance. I am grateful for the help and support of Christian Nestler (IHK Berlin) and the archive of the Berlin state parliament (Berliner Abgeordnetenhaus).

I had the good fortune to have a number of colleagues and specialists who were prepared to read early versions of the manuscript and gave me valuable advice. Above all, I would like to thank János Kovács and the former Austrian finance minister Ferdinand Lacina, as well as my good friend (and guinea-pig reader) Thomas Vierich, and Martina Steer (Vienna University). Iris Engemann (who runs the agency Berlin-Text) created all the graphs, researched a tremendous amount of data, and saved me from a number of errors over the years. The quality of the book owes much to her research, questions, and entrepreneurial spirit. The questions and comments of my students in Vienna and at the CEU in Budapest in winter 2015 were also an important source of stimulation. In addition, I learned quite a lot from comments made on the previous Polish and Czech translations of this book.

I owe a particular debt of gratitude to the publisher Suhrkamp, and especially my lector, Heinrich Geiselberger. His excellent professional advice on the initial German version inspired me to make various changes and pursue new trains of thought. Literary agent Hanna Leitgeb (Agentur Rauchzeichen, Berlin) also had an important impact on the book. And my thanks go to Anita Biricz for her invaluable support during the correction phase.

Finally, I would like to thank Princeton University Press and especially chief lector Brigitta van Rheinberg, and Quinn Fusting for her excellent mentoring. Our cooperation has been very smooth and has lifted my spirits on various occasions.

It remains to mention the University of Vienna and our rector, Heinz Engl. Without the sabbatical granted in winter 2013/14 and the subsequent reduction of my teaching responsibilities I would not have been able to complete the book and supervise its translations. The cooperation with my translator Charlotte

Hughes-Kreutzmüller was, as always, excellent. Her questions and inventiveness have helped transform this book from a mere translation into a more refined English version.

This book was made possible not least by the support of my family. I am especially grateful to my wife, Martina, for her inspiration on many levels. I hope that when my children, Oskar, Anton, Raphael, and Eva, grow up, they will live in a Europe that offers them as many chances as the one formed in 1989.

# NOTES

## Chapter 1. Introduction

1. For the exact figures, see Iván T. Berend, *From the Soviet Bloc to the European Union: The Economic and Social Transformation of Central and Eastern Esurope since 1973*, Cambridge: Cambridge University Press, 2009, p. 69.
2. The original text is translated in Milan Kundera, "The Tragedy of Central Europe (April 26, 1984)," in Gale Stokes, ed., *From Stalinism to Pluralism: A Documentary History of Eastern Europe since 1945*, New York: Oxford University Press, 1991, pp. 217–23.
3. On the demise of Keynesianism and the breakthrough of neoliberalism, see Daniel Stedman Jones, *Masters of the Universe: Hayek, Friedman and the Birth of Neoliberal Politics*, Princeton: Princeton University Press, 2012, pp. 215–72.
4. The Canadian historian James Krapfl, who has written an excellent book about the ideals behind the revolution of 1989, calls this its "romantic" representation and reception. See his *Revolution with a Human Face: Politics, Culture, and Community in Czechoslovakia, 1989–1992*, Ithaca: Cornell University Press, 2013, pp. 14–18.
5. See the reports by the Vienna Institute for International Economic Studies (WIIW), which have been an important resource for this book. On price increases in Czechoslovakia, see *WIIW-Mitgliederinformation* 1990/6, pp. 22–23. Most of the statistical data on the post-1989 development of the individual countries are taken from the *WIIW Handbook of Statistics 2012* (Vienna: WIIW, 2013) and the supplementary CD-ROM (see especially the section "Countries by indicator"). The 2013 edition of the *WIIW Handbook of Statistics* was published shortly after the original edition of the present book was completed.
6. This is how Hans Rothfels, a founding father of contemporary history in postwar West Germany (who had taught in exile at Brown University and the University of Chicago from 1940 to 1951), put it. He spoke of an "Epoche der Mitlebenden."
7. On these celebrations, see Matthias Schlegel and Andrea Dernbach, "Die Welt schaut auf Berlin." *Zeit online* 9 November 2009. http://www.zeit.de/politik/2009–11/berlin-mauerfall. Accessed May 2014.

8. On urban-rural divergence, see Michael Förster, David Jesuit, and Timothy Smeeding, "Regional Poverty and Income Inequality in Central and Eastern Europe: Evidence from the Luxembourg Income Study." In Ravi Kanbur and Anthony J. Venables, eds., *Spatial Inequality and Development*, Oxford: Oxford University Press, 2005, pp. 311–47; Karen Macours and Johan F. M. Swinnen, "Rural-Urban Poverty Differences in Transition Countries." *LICOS Discussion Paper* 169, 2007. http://www.econ.kuleuven.be/licos/publications/dp /dp169.pdf. Accessed May 2014.

9. The internet's short memory is a problem where all these sources are concerned. Some information accessed at the outset of writing this book, around three or four years ago, has since been deleted or is no longer accessible (e.g., on Eurostat). This is pointed out where applicable.

10. Print media consulted for this book include the *Economist*, the *New York Times*, *Der Spiegel*, *Die Zeit*, *Frankfurter Allgemeine Zeitung*, *Süddeutsche Zeitung* (Germany), *Presse*, *Standard*, *Wiener Wirtschaftsblatt* (Austria), *Polityka*, *Gazeta Wyborcza* and *Rzeczpospolita* (Poland), *Respekt* (Czech Republic), and *Hospodárske Noviny* (Slovakia). Media sources that are accessible on the internet are not separately listed in the bibliography to avoid taking up too much space.

11. According to long-term CDU parliamentary party leader Klaus-Rüdiger Landowsky in a speech he gave to the Berlin House of Representatives. Cf. Abgeordnetenhaus von Berlin, 13. Wahlperiode, Plenarprotokoll 13/37, 37. Sitzung, 11. Dezember 1997, p. 2386. http://pardok.parlament-berlin.de/starweb/adis/citat/VT /13/PlenarPr/p13037.pdf#page=10. Accessed May 2014.

12. I initially considered consulting the Human Development Index (HDI) for this book. The HDI has been used by the UN since 1990 and is broadly considered a more meaningful measure of social prosperity than statistics on GDP. However, there are very few regional and local statistics on HDI. For this reason, I have relied predominantly on data on GDP, economic growth, and other indicators.

13. On the Mont Pèlerin Society's founding principles, see Dieter Plehwe, "Introduction." In Philip Mirowski and Dieter Plehwe, eds., *The Road from Mont Pèlerin: The Making of the Neoliberal Thought Collective*, Cambridge, MA: Harvard University Press, 2009, pp. 1–44. Hayek, who worked at the London School of Economics for many years, was regarded as John Maynard Keynes's principal adversary; their

academic rivalry was a definitive factor in promoting neoliberalism. Lippmann stayed in the society for only a short time.

14. On the history of economics as an academic discipline, see Warren Samuels, Jeff Biddle, and John Davis, *A Companion to the History of Economic Thought*, Oxford: Oxford University Press, 2003.

15. The paper's actual author was the economist John Williamson, who acted as expert consultant to the institutions involved. For the original text, see John Williamson, ed., *Latin American Readjustment: How Much Has Happened*, Washington, DC: Institute for International Economics, 1990; on its adaptation to postcommunist Europe, see Paul Dragos Aligica and Anthony John Evans, *The Neoliberal Revolution in Eastern Europe: Economic Ideas in the Transition from Communism*, Cheltenham: Elgar, 2009.

16. Joseph Stiglitz, *Freefall: America, Free Markets, and the Sinking of the World Economy*, New York: Penguin, 2010, pp. xiii, 12–15, 248–53.

17. See the review by John Williamson, "A Short History of the Washington Consensus." http://www.iie.com/publications/papers/williamson0904-2.pdf. Accessed May 2014. On the tendency among neoliberalism's proponents to distance themselves from the term, see the first footnote in the above paper; on the (very broad) definition of neoliberalism, see Johanna Bockman, *Markets in the Name of Socialism: The Left-Wing Origins of Neoliberalism*, Stanford: Stanford University Press, 2011, pp. 4–10. On the dissemination and internal logic of neoliberalism, see e.g., David Harvcy, *A Brief History of Neoliberalism*, Oxford: Oxford University Press, 2005.

18. Plehwe, "Introduction," p. 2.

19. However, this, too, is disputed. Aligica and Evans contend that the measures applied in the transitional countries were merely in the economic mainstream: see their *The Neoliberal Revolution*, pp. 157–58. Other economists (mostly those who sympathized with the economic reforms of the nineties) also reject the term "neoliberalism" for classifying economic policies and schools of thought.

20. See, among others, Juan J. Linz and Alfred Stepan, *Problems of Democratic Transition and Consolidation: Southern Europe, South America, and Post-Communist Europe*, Baltimore: Johns Hopkins University Press, 1996.

21. David Lipton and Jeffrey D. Sachs, "Poland's Economic Reform." *Foreign Affairs* 69.3 (1990), pp. 47–66.

22. Interestingly, these influences have mostly been seen to run from West to East, and not vice versa. On the "fourth dimension," see Mitchell A. Orenstein, Stephen Bloom, and Nicole Lindstrom, eds.,

*Transnational Actors in Central and East European Transitions*, Pittsburgh: University of Pittsburgh Press, 2008; Rachel A. Epstein, *In Pursuit of Liberalism: International Institutions in Postcommunist Europe*, Baltimore: Johns Hopkins University Press, 2008; Heather Grabbe, *The EU's Transformative Power: Europeanization through Conditionality in Central and Eastern Europe*, Basingstoke: Palgrave, 2008; Milada Vachudova, *Europe Undivided: Democracy, Leverage and Integration after Communism*, Oxford: Oxford University Press, 2005.

23. Samuel P. Huntington, *The Third Wave: Democratization in the Late Twentieth Century*, Norman: University of Oklahoma Press, 1991; on political system change, see also Philippe Schmitter and Nicolas Guilhot, "From Transition to Consolidation: Extending the Concept of Democratization and the Practice of Democracy." In Michel Dobry, ed., *Democratic and Capitalist Transitions in Eastern Europe*, Dordrecht: Kluwer, 2000, pp. 131–46; see also Klaus von Beyme, *Systemwechsel in Osteuropa*, Frankfurt am Main: Suhrkamp, 1994; Wolfgang Merkel, *Systemtransformation. Eine Einführung in die Theorie und Empire der Transformationsforschung*, Wiesbaden: VS Verlag für Sozialwissenschaften, 2010.

24. Padraic Kenney, *The Burdens of Freedom: Eastern Europe since 1989*, Black Point: Zed Books, 2006.

25. Revolution theories are considered in greater depth below in chapter 3, on the revolutions of 1989–91.

26. Zygmunt Bauman, "A Revolution in the Theory of Revolution." *International Political Science Review* 15 (1994), pp. 15–24.

27. See Hannah Arendt, *On Revolution*, New York: The Viking Press, 1963, pp. 13–52.

28. See Alexis de Tocqueville, *The Ancien Régime and the French Revolution*, edited by John Elster, translated by Arthur Goldhammer, Cambridge: Cambridge University Press, 2011; Edmund Burke, *Reflections on the Revolution in France and on the Proceedings in Certain Societies in London Relative to That Event* (1790), London: Penguin Books, 1968.

29. The level of simultaneity in the mid-nineties gave Claus Offe cause to doubt whether the transformation could succeed at all. See his *Der Tunnel am Ende des Lichts. Erkundungen der politischen Transformation im Neuen Osten*, Frankfurt am Main: Campus, 1994.

30. Maria Dąbrowska, "Tagebücher." In Karl Dedecius, ed., *Bube, Dame, König. Geschichten aus Polen*, Frankfurt am Main: Suhrkamp, 1990, pp. 143–54.

31. See Douglas Coupland, *Generation X: Tales for an Accelerated Culture*, New York: St. Martin's Press, 1991, p. 7. He writes of "historical

overdosing—to live in a period of time when too much seems to happen. Major symptoms include addiction to newspapers, magazines, and TV news broadcasts."

32. See Lynn Hunt, ed., *The New Cultural History*, Berkeley: University of California Press, 1989.

33. See, e.g., Philipp Ther, "Das 'neue Europa' seit 1989. Überlegungen zu einer Geschichte der Transformationszeit." *Zeithistorische Forschungen* 6 (2009), pp. 105–14.

34. See the eponymous book by Peter A. Hall and David Soskice, eds., *Varieties of Capitalism: The Institutional Foundation of Comparative Advantage*, Oxford: Oxford University Press, 2001. Further literature is recommended in the section of this book titled "A Typology of Reform Outcomes."

35. See, e.g., the Index of Economic Freedom that has been compiled since 1995 by the Heritage Foundation and the *Wall Street Journal*, in which private ownership plays a central role. The current index is accessible online at http://www.heritage.org/index/ranking.aspx. Accessed May 2014. Despite its bias, this index is of interest due to its global comparisons (including Europe), as well as the fact that it proves the hegemony of neoliberalism during the transformation period.

36. On the economic transformation, see, e.g., the overviews by Marie Lavigne, *The Economics of Transition: From Socialist Economy to Market Economy*, 2nd edition, Basingstoke: Palgrave Macmillan, 2007; Hans-Jürgen Wagener, *Wirtschaftsordnung im Wandel. Zur Transformation 1985–2010*, Marburg: Metropolis Verlag, 2011. On the Russian Federation's Land Act, see Grigoriy Joffe, Tatyana Nefedova, and Ilya Zaslavsky, *The End of Peasantry? The Disintegration of Rural Russia*, Pittsburgh: University of Pittsburgh Press, 2006, pp. 28–29.

37. See Dorothee Bohle and Béla Greskovits, "Neoliberalismus, eingebetteter Neoliberalismus, und Neo-Korporatismus. Sozialistische Hinterlassenschaften, transnationale Integration und die Diversität osteuropäischer Kapitalismen." In Dieter Segert, ed., *Postsozialismus. Hinterlassenschaften des Staatssozialismus und neue Kapitalismen in Europa*, Vienna: Braumüller, 2007, pp. 185–205. The authors applied the same typology to their more recent acclaimed study, *Capitalist Diversity on Europe's Periphery*, Ithaca: Cornell University Press, 2012.

38. On such criticisms, see Peter Katzenstein, "Small States and Small States Revisited," *Political Economy* 1.8 (2003), pp. 9–30. Katzenstein (whom Bohle and Greskovits cite) argues against defining the East

Central European countries as neoliberal in view of their high social security spending.

39. See Wolfgang Merkel, "Gegen alle Theorie? Die Konsolidierung der Demokratie in Ostmitteleuropa," *Politische Vierteljahresschrift* 48.3 (2007), pp. 413–33; idem, *Systemtransformation*; Grzegorz Ekiert, "The State after State Socialism: Poland in Comparative Perspective," In John Hall and John Ikenberry, eds., *The Nation-State in Question*, Princeton: Princeton University Press, 2003, pp. 291–320. On the role of education for the course of reforms and the persistence of postcommunist parties, see Keith Darden and Anna Grzymała-Busse, "The Great Divide: Literacy, Nationalism, and the Communist Collapse," *World Politics* 59.1 (October 2006), pp. 83–115.

40. On transformation in the former Yugoslavia, see Duško Sekulić and Željka Šporer, "Croatia: Managerial Elite Circulation or Reproduction?," in John Higley and György Lengyel, eds., *Elites after State Socialism: Theories and Analysis*, Lanham: Rowman & Littlefield, 2000, pp. 143–62; Sabrina P. Ramet and Davorka Matić, eds., *Democratic Transition in Croatia: Value Transformation, Education & Media*, College Station: Texas A&M University Press, 2007.

41. Perhaps the best book on Yugoslavia's collapse is Holm Sundhaussen, *Jugoslawien und seine Nachfolgestaaten 1943-2011*, Vienna: Böhlau, 2012.

42. See Peter Siani-Davies, *The Romanian Revolution of December 1989*, Ithaca: Cornell University Press, 2005.

43. See Lilia Shevtsova, *Russia: Lost in Transition: The Yeltsin and Putin Legacies*, Washington, DC: Carnegie Endowment, 2007. In this book, well-known Russian and Ukrainian names, e.g. Vladimir Putin, are transliterated according to English conventions; lesser-known names are rendered according to the scholarly system of transliteration.

44. On the Chinese path of transformation, see, e.g., Kellee S. Tsai, *Capitalism without Democracy: The Private Sector in Contemporary China*, Ithaca: Cornell University Press, 2007.

45. On this concept (in German: "nachholende Modernisierung") and the development of the Eastern Bloc in the postwar era, see Dieter Segert, *Transformation in Osteuropa im 20. Jahrhundert*, Vienna: Facultas, 2013, pp. 63–65, 71.

46. The chief proponent of such regional studies is the Polish social scientist Grzegorz Gorzelak. See his book *The Regional Dimension of Transformation in Central Europe: Regions and Cities*, 2nd edition, London:

Routledge, 2002 [1996], and Grzegorz Gorzelak, John Bachtler, and Maciej Smętkowski, eds., *Regional Development in Central and Eastern Europe: Development Processes and Policy Challenges*, London: Routledge, 2010; see also Heinz Fassmann, "Die Rückkehr der Regionen—regionale Konsequenzen der Transformation in Ostmitteleuropa. Eine Einführung," in idem, ed., *Die Rückkehr der Regionen. Beiträge zur regionalen Transformation Ostmitteleuropas*, Vienna: Verlag der ÖAW, 1997, pp. 13–34. On the causes of this divergence, see Petr Pavlínek, "Regional Development Implications of Foreign Direct Investment in Central Europe," *European Urban and Regional Studies* 11.1 (2004), pp. 47–70.

47. For an introduction, see Grigoriy Kostinskiy, "Post-Socialist Cities in Flux," in Ronan Paddison, ed., *Handbook of Urban Studies*, London: Sage, 2001, pp. 450–85.

48. See, among others (in order of publication date), Katherine Verdery, *What Was Socialism and What Comes Next?*, Princeton: Princeton University Press, 1996; Michał Buchowski, *Rethinking Transformation: An Anthropological Perspective on Postsocialism*, Poznań: Humaniora, 2001; Michael Burawoy and Katherine Verdery, eds., *Uncertain Transition: Ethnographies of Change in the Postsocialist World*, Lanham, Rowman & Littlefield, 1999; Elizabeth C. Dunn, *Privatizing Poland: Baby Food, Big Business, and the Remaking of Labor*, Ithaca: Cornell University Press, 2004; Chris Hann, *Postsocialism: Ideals, Ideologies and Practices in Eurasia*, London: Routledge, 2002; Tatjana Thelen, Andrew Cartwright, and Thomas Sikor, *Local State and Social Security in Rural Communities: A New Research Agenda and the Example of Postsocialist Europe*, Halle: Max-Planck Institut für ethnologische Forschung, 2008; Aleksandra Galasińska, Michał Krzyżanowski, Sue Wright, and Helen Kelly-Holmes, eds., *Discourse and Transformation in Central and Eastern Europe: Language and Globalization*, Basingstoke: Palgrave Macmillan, 2009.

49. Some examples of such syntheses of twentieth-century history are Eric Hobsbawm, *The Age of Extremes: The Short Twentieth Century, 1914–1991*, London: Michael Joseph, 1994; Norman Davies, *Europe: A History*, Oxford: Oxford University Press, 1996; Mark Mazower, *Dark Continent: Europe's Twentieth Century*, New York: Vintage, 2000; Tony Judt, *Postwar: A History of Europe since 1945*, New York: Penguin, 2005; Hartmut Kaelble, *Sozialgeschichte Europas. 1945 bis zur Gegenwart*, Munich: Beck, 2007; Konrad Jarausch, *Out of Ashes: A New History of Europe in the Twentieth Century*, Princeton, Princeton University Press, 2015.

50. For another German-language book that begins its inquiry in the 1980s, see Andreas Wirsching, *Der Preis der Freiheit. Geschichte Europas in unserer Zeit*, Munich: Beck, 2012.

## Chapter 2. Where the East Meets the West: Crisis and Reform Debates in the 1980s

1. Klaus Segbers, *Der sowjetische Systemwandel*, Frankfurt am Main: Suhrkamp, 1989; Anders Åslund, *Gorbachev's Struggle for Economic Reform: The Soviet Reform Process, 1985-1988*, Ithaca: Cornell University Press, 1989.
2. Cf. the original slogan "Überholen, ohne einzuholen," cited in Raymond G. Stokes, "Von Trabbis und Acelyten—die Technikentwicklung," in Andre Steiner, ed., *Überholen ohne Einzuholen. Die DDR-Wirtschaft als Fußnote der deutschen Geschichte?*, Berlin: C. Links, 2006, pp. 105–26, here 114.
3. For a comparison of welfare states in East and West, see Christoph Boyer, "Zwischen Pfadabhängigkeit und Zäsur. Ost- und westeuropäische Sozialstaaten seit den siebziger Jahren des 20. Jahrhunderts," In Konrad Jarausch, ed., *Das Ende der Zuversicht? Die siebziger Jahre als Geschichte*, Göttingen: Vandenhoeck & Ruprecht, 2008, pp. 103–19.
4. Paul Villaume and Odd Arne Westad, eds., *Perforating the Iron Curtain: European Détente, Transatlantic Relations, and the Cold War, 1965-1985*, Copenhagen: Museum Tusculanum Press, 2010.
5. On trade relations and other contacts within the Eastern Bloc, see Włodzimierz Borodziej, Jerzy Kochanowski, and Joachim von Puttkamer, eds., *"Schleichwege." Inoffizielle Begegnungen sozialistischer Staatsbürger zwischen 1956 und 1989*, Vienna: Böhlau, 2010.
6. Cf. Christian Domnitz, *Hinwendung nach Europa. Neuorientierung und Öffentlichkeitswandel im Staatssozialismus 1975-1989*, Bochum: Winkler, 2015.
7. See also the conference titled "Loopholes in the Iron Curtain: Economic Contacts between Eastern and Western Europe since the 1970s," held on 18–19 April 2013 in Vienna, documented at the H-Soz-u-Kult website: http://hsozkult.geschichte.hu-berlin.de /tagungsberichte/id=4996. Accessed May 2014.
8. See John Lewis Gaddis, *We Now Know: Rethinking Cold War History*, Oxford: Oxford University Press, 1997. For a more comprehensive account, though also focused on the major conflicts, see Melvin Leffler

and Odd Arne Westad, eds., *The Cambridge History of the Cold War*, 3 vols., Cambridge: Cambridge University Press, 2010.

9. See Frédéric Bozo, Marie-Pierre Rey, Piers Ludlow, and Leopoldo Nuti, *Europe and the End of the Cold War: A Reappraisal*, London: Routledge, 2008; on the Cold War in Europe, see also Bernd Stöver, *Der Kalte Krieg. Geschichte eines radikalen Zeitalters, 1947–1991*, Munich: Beck, 2011, pp. 386–409.

10. All ten episodes of the series can be viewed online: http://www.youtube.com/watch?v=f1Fj5tzuYBE. Accessed May 2014. Friedman also published a book on the subject, written with his wife, which was a similar popular success. See Milton Friedman and Rose Friedman, *Free to Choose: A Personal Statement*, New York: Harcourt, 1980.

11. Quoted from Konrad H. Jarausch, "Zwischen 'Reformstau' und 'Sozialabbau'" Anmerkungen zur Globalisierungsdebatte in Deutschland 1973–2003," in idem, ed., *Das Ende der Zuversicht? Die siebziger Jahre als Geschichte*, Göttingen: Vandenhoeck & Ruprecht, 2008, pp. 330–52, here 335. The original citation was: "Weg von mehr Staat, hin zu mehr Markt; weg von kollektiven Lasten, hin zur persönlichen Leistung; weg von verkrusteten Strukturen, hin zu mehr Beweglichkeit, Eigeninitiative und verstärkter Wettbewerbsfähigkeit."

12. See Geoff Eley, *Forging Democracy: The History of the Left in Europe, 1850–2000*, Oxford: Oxford University Press, 2002.

13. Harold James, *Europe Reborn: A History 1914–2000*, London: Longman, 2003; on the "conservative revolution" and Thatcherism, see Dominik Geppert, *Thatchers konservative Revolution. Der Richtungswandel der britischen Tories 1975–1979*, Munich: Oldenbourg, 2002.

14. Cf. Jarausch, *Das Ende der Zuversicht*; also Anselm Doering-Manteuffel and Raphael Lutz, *Nach dem Boom. Perspektiven auf die Zeitgeschichte seit 1970*, Göttingen: Vandenhoeck & Ruprecht, 2008.

15. On the black market in Poland under state socialism, see Jerzy Kochanowski, *Jenseits der Planwirtschaft. Der Schwarzmarkt in Polen 1944–1989*, Göttingen: Wallstein, 2013; on Poland's history during this difficult time, see Włodzimierz Borodziej, *Geschichte Polens im 20. Jahrhundert*, Munich: Beck, 2010.

16. Cf. Marek Borkowski, "Sprzedać, oddać, wydzierżawić," *Polityka* 32.49 (3 Dezember 1988), pp. 1, 4. Borkowski was a head of department in the domestic market ministry at the time. He rose to become deputy minister in the ministry under the first two Solidarność-led administrations, where he was responsible for the privatization of trade and tourism enterprises. In 1993 he became finance minister of

the first postcommunist government. His career is a prime example of the continuities in Poland's reform and privatization policy. On the supporters of radical reforms, see also Borodziej, *Geschichte Polens im 20. Jahrhundert*, pp. 376–80. Cf. the personal account by Karol Modzelewski, *Zajeździmy kobyłę historii. Wyznania poobijanego jeźdźca*, Warsaw: Iskry, 2013, p. 362.

17. See Roman Szporluk, *Russia, Ukraine and the Breakup of the Soviet Union*, Stanford: Hoover Institution Press, 2000, pp. 395–429; Mark R. Beissinger, "Nationalism and the Collapse of Soviet Communism," *Contemporary European History* 18.3 (2009), pp. 331–47.

18. On responses to neoliberalism among economists and economic policymakers in Eastern Europe (especially Yugoslavia), see Bockman, *Markets in the Name of Socialism*, pp. 76–132.

19. Robert Heilbroner, "The Triumph of Capitalism," *The New Yorker* 23 January 1989, p. 98.

20. The episode dealing with the breakdown of state socialism and the postcommunist transformation can be viewed online: http://www.youtube.com/watch?v=l2h5OR1QX3Y. Accessed May 2014. Cf. the Reagan citation starting at 40 seconds.

## Chapter 3. The Revolutions of 1989–91

1. On the use of the term "revolution" in the GDR in fall 1989, see Bernd Lindner, "Begriffsgeschichte der Friedlichen Revolution. Eine Spurensuche," *Aus Politik und Zeitgeschichte* 24–26/2014, pp. 33–39. On the same in Czechoslovakia, see Krapfl, *Revolution with a Human Face*, p. 8.

2. See Charles Tilly, *European Revolutions 1492-1992*, Oxford: Oxford University Press, 1992; Theda Skocpol, *Social Revolutions in the Modern World*, Cambridge: Cambridge University Press, 1994; Arendt, *On Revolution*. More recent attempts at defining revolutions have been provided by David Parker, ed., *Revolutions and the Revolutionary Tradition in the West 1560-1991*, London: Routledge, 2000; George Lawson, *Negotiated Revolutions: The Czech Republic, South Africa and Chile*: London: Ashgate, 2004.

3. For a good chronological overview, see Victor Sebestyen, *Revolution 1989: The Fall of the Soviet Empire*, New York: Random House, 2009. On the course of the revolutions and the controversial responses they elicited, see also the special edition edited by Manfred Sapper and Volker Weichsel of the magazine *Osteuropa, Freiheit im Blick. 1989 und der Aufbruch in Europa* (= *Osteuropa* 2/3 [2009]).

4. Putin's speech is documented in the Kremlin archive: http://archive.kremlin.ru/text/appears/2005/04/87049.shtml. Accessed May 2014.

5. Cf. Milada Vachudova and Timothy Snyder, "Are Transitions Transitory? Two Models of Political Change in East Central Europe since 1989," *East European Politics & Society* 11 (1997), pp. 1–35, here 3. ("Ethnic geography" is identified here as one of three main factors contributing to the success or failure of a country's transformation.)

6. See Jan Zielonka, *Europe as Empire: The Nature of the Enlarged European Union*, Oxford: Oxford University Press, 2006.

7. On Czechoslovakia, where the word "reform" was avoided as a rejection of the reform communists of 1968, see Michal Pullmann, *Konec experimentu. Představba a pad komunismu v Československu*, Prague: Scriptorium, 2011, pp. 63–70.

8. Timothy Garton Ash, *We the People: The Revolution of '89 Witnessed in Warsaw, Budapest, Berlin & Prague*, Cambridge: Granta Books, 1990.

9. György Dalos, *Der Vorhang geht auf. Das Ende der Diktaturen in Osteuropa*, Munich: Beck, 2009.

10. Padraic Kenney, *A Carnival of Revolution: Central Europe 1989*, Princeton: Princeton University Press, 2002.

11. On this debate, see Timothy Garton Ash, "1989!" *New York Review of Books* 56.17 (5 November 2009), p. 6.

12. Stephen Kotkin, with the cooperation of Jan T. Gross, *Uncivil Society: 1989 and the Implosion of the Communist Establishment*, New York: Random House, 2009.

13. On the local proliferation of civil rights committees, see Krapfl, *Revolution with a Human Face*, pp. 115, 201–16.

14. See the divergent interpretations in Tom Gallagher, *Theft of a Nation: Romania since Communism*, London: Hurst & Company, 2005, pp. 70–109, who supports the putsch thesis, and Siani-Davies, *The Romanian Revolution of December 1989*, pp. 267–86.

15. See Valère P. Gagnon, *The Myth of Ethnic War: Serbia and Croatia in the 1990s*, Ithaca: Cornell University Press, 2004.

16. See, for example, Anders Åslund, *Gorbachev's Struggle for Economic Reform*, and idem, *How Capitalism Was Built: The Transformation of Central and Eastern Europe, Russia, and Central Asia*, Cambridge: Cambridge University Press, 2007.

17. See Berend, *From the Soviet Bloc*, pp. 20–38.

18. The Vienna Institute for International Economic Studies (WIIW) recognized the severity of the problem at the time. See *WIIW-Mitgliederinformation* 1990/6, pp. 24–25. On Gorbachev's fatal

economic and budget policy, see also Gerald M. Easter, *Capital, Coercion, and Postcommunist States*, Ithaca: Cornell University Press, 2012, pp. 23–50.

19. See Boyer, "Zwischen Pfadabhängigkeit und Zäsur," pp. 103–19.

20. See the comprehensive record by Mark Kramer, "Ukraine and the Czechoslovak Crisis of 1968 Part 2: New Evidence from the Ukrainian Archives." *Cold War International History Project Bulletin* 14/15 (2004), pp. 273–368.

21. See Mary Elise Sarotte, *The Collapse: The Accidental Opening of the Berlin Wall*, New York: Basic Books, 2014, pp. 63, 73.

22. See Ronald G. Suny and Terry Martin, eds., *A State of Nations: Empire and Nation Making in the Age of Lenin and Stalin*, Oxford: Oxford University Press, 2001.

23. For the exact statistics, see Graham Smith, "The Resurgence of Nationalism," in idem, ed., *The Baltic States: The National Self-Determination of Estonia, Latvia and Lithuania*, New York: St. Martin's, 1994, pp. 121–43.

24. See Yaroslav Hrytsak, "On the Relevance and Irrelevance of Nationalism in Contemporary Ukraine," in Georgiy Kasianov and Philipp Ther, eds., *A Laboratory of Transnational History: Ukraine and Recent Ukrainian Historiography*, Budapest: CEU Press, 2009, pp. 225–48.

25. See Mark Kramer, "The Collapse of East European Communism and the Repercussions within the Soviet Union, Part 1," *Journal of Cold War Studies* 5/4 (fall 2003), pp. 178–256. On the internal Soviet dynamics, see Serhii Plokhy, *The Last Empire: The Final Days of the Soviet Union*, New York: Basic Books, 2014.

26. Sundhaussen, *Jugoslawien und seine Nachfolgestaaten*.

27. Sarotte, *The Collapse*, pp. 177–79.

28. On the concept of revolution and its internal differentiations, see Tilly, *European Revolutions*, p. 8.

29. One good biography has been published, though without footnotes to facilitate further research. See György Dalos, *Gorbatschow—Mensch und Macht. Eine Biografie*, Munich: Beck, 2010.

30. See Michael Zantovsky, *Havel: A Life*, New York: Grove Press, 2014.

31. See Lars Fredrik Stöcker, *Bridging the Baltic Sea: Networks of Resistance and Opposition during the Cold War Era*, Ph.D. thesis, EUI Florence, Department of History and Civilization, 2013.

32. On 1989 in a global perspective, see: Lawson, *Negotiated Revolutions*; George Lawson, Chris Armbruster, and Michael Cox, eds., *The Global 1989: Continuity and Change in World Politics*, Cambridge: Cambridge University Press, 2010; also Jacques Rupnik, ed., *1989 as a Political*

*World Event: Democracy, Europe and the New International System in the Age of Globalization*, London: Routledge, 2014.

33. On support for the Chinese party leadership in the GDR, see Sarotte, *The Collapse*, p. 43. According to Timothy Garton Ash, however, the massacre on Tiananmen Square had an overall negative impact; see "1989!," p. 6.

34. One of the first books to describe this tendency, in the 1950s, was Robert R. Palmer, *The Age of the Democratic Revolution: A Political History of Europe and America, 1760–1800*, Princeton: Princeton University Press, 1959; see also Tilly, *European Revolutions*; Theda Skocpol, *Social Revolutions in the Modern World*, Cambridge: Cambridge University Press, 1994.

35. See Sarotte, *The Collapse*, pp. 30–32. Jens Gieseke, "Der entkräftete Tschekismus. Das MfS und seine ausgebliebene Niederschlagung der Konterrevolution 1989/90," in Martin Sabrow, ed., *1989 und die Rolle der Gewalt*, Göttingen: Wallstein, 2012, pp. 56–81, here 60–61.

36. Russian writer Y. Yevtushenko has incorporated an account of this incident in a compelling novel, *Don't Die before You Are Dead*, New York: Random House, 1995.

37. See, for example, Heinz-Gerhard Haupt, *Gewalt und Politik im Europa des 19. und 20. Jahrhunderts*, Göttingen: Wallstein, 2012.

38. See Miroslav Vaněk, "Der 17. November und seine Ursachen in den Erzählungen kommunistischer Funktionäre," in Niklas Perzi, Beata Blehová, and Peter Bachmeier, eds., *Die samtene Revolution. Vorgeschichte–Verlauf–Akteure*, Frankfurt am Main: Peter Lang, 2009, pp. 147–64.

39. See Sarotte, *The Collapse*, p. 54.

40. On this concept of revolution, see Tilly, *European Revolutions*, p. 8. In view of the "revolutionary outcomes," Tilly holds that the events of 1989 amounted to a chain of revolutions; see idem, p. 235; on the definition of revolutions, see also Skocpol, *Social Revolutions in the Modern World*, p. 133.

41. See Jadwiga Staniszkis, *Pologne. La révolution autolimitée*, Paris: Presses universitaires de France, 1982. (An English translation entitled *Poland's Self-Limiting Revolution* was published in 1984 by Princeton University Press.) After 1989 Staniszkis frequently criticized the endurance of ties with communism in Poland; see her critical view of postcommunism in idem, *Postkomunizm. Próba opisu*, Gdańsk: Wydawnictwo słowo/obraz terytoria, 2001. For a broader consideration of the concept of the "negotiated revolution," see also Lawson, *Negotiated Revolutions*.

42. Arendt, *On Revolution*, pp. 13–52.
43. On Hungarian criticism and denial of the revolution, see the eye-opening texts by Joachim von Puttkamer, Ellen Bos, and András Bozoki in a special edition devoted to Orbán of the magazine *Osteuropa* (*Osteuropa* 61/12 [December 2011]).
44. See Jürgen Habermas, "What Does Socialism Mean Today? The Rectifying Revolution and the Need for New Thinking on the Left," *New Left Review* 1.183 (September–October 1990), pp. 3–21; Jacques Rupnik, "1968: The Year of Two Springs," *Eurozine* 16 May 2008. http://www.eurozine.com/articles/2008-05-16-rupnik-en.html. Accessed May 2014. Rupnik holds that 1989 was a "counter-'68."
45. On the Prague protesters' original values and the endurance of positive attitudes to socialism, see Pullmann, *Konec experimentu*, pp. 189–90.

## Chapter 4. Getting on the Neoliberal Bandwagon

1. See Bauman, "A Revolution in the Theory of Revolution," pp. 15–24.
2. An earlier critique of the Washington Consensus was published in Moisés Naím, "Fads and Fashion in Economic Reforms: Washington Consensus or Washington Confusion?," 26 October 1999. http://www.imf.org/external/pubs/ft/seminar/1999/reforms/Naim.HTM. Accessed May 2014. Interestingly, this critique was published by the World Bank, indicating that it was beginning to distance itself from its own policies of 1989.
3. See N. N., "Unwort des Jahres 'alternativlos.'" *Die Zeit* 18 January 2011. http://www.zeit.de/gesellschaft/zeitgeschehen/2011-01/unwort-2010-alternativlos. Accessed May 2014. *Die Zeit* is Germany's most respected weekly newspaper.
4. Strictly speaking, this was preceded by the 1992 election victory of Algirdas Brazauskas in Lithuania. However, this first instance of a postcommunist politician winning out over former opposition parties garnered less interest in the West.
5. Later, Balcerowicz and his circle also used the terms "shock" and "shock therapy," making a political mistake for which they paid at the 1993 elections. See Leszek Balcerowicz, *800 Dni Szok Kontrolowany. Zapisał: Jerzy Baczyński*, Warsaw: BGW, 1992.
6. On the reformers' original assumptions, see the comments by Leszek Balcerowicz in an interview with the weekly newspaper *Polityka* in December 1989, when he still assumed that there would be only a

slight drop in demand and high unemployment could be avoided. See "Albo szybko, albo wcale," *Polityka* 33/48 (2 December 1989), pp. 1, 5 (here especially column 2 on p. 1).

7. See the statistics in *WIIW Handbook 2012*, Countries by indicator, Table II/1.7. At the time, the slump provoked serious doubts among international observers whether the reforms in Poland would succeed at all. See, e.g., the IMF Staff Report from July 8, 1992, which is accessible in the World Bank Archive, World Bank File 30029780 (Poland – Privatization – Volume 2): n.p. These doubts do not confirm today's idolization of the shock therapy.

8. Modzeleweski, *Zajeździmy*, p. 393.

9. In Poland, Grzegorz Kołodko championed this idea. He was finance minister under several SLD-led governments and an internationally renowned economic expert. He also published in English, testifying to his international reputation. See, e.g., his *From Shock to Therapy: The Political Economy of the Postsocialist Transformation*, Oxford: Oxford University Press, 2000.

10. See Adam Michnik, "Ten straszny Balcerowicz," *Gazeta Wyborcza* 28 November 1992, p. 10. In this article, Michnik writes: "One might ask whether in the current situation there is any possibility of gaining broad acceptance at all—but one cannot simply assume that the majority of the population would have understood the sense and consequences of Balcerowicz's policies in the first place" (my translation). Balcerowicz expressed the same view, saying that it was necessary to present the reforms as a "fait accompli" to carry them out. See Leszek Balcerowicz, *Socialism, Capitalism, Transformation*, Budapest: CEU Press, 1995, p. 307. On the paradoxes of liberalism in Poland, see Jerzy Szacki, *Liberalism after Communism*, Budapest: CEU Press, 1995.

11. See the chapter "How Liberals Lost Labour" in David Ost, *The Defeat of Solidarity: Anger and Politics in Postcommunist Europe*, Ithaca: Cornell University Press, 2005, pp. 94–120.

12. On the validity of this term, see Anne Goedicke, "A 'Ready-Made State': The Mode of Institutional Transition in East Germany after 1989," In Martin Diewald, Anne Goedicke, and Karl Ulrich Mayer, eds., *After the Fall of the Wall: Life Courses in the Transformation of East Germany*, Stanford: Stanford University Press, 2006, p. 63.

13. See H. Jörg Thieme, "Notenbank und Währung in der DDR," in Deutsche Bundesbank, ed., *Fünfzig Jahre Deutsche Mark. Notenbank und Währung in Deutschland seit 1948*, Munich: Beck, 1998, pp. 609–54, here 628, 648. On the GDR's economic problems, see Hartmut Berghoff

and Uta Andrea Balbier, *The East German Economy, 1945–2010: Falling Behind or Catching Up?*, Cambridge: Cambridge University Press, 2013.

14. The economist Hans-Werner Sinn calculated on the basis of purchasing power parity. Indeed, it was possible to buy almost as much for one East German mark as for one West German mark. But wages and salaries were distinctly lower in the GDR than in West Germany. See Gerlinde Sinn and Hans-Werner Sinn, *Kaltstart. Volkswirtschaftliche Aspekte der deutschen Vereinigung*, 2nd edition, Tübingen: Mohr, 1992, pp. 54–64.

15. Representatives of the GDR state bank warned against this revaluation and argued for an exchange rate of 7:1 to keep the East German economy competitive. See an interview of 28 February 2015 with the vice president of the GDR state bank, Edgar Most, broadcast by the radio station Deutschlandfunk: http://www.deutschlandfunk.de/25 -jahre-treuhandanstalt-eine-einzige-schweinerei.694.de.html?dram: article_id=312882. Accessed March 2015.

16. See Andreas Rödder, *Deutschland einig Vaterland. Die Geschichte der Wiedervereinigung*, Munich: Beck, 2009, p. 193.

17. See Goedicke: "A 'Ready-Made State,'" pp. 44–64, here 48.

18. Karl-Heinz Paqué, "Transformationspolitik in Ostdeutschland. Ein Teilerfolg," *Aus Politik und Zeitgeschichte 28* (2009), pp. 22–27, here 23.

19. See Paqué, *Die Bilanz. Eine wirtschaftliche Analyse der Deutschen Einheit*, Munich: Hanser, 2009, p. 73. Estimates of East German productivity in comparison to West Germany varied between 17 and 50 percent (ibid., pp. 20–21).

20. See Sinn and Sinn, *Kaltstart*, vii.

21. On migration from the former GDR, see Bernd Martens, "Der Zug nach Westen—Anhaltende Abwanderung" (30 March 2010). http:// www.bpb.de/geschichte/deutsche-einheit/lange-wege-der-deutschen -einheit/47253/zug-nach-westen?p=all. Accessed May 2014.

22. See Paqué, *Die Bilanz*, p. 20.

23. Adam Przeworski, *Democracy and the Market: Political and Economic Reforms in Eastern Europe and Latin America*, New York: Cambridge University Press, 1991, p. 174, cit. from Merkel, *Systemtransformation*, p. 339. The author has started an international research project on the transformation of shipyards in 2016. More information can be found on the webpage of the Institute of East European History: http://iog.univie .ac.at/ueber-uns/personal/professoren/?no_cache=1.

24. See Preston Keat, "Fallen Heroes: Explaining the Failure of the Gdansk Shipyard, and the Successful Early Reform Strategies in

Szczecin and Gdynia," *Communist and Postcommunist Studies* 36 (2003), pp. 209–30. This policy was introduced by the otherwise neoliberal-oriented government under Barbara Suchocka.

25. On unemployment figures in Eastern Europe, see János Kornai, "The Great Transformation of Central Eastern Europe: Success and Disappointment," *Economics of Transition* 14.2 (2006), pp. 207–44, here 231. In 1996 the unemployment rate in the Czech Republic was 3.5 percent. It rose over the next three years as a result of the transformation crisis to 9.4 percent.

26. On Russia, see Neill Robinson, "The Context of Russia's Political Economy," in idem, ed., *The Political Economy of Russia*, Lanham: Rowman & Littlefield, 2013, pp. 15–50, here 34.

27. An analogous explanation can be found in the above-mentioned essay by Neill Robinson, who blames the Soviet tradition of "particularistic exchange," i.e., personalized networks for Russia's economic plight in the 1990s rather than fiscal, profit-oriented ties between economic actors (a problem of cultural traditions and attitudes). See Robinson, "The Context," p. 22.

28. See Anders Åslund, *Building Capitalism: The Transformation of the Former Soviet Bloc*, Cambridge: Cambridge University Press, 2002, p. 118.

29. See the population statistics in Peter Fässler, Thomas Held, and Dirk Sawitzki, *Lemberg—Lwow—Lviv. Eine Stadt im Schnittpunkt europäischer Kulturen*, Cologne: Wissenschaft und Politik, 1995, p. 183. The population data for the year 2001 are accessible online on the website of the Ukrainian state statistical office: http://www.ukrcensus.gov.ua. Accessed May 2014.

30. See again the calculations in Åslund, *Building Capitalism*, p. 118.

31. On Russia, see Robinson, "The Context," pp. 29–31.

32. On the rise and recent slackening of neoliberalism, see Hilary Appel and Mitchell A. Orenstein, "Why Did Neoliberalism Triumph and Endure in the Post-Communist World?" *Comparative Politics*, 48.3 (April 2016).

33. See Dieter Plehwe, "Introduction," pp. 1–44, here 2.

34. On the academic debate concerning this issue, see the publications by two members of the Russian Academy of Sciences: Boris Kuzyk and Yuriy Yakovets, *Rossiya 2050. Strategiya innovatsionnogo proryva*, Moscow: Ekonomika, 2004.

35. Balcerowicz, *Socialism, Capitalism*, pp. 303–7.

36. See Shmuel N. Eisenstadt, ed., *Multiple Modernities*, New Brunswick: Transaction, 2002.

37. See Lawrence King, "Postcommunist Divergence: A Comparative Analysis of the Transition to Capitalism in Poland and Russia," *Studies in Comparative International Development* 37.3 (2002), pp. 3–34. Another influential distinction has been made between "liberal market economies," where intercompany relations and relations between employees and management are barely regulated and the state is limited to its elementary functions, and the more regulated "coordinated market economies," where consensus-forming, trade unions, and corporative structures play a greater role and the state provides more social security. See Hall and Soskice, *Varieties of Capitalism*. For an overview of the longer-term antecedents of capitalism, see Jürgen Kocka, *Capitalism: A Short History*, Princeton: Princeton University Press, 2016.

38. See Lawrence P. King and Iván Szelényi, "Post-Communist Economic Systems," In Neil J. Smelser and Richard Swedberg, eds., *Handbook of Economic Sociology*, 2nd edition, Princeton: Princeton University Press, 2005, pp. 206–29.

39. In Poland and Czechoslovakia alone they totalled three million by 1993, and 660,000 in Hungary. See the figures in Berend, *From the Soviet Bloc*, p. 61.

40. On FDI, see Berend, *From the Soviet Bloc*, pp. 108–33.

41. Grzegorz Ekiert attributes key importance to these reforms for the success of transformation in Poland. See his "The State after State Socialism," pp. 291–320.

42. See Iván T. Berend and György Ranki, *The European Periphery and Industrialization 1780–1914*, Cambridge: Cambridge University Press, 1982.

43. See Jeffrey Sachs, *The End of Poverty: Economic Possibilities for Our Time*, New York: Penguin, 2005, pp. 109–30.

44. See *WIIW Handbook 2012*, Countries by indicator, Tables II/1.8 and II/1.1.

45. See Bohle and Greskovits, *Capitalist Diversity*, pp. 223–57; also chapter 7 in the present book.

## Chapter 5. Second-Wave Neoliberalism

1. On these two countries, see the Eurostat data: "Gross Domestic Product at Market Prices," http://epp.eurostat.ec.europa.eu /tgm/refreshTableAction.do?tab=table&plugin=1&pcode=tec00001 &language=en. On Microsoft, see the overview of the company's worldwide turnover in the years 2002 to 2013 on the Statista website:

http://www.statista.com/statistics/267805/microsofts-global
-revenue-since-2002/. Both accessed May 2014.

2. See the website of the Warsaw Stock Exchange: http://www
.annualreport2011.gpw.pl/en/activities/business-lines/listing. Accessed May 2014. Of course, compared to Wall Street this is a minimal sum of trading.

3. On the introduction of the flat tax system in these and all other Eastern European countries (Romania, Macedonia, and Bulgaria followed suit in 2005–8), see Aligica and Evans, *The Neoliberal Revolution in Eastern Europe*, pp. 185–87.

4. On the further development of private and corporate income tax rates, see Alvin Rabushka, "Amendments to Serbia's Personal Income Tax." (16 August 2010). http://flattaxes.blogspot.de/2010/08/amendments-to-serbias-personal-income.html. Accessed May 2014.

5. On the proportion of welfare spending in the Baltic states' and Slovakia's GDPs, see Segert, *Transformationen in Osteuropa*, p. 233.

6. For some examples of the "tiger" discourse, see Matthew Reynolds, "Once a Backwater, Slovakia Surges," *New York Times* 28 December 2004. http://www.nytimes.com/2004/12/28/business/worldbusiness/28slovakia.html?sq=&st=nyt&adxnnl=1&scp=1&adxnnlx=1360847963-uYRNvkWVYaKYtkSC6ynu8A. Accessed May 2014. For an example from German print media, see Karl-Peter Schwarz, "Vom Siebenschläfer zum Tiger der Karpaten," *Frankfurter Allgemeine Zeitung* 26 August 2005. http://www.faz.net/aktuell/wirtschaft/wirtschaftspolitik/einheitssteuer-vom-siebenschlaefer-zum-tiger-der-karpaten-1254535.html. Accessed May 2014. On Slovenia and other new EU countries, see Marion Kraske and Jan Puhl, "Eastern Europe's Economics Boom: The Tiny Tigers," *Der Spiegel* 21 December 2005. http://www.spiegel.de/international/spiegel/eastern-europe-s-economic-boom-the-tiny-tigers-a-391649.html. Accessed May 2014.

7. Between 1991 and 2012, average election turnouts in Eastern Europe dropped from 72 to 57 percent. On this problem, which has come to affect all Western democracies, see Jürgen Kocka and Wolfgang Merkel, "Neue Balance gesucht. Gefährdet der Finanzkapitalismus die Demokratie?" *WZB-Mitteilungen* 144 (June 2014), pp. 41–44. http://www.wzb.eu/sites/default/files/publikationen/wzb_mitteilungen/s41–44_kocka_merkel.pdf. Accessed May 2014.

8. Merkel, *Systemtransformation*, pp. 394–435. Estonia and Poland formed exceptions to the aforementioned vote-out rule. Their respective prime ministers were reelected in 2009 and 2011.

9. University education for the lower classes was made possible to a large extent by discrimination against the former elites or their children, especially in the 1950s. On the education drive, see Segert, *Transformationen in Osteuropa*, p. 73. In the seventies, over 50 percent of students in the ČSSR came from working-class or farming backgrounds.

10. See on this term Gary S. Becker, *Human Capital: A Theoretical and Empirical Analysis, with Special Reference to Education*, Chicago: University of Chicago Press, 1964. (The last edition was published in 1993, after which interest dwindled.)

11. On income levels and different types of investment, see Berend, *From the Soviet Bloc*, pp. 121, 118–24.

12. Elisabeth Dunn has examined the differences in pre- and postsocialist production using the example of a Polish baby-food factory. See Elizabeth C. Dunn, *Privatizing Poland: Baby Food, Big Business, and the Remaking of Labor*, Ithaca: Cornell University Press, 2004, pp. 94–129.

13. See Agnieszka Knyt and Alicja Wancerz-Gluza, eds., *Prywaciarze 1945-89*, Warsaw: Karta, 2001.

14. On the "Polonia" enterprises, see Jerzy Kochanowski, "Pioneers of the Market Economy? Unofficial Commercial Exchange between People from the Socialist Bloc Countries (1970s and 1980s)," *Journal of Modern European History* 8 (2010), pp. 196–220. On *komputeryzacja*, see Patryk Wasiak, "Komputeryzujemy się!" in Natalia Jarska and Jan Olaszek, *Społeczeństwo polskie w latach 1980-1989*, Warsaw: IPN, 2015, pp. 159–69. See also the report on the conference 'Loopholes in the Iron Curtain. Economic Contacts between Eastern and Western Europe since the 1970s" (Vienna, 18–19 April 2013) at the H-Soz-u-Kult website: http://hsozkult.geschichte.hu-berlin.de/tagungsberichte/id=4996. Accessed May 2013. On the general deficit in computer technology in socialist countries, see Berend, *From the Soviet Bloc*, p. 25.

15. On these figures, see Kochanowski, *Jenseits der Planwirtschaft*, pp. 427–28.

16. Ibid., pp. 200–50, and on vain attempts at state controls, pp. 117–53.

17. On this company, see the in-depth interview "Mój biznes" in the financial supplement of *Gazeta Wyborcza*, 30 September 2008, pp. 1–3. Other Polish companies were also able to get a foothold in this market niche, including the previously founded Inter-Fragrance and the juice and perfumes manufacturer Comindeks. The latter were among the "Polonia" enterprises.

18. See Knyt and Wancerz-Gluza, *Prywaciarze 1945-89*, pp. 105–8, 145–48. On the expanding underground economy in the ČSSR, see

*WIIW-Mitgliederinformation*, 1989/10, pp. 8–15 ("The second economy in Czechoslovakia").

19. Research has not confirmed whether this helped them after 1989. Małgorzata Mazurek traces a number of individual biographies (in *Społeczeństwo kolejki. O doświadczeniach niedoboru 1945–1989*, Warsaw: Trio, 2010, pp. 62, 67) to support the thesis that the pioneers of the market economy of the 1980s often foundered as entrepreneurs in later years. Some were successful, but statistics show that this group's income generally dwindled; for many of them bazaar trading was a daily struggle for survival.

20. On Poland, Hungary, and the Czech Republic, see Pál Tamás and Helmut Steiner, eds., *The Business Elites of East Central Europe*, Berlin: Trafo, 2005. For a more detailed study of Poland, see Krzysztof Jasiecki, *Elita biznesu w Polsce. Drugie narodziny kapitalizmu*, Warsaw: IFIS, 2002. Jasiecki stresses the pluralism of the new economic elite; according to his estimates, over half of its members had been top managers of former state enterprises.

21. On the social mobility of former SED members, see Martin Diewald, Heike Solga, and Anne Goedicke, "Old Assets, New Liabilities? How Did Individual Characteristics Contribute to Labor Market Success or Failure After 1989," in Diewald et al., eds., *After the Fall of the Wall*, pp. 65–88, here 78. Remarkably, a relatively high number of former party officials became self-employed and set up their own businesses.

22. See the statistics in Gabor Hunya, *Shift to the East: WIIW Database on Foreign Direct Investment in Central, East and Southeast Europe*, Vienna: WIIW, 2007; see also the slightly deviating figures in N. N., "Over the Hill? Foreign Investment in Eastern Europe May Be at a Peak," *Economist* 25 June 2007, http://www.economist.com/node/9392733. Accessed May 2014.The volume of FDIs on a global level increased fourfold between 1980 and 2000. See Berend, *From the Soviet Bloc*, p. 40. The Polish National Bank (NBP) arrives at a lower sum of FDIs, partly because property investments were not calculated before 2006. (In some respects this was the more meaningful mode of calculation; the property bubbles which affected the Baltic states, especially, did not have such a strong impact on the FDI statistics.) See the data on foreign direct investments on the NBP website: http://www.nbp.pl/homen.aspx?f=/en/publikacje/ziben/ziben.html. Accessed May 2014. According to the NBP, FDIs totaled almost ten billion euros in 2008 and 2009, but less than five billion in 2012.

23. See the IMF data on Poland's GDP adjusted to purchasing power parity: http://www.imf.org/external/pubs/ft/weo/2012/01/weodata

/weorept.aspx?sy=1991&ey=2012&scsm=1&ssd=1&sort=country&ds
=%2C&br=1&pr1.x=53&pr1.y=4&c=964&s=PPPGDP&grp=0&a=;
also the IMF data on the per capita GDP after purchasing power
parity: http://www.imf.org/external/pubs/ft/weo/2012/01/weodata
/weorept.aspx?pr.x=80&pr.y=18&sy=1988&ey=2012&scsm=1&ssd=1
&sort=country&ds=.&br=1&c=964&s=PPPPC&grp=0&a=. Both accessed May 2014.

24. See Berend, *From the Soviet Bloc*, p. 260.
25. The data on GDPs and FDIs in this paragraph are drawn from the
    *WIIW Handbook 2012*, Table I/1.6; also *WIIW Handbook 2012*, Coun-
    tries by indicator, Table II 1.8 (Romania), II/1.5 (Latvia), II/1.18
    (Ukraine).
26. See Andrei Shleifer and Daniel Treisman, "Normal Countries: The
    East 25 Years after Communism," *Foreign Affairs* 93 (2014). http://
    www.foreignaffairs.com/articles/142200/andrei-shleifer-and-daniel
    -treisman/normal-countries. Accessed March 2015.
27. Bohle and Greskovits, *Capitalist Diversity*, p. 225.
28. See the report by N. N., "Volkswagen chystá znižovanie platov,"
    *Hospodárske noviny*. http://hn.hnonline.sk/ekonomika-a-firmy-117
    /zistenie-hn-volkswagen-chysta-znizovanie-platov-602149. Accessed
    May 2014.
29. See "Länderbericht Rumänien," *Frankfurter Allgemeine Zeitung* 16 De-
    cember 2013, p. 20.
30. On rates of unemployment in Slovakia and other EU countries, see
    the Eurostat data: "Unemployment statistics." http://epp.eurostat
    .ec.europa.eu/statistics_explained/index.php/Unemployment
    _statistics#Recent_developments_in_unemployment_at_a
    _European_and_Member_State_level. Accessed May 2014.
31. On eastern Slovakia, see the report in *Wiener Wirtschaftsblatt* of 4 No-
    vember 2013, p. 14. For a comparison of average incomes in Europe,
    see Eurostat: "Haushaltseinkommen nach NUTS-2-Regionen."
    http://appsso.eurostat.ec.europa.eu/nui/show.do?dataset=nama
    _r_ehh2inc&lang=de. On the wages of workers in the automobile
    industry, see: "Slovenské automobilky zvýší mzdy zaměstnancům,
    nejvíce přidá VW." http://www.auto.cz/slovenske-automobilky
    -zvysi-mzdy-zamestnancum-nejvice-prida-vw-55192. Both accessed
    May 2014.
32. The debate over the extent of Poland's modernization in the postwar
    period is especially controversial. For an overview of this debate in
    recent years and a critical view of the People's Republic of Poland,

see Dariusz Jarosz, "Problemy z peerelowską modernizacją," *Kwartalnik Historyczny* 120 (2013), pp. 365–84.

33. However, city residents looked down on country dwellers on account of the prevalent stereotype of backwardness rather than actual differences in living standards. See *Zeithistorische Forschungen* 10.2 (2013) and Klaus Bachmann's article about social inequality in Poland under late state socialism in this special edition of the German historical journal.

34. All the figures in this paragraph are taken from Eurostat regional statistics: http://epp.eurostat.ec.europa.eu/portal/page/portal/region _cities/regional_statistics/data/database. Accessed May 2014. Even at the time, the data for 1995 were not complete for all administrative districts, and the state of availability has worsened since, as Eurostat started deleting data from previous years in 2013–14. Current (though sometimes divergent) figures can be found in Eurostat, "Bruttoinlandsprodukt (BIP) zu laufenden Marktpreisen nach NUTS-3-Regionen." http://appsso.eurostat.ec.europa.eu/nui/show .do?dataset=nama_r_e3gdp&lang=de. Accessed May 2014.

35. Again, see the Eurostat regional statistics: http://epp.eurostat.ec .europa.eu/portal/page/portal/region_cities/regional_statistics /data/database. Accessed May 2014.

36. See OECD, "Regional labour market TL3." http://stats.oecd.org /Index.aspx?DataSetCode=REG_LAB_TL3. Accessed May 2014.

37. Eurostat does not provide any statistics on Ukraine. The Ukrstat data were made comparable by providing the equivalent value in euros under consideration of the changing purchasing power parities.

38. The statistics in this section on regional GDP in the western districts of the Ukraine and in Kyiv were calculated as follows: gross regional product (in the currency of the Ukraine, Hryvnia) in the years 2000, 2005, and 2008 according to the information provided by the *Статистичний збірник "Регіони України" 2010 Частина II* (Statistical anthology of the regions of the Ukraine 2010). The data can be accessed on the website of the State Statistical Office of the Ukraine (http://www.ukrstat.gov.ua/, and following the links "publikacii," "regionalna statistika" and for earlier years "arkhiv"). Values in euro, adjusted to purchasing power parity, were calculated according to the purchasing power parities in *WIIW Handbook 2012*, Countries by indicator, Table II/4.18, Position/Table 64. It is important to note that wages earned abroad by migrant laborers are not factored into their regions' domestic GDP. The regions may, then, be wealthier

than their GDPs suggest. Tax evasion and clandestine work are also widespread phenomena that are not reflected in official statistics on GDP. Nevertheless, these remain an important indicator of economic performance.

39. See the report by the Warsaw Center for Migration Studies (Ośrodek Badań nad Migracjami): Zuzanna Brunarska, Małgorzata Grotte, and Magdalena Lesińska, *Migracje obywateli Ukrainy do Polski w kontekście rozwoju społeczno-gospodarczego: stan obecny, polityka, transfery pieniężne*, Warsaw: CMR, 2012, p. 61. The report is accessible online: http://www.migracje.uw .edu.pl/download/publikacja/2017/. Accessed May 2014.

40. Ibid., p. 13. In 2011, only 18,700 Ukrainians possessed an official work permit. On Ukrainian workers in the Czech Republic, see the website of the local diaspora organization: http://www.ukrajinci.cz/. Accessed May 2014.

41. Stanisław Szczepanowski, *Nędza Galicji w cyfrach i program energicznego rozwoju gospodarstwa krajowego*, Lwów: Gubrynowicz und Schmidt, 1888. Szczepanowski compared Galicia with Ireland and Italy, and in some points with Bengal and China (see p. 3).

42. For data on these countries, see the website of the World Bank: http://data.worldbank.org/country/india; http://data.worldbank .org/country/morocco; http://data.worldbank.org/country/turkey. Accessed May 2014.

43. In the last year before the crisis, 2008, the per capita GDP in Dresden was €29,900; in Görlitz, €18,400; in the Erzgebirge district, only €16,800—this is evidence of regional divergence on a small scale. As above, see the data in the Eurostat regional statistics: http://epp .eurostat.ec.europa.eu/portal/page/portal/region_cities/regional _statistics/data/database; also Eurostat, "Bruttoinlandsprodukt (BIP) zu laufenden Marktpreisen nach NUTS-3-Regionen." http:// appsso.eurostat.ec.europa.eu/nui/show.do?dataset=nama_r_e3gdp &lang=de. Both accessed May 2014. Since the nineties, class-related inequality has also increased. For a historical perspective on urban-rural divergence in Germany, see Wendelin Strubelt, "'Stadt und Land'— The Relation between City and Countryside. (Non-Urban Territories) The German Case—a German case? Reflections and Facts," in Wendelin Strubelt and Grzegorz Gorzelak, *City and Region: Papers in Honour of Jiří Musil*, Opladen: Budrich UniPress, 2008, pp. 233–67.

44. See N. N., "SAV: Number of Slovak Caregivers in Austria Has Tripled," *Tasr* 31 January 2012. http://195.46.72.16/free/jsp/search/view /ViewerPure_en.jsp?Document=..%2F..%2FInput_text%2Fonline

%2F12%2F01%2Ftbbw1vd302533.dat.1%40Fondy&QueryText=.
Accessed May 2014.

45. Kuznets argued that in previous phases of economic growth (such as industrialization) income inequality grew, but shrank again in later development cycles. See Simon Kuznets, "Economic Growth and Income Inequality," *American Economic Review* 45 (1955), pp. 1–28. I am grateful to Mária Hidvégi (Universität Konstanz) and Uwe Müller (GWZO Leipzig) for advice on literature concerning economic history.

46. For a long list of companies in the Polish food industry that went bankrupt, see: Andrzej Karpiński, Stanisław Paradysz, Paweł Soroka, and Wiesław Żółtkowski, *Jak powstawały i jak upadały zakłady przemysłowe w Polsce*, Warsaw: Muza, 2013, pp. 323–26.

47 Berend, *From the Soviet Bloc*, p. 74.

48. On agricultural policy in Vietnam, see Pham Quang Minh, *Zwischen Theorie und Praxis. Agrarpolitik in Vietnam seit 1945*, Berlin: Logos, 2003.

49. The number of unemployed almost doubled after 1997, reaching a record level of 20 percent in Poland (2002) and 19.5 percent in Slovakia (2001). See the data (in a long-term series) in Eurostat, "Arbeitslosenquoten nach Geschlecht, Alter und NUTS-2-Regionen (%)," http://appsso.eurostat.ec.europa.eu/nui/show.do?dataset=lfst _r_lfu3rt&lang=de. On regional unemployment, see the Eurostat regional statistics: http://epp.eurostat.ec.europa.eu/portal/page /portal/region_cities/regional_statistics/data/database. Both accessed May 2014.

50. See Goedicke, "A 'Ready-Made State,'" p. 50.

51. Swetlana Alexejewitsch, *Secondhand-Zeit. Leben auf den Trümmern des Sozialismus*, Munich: Hanser, 2013, p. 125.

52. On PHARE, see Berend, *From the Soviet Bloc*, p. 87. On later programs, see also Andrzej Chwalba, *Kurze Geschichte der Dritten Republik Polen*, Wiesbaden: Harrassowitz, 2010, p. 184.

53. On the amount of funds granted and paid, see N. N., "EU Polen behauptet sich am Fördertrog," *Wiener Wirtschaftsblatt* 18 February 2014, pp. 1, 8; also a Polish government document on the structural fund: "Wykorzystanie środków z funduszy strukturalnych w Polsce i w nowych państwach członkowskich UE." http://www.funduszestrukturalne.gov .pl/NR/rdonlyres/508CE9F0–7FD9–484A-B093–1559BDF0E4D3 /28926/pl_a_inne_kraje_0802091.pdf. Accessed May 2014.

54. For this calculation, the capital outflow abroad was deducted from the FDIs. On FDI in- and outflows, see *WIIW Handbook 2012*,

Countries by indicator, Table II/1.17. On the figures for 2012, see the data collated by the Polish national bank on foreign direct investments in Poland: http://www.nbp.pl/homen.aspx?f=/en/publikacje /ziben/ziben.html. Accessed May 2014. Between 2007 and 2012, the capital inflow totalled 44.4 billion euros; according to the Polish Finance Ministry's estimates in 2013 the volume of FDIs increased slightly on 4.8 billion the previous year. This makes a total of approximately fifty billion. On EU programs in the nineties, see Berend, *From the Soviet Bloc*, p. 87.

55. See the press release on cohesion policy in the EU by the European Commission of 30 May 2007: http://europa.eu/rapid/press-release _IP-07-721_de.htm. Accessed May 2014.

56. For an overview, see Kornai, "The Great Transformation," pp. 207–44, here 229. On revenues in cities and rural areas of Poland, see Główny Urząd Statystyczny, *Dochody i warunki życia ludności Polski* (raport z badania EU-SILC 2011), Warsaw: GUS, 2012, p. 132. The difference in wages and salaries has been shrinking since 2008.

57. Galicia was an exception, lagging far behind, as did Hungary and especially the Carpathians—poverty here, then, is a long-term, enduring problem. On economic and social history in the latter period Austro-Hungarian Empire, see Volumes IX (2010) and I (1973) of the series edited by Peter Urbanitsch and Helmut Rumpler, *Die Habsburgermonarchie 1848–1918*, published by ÖAW.

58. The difference between the capital and the rural regions along the Russian border in per capita GDP is, similarly to Poland, about 5:1. See Macours and Swinnen, "Rural-Urban Poverty Differences"; Michael Harter and Reiner Jaakson, "Economic Success in Estonia: The Centre versus Periphery Pattern of Regional Inequality," *Communist Economies and Economic Transformation* 9.4 (1997), pp. 469–90.

59. In the hypothetical case that a country's Gini coefficient is zero, all its citizens would have the same amount of income at their disposal. A Gini coefficient at the highest possible rate of 100 (or 1, by an alternative mode of calculation) would indicate that one single individual possesses the country's entire income. De facto, the Gini fluctuates in emerging and industrialized countries between rates of around 23 in more equitable societies (e.g. Sweden) and 60 in extremely inequitable societies (e.g. Brazil). On the Russian Gini, see Robinson, "The Context of Russia's Political Economy," pp. 15–50, here 32; see also the (partly divergent) data on the Gini coefficient in Russia published by Trading Economics: http://www.tradingeconomics .com/russia/gini-index-wb-data.html. Accessed May 2014.

60. See the Gini calculations in Eurostat, "Gini-Koeffizient des verfügbaren Äquivalenzeinkommens." http://appsso.eurostat.ec.europa .eu/nui/show.do?dataset=ilc_di12&lang=de. Accessed May 2014. UN information (see table 5.3.b) is, again, slightly incongruent.

61. See World Bank, "Life Expectancy at Birth, Male (Years)." http:// data.worldbank.org/indicator/SP.DYN.LE00.MA.IN. Accessed May 2014.

62. See Jonathan Tirone and Alexander Weber, "Ukraine Billionaire Firtash Jailed in Vienna on FBI Warrant," *Bloomberg* 13 March 2014. http://www.bloomberg.com/news/2014–03–13/ukraine-billionaire -firtash-arrested-in-vienna-on-fbi-warrant.html. Accessed May 2014.

63. On welfare spending, see Segert, *Transformationen in Osteuropa*, p. 233.

64. The worst-off 20 percent of Russian society earned only 6 percent of national revenue in 2010; the wealthiest 10 percent, by contrast, had over a third of national revenue at their disposal, the top 20 percent just over half. See Trading Economics: http://www.tradingeconomics .com/russia/gini-index-wb-data.html. Accessed May 2014.

65. On deeper-rooted reasons for criticizing the EU (and the West in general), see the still-relevant essay by Andrew C. Janos, "From Eastern Empire to Western Hegemony: East Central Europe under Two International Regimes," *East European Politics and Societies* 15.2 (2001), pp. 221–49.

66. Zenonas Norkus has identified ten different patterns and sixty-four potential paths of change in his comparative analysis of political and economic transformation. See his *On Baltic Slovenia and Adriatic Lithuania*, Budapest: Central European University Press, 2012, p. 140 (also the following chapter to p. 198).

67. Keane and Prasad were commissioned by the IMF to compare paths of transformation. See Michael P. Keane and Eswar S. Prasad, "Poland: Inequality, Transfers, and Growth in Transition," *Finance & Development: A Quarterly Magazine of the IMF* 38.1 (March 2001). http:// www.imf.org/external/pubs/ft/fandd/2001/03/keane.htm. Accessed May 2014.

68. On this data (and the data in the following paragraph), see Segert, *Transformationen in Osteuropa*, p. 233.

## Chapter 6. Central European Cities: A Metropolitan Comparison

1. "Der Westn is besser / Der Westn is bunter / Und schöner und schauer / Und reicher und frei . . . Der Ostn is schlechter / Der Ostn is grauer / Und klein sind die Chancen / Und groß ist die Not."

(English translation by Charlotte Hughes-Kreutzmüller.) The song appears on the Wolf Biermann LP *Gut Kirschenessen. DDR—Ça Ira!* Hamburg: Electrola, 1990.

2. On the basic principles of historical comparison, see Heinz-Gerhard Haupt and Jürgen Kocka, eds., *Geschichte und Vergleich. Ansätze und Ergebnisse international vergleichender Geschichtsschreibung*, Frankfurt am Main: Campus, 1996; Hartmut Kaelble and Jürgen Schriewer, eds., *Vergleich und Transfer. Komparatistik in den Sozial, Geschichts- und Kulturwissenschaften*, Frankfurt am Main: Campus, 2003.

3. On average, food prices in Czechoslovakia increased by 24.6 percent in 1990 alone. See *WIIW-Mitgliederinformation* 1990/6, pp. 22–23.

4. Despite being an employee-friendly policy, it is one of the causes of the southern eurozone's economic plight. These countries largely retained their customary indexation from the pre-euro era, resulting in higher inflation than in countries like Germany, where index-linking is uncommon.

5. On Poland, see *WIIW-Mitgliederinformation* 1990/8, p. 28 (stating a drop in real wages of 46 percent).

6. See *Rocznik Statystyczny Województwa Warszawskiego 1991*, Warsaw: Wojewódzki Urząd Statystyczny (henceforth WUS), 1991, p. 119. The earlier statistics refer to the entire voivodeship; data specifically on the city of Warsaw only exist from 1992. The exact figures are: average monthly household income of 2,276,000 złotys, of which 1,796,000 were wages, against monthly household expenditure of 1,882,000 złotys, of which 848,000 was for food (excepting alcoholic beverages). According to information from the Polish central bank, the rate of exchange in mid-1990 was 11,458 złotys for one US dollar. (In 1995, four zeros were deleted, resulting in the much lower rate of exchange.)

7. See, e.g., Jacek Kurczewski, Mariusz Cichomski, and Krzysztof Wiliński, *Wielkie bazary warszawskie*, Warsaw: Trio, 2010; Roch Sulima, "The Laboratory of Polish Postmodernity: An Ethnographic Report from the Stadium Bazaar," in Monika Grubbauer and Joanna Kusiak, eds., *Chasing Warsaw: Socio-Material Dynamics of Urban Change Since 1990*, Frankfurt am Main: Campus, 2012, pp. 241–68; Janusz Dąbrowski, ed., *Wybrane aspekty funkcjonowania targowiska "Jarmark Europa" na Stadionie X—lecia. Wyniki badań ankietowych przeprowadzonych na zlecenie firmy Damis*, Warsaw: Instytut Badań nad Gospodarką Rynkową, 1996; Marcin Peterlik, *Handel targowiskowy w roku 1999*, Warsaw: Instytut Badań nad Gospodarką Rynkową, 2000.

8. Kochanowski, *Jenseits der Planwirtschaft*, p. 161, also 419–36.

9. On these and the following statistics, and the market's development, see Ursula Weber, *Der Polenmarkt in Berlin. Zur Rekonstruktion eines kulturellen Kontakts im Prozess der politischen Transformation Mittel- und Osteuropas*, Neuried: Ars Una, 2002, p. 69.

10. A number of traders' memoirs are included in the following documentation about Polish "prywaciarze" (self-employed) in the postwar era. See Knyt and Wancerz-Gluza, *Prywaciarze 1945-89*, pp. 105–8, 145–48.

11. See Mazurek, *Społeczeństwo kolejki*, pp. 107–42.

12. Weber, *Der Polenmarkt in Berlin*, p. 17.

13. Peterlik, *Handel targowiskowy*, p. 9.

14. Ibid., p. 21. On the number of market-related jobs, see ibid., pp. 16–19.

15. For a journalistic impression of Mexikoplatz, see Roland Girthler, *Abenteuer Grenze. Von Schmugglern und Schmugglerinnen, Ritualen und "heiligen" Räumen*, Vienna: Lit-Verlag, 2006, pp. 126–52. On raids and customs investigations conducted here, see pp. 139–40, 143.

16. The broader term is used here in contrast to "*capitalism* from below," which focuses on aspects of the reforms, or system change "from above." The traders not only did business and (at best) accumulated capital, but also transformed their mindsets and behaviors. On the categorization of capitalism as "from without," "from above," or "from below," see King and Szelényi, "Post-Communist Economic Systems," pp. 206–29.

17. Cf. *WIIW-Mitgliederinformation* 1990/8, p. 27.

18. See the data in *130 Lat Statystyki Warszawy 1864-1994*, Warsaw: Wojewódzki Urząd Statystyczny w M. St. Warszawie, 1994; *Przegląd Statystyczny Warszawa* 2/12 (December 1993), p. 34. Unfortunately, the use of terms is not entirely consistent but varies between "enterprise" (*zakłady*) and "economic unit" (*podmioty gospodarki*). The term *podmioty gospodarki narodowej* also applies to legal entities (e.g., associations). Therefore the statistics cannot be precisely equated with the number of enterprises. Reliable data on Warsaw only exist from 1992, collated especially for this book.

19. See the special privatization supplement of the weekly newspaper *Polityka* (February 1993), "Prywatizacja IV, Dodatek poświęcony przekształceniom własnościowym," pp. I, IV.

20. "Jedna dziewczyna w wielkiej desperacji / Chciała się oddać prywatizacji / A że nie była to tęga głowa / Wyszła jej spółka jednoosobowa," Ibid., p. I (column 2).

21. See Investitionsbank Berlin, "Gründungsaktivitäten im Städte-vergleich," *Berlin aktuell* 28 Februar 2008, p. 1. https://www.ibb .de/portaldata/1/resources/content/download/newsletter/berlin _aktuell/kn_ba_gruendungen_080228.pdf. Accessed May 2014. On the development of East German private enterprise after 1989, see Karl Ulrich Mayer, "After the Fall of the Wall: Living through the Post-Socialist Transformation in East Germany," in Diewald et al., *After the Fall*, pp. 1–28, here 27.

22. Statistical evidence of this can be found in: Martin Diewald and Bogdan W. Mach, "Comparing Paths of Transition: Employment Opportunities and Earnings in East Germany and Poland during the First Ten Years of Transformation Process," in Diewald, *After the Fall*, pp. 237–68, here pp. 261 and 267. Diewald and Mach conclude that Poland developed a tendency toward "owner capitalism" while the GDR was outgunned by West Germany.

23. See the data on business formations in Poland, Czechoslovakia, Hungary, and Bulgaria in Berend, *From the Soviet Bloc*, p. 61.

24. All the following figures are taken from Eurostat, "Bruttoinland-sprodukt (BIP) zu laufenden Marktpreisen nach NUTS-3-Regionen." http://appsso.eurostat.ec.europa.eu/nui/show.do?dataset=nama_r _e3gdp&lang=de. Accessed May 2014. In 2014 the figures on Berlin were revised upward somewhat to correspond with the retrospectively downward-corrected population figures.

25. Cf. *Rocznik Statystyczny Warszawy* (henceforth *RSW*), Warsaw: Urząd Statystyczny w Warszawie (henceforth USW), 1996, p. 144.

26. Cf. Bundesagentur für Arbeit, "Arbeitsmarkt in Zahlen. Entwick-lung der Arbeitslosenquote für Deutschland, West- und Ostdeutsch-land von 1991 bis heute (2007)." http://www.khd-research.net/Docs /BAfA_Arbeitslose_1991–2007.pdf. Accessed May 2014.

27. See Grzegorz Kołodko, *From Shock to Therapy: The Political Economy of Postsocialist Transformation*, Oxford: Oxford University Press, 2000.

28. See the figures in Berend, *From the Soviet Bloc*, p. 169. Unfortunately there are no comparable data available on Warsaw. The present au-thor's inquiries and archival research remained fruitless.

29. For unemployment statistics on the capitals considered here, see Eu-rostat, "Arbeitsmarkt, jährlich—Städte und Ballungsräume." http:// appsso.eurostat.ec.europa.eu/nui/show.do?dataset=urb_clma&lang =de. Accessed May 2014. The unemployment rate among women was 9.8 percent compared to 7.9 percent among men, indicating that women were more often losers during transformation.

30. The data on income distribution is taken from Eurostat Urban Audit: http://epp.eurostat.ec.europa.eu/portal/page/portal/region_cities /city_urban/data_cities/database_sub1. Accessed July 2011. Unfortunately some of the previously available data are no longer accessible, therefore the 2011 status is given here. (For current data, see http://epp.eurostat.ec.europa.eu/portal/page/portal/product _details/generic_url_page/?pcode=urb_vcity&pmode=DETAIL& planguage. Accessed May 2014.)

31. Dieter Stiefel and Schumpeter-Gesellschaft, eds., *Der "Ostfaktor." Österreichs Wirtschaft und die Ostöffnung 1989 bis 2009*, Vienna: Böhlau, 2010.

32. See the WKO website: http://www.standort-wien.at/WienUeberblick /Wirtschaftsstandort/#oben. Accessed May 2014.

33. On population development in Vienna, see the municipal authority statistics: http://www.wien.gv.at/statistik/bevoelkerung /bevoelkerungsstand/. Accessed May 2014. (The population of Vienna grew in the period 2000–2005 by ninety-four thousand; in 2006 by another twenty thousand.) On demographic development in the nineties, see the information provided by the Austrian Center for Democracy (Demokratiezentrum): Hansjörg Hansely and Manfred Schopper, "Wien im Aufbruch." http://www.demokratiezentrum .org/fileadmin/media/pdf/aufbruch_schopper_hansely.pdf. Accessed May 2014. Some of the figures given here are higher.

34. As above, these data are based on the Eurostat regional statistics: http://epp.eurostat.ec.europa.eu/portal/page/portal/region_cities /regional_statistics/data/database. Accessed May 2014.

35. The figures on Kyiv are based on information (in the national currency, hryvnia) from the state statistical agency of the Ukraine: http://www.ukrstat.gov.ua/. Accessed May 2014. The equivalent value in euros, adjusted to purchasing power parity, was calculated by means of the rates of exchange and purchasing power parities in the *WIIW Handbook 2012*, Countries by indicator, Table II/4.18, Position 64.

36. On urban development on a global level, see e.g. Saskia Sassen, *The Global City: New York, London, Tokyo*, Princeton: Princeton University Press, 2001.

37. For statistics on Berlin and the other capitals, see Eurostat, "Bruttoinlandsprodukt (BIP) zu laufenden Marktpreisen nach NUTS-3-Regionen." http://appsso.eurostat.ec.europa.eu/nui/show.do?dataset =nama_r_e3gdp&lang=de. Accessed May 2014. In 2014 these figures were partly revised upward, suggesting that Berlin's per capita GDP

stagnated, rather than decreased, between 1995 and 2005. I was not able to ascertain exactly why the figures were revised, but it was probably because the population statistics were revised downward in 2013, implying that Berlin's GDP was dispersed among fewer people. On Berlin's long-term economic weakness, see IHK Berlin and Handwerkskammer Berlin, *Berliner Wirtschaft in Zahlen. Ausgabe 2009*, Berlin: Heenemann, 2009, p. 9. http://www.ihk-berlin.de/linkableblob /bihk24/standortpolitik/ZahlenundFakten/downloads/1890712/ .5./data/Berliner_Wirtschaft_in_Zahlen_2009-data.pdf. Accessed May 2014.

38. For unemployment statistics on Berlin (and other EU cities), see Eurostat, "Arbeitsmarkt, jährlich—Städte und Ballungsräume." http:// appsso.eurostat.ec.europa.eu/nui/show.do?dataset=urb_clma&lang =de. Accessed May 2014. The data here are calculated according to ILO standards, or the percentage of persons in civilian employment. The figure 19.2 percent is taken from the German Federal Insurance Fund for Salaried Employees (BfA) and differs slightly from Eurostat information.

39. See Martens, "Der Zug nach Westen."

40. A few exceptions were the French company JC Decaux (the largest European supplier of outdoor advertising) and ALSTOM Grid (an electricity grid specialist). The Berlin senate website describes the city as a "gateway to Central and Eastern Europe" but does not support the claim with any in-depth information or details of existing companies. See the information at http://www.berlin.de/wirtschaft /wirtschaftsstandort/index.de.php. Accessed May 2014.

41. On the Berlin bank scandal, see Hans-Peter Schwintowski, "Berliner Bankenskandal—und was wir daraus lernen könnten," *Humboldt Forum Recht* 7 (2005), pp. 60–184. http://www.humboldt-forum-recht.de /druckansicht/druckansicht.php?artikelid=8. Accessed May 2014.

42. See the online plenary records of the Berlin parliament. Sometimes doubts about whether Berlin is actually a metropolis were expressed, but rarely by CDU politicians. See, e.g., the argument put forward by long-serving senator, CDU parliamentary party leader, and chief executive of the mortgage bank Berlin Hyp (thus one of the main culprits responsible for the Berlin bank crisis) Klaus-Rüdiger Landowsky, "Von der Großstadt zur Weltstadt zur Metropole" (From a City to a Cosmopolitan City to a Metropole), in Abgeordnetenhaus von Berlin, 13. Wahlperiode, Plenarprotokoll 13/37, 37. Sitzung, 11. Dezember 1997, p. 2386. http://pardok.parlament-berlin

.de/starweb/adis/citat/VT/13/PlenarPr/p13037.pdf#page=10. Accessed May 2014.

43. Wowereit's actual words, spoken in an interview with *Focus Money* in November 2003, translate as: "We are indeed poor, but we're still sexy" ("Wir sind zwar arm, aber trotzdem sexy"). See N. N., "Arm, aber sexy," *Focus online* 19 October 2006. http://www.focus.de/politik/deutschland/wowereits-berlin-slogan_aid_117712.html. Accessed May 2014.

44. See, e.g., the analysis published in 2003 by the Institut für Wirtschaftsforschung Halle: http://www.iwh-halle.de/d/publik/wiwa/1-03-1.pdf. Accessed February 2015.

45. On transfer payments to East Germany, see Oliver Holtemöller and Martin Altemayer-Bartscher, "Auf welche Frage sind zwei Billionen die Antwort," *Wirtschaft im Wandel*, 3/2014. http://www.iwh-halle.de/d/publik/wiwa/3-14-1.pdf. Accessed February 2015. According to the lower estimate by the Bundeszentrale für Politische Bildung, the transfer payments ran to 1.6 billion euros in the two decades following German reunification. See Jürgen Kühl, "25 Jahre deutsche Einheit: Annäherungen und verbliebene Unterschiede zwischen West und Ost," *Bundeszentrale für Politische Bildung* 2014. Accessed February 2015. http://www.bpb.de/politik/innenpolitik/arbeitsmarktpolitik/55390/25-jahre-deutsche-einheit?p=all. The problem with these estimates is that the German government has not collated any exact statistics on transfer payments since 1999, and allowance must be made for the distinction between gross and net payments (deducting the return flow from the East to the federal government and the welfare state). Transfer payments were also made in the form of development assistance (which, however, West German entities could also apply for) and special funds (e.g., in the context of economic support programs). For a comprehensive evaluation, see Ulrich Blum, Joachim Ragnitz, Sabine Freye, Simone Scharfe, and Lutz Schneider, *Regionalisierung öffentlicher Ausgaben und Einnahmen—Eine Untersuchung am Beispiel der Neuen Länder*, Halle: IWH, 2009 (= IWH Sonderheft 4).

46. See Grubbauer and Kusiak, *Chasing Warsaw*.

47. On the average amount of living space per person in Berlin, see the information published by the senate administration: http://www.stadtentwicklung.berlin.de/wohnen/wohnenswerte_stadt/de/marktuebersicht.shtml. Accessed October 2013. (In 2014 the link unfortunately no longer functioned.) Up-to-date information on the Berlin housing market is available at the following address: http://

www.stadtentwicklung.berlin.de/wohnen/wohnungsmarktbericht/. Accessed May 2014. On the situation in Warsaw in 1988 (based on data on the cities in the Warsaw voivodeship), see *Rocznik Statystyczny Województwa Warszawskiego*, p. 219.

48. See the statistics in *130 lat statystyki*, p. 291; *RSW 2012*, Warsaw: Urząd Statystyczny w Warszawie 2012, p. 183. With a surface area of 180 feet, the average apartment here is still distinctly smaller than in Berlin or Vienna, but almost thirty-two feet larger than the average in 1988. The number of people per room has fallen from one to 0.66, making it easier to keep out of each other's way. The differences within Warsaw are interesting. In working-class districts such as Ursynów and Praga, the population still lives more densely packed. On Warsaw's gated communities, see Jacek Gądecki, "Gating Warsaw: Enclosed Housing Estates and the Aesthetics of Luxury," in Grubbauer and Kusiak, *Chasing Warsaw*, pp. 109–32, here 115. Gądecki estimates that about 75 percent of the apartments built since 1989 are in gated communities.

49. All the data in this paragraph are based on the statistical yearbooks published by the statistical agency of the city of Warsaw and the midyear rate of exchange from złotys to dollars (according to the Polish national bank). See *RSW*, Warsaw: Urząd Statystyczny w Warszawie (henceforth USW), 1996 (for 1995), 2002 (for 2000), 2006 (for 2005), 2010 (for 2008) and 2012. The figures on GDP are taken from Eurostat, "Bruttoinlandsprodukt (BIP) zu laufenden Marktpreisen nach NUTS-3-Regionen." http://appsso.eurostat.ec.europa.eu/nui/show .do?dataset=nama_r_e3gdp&lang=de. Accessed May 2014.

50. These figures are based on Warsaw's car registration statistics. See *Rocznik Statystyczny Województwa Warszawy 1991*, p. LXV; *RSW 2002*, p. 404 (for 2000); *RSW 2006*, p. 285; *RSW 2010*, p. 286. On Vienna, see *Statistisches Jahrbuch der Stadt Wien 2013*, p. 274.

51. For the statistics on the years 1995–2005, see *RSW 2006*, p. 285.

52. See *Gazeta Wyborcza*; "Dwa i pół metra," *Gazeta Stołeczna* 8 June 2001, p. 4.

53. See *RSW 2002*, p. 221. On a more positive note, investments have been made in daycare for toddlers since 2005, and the number of daycare places has risen, but is still some 25 percent lower than in 1989. For recent figures, see *RSW 2012*, p. 231.

54. *RSW 2012*, p. 181.

55. Recently an increasing number of commentators have spoken out in favor of high-rise development on Alexanderplatz. See Niklas Maak, "Berlin Alexanderplatz die Wahrheit der Türme," *Frankfurter Allgemeine*

*Zeitung* 14 April 2013. http://www.faz.net/aktuell/feuilleton/berlin
-alexanderplatz-die-wahrheit-der-tuerme-12147588.html. Accessed
May 2014.

56. In 2012, Berlin recorded almost twenty-five million overnight stays
and a steady increase in the number of foreigner visitors. See the
information published by Senatsverwaltung für Wirtschaft, Tech-
nologie und Forschung: http://www.berlin.de/sen/wirtschaft/abisz
/tourismus.html. Accessed May 2014.

57. The difference is due to the appreciation of the Ukrainian currency
caused by a distinctly higher rate of inflation in parallel with a more
or less constant rate of exchange for euros. The rapid appreciation
presaged the crisis of 2008–9, as Ukraine, or rather Kyiv, grew more
and more expensive. In absolute numbers, Kyiv's per capita GDP,
adjusted to purchasing power parity, grew by 24.4 percent from the
equivalent of €14.339 to €17.837. As previously, these figures are
based on Ukrainian statistics and WIIW parity estimates.

58. Unfortunately, no exact figures are available from Eurostat, which
collates by "NUTS 2 regions" which are greater than just the capitals. See Eurostat, "Haushaltseinkommen nach NUTS-2-Regionen."
http://appsso.eurostat.ec.europa.eu/nui/show.do?dataset=nama
_r_ehh2inc&lang=de. Accessed May 2014. The figures are even
more disparate if one compares disposable incomes rather than net
primary incomes. This is due partly to the tax bracket creep, which
starts much lower in Poland, the Czech Republic, and Hungary. By
German or Austrian standards, then, they place a relatively high burden on low- and mid-level incomes.

59. See Eurostat, "Arbeitslosenquoten nach Geschlecht und Alter (%)."
http://appsso.eurostat.ec.europa.eu/nui/show.do?dataset=met
_lfu3rt&lang=de. Accessed May 2014.

60. See N. N., "Berlin—Hauptstadt der Armen," *Neue Zürcher Zeitung* 25 October 2002. http://www.nzz.ch/aktuell/startseite/article8HDV4-1
.434038. Accessed May 2014.; Rainer Woratschka, "Berlin ist
Armuts-Hochburg," *Der Tagesspiegel* 20 December 2012. http://www
.tagesspiegel.de/politik/armutsbericht-berlin-ist-armuts-hochburg
/7549014.html. Accessed May 2014. For more in-depth information, see Berliner Senatsverwaltung für Gesundheit, Umwelt und
Verbraucherschutz, *Gesundheitsberichterstattung Berlin. Spezialbericht. Sozialstrukturatlas Berlin 2008.* http://www.berlin.de/imperia/md/content
/sen-statistik-gessoz/gesundheit/spezialberichte/gbe_spezial_2009
_1_ssa2008.pdf?start&ts=1308132950&file=gbe_spezial_2009

_1_ssa2008.pdf. Accessed May 2014. Vienna does not publish an official poverty report, but the number of poor residents is lower than in Germany and did not rise significantly after the crisis. See the report from the Austrian conference on poverty: http://www .armutskonferenz.at/index.php?option=com_content&task=view& id=447&Itemid=166. Accessed May 2014.

61. See N. N., "Großer Vergleich: Leipzig ist Deutschlands Armuts-hauptstadt," *Spiegel Online* 30 June 2010. http://www.spiegel.de /wirtschaft/soziales/grosser-vergleich-leipzig-ist-deutschlands -armutshauptstadt-a-703787.html. Accessed May 2014; N. N., "Ländervergleich: Berlin ist Deutschlands Armutshauptstadt," *Spiegel Online* 18 January 2010. http://www.spiegel.de/wirtschaft /soziales/laendervergleich-berlin-ist-deutschlands-armutshauptstadt -a-672495.html. Accessed May 2014. It should be noted that the poverty statistics are calculated according to average German in-comes and prices, which are far lower in Berlin than in Munich or Hamburg. However, the level of poverty in Berlin is also illustrated by the number of social benefit claimants, almost 20 percent of the population.

62. See *RSW 2012*, p. 172. In 2010 the average wage in the food services in-dustry and for "supportive activities" was 2700 złotys (or about $680).

63. Cf. "Berlin lernt das Geldverdienen," *Frankfurter Allgemeine Sonntagszei-tung* 17 November 2013, p. 30.

64. On recent population development, see the information published by the Berlin state office for statistics: https://www.statistik-berlin -brandenburg.de/statis/login.do?guest=guest&db=BevBBBE. Ac-cessed May 2014.

65. On business registrations and cancellations, see the report by Ber-liner Investitionsbank: "Gründungsaktivitäten im Städtevergleich," *Berlin aktuell* 28 February 2008, p. 2. https://www.ibb.de/portaldata /1/resources/content/download/newsletter/berlin_aktuell/kn_ba _gruendungen_080228.pdf. Accessed May 2014.

66. See the information in Stadt Wien, Magistratsabteilung 17—Integration und Diversität, *Monitoring. Integration. Diversität. Wien 2009-2011*, p. 10. https://www.wien.gv.at/menschen/integration /pdf/monitor-2012.pdf. Accessed May 2014.

67. See Eurostat, "Bruttoinlandsprodukt (BIP) zu laufenden Markt-preisen nach NUTS-3-Regionen." http://appsso.eurostat.ec.europa .eu/nui/show.do?dataset=nama_r_e3gdp&lang=de. Accessed May 2014.

68. Cf. the Eurostat press release 29/2014 of 27 February 2014, "Regional GDP. GDP per Capita in the EU in 2011: Seven Capital Regions among the Ten Most Prosperous." http://epp.eurostat.ec.europa.eu /cache/ITY_PUBLIC/1-27022014-AP/EN/1-27022014-AP-EN .PDF. Accessed May 2014. I am grateful to Dr. Roman Römisch of the Vienna Institute for International Economic Studies for drawing my attention to this press release.

69. On the consequences of structurally weak regions for growth centers, see Paul Krugman, "Increasing Returns and Economic Geography," *The Journal of Political Economy* 99.3 (June 1991), pp. 483–99.

70. See Branko Milanovic, "Reform and Inequality in the Transition: An Analysis Using Panel Household Survey." In Gerard Roland, ed.: *Economies in Transition: The Long Run View*, London: Palgrave, 2013, pp. 84–108, here 101.

## Chapter 7. The Great Recession: 2008–9 and Its Consequences

1. See Norkus: *On Baltic Slovenia*, p. 130. In 2006 the Baltic states and the European successor states of the Soviet Union achieved an average economic growth of 10 percent.

2. See the data on GDP in the EU countries in Eurostat, "BIP pro Kopf in KKS." http://epp.eurostat.ec.europa.eu/tgm/table.do?tab =table&init=1&plugin=1&language=de&pcode=tec00114. Accessed May 2014. The data on East Germany refer to the five new German states without Berlin. Including East Berlin, which the state-premise of the database prohibits, the East German GDP would approach that of the Czech Republic, as always, adjusted to purchasing power parity.

3. See *WIIW Handbook* 2012, p. 11.

4. By 1914, the Austro-Hungarian Empire had partially caught up with the West, i.e., the pioneers of industrialization. The preceding period is, then, comparable with the transformation era. On the catch-up process in the nineteenth century, see Angus Maddison, *Monitoring the World Economy, 1820–1992*, Paris: OECD, 1995. On East Central Europe more specifically, see Andrew C. Janos, *East Central Europe in the Modern World: The Small States of the Borderlands from Pre- to Postcommunism*, Stanford: Stanford University Press, 2000, pp. 130, 138, 349.

5. See the data in Eurostat, "BIP pro Kopf in KKS." http://epp .eurostat.ec.europa.eu/tgm/table.do?tab=table&init=1&plugin=1& language=de&pcode=tec00114. Accessed May 2014.

6. It wouldn't be the first time. Before the Second World War, Poland's GDP was higher than that of Spain and Portugal, although it plummeted in the communist era to only 49 percent of Spain's GDP; see Jarosz, "Problemy z peerelowską modernizacją," p. 366.

7. The figures (which are not adjusted to purchasing power parity) are accessible on the UN website at http://data.un.org/Data.aspx?d= SNAAMA&f=grID%3A101%3BcurrID%3AUSD%3BpcFlag%3A1. Accessed May 2014. Adjusted for purchasing power, the WIIW estimated the Polish per capita GDP of 1990–91 to be around 4600 euros (at 1995 rates). See *WIIW Handbook 2012*, Countries by indicator, Table II/1.7.

8. See *WIIW Handbook 2012*, Countries by indicator, Table II/1.7. These statistics are based on prices in 1995 converted into euros. On Germany, see also "Bruttoinlandsprodukt Deutschlands ab 1970 (in konstanten Preisen von 1995) nach Angaben des Stat. Bundesamtes und des Arbeitskreises Volkswirtschaftliche Gesamtrechnungen der Länder." http://pdwb.de/w_biprei.htm. Accessed May 2014.

9. See the data in *WIIW Handbook 2012*, pp. 66–96, and the (slightly divergent) GDP statistics compiled by the World Bank: http://data .worldbank.org/indicator/NY.GDP.MKTP.KD.ZG. Accessed May 2014.

10. See *WIIW Handbook 2012*, Countries by indicator, Table II/1.3.

11. Berlin is included with the former West German states for this intra-German comparison, which of course alters the premise; see DIHK, "Ost-Wirtschaft kämpft auch 2014 um Anschluss." http://www.dihk .de/presse/meldungen/2013–11–14-ostkonjunktur. Accessed May 2014. On recent trends in the East Germany economy, see also the final section of Berghoff/Balbier, *East German Economy*.

12. See Bohle and Greskovits: *Capitalist Diversity*, p. 256 (also for recommendations for further reading).

13. See *WIIW Handbook 2012*, pp. 66, 70. In 2008 Lithuania still achieved nominal growth, but it fell into an equally deep recession in 2009.

14. For a comparison of FDI inflows, see Bohle and Greskovits, *Capitalist Diversity*, p. 225.

15. On migration from Poland before and after EU accession, see Izabela Niemirska, "Migracje zarobkowe Polaków w dobie kryzysu," in *Młodzi ekonomiści wobec kryzysu. Gospodarka. Finanse. Rynek Pracy*, Szczecin: Uniwersytet Szczeciński, 2010, pp. 221–32.

16. On this concept and the comparable mortgage allocation practices in the United States before 2008, see Stiglitz: *Freefall*, pp. 175–76.

17. The phenomenon of foreign currency loans became widely known in Poland after about 1997, when the number of personal loans in general, and the proportion in foreign currencies, rose sharply. See N. N., "Wstępne wyniki," *Rzeczpospolita* 11 January 1997, p. X1. By 2000 the Polish media were reporting enthusiastic feedback from bank clients, pleased to have made large savings or taken out much larger loans than they would otherwise have been able to. See N. N., "Dollar, euro czy złoty," *Rzeczpospolita* 19 May 2000, p. X1.

18. This commercial is accessible online on YouTube: http://www .youtube.com/watch?v=OjXl61uKq8c. Accessed May 2014. My attention was drawn to it by Roland Adrowitzer and Ernst Gelegs, *Schöne Grüße aus dem Orbán-Land. Die rechte Revolution in Ungarn,* Graz: Styria, 2013, p. 108. Similar (although not quite as brazen) Polish commercials are also accessible online on YouTube: http://www .youtube.com/watch?v=xX6QnOqIC5s, http://www.youtube.com /watch?v=u8EVhBmdi5Q. Accessed May 2014.

19. See, for example, an article of 2001 in *Rzeczpospolita* entitled "Nobody Considers the Risks": N. N., "Nikt nie patrzy na ryzyko," *Rzeczpospolita* 2 May 2001, p. X1. (The article was hidden in a very specialist business supplement of this finance-oriented, conservative daily newspaper with a limited readership.)

20. See the exchange rates on the websites of the Polish and Hungarian national banks: http://nbp.pl/home.aspx?c=/ascx/archa .ascx; http://english.mnb.hu/Root/ENMNB/Statisztika/data-and -information/mnben_statisztikai_idosorok/mnben_elv_exchange _rates. Accessed May 2014.

21. See N. N., "Fremdwährungskredite. Wege aus der Franken-Falle," *Konsument* (11 November 2010). Accessed May 2014. http://www.konsument.at/cs/Satellite?pagename=Konsument %2FMagazinArtikel%2FDetail&cid=318873919185. Accessed May 2014. In 2011 the financial market authority intervened to regulate the market. See the FMA documents on minimum standards: http://www.fma.gv.at/de/rechtliche-grundlagen/mindeststandards /banken.html. Accessed May 2014.

22. See APA, "Ungarn beschließt Gesetzt zu Fremdwährungs-krediten," *Die Presse* 20 December 2012. http://diepresse.com/home /wirtschaft/international/694445/Ungarn-beschliesst-Gesetz-zu -Fremdwaehrungskrediten. Accessed May 2014.

23. See András Szigetvari, "Kartenhaus aus Euro, Franken und Yen wackelt," *Der Standard* 24 November 2010. http://derstandard.at

/1289608695744/Fremdwaehrungskredite-Kartenhaus-aus-Euro
-Franken-und-Yen-wackelt. Accessed May 2014.

24. On this law of September 2011, see APA, "Ungarn beschließt Gesetz zu Fremdwährungskrediten."

25. The original wording is: "nicht als Massenprodukt geeignet," cited from FMA: "Ergänzung zu den FMA Mindeststandards zur Vergabe und Gestionierung von Fremdwährungskrediten und Krediten mit Tilgungsträgern vom 16. Oktober 2003. Ergänzung vom 22. März 2010 (FMA-FXTT-EMS)," p. 5. http://www.fma.gv.at/typo3conf /ext/dam_download/secure.php?u=0&file=1869&t=1338270132 &hash=801e2a31b10ee8a4fab55379e9acf13b. Accessed May 2014. Companies and governments have used foreign currency loans for many years. (For example, the city of Vienna has borrowed francs from Switzerland for decades because of the lower interest rates.) The "innovation" after 1989 was the extension of the practice to masses of private debtors.

26. Cf. the data in *RSW 2010*, p. 286.

27. All the population statistics cited in this paragraph are taken from the WIIW. See *WIIW Handbook 2012*, Countries by indicator, Table II/1.1, 3, 5, 6, 8. The decline in the population is not necessarily due entirely to migration; according to the *Economist*, 6 percent of the Latvian population migrated in search of work between 2008 and 2012, accounting for two-thirds of the country's crisis-related population shrinkage. See N. N., "European Labour Mobility: On the Move." http://www.economist.com/blogs/freeexchange/2014/01/european -labour-mobility. Accessed May 2014.

28. Cf. the figures in *WIIW Handbook 2012*, Countries by indicator, Table II/1.8. According to these, the population decreased from 21,438,000 to 1,991,000 in 2010–11.

29. On emigration and immigration trends in Ireland, see OECD, *International Migration Outlook 2014*, Paris: OECD Publishing, 2014, pp. 262– 63; also specifically on emigration. http://www.cso.ie/multiqicktables /quickTables.aspx?id=pea18_2. Accessed February 2015.

30. FDI capital stock amounted to over fifty billion euros in 2011. Cf. *WIIW Handbook 2012*, Table I/2.9 (FDI inward stock, p. 49).

31. On Russia's ousting of foreign corporations, see the dossier covering several years by the magazine *Spiegel*: http://www.spiegel.de/thema /tnk_bp/dossierarchiv-2.html. Accessed May 2014.

32. The speech is documented on the Russian government website. See N. N., "Der Präsident von Russland auf der Münchner Konferenz zu

Fragen der Sicherheitspolitik-Teil 1." http://russland.ru/rupol0010 /morenews.php?iditem=15254. Accessed May 2014.

33. See Neill Robinson, "Introduction," in idem, ed., *The Political Economy of Russia*, Lanham: Rowman & Littlefield, 2013, pp. 1–14; also the essay contained in this anthology by Gerald Easter, "Revenue Imperatives: State over Market in Postcommunist Russia," pp. 51–68.

34. The Western press seems to have misconstrued the nature of Russia's state-run economy, erroneously referring to RosAtom as a "corporation." See inter alia N. N.: "Atomkraftwerksbau: Ungarn vergibt milliardenschweren Auftrag an Russland," *Der Spiegel* 14 January 2014. http://www.spiegel.de/politik/ausland/ungarn-vergibt -milliardenschweren-atomauftrag-an-russland-a-943568.html. Accessed May 2014.

35. On these taxes and Hungarian discrimination against foreign companies, see Adrowitzer and Gelegs, *Schöne Grüße*, pp. 99–107.

36. See Sándor Richter, "Im Würgegriff des Populismus. Ungarns Volkswirtschaft," *Osteuropa* 61/12 (2012), pp. 213–24.

37. According to official statistics, two hundred and fifty thousand Hungarian citizens lived and worked abroad in June 2013, up from only six thousand in 2010 (see Adrowitzer and Gelegs: *Schöne Grüße*, p. 112). The actual number of labor migrants is probably higher as the statistics do not include seasonal workers or employees of Hungarian subcontractors abroad.

38. On Orbán and Fidesz, see Edith Oltay, *Fidesz and the Reinvention of the Hungarian Center-Right*, Budapest: Századvég, 2013.

## Chapter 8. Southern Europe: The New East?

1. See the statistics provided by the education union FLC CGIL on the "Legge di stabilità": http://www.flcgil.it/attualita/sindacato /legge-di-stabilita.-confermati-i-tagli.-pochi-interventi-a-favore-della -conoscenza. Accessed May 2014.

2. In early 2014, Italian private enterprise still had outstanding invoices worth 91 billion euros. See N. N., "Fallimenti record per colpa dei debiti Pa," *La Repubblica* 3 February 2014. http://www.repubblica .it/economia/2014/02/03/news/fallimenti_record_per_colpa _dei_debiti_pa_cgia_alle_imprese_mancano_ancora_100_mld -77592615/. Accessed May 2014.

3. The statistics on Italy refer to industrial production, not including the construction industry, and are taken from the Italian government's

statistical agency (Istat). Unfortunately, it is not possible to reconstruct my online research via a specific link. One must take the more arduous route of going to the Istat website (http://dati.istat.it/Index .aspx) and clicking through to "Industria e Costruzioni," "Produzione," and "Indice della produzione industriale," entering the corresponding years. For the statistics on Poland, see *WIIW Handbook 2012*, Countries by indicator, Table II/1.17.

4. In the book *Case Studies on Modern European Economy. Entrepreneurs, Invention, Institutions*, London: Routledge, 2013, Iván Berend briefly considers the crisis in conclusion, but attributes it primarily to "cultural-behavioral factors" and criticizes southern European tendencies toward extravagance, corruption, and tax evasion. It is striking how often economists refer to cultural factors when other explanations fail. Unfortunately the standard English-language work, the *Cambridge Economic History of Modern Italy*, does not extend to recent years.

5. Cf. Wirtschaftskammer Österreich, "Öffentliche Verschuldung. Staatsschuldenquote (Schuldenstand des Gesamtstaates in % des BIP)." http://wko.at/statistik/eu/europa-verschuldung.pdf. Accessed May 2014. An additional difference is that the Hungarian national debt has not grown further relative to the GDP since the outbreak of the crisis.

6. On the FDI (including those from Italy) in the new EU member states, see Łukasz Białek, "Przegląd bezpośrednich inwestycji zagranicznych w Europie Środkowej i Wschodniej." http://ceedinstitute.org /attachments/281/d44b6519328278fe999108afe767da4b.pdf. Accessed May 2014.

7. The figures on the share of Western European capital in Eastern European FDI vary. According to information from the National Bank of Poland, 90 percent of FDI invested in Poland by 2011 came from Western Europe; see "Zagraniczne inwestycje bezpośrednie w Polsce w 2010 roku" (October 2011). http://www.nbp.pl/publikacje/zib /zib2010.pdf, especially pp. 23, 143; accessed May 2014. On further developments, see the data on the website of the NBP: http://www .nbp.pl/home.aspx?f=/publikacje/zib/zib.html. Accessed May 2014. Berend puts the proportion in Hungary at 80 percent; see Berend, *From the Soviet Bloc*, p. 117. A Polish-language survey of the entire region estimates the share of all FDI from the eurozone at between 70 and 90 percent; see Białek, "Przegląd bezpośrednich inwestycji zagranicznych w Europie Środkowej i Wschodniej." In Russia the EU countries' share of FDI is 64 percent; see Ernst & Young, "Russia

2014: Shaping Russia's Future." http://www.ey.com/Publication /vwLUAssets/2013-Russia-attractiveness-survey-Eng/$FILE/2013 -Russia-attractiveness-survey-Eng.pdf. Accessed May 2014.

8. See Berend: *From the Soviet Bloc*, p. 126. There is, however, no direct connection between the FDI in the new European Union countries and the level of domestic investment, which is often criticized as too low in Germany and is even lower in Italy, although it was thought that the high inflow of FDI in eastern Europe might be linked to an outflow of domestic capital; see Kálmán Kalotay, "Investment Creation and Diversion in an Integrating Europe," in Peeter Vahtra and Elina Pelto, eds.: *The Future Competitiveness of the EU and Its Eastern Neighbours: Proceedings of the Conference*, Turku: Pan-European Institute, 2007, pp. 49–65.

9. On the lower costs in Bulgaria and Romania, see Kirsten Reinhold, "Textile Quelle Schwarzes Meer," *TextilWirtschaft* 19 (19 May 2002). http://www.textilwirtschaft.de/suche/show.php?ids[]=170615. Accessed May 2014.

10. For the results of the various studies, see OECD, "PISA—Internationale Schulleistungsstudie der OECD." http://www.oecd.org/berlin /themen/pisa-internationaleschulleistungsstudiederoecd.htm. Accessed May 2014. The Italian (and Spanish) PISA results showed a striking deterioration between 2000 and 2006. Since then, their results in most categories (reading, math) have improved. The same is true of Poland, which attained particularly good results in math.

11. On broadband internet access and provision to private households, see Heidi Seybert, "Internet Use in Households and by Individuals in 2012," *Eurostat. Statistics in Focus* 50/2012. http://epp.eurostat .ec.europa.eu/cache/ITY_OFFPUB/KS-SF-12–050/EN/KS-SF -12–050-EN.PDF. Accessed May 2014.

12. On the rise and later decline of Olivetti, see Giovanni De Witt, *Le fabbriche ed il mondo. L'Olivetti industriale nella competizione globale, 1950– 90*, Milan: Franco Angeli, 2005. On the individual devices, see the comprehensive documentation by Storiaolivetti: http://www .storiaolivetti.it/. Accessed March 2014. (At the last attempt in May 2014, the website was unfortunately no longer accessible.) On the growth phase in the Italian economy during the eighties, see Paul Ginsborg, *Storia d'Italia 1943–1996. Famiglia, società, stato*, Turin, Einaudi, 1998.

13. On the development of the spread in 2011, see Michela Scacchioli, "Da Berlusconi a Monti. La drammatica estate 2011 tra spread e rischi

d bancarotta," *La Repubblica* 10 February 2014. http://www.repubblica
.it/politica/2014/02/10/news/estate_2011_spread_berlusconi_bce
_monti_governo_napolitano-78215026/. Accessed May 2014.

14. For a critical view on austerity, see Giulio Marcon and Mario Pianta, *Sbilanciamo l'economia. Una via d'uscita dalla crisi*, Rome: Laterza, 2013. However, like many left-wing Italians, these authors also question European integration after the Maastricht Treaty.

15. On these figures, see Eurostat, "Arbeitslosenquote nach Altersgruppe." http://epp.eurostat.ec.europa.eu/tgm/table.do?tab=table&init=1&language=de&pcode=tsdec460&plugin=1. Accessed May 2014.

16. On these figures, see OECD, "Country Statistical Profile: Italy." http://www.oecd-ilibrary.org/economics/country-statistical-profile -italy_20752288-table-ita. Accessed May 2014.

17. On regional divergence in Italy since the crisis, see Inequalitywatch, "Income Inequalities in Italy: Trend over Time." http://www .inequalitywatch.eu/spip.php?article139&id_mot=87&lang=en. Accessed May 2014. On the more long-term decline in southern Italy, see Carlo Borgomeo, *L'equivoco del Sud. Sviluppo e coesione sociale*, Rome: Laterza, 2013.

18. See Francesco Barbagallo, *La questione italiana. Il Nord e il Sud dal 1860 a oggi*, Rome: Laterza, 2013, p. 218.

19. Borgomeo attributes Italy's current problems primarily to the bias of regional aid since the mid-fifties toward industrializing the South (in a similar manner to previous regimes' efforts to industrialize rural regions of Poland and the ČSSR); see Borgomeo, *L'equivoco del Sud*, pp. 14–23.

20. On the alternative use of regional aid (the funds were redirected to areas such as the health system), see Barbagallo, *La questione italiana*, pp. 207–8; on social expenditure, see ibid., p. 218; on the development of regional GDP in Italy until 2012, see Raffaele Ricciardi, "Il Pil del Sud è il 42 % meno del Nord. Così la crisi ha segnato il Mezzogiorno," *La Repubblica* 27 November 2013. http://www.repubblica .it/economia/2013/11/27/news/conti_economici_regionali_istat _nord_sud-72073979/. Accessed May 2014. According to this report, the regional GDP in Sicily, Calabria, and Campania in 2012 was between 16,400 and 16,800 euros per capita; and 17,400 euros in the Mezziogiorno region as a whole. (Some 2 percent should be deducted after adjustment to purchasing power, to reflect the lower purchasing power of a euro in Italy than the EU average.) Poland's

purchasing-power-adjusted GDP in 2012 was almost 18,000 euros; see Trading Economics, "Polen—BIP pro Kopf PPP." http://de .tradingeconomics.com/poland/gdp-per-capita-ppp. Accessed May 2014. The comparison is relativized by equal consideration of the poorer parts of Poland. Moreover, the Italian GDP was still eight-fold that of Poland in absolute terms.

21. On attitudes to returning home (e.g., to Poland), see Izabela Grabowska-Lusińska, *Poakcesyjne powroty Polaków*, Warsaw: Ośrodek Badan nad Migracjami, 2010, pp. 27–36 (= *CMR Working Papers* 43/101).

22. Frithjof B. Schenk and Martina Winkler, eds., *Der Süden. Neue Perspektiven auf eine europäische Geschichtsregion*, Frankfurt am Main: Campus, 2007.

23. See Larry Wolff, *Inventing Eastern Europe: The Map of Civilization on the Mind of the Enlightenment*, Stanford: Stanford University Press, 1994.

24. Cited in Andrew Higgins, "Used to Hardship, Latvia Accepts Austerity, and Its Pain Eases." *New York Times* 1 January 2013. http://www .nytimes.com/2013/01/02/world/europe/used-to-hardship-latvia -accepts-austerity-and-its-pain-eases.html?_r=0. Accessed May 2014.

25. For a counternarrative against the Chilean neoliberal success story, see Ricardo Ffrench-Davis, *Economic Reforms in Chile: From Dictatorship to Democracy*, third edition, London: Macmillan 2010. There are of course many more experts on Chile, such as Michael J. Kurtz and Peter Winn, but Ffrench-Davis is especially interesting because he was trained as an economist at the University of Chicago and therefore knows both viewpoints, the neoliberal and the Christian Democratic. Many expert reports criticizing Pinochet's neoliberal policies around 1989–90 can also be found in: World Bank Archive, World Bank File 16435 (Chile—Lending, Economy and Program (LEAP)— General—volume 2); World Bank File 16436 (Chile—Lending, Economy and Program (LEAP)—General—volume 3).

26. Cf. Dietmar Neuerer, "Von Lettland lernen, heißt siegen lernen," *Handelsblatt* 28 February 2012. http://www.handelsblatt.com/politik /international/vorbild-fuer-krisenstaaten-von-lettland-lernen-heisst -siegen-lernen/7063756.html. Accessed May 2014.

27. They are calculated by taking the number of labor migrants relative to total populations; see W. P., "European Labour Mobility," *Economist* 13 January 2014. http://www.economist.com/blogs/freeexchange /2014/01/european-labour-mobility. Accessed May 2014.

28. See Kaelble, *Sozialgeschichte Europas*; Béla Tomka, *A Social History of Twentieth-Century Europe*, Abingdon: Routledge, 2013.

29. See the figures specifically concerning young people compiled by the agency Datagiovani: "Sempre meno giovani contribuenti in Italia." http://www.datagiovani.it/newsite/wp-content/uploads/2012/05 /Comunicato-Dichiarazioni-dei-redditi-2011-dei-giovani.pdf. Accessed May 2014. Incomes of young people in southern Italy were lower. Even factoring in undeclared incomes (the calculations were made on the basis of tax declarations, or tax office information) and the number of young people in education programs and vocational training, the average income is still extremely low.

30. See N. N., "L'allarme dell'Eurispes sull'Italia," *La Repubblica* 30 January 2012. http://www.repubblica.it/economia/2014/01/30/news/eurispes _3_italiani_su_10_non_arrivano_a_fine_mese-77273192/. Accessed May 2014. See also N. N., "Impossibile arrivare a fine mese, uno su tre chiede aiuto a mama e papa," *Rai News 24* (9 November 2013). http://www.rainews.it/it/news.php?newsid=183983. Accessed May 2014.

31. See Peter Spahn, "Die Schuldenkrise der Europäischen Währungs-union," *WISO direkt* (December 2010). http://library.fes.de/pdf-files /wiso/07686.pdf. Accessed May 2014. The figures look different if one factors in corporate and private loans, which were negligble in socialist countries. Foreign debt in Spain, Portugal, and Greece is worth 100 percent of the GDP or more.

32. Waldemar Kuczyński, "Czy Polska zbiedniała?," *Tygodnik Powszechny* 11 September 2005, p. 11.

33. See N. N., "Die große Enteignung. Zehn Prozent 'Schulden-Steuer' auf alle Spar-Guthaben," *Deutsche Wirtschaftsnachrichten* 17 October 2013. http://deutsche-wirtschafts-nachrichten.de/2013/10/17 /die-grosse-enteignung-zehn-prozent-schulden-steuer-auf-alle-spar -guthaben/. Accessed May 2014. Later the IMF backtracked and claimed the paper had only contained reflections.

## Chapter 9. Cotransformation: The Case of Germany

1. Cultural transfer research is too broad a field to sum up in one footnote. The standard works by Michael Werner and Michel Espagne are discussed in Philipp Ther, "Comparisons, Cultural Transfers and the Study of Networks: Towards a Transnational History of Europe," in Heinz-Gerhard Haupt and Jürgen Kocka, eds., *Comparative and Transnational History: Central European Approaches and New Perspectives*, New York: Berghahn, 2010, pp. 204–25.

2. On cultural transfers via dissociation, see Martin Aust and Daniel Schönpflug, eds., *Vom Gegner lernen. Feindschaften und Kulturtransfers im Europa des 19. und 20. Jahrhunderts*, Frankfurt am Main: Campus, 2007.

3. On the concept of "speech acts," see Quentin Skinner, "Conventions and the Understanding of Speech Acts," *The Philosophical Quarterly* 20.79 (April 1970), pp. 118–38.

4. Cf. http://www.gesetze-im-internet.de/gg/art_146.html. Accessed February 2015.

5. See Goedicke, "A 'Ready-Made State,'" p. 49.

6. On the overburdening of the prospects of success of the German welfare state, see Gerhard A. Ritter, *Der Preis der deutschen Einheit. Die Wiedervereinigung und die Krise des Sozialstaates*, Munich: Beck, 2006.

7. See Edgar Wolfrum, *Rot-Grün an der Macht. Deutschland 1998–2005*, Munich: Beck, 2013, pp. 34–35.

8. See the interview conducted by *Spiegel* editors Olaf Ilhau, Stefan Aust, and Gabor Steingart with Gerhard Schröder, "Wir haben bessere Karten." *Der Spiegel* 21 September 1998. http://www.spiegel.de/spiegel/print/d-8002130.html. Accessed May 2014.

9. See N. N. "The Sick Man of the Euro," *Economist* 3 June 1999. http://www.economist.com/node/209559. Accessed May 2014.

10. On the "Riester-Rente" pension scheme, see Wolfrum, *Rot-Grün*, pp. 203–9.

11. On global debates over privately financed pension systems, see Mitchell Orenstein, *Privatizing Pensions: The Transnational Campaign for Social Security Reform*, Princeton: Princeton University Press, 2008.

12. Retirement age was fifty-five for women and sixty for men, which is almost unimaginable today but tallied with life expectancy at the time. See Louise Fox and Edward Palmer, "Latvian Pension Reform" (= The World Bank, *Social Protection Discussion Paper Series* 9922). http://siteresources.worldbank.org/SOCIALPROTECTION/Resources/SP-Discussion-papers/Pensions-DP/9922.pdf Accessed May 2014; OECD, "Pension Reform in the Baltic Countries" (= *Private Pension Series* 5). http://www.oecd-ilibrary.org/finance-and-investment/pension-reform-in-the-baltic-countries_9789264021068-en. Accessed May 2014.

13. On the Swedish pension reform, see Annika Sundén, "The Swedish Experience with Pension Reform," *Oxford Review on Economic Policy* 22 (2006), pp. 133–48.

14. The Estonian pension scheme website is accessible online at http://www.pensionikeskus.ee/?id=628. Accessed May 2014.

15. See Wolfrum, *Rot-Grün*, p. 153.

16. On the semantics of the labor market reform and the individual Hartz laws, see Elena Buck and Jana Hönke, "Pioniere der Prekarität— Ostdeutsche als Avantgarde des neuen Arbeitsmarktregimes," in Rebecca Pates and Maximilian Schochow, eds., *Der "Ossi." Mikropolitische Studien über einen symbolischen Ausländer*, Wiesbaden: Springer, 2013, pp. 23–53, here 27.

17. See, e.g., Friedman and Friedman, *Free to Choose*, pp. 120–26; also the 2002 edition of Friedman's *Capitalism and Freedom*, Chicago: University of Chicago Press, 2002, pp. 192–94.

18. Wolfrum, *Rot-Grün*, p. 545.

19. This was the number receiving additional payments for regular occupations under Hartz IV in 2013; see N. N., "Hartz IV: Aufstocker kommen oft nicht aus Grundsicherung heraus," *Spiegel online* 18 July 2013. http://www.spiegel.de/wirtschaft/soziales/studie-aufstocker -kommen-nur-schwer-aus-hartz-iv-a-911813.html. Accessed May 2014.

20. See Yasmin El-Sharif, "Aufstocker. Callcenter kosten den Staat jährlich 36 Millionen Euro," *Spiegel online* 11 March 2013. http://www .spiegel.de/wirtschaft/soziales/callcenter-kosten-den-staat-jaehrlich -36-millionen-euro-a-888076.html. Accessed May 2014.

21. See James, *Europe Reborn*, pp. 352–60.

22. On the history of civil society concepts in east-west transfers, see Agnes Arndt, *Intellektuelle in der Opposition. Diskurse zur Zivilgesellschaft in der Volksrepublik Polen*, Frankfurt am Main: Campus, 2007.

23. See Robert D. Putnam, "Bowling Alone: America's Declining Social Capital," *Journal of Democracy* 6 (1995), pp. 65–78. In 2000, Putnam published a similarly titled book, *Bowling Alone: The Collapse and Revival of American Community*, New York: Simon & Schuster.

24. Cf. Gerhard Schröder, "Die zivile Bürgergesellschaft. Zur Neubestimmung der Aufgaben von Staat und Gesellschaft," *Neue Gesellschaft* 4 (2000), pp. 200–7; also Ulrich Beck, "Mehr Zivilcourage bitte," *Die Zeit* 25 May 2000. http://www.zeit.de/2000/22/200022.der _gebaendigte_.xml. Accessed May 2014.

25. On social problems in the Mezzogiorno, see also Borgomeo, *L'equivoco del Sud*, p. 8.

26. This speech is documented on the website *Zeit online*: Angela Merkel, "Was wir vorhaben, ist ein Befreiungsschlag zur Senkung der Arbeitskosten," *Zeit online* 23 July 2003. http://www.zeit.de/reden /deutsche_innenpolitik/200349_merkelcduparteitag. Accessed May 2014.

27. See Monika Queisser, "Die Rente mit Kapital unterlegen," *Frankfurter Allgemeine Zeitung* 24 January 1998; also N. N., "Aktien statt Almosen," *Der Spiegel* 3 August 1998. http://www.spiegel.de/spiegel/print/d -7956090.html. Accessed May 2014. The catchword "bankruptcy" (*Bankrott*) reflected the contemporary alarmist mood; in a sober light, pension systems based on an intergenerational contract cannot go bankrupt unless the contributors collectively refuse to pay in. The reference to Poland in the *Spiegel* article is brief.

28. See Katharina Müller, "Vom Staat zum Markt? Rentenreformen in Mittelosteuropa," *Staatswissenschaften und Staatspraxis* 9.2 (1998), pp. 163–89.

29. See Markus Schneider, "Warum die Flat Tax sozial ist," *Die Welt* 31 August 2005. http://www.welt.de/print-welt/article162199/Warum -die-Flat-Tax-sozial-ist.html. Accessed May 2013. Also Schwarz, "Vom Siebenschläfer zum Tiger der Karpaten." Left-liberal and left-wing newspapers were more critical; see Nicola Liebert, "Die Flat Tax ist nur ein Verschiebebahnhof," *Die Tageszeitung* 29 November 2005. http://www.taz.de/1/archiv/archiv/?dig=2005/11/29/a0106. Accessed May 2014.

30. See especially the writings by Swedish pension expert Edward Palmer, who advised a number of other postcommunist countries as well as the Latvian government and was subsequently made research director of the Swedish social security agency, partly on account of the international recognition he had gained.

31. On discursive globalization and the World Polity theory of John W. Meyer, see, e.g., Georg Krücken and Gili S. Drori, eds., *World Society: The Writings of John W. Meyer*, New York: Oxford University Press, 2009.

32. See N. N., "Schulden explodieren: Polen konfisziert private Renten-Fonds," *Deutsche Wirtschafts Nachrichten* 8 September 2013. http://deutsche-wirtschafts-nachrichten.de/2013/09/08/schulden -explodieren-polen-enteignet-private-renten-fonds/comment-page -3/. Accessed June 2014.

33. See N. N., "'Zum Kotzen'. Helmut Schmidt wettert gegen Jammer-Ossis," *Spiegel online* 11 October 2003. http://www.spiegel.de/politik /deutschland/zum-kotzen-helmut-schmidt-wettert-gegen-jammer -ossis-a-269386.html. Accessed May 2014.

34. See Wolfgang Engler, *Die Ostdeutschen als Avantgarde*, Berlin: Aufbau, 2002; also Thomas Kralinski, "Die neuen Ostdeutschen," *Berliner Republik. Das Debattenmagazin* 4 (2000). http://www.b-republik.de/archiv /die-neuen-ostdeutschen. Accessed May 2014.

35. Schröder said this in a speech on the solidarity agreement, which is documented on the website *Ruhrpost online*; see N. N., "Schröder halt am Solidarpakt II fest," *RP-online* 18 April 2004. http://www.rp-online.de/politik/deutschland/schroeder-haelt-am-solidarpakt-ii-fest-aid-1.2280078. Accessed May 2014.

36. See Claus-Dieter Steyer, "Schröder auf Osttour: Der Kanzler wirft einen Blick auf die ostdeutsche Landwirtschaft," *Der Tagesspiegel* 30 August 2000. http://www.tagesspiegel.de/berlin/brandenburg/schroeder-auf-osttour-der-kanzler-wirft-einen-blick-auf-die-ostdeutsche-landwirtschaft/162802.html. Accessed May 2014.

37. Cited from Buck and Hönke, "Pioniere der Prekarität," p. 40.

38. See a (negative) statement made by the deputy party chairman, Wolfgang Thierse, at an event hosted by the SPD-related Friedrich Ebert Foundation in November 2004: "Das Potenzial des Ostens—wo stehen wir im deutsch-deutschen Prozess?" http://www.fes-forumberlin.de/pdf_2004-2003/4_11_5_thierse.pdf. Accessed May 2014.

39. See Borgomeo, *L'equivoco des Sud*, pp. 14–23.

## Chapter 10. The Roads Not Taken

1. On the internationalist aspect of the revolution in the ČSSR and the cross-border actions in this and the following paragraphs, see Krapfl, *Revolution with a Human Face*, pp. 57–59; see also Arnold Suppan, "Austria and Its Neighbours in Eastern Europe, 1955–89," in Wolfgang Mueller, Michael Gehler, and Arnold Suppan, eds., *The Revolutions of 1989: A Handbook*, Vienna: Verlag der ÖAW, 2014, pp. 419–36.

2. The term "reckoning" (German: "Abrechnung"; Polish: "rozrachunek") has been consciously chosen over that of "reappraisal" of the past (German: "Aufarbeitung"). History as a rule cannot be profoundly reappraised immediately after the end of a certain regime. The victims' trauma is too fresh and the perpetrators too preoccupied with evading prosecution, property confiscations, and other sanctions to allow an honest dialog about the past to take place. For example, it took some two decades for West Germans to be able to start "reappraising" the Nazi past. This leads us to the second reason for avoiding the term "reappraisal": It suggests a questionable parallel between the history of the GDR and that of Nazi Germany. Third, the special status of the former GDR achieved by unification with the Federal Republic of Germany must be taken into account. This allowed an almost complete changeover of elites to take place. All the other former

Eastern Bloc countries, like West Germany in the 1950s and '60s, had the task of transforming erstwhile supporters of dictatorship into good democrats, or at least into compliant fellow travelers.

3. Cf. Jürgen Habermas, "Die nachholende Revolution," in Habermas, *Kleine Politische Schriften VII*, Frankfurt am Main: Suhrkamp, 1990, pp. 177–204. An English translation was published some six months later. See Habermas, "What Does Socialism," pp. 3–21.

4. See Habermas, "What Does Socialism," p. 5.

5. Ibid., p. 4.

6. See Timothy Garton Ash, "Apres le deluge, nous," *Transit. Europäische Revue* 1 (1990), pp. 11–34.

7. "tiefes Tal der Tränen." Cf. Ralf Dahrendorf, "Übergänge: Politik, Wirtschaft und Freiheit," *Transit. Europäische Revue* 1 (1990), pp. 35–47, here 41–42. Polish liberals advanced similar arguments. See Szacki, *Liberalism after Communism*.

8. See the references to transition (in German: "Übergang") in East Asian civil society in Dahrendorf, pp. 36–37. In his German-language text, Dahrendorf wrote of "Bürgergesellschaft."

9. François Furet, "1789–1917, 'Rückfahrkarte'," *Transit. Europäische Revue* 1 (1990), pp. 48–64, here 60. Interestingly, Furet, who died in 1997, had not been a conservative all his life. As a young man, he was a member of the French Communist Party, and later held liberal views for a time.

10. See Furet, "1789–1917, 'Rückfahrkarte'," pp. 52, 60–61.

11. Excerpts of films of these two demonstrations can be viewed on YouTube under the Czech titles "První obří demonstrace na Letné" (http://www.youtube.com/watch?v=x0aUIjCdp74) and "Druhá obří demonstrace na Letné" (http://www.youtube.com/watch?v=yxmthRAIrGM). Both accessed May 2014.

12. See Patočka's collected works on Comenius: Jan Patočka, *Komeniologické studie I, Soubor textů o J. A. Komenském, Texty publikované v letech 1941–1958*, edited by Vera Schifferová, Prague: Oikúmené, 1997. On this reception of Patočka, see also Jan-Werner Müller, *Das demokratische Zeitalter. Eine politische Ideengeschichte Europas im 20. Jahrhundert*, Berlin: Suhrkamp, 2013, pp. 388–89.

13. See, e.g., Václav Havel, *Do ruzných stran*, Prague: Lidové noviny, 1990. These writings date predominantly from the period before 1989, around the time of Charter 77, and are therefore not to be unequivocally associated with the revolution.

14. For Garton Ash's criticism of Havel, see "Après le déluge," p. 14.

15. On the actors of the revolution and their demands, see Krapfl, *Revolution with a Human Face*, and the Czech-language literature, including Jiří Suk, *Labyrintem revoluce. Aktéři, zápletky a křižovatky jedné politické krize (Od listopadu 1989 do června 1990)*, Prague: Prostor, 2003; Milan Otáhal and Miroslav Vaněk, *Sto studentských revolucí. Studenti v období pádu komunismu—životopisná vyprávění*, Prague: Lidové noviny, 1999.

16. On this debate in Poland, which to some extent referred to an idealized past and a common set of values, see Aleksander Smolar, *Tabu i niewinność*, Kraków: Universitas, 2010, p. 130.

17. On this legacy of 1989, see ibid., pp. 127–28.

18. See Isaiah Berlin, *Liberty: Incorporating Four Essays on Liberty*, edited by Henry Hardy, Oxford: Oxford University Press, 2002.

19. See Charles Taylor, *The Ethics of Authenticity*, Cambridge: Harvard University Press, 1992.

20. With respect to the ČSSR, see Krapfl, *Revolution with a Human Face*, pp. 74–110; on Poland, see Smolar, *Tabu i niewinność*, pp. 89–90.

21. Nevertheless, Gaidar, who died in 2009, is revered in Russian business circles to this day. The Gaidar Forum (Гайдаровский форум), which debates problems of the Russian economy, is named in his honor.

22. Rupnik, "1968: The Year of Two Springs."

23. See OECD, "Gender Wage Gap." http://www.oecd.org/gender/data /genderwagegap.htm. Accessed May 2014. In Hungary, women have more or less achieved equality in terms of pay; in the Czech Republic, Slovakia, and Estonia, they have not.

24. The most positive potential scenario is that China will take the Hungarian path and allow party-political pluralization, or different factions under the umbrella of the Chinese Communist Party. This idea was briefly considered in 2012–13, but overruled for the time being.

25. The original German reads: "Polnische Schwarzhändler, Schmuggler und Ladendiebe in West-Berlin heizen die Ausländerfeindlichkeit unter Einheimischen an." Cf. N. N., "Arme Teufel," *Der Spiegel* 17/1990, pp. 105–7.

26. See N. N., "Österreich. Volles Boot, leeres Hirn," *Der Spiegel* 28/1990, p. 122; on the visa requirement, see Joanna Jajdek, "Der mittelbare Nachbar. Österreichvorstellungen in Polen 1970–1995," in Oliver Rathkolb, Otto M. Maschke, and Stefan August Lütgenau, eds., *Mit anderen Augen gesehen. Internationale Perzeptionen Österreichs 1955–1990*, Vienna: Böhlau, 2002, pp. 647–76, here 666–67.

27. See Heinz Fassmann and Rainer Münz, *Ost-West-Wanderungen in Europa. Rückblick und Ausblick*, Vienna: Böhlau, 2000.

28. See Ronald Freudenstein, "Angst essen Seele auf. Die Deutschen und die Osterweiterung der Europäischen Union," *DPI Jahrbuch* 12 (2001). http://dpi.de1.cc/Publikationen/Jahrbuch-Ansichten /jahrbuch12_2001.php. Accessed May 2014. For the Stoiber citation, see p. 3.

29. Issen said this on several occasions, including in a comment in 2001 on the imminent expansion of the European Union. He was subsequently quoted in the Bundestag; one SPD member of parliament echoed his visions of doom; see Deutscher Bundestag, Stenographischer Bericht. 99. Sitzung, 13. April 2000, p. 31. http://dip21 .bundestag.de/dip21/btp/14/14099.pdf. Accessed May 2014.

30. See N. N., "Stoiber will EU-Beitrittsverträge nachbessern," *Handelsblatt* 23 April 2005. http://www.handelsblatt.com/politik/deutschland /uebergangsregelungen-gefordert-stoiber-will-eu-beitrittsvertraege -nachbessern/2497098.html. Accessed May 2014.

31. See Manuel Bewarder, "'Wer betrügt, der fliegt'—die CSU im Faktencheck," *Die Welt* 31 December 2013. http://www.welt.de/politik /deutschland/article123419505/Wer-betruegt-der-fliegt-die-CSU-im -Faktencheck.html. Accessed May 2014.

32. "Je reste en Pologne. Venez nombreux"; see Kornelia Kończal, "Vom Schreckgespenst zum Dressman. Le plombier polonais und die Macht der Imagination," in Kiran Patel, Veronika Lipphardt, and Lorraine Bluche, eds., *Der Europäer—ein Konstrukt. Wissensbestände und Diskurse*, Göttingen: Wallstein, 2008, pp. 299–325.

33. See N. N., "Irak-Krieg: Chirac knöpft sich die EU-Kandidaten vor," *Der Spiegel* 17 February 2003. http://www.spiegel.de/politik/ausland /irak-krieg-chirac-knoepft-sich-die-eu-kandidaten-vor-a-236530 .html. Accessed May 2014.

34. On relations between the European Union and Ukraine at the time, see Serhii Yekelczyk and Oliver Schmidtke, eds., *Europe's Last Frontier? Belarus, Moldova, and Ukraine between Russia and the European Union*. New York: Palgrave, 2008.

35. "nur untereinander verwandte kulturelle Entwicklung durchlaufen"; "russischen Kulturkreis." See Helmut Schmidt, *Die Selbstbehauptung Europas. Perspektiven für das 21. Jahrhundert*, Munich: DVA, 2000. The citations are from the excerpts of the book that were published in the newspaper *Die Zeit*; see Helmut Schmidt, "Wer nicht zu Europa gehört," *Die Zeit* 5 October 2000, especially p. 2. http://www.zeit.de /2000/41/Wer_nicht_zu_Europa_gehoert. Accessed May 2014.

36. Shortly before the "referendum" in Crimea in March 2014 (which occurred in violation of international law), the Berlin-based historian

Jörg Baberowski questioned whether Ukraine was a nation at all. He described the country as a "child of the Soviet nationalities' policy" and claimed that it had been condemned to become a nation in 1991; see Jörg Baberowski, "Geschichte der Ukraine. Zwischen den Imperien," *Die Zeit* 13 March 2014. http://www.zeit.de/2014/12 /westen-russland-konflikt-geschichte-ukraine. Accessed May 2014. Following Russia's annexation of Crimea and initial destabilization of East Ukraine, the editor-in-chief of *Die Zeit*'s arts pages, Jens Jessen, topped this, portraying Ukraine as the result of German warfare in the First and Second World Wars; see Jens Jessen, "Krimkrise. Teufelspakt für die Ukraine," *Die Zeit* 28 March 2014. http://www .zeit.de/2014/14/ukraine-unabhaengigkeit. Accessed May 2014. For those interested in the formation of the Ukrainian nation, the following is a recommended read: Andreas Kappeler, ed., *Die Ukraine. Prozesse der Nationsbildung*, Cologne: Böhlau, 2011. A remarkable feature of the debate over Ukraine is the number of German "experts" offering opinions who have never before given the country serious consideration and do not even understand the Ukrainian language.

37. On this speech and the further progress of the state visit, see Johannes Leithäuser, "Dank, Hoffnung und die Bitte um Visa-Erleichterung," *Frankfurter Allgemeine Zeitung* 9 March 2005. http://www.faz.net/aktuell /politik/juschtschenko-in-berlin-dank-hoffnung-und-die-bitte-um -visa-erleichterungen-1209774.html. Accessed May 2014.

38. See Commission of the European Communities, "Wider Europe— Neighbourhood: A New Framework for Relations with Our Eastern and Southern Neighbours" (11 March 2003). http://eeas.europa .eu/enp/pdf/pdf/com03_104_en.pdf. Accessed May 2014. See for background information Richard G. Whitman and Stefan Wolff, eds., *European Neighbourhood Policy in Perspective: Context, Implementation and Impact*, London: Palgrave Macmillan, 2010; Elena A. Korosteleva, *The European Union and Its Eastern Neighbours: Towards a More Ambitious Partnership?*, London: Routledge, 2012.

39. See Jurii Durkot, "Trügerische Normalität," *Die Tageszeitung* 5 May 2014. http://www.taz.de/!137856/. Accessed May 2014.

40. See Josef Zisels, et al., "Open Letter of Ukrainian Jews to Russian Federation President Vladimir Putin." http://eajc.org/page32 /news43672.html. Accessed May 2014.

41. See Andrei Lipskii, "Predstavlayetsia pravil'niim initsirovat' prisoyedenenie vostochnykh oblastei Ukraini k Rossii," *Novaya Gazeta* 25 February 2015. http://www.novayagazeta.ru/politics/67389.html. Accessed March 2015.

42. On the political semantics of these terms, see Anna Veronika Wendland, "Hilflos im Dunkeln. 'Experten' in der Ukraine-Krise: eine Polemik," *Osteuropa* 9–10 (2014), pp. 13–34.

43. This address of 25 April 2004 is published in Russian on the website of the Russian president at: http://archive.kremlin.ru/text/appears /2005/04/87049.shtml. Accessed May 2014. Putin spoke of millions of Russians who are now forced to live outside Russian territory. For an analysis of Russian politics, see also the blog "Ukraine in Focus" on the website of the IWM in Vienna; specifically the article by Ivan Krastev, "Putin's World." http://www.iwm.at/read-listen-watch /transit-online/putins-world/. Accessed May 2014.

44. See the various articles on the topic by Mykola Riabchuk on the blog "Ukraine in Focus."

45. See Andrew E. Kramer, "Ukraine Turns to Its Oligarchs for Political Help." *New York Times* 2 March 2014. http://www.nytimes.com/2014 /03/03/world/europe/ukraine-turns-to-its-oligarchs-for-political -help.html. Accessed May 2014.

46. On Ukraine's various oligarchs, see Serhii Leshchenko, "Hinter den Kulissen. Eine Typologie der ukrainischen Oligarchen," *Transit. Europäische Revue* 45 (2014), pp. 102–17.

47. This is the conclusion drawn in 2001 by the two American authors of an IMF-commissioned comparison of paths of transformation. See Keane and Prasad, "Poland: Inequality, Transfers, and Growth in Transition."

48. See Shleifer and Treisman, "Normal Countries." The authors were obviously unaware that the term "normal" has been tainted by the use of the word "normalization" to denote the process instituted in the ČSSR after the invasion of Warsaw Pact troops.

49. See N. N., "Reforms Are the Best Antidote to Exogenous Shocks Confronting Ukraine." http://www.worldbank.org/en/news/press -release/2015/04/29/reforms-are-the-best-antidote-to-exogenous -shocks-confronting-ukraine-says-world-bank. Accessed April 2015.

50. On Italy, for example, see Marcon and Pianta, *Sbilanciamo L'economia*.

51. See "Protest gegen Umweltverschmutzung. Wütende Chinesen stoppen Industrieprojekt," *Spiegel online* 28 July 2012. http://www.spiegel .de/wirtschaft/service/massenproteste-in-china-wuetende-anwohner -stoppen-abwasserleitung-a-846898.html. Accessed May 2014.

# SELECTED BIBLIOGRAPHY

Adrowitzer, Roland, and Ernst Gelegs. 2013. *Schöne Grüße aus dem Orbán-Land. Die rechte Revolution in Ungarn.* Graz: Styria.

Alexejewitsch, Swetlana. 2013. *Secondhand-Zeit. Leben auf den Trümmern des Sozialismus.* Munich: Hanser.

Aligica, Paul Dragos, and Anthony John Evans. 2009. *The Neoliberal Revolution in Eastern Europe: Economic Ideas in the Transition from Communism.* Cheltenham: Elgar.

Arendt, Hannah. 1963. *On Revolution.* New York: Viking Press.

Arndt, Agnes. 2007. *Intellektuelle in der Opposition. Diskurse zur Zivilgesellschaft in der Volksrepublik Polen.* Frankfurt: Campus.

Åslund, Anders. 1989. *Gorbachev's Struggle for Economic Reform: The Soviet Reform Process, 1985–1988.* Ithaca, NY: Cornell University Press.

——. 2002. *Building Capitalism: The Transformation of the Former Soviet Bloc.* Cambridge: Cambridge University Press.

——. 2007. *How Capitalism Was Built: The Transformation of Central and Eastern Europe, Russia, and Central Asia.* Cambridge: Cambridge University Press.

Aust, Martin, and Daniel Schönpflug, eds. 2007. *Vom Gegner lernen: Feindschaften und Kulturtransfers im Europa des 19. und 20. Jahrhunderts.* Frankfurt: Campus.

Bachmann, Klaus. 2013. "Gleichheit und Ungleichheit in der Volksrepublik Polen. Eine Untersuchung auf der Basis zeitgenössischer Meinungsumfragen." *Zeithistorische Forschungen* 10(2): 219–42.

Balcerowicz, Leszek. 1992. *800 Dni Szok Kontrolowany. Zapisał Jerzy Baczyński.* Warsaw: BGW.

——. 1995. *Socialism, Capitalism, Transformation.* Budapest: CEU Press.

Barbagallo, Francesco. 2013. *La questione italiana. Il Nord e il Sud dal 1860 a oggi.* Rome: Laterza.

Bauman, Zygmunt. 1994. "A Revolution in the Theory of Revolution." *International Political Science Review* 15: 15–24.

Baumeister, Martin, and Roberto Sala, eds. 2015. *Southern Europe? Italy, Spain, Portugal and Greece from the 1950s until the Present Day.* Frankfurt: Campus.

Becker, Gary S. 1964. *Human Capital: A Theoretical and Empirical Analysis, with Special Reference to Education.* Chicago: University of Chicago Press.

Beissinger, Mark R. 2009: "Nationalism and the Collapse of Soviet Communism." *Contemporary European History* 18(3): 331–47.

Berend, Iván T. 2009. *From the Soviet Bloc to the European Union: The Economic and Social Transformation of Central and Eastern Europe since 1973*. Cambridge: Cambridge University Press.

Berend, Iván T., and György Ranki. 1982. *The European Periphery and Industrialization 1780–1914*. Cambridge: Cambridge University Press.

Berghoff, Hartmut, and Uta Andrea Balbier, eds. 2013. *The East German Economy, 1945–2010: Falling Behind or Catching Up?*. Cambridge: Cambridge University Press.

Berlin, Isaiah. 2002. *Liberty: Incorporating Four Essays on Liberty*, edited by Henry Hardy. Oxford: Oxford University Press.

Berliner Senatsverwaltung für Gesundheit, Umwelt und Verbraucherschutz. 2009. *Gesundheitsberichterstattung Berlin: Spezialbericht. Sozialstrukturatlas Berlin 2008*. Accessed May 2014. http://www.berlin.de/imperia /md/content/sen-statistik-gessoz/gesundheit/spezialberichte/gbe _spezial_2009_1_ssa2008.pdf?start&ts=1308132950&file=gbe _spezial_2009_1_ssa2008.pdf.

Beyme, Klaus von. 1994. *Systemwechsel in Osteuropa*. Frankfurt: Suhrkamp.

Białek, Łukasz. *Przegląd bezpośrednich inwestycji zagranicznych w Europie Środkowej i Wschodniej (Biuletyn Europy Środkowej i Wschodniej. Puls Regionu Nr. 3)*. Accessed May 2014. http://ceedinstitute.org/attachments /281/d44b6519328278fe999108afe767da4b.pdf.

Blum, Ulrich, Joachim Ragnitz, Sabine Freye, Simone Scharfe, and Lutz Schneider. 2009. *Regionalisierung öffentlicher Ausgaben und Einnahmen – Eine Untersuchung am Beispiel der Neuen Länder*. Sonderheft 4. Halle: IWH.

Bockman, Johanna. 2011. *Markets in the Name of Socialism: The Left-Wing Origins of Neoliberalism*. Stanford, CA: Stanford University Press.

Bohle, Dorothee, and Béla Greskovits. 2007. "Neoliberalismus, eingebetteter Neoliberalismus, und Neo-Korporatismus. Sozialistische Hinterlassenschaften, transnationale Integration und die Diversität osteuropäischer Kapitalismen." In *Postsozialismus. Hinterlassenschaften des Staatssozialismus und neue Kapitalismen in Europa*, edited by D. Segert, 185–205. Vienna: Braunmüller.

———. 2012. *Capitalist Diversity on Europe's Periphery*. Ithaca, NY: Cornell University Press.

Borgomeo, Carlo. 2013. *L'equivoco des Sud. Sviluppo e coesione sociale*. Rome: Laterza.

Borodziej, Włodzimierz. 2010. *Geschichte Polens im 20. Jahrhundert*. Munich: C. H. Beck.

Borodziej, Włodzimierz, Jerzy Kochanowski, and Joachim von Putt-kamer, eds. 2010. *"Schleichwege". Inoffizielle Begegnungen sozialistischer Staatsbürger zwischen 1956 und 1989*. Vienna: Böhlau.

Boyer, Christoph. 2008. "Zwischen Pfadabhängigkeit und Zäsur: Ost- und westeuropäische Sozialstaaten seit den siebziger Jahren des 20. Jahrhunderts." In *Das Ende der Zuversicht? Die siebziger Jahre als Geschichte*, edited by K. Jarausch, 103–19. Göttingen: Vandenhoeck & Ruprecht.

Bozo, Frédéric, Marie-Pierre Rey, Piers Ludlow, and Leopoldo Nuti. 2008. *Europe and the End of the Cold War: A Reappraisal*. London: Routledge.

Bozoki, András. 2011. "Autoritäre Versuchung. Die Krise der un-garischen Demokratie." *Osteuropa* 61(12): 65–88.

Brunarska, Zuzanna, Małgorzata Grotte, and Magdalena Lesińska. 2012. *Migracje obywateli Ukrainy do Polski w kontekście rozwoju społeczno-gospodarczego: stan obecny, polityka, transfery pieniężne*. Warsaw: CMR. Accessed May 2014. http://www.migracje.uw.edu.pl/download /publikacja/2017/.

Buchowski, Michał. 2001. *Rethinking Transformation: An Anthropological Per-spective on Postsocialism*. Poznań: Humaniora.

Buck, Elena, and Jana Hönke. 2013. "Pioniere der Prekarität— Ostdeutsche als Avantgarde des neuen Arbeitsmarktregimes." In *Der "Ossi". Mikropolitische Studien über einen symbolischen Ausländer*, edited by R. Pates and M. Schochow, 23–53. Wiesbaden: Springer.

Burawoy, Michael, and Katherine Verdery, eds. 1999. *Uncertain Transition: Ethnographies of Change in the Postsocialist World*. Lanham, MD: Rowman & Littlefield.

Burgin, Angus. 2012. *The Great Persuasion: Reinventing Free Markets since the Depression*. Cambridge, MA: Harvard University Press.

Burke, Edmund. 1968 (1790). *Reflections on the Revolution in France and on the Proceedings in Certain Societies in London Relative to That Event*. London: Penguin Books.

Chwalba, Andrzej. 2010. *Kurze Geschichte der Dritten Republik Polen*. Wies-baden: Harrassowitz.

Commission of the European Communities. 2003. *Wider Europe— Neighbourhood: A New Framework for Relations with our Eastern and Southern Neighbours*. Accessed May 2014. http://eeas.europa.eu/enp/pdf/pdf /com03_104_en.pdf.

Coupland, Douglas. 1991. *Generation X: Tales for an Accelerated Culture*. New York: St. Martin's Press.

Dąbrowska, Maria. 1990. "Tagebücher." In *Bube, Dame, König: Geschichten und Gedichte aus Polen*, edited by K. Dedecius, 143–54. Frankfurt: Suhrkamp.

Dąbrowski, Janusz, ed. 1996. *Wybrane aspekty funkcjonowania targowiska 'Jarmark Europa' na Stadionie X-lecia*. Warsaw: Instytut Badań nad Gospodarką Rynkową.

Dahrendorf, Ralph. 1990. "Übergänge. Politik, Wirtschaft und Freiheit." *Transit. Europäische Revue* 1: 35–47.

Dalos, György. 2009. *Der Vorhang geht auf. Das Ende der Diktaturen in Osteuropa*. Munich: C. H. Beck.

———. 2010. *Gorbatschow—Mensch und Macht. Eine Biografie*. Munich: C. H. Beck.

Darden, Keith, and Anna Grzymała-Busse. 2006. "The Great Divide: Literacy, Nationalism, and the Communist Collapse." *World Politics* 59(1): 83–115.

Davies, Norman. 1996. *Europe: A History*. Oxford: Oxford University Press.

De Witt, Giovanni. 2005. *Le fabbriche ed il mondo. l'Olivetti industriale nella competizione globale, 1950–90*. Milan: Franco Angeli.

Diewald, Martin, Anne Goedicke, and Karl Ulrich Mayer, eds. 2006. *After the Fall of the Wall: Life Courses in the Transformation of East Germany*. Stanford, CA: Stanford University Press.

Diewald, Martin, and Bogdan W. Mach. 2006. "Comparing Paths of Transition: Employment Opportunities and Earnings in East Germany and Poland during the First Ten Years of Transformation Process." In Diewald, Goedicke, and Mayer 2006, 237–68.

Diewald, Martin, Heike Solga, and Anne Goedicke. 2006. "Old Assets, New Liabilities? How Did Individual Characteristics Contribute to Labor Market Success or Failure after 1989?" In Diewald, Goedicke, and Mayer 2006, 65–88.

Doering-Manteuffel, Anselm, and Lutz Raphael, eds. 2008. *Nach dem Boom. Perspektiven auf die Zeitgeschichte seit 1970*. Göttingen: Vandenhoeck & Ruprecht.

Domnitz, Christian. 2015. *Hinwendung nach Europa. Neuorientierung und Öffentlichkeitswandel im Staatssozialismus 1975-1989*. Bochum: Winkler.

Dudek, Antoni. 2004. *Reglamentowana rewolucja. Rozkład dyktatury komunistycznej w Polsce 1988-1990*. Kraków: Arcana.

Dunn, Elizabeth C. 2004. *Privatizing Poland: Baby Food, Big Business, and the Remaking of Labor*. Ithaca, NY: Cornell University Press.

Easter, Gerald M. 2012. *Capital, Coercion, and Postcommunist States*. Ithaca, NY: Cornell University Press.

——. 2013. "Revenue Imperatives: State over Market in Postcommunist Russia." In *The Political Economy of Russia*, edited by N. Robinson, 51–68. Lanham, MD: Rowman & Littlefield.

Eisenstadt, Shmuel N., ed. 2002. *Multiple Modernities*. New Brunswick, NJ: Transaction.

Ekiert, Grzegorz. 2003. "The State after State Socialism: Poland in Comparative Perspective." In *The Nation-State in Question*, edited by J. Hall and J. Ikenberry, 291–320. Princeton, NJ: Princeton University Press.

Eley, Geoff. 2002. *Forging Democracy: The History of the Left in Europe. 1850–2000*. Oxford: Oxford University Press.

Engler, Wolfgang. 2002. *Die Ostdeutschen als Avantgarde*. Berlin: Aufbau.

Epstein, Rachel A. 2008. *In Pursuit of Liberalism: International Institutions in Postcommunist Europe*. Baltimore: Johns Hopkins University Press.

Fässler, Peter, Thomas Held, and Dirk Sawitzki, eds. 1995. *Lemberg – Lwow – Lviv. Eine Stadt im Schnittpunkt europäischer Kulturen*. Cologne: Wissenschaft und Politik.

Fassmann, Heinz. 1997. "Die Rückkehr der Regionen – regionale Konsequenzen der Transformation in Ostmitteleuropa. Eine Einführung." In *Die Rückkehr der Regionen. Beiträge zur regionalen Transformation Ostmitteleuropas,* 13–34. Vienna: Verlag der ÖAW.

Fassmann, Heinz, and Rainer Münz, eds. 2000. *Ost-West-Wanderungen in Europa. Rückblick und Ausblick*. Vienna: Böhlau.

Förster, Michael, David Jesuit, and Timothy Smeeding. 2005. "Regional Poverty and Income Inequality in Central and Eastern Europe: Evidence from the Luxembourg Income Study." In *Spatial Inequality and Development*, edited by R. Kanbur and A. J. Venables, 311–47. New York: Oxford University Press.

Fox, Louise, and Edward Palmer. 1999. "Latvian Pension Reform." World Bank Social Protection Discussion Paper Series 9922. Accessed May 2014. http://siteresources.worldbank.org/SOCIALPROTECTION/Resources/SP-Discussion-papers/Pensions-DP/9922.pdf.

Freudenstein, Ronald. 2001. "Angst essen Seele auf. Die Deutschen und die Osterweiterung der Europäischen Union." *DPI Jahrbuch* 12/2001. Accessed May 2014. http://dpi.de1.cc/Publikationen/Jahrbuch-Ansichten/jahrbuch12_2001.php.

Friedman, Milton. 2002. *Capitalism and Freedom: Fortieth Anniversary Edition*. Chicago: University of Chicago Press.

Friedman, Milton, and Rose Friedman. 1980. *Free to Choose: A Personal Statement*. New York: Harcourt.

Frischke, Andrzej. 2014. *Rewolucja Solidarności 1980–1981*. Kraków: Znak.

Furet, François. 1990. "1789–1917: 'Rückfahrkarte'." *Transit. Europäische Revue* 1: 48–64.

Gaddis, John Lewis. 1997. *We Now Know: Rethinking Cold War History.* Oxford: Oxford University Press.

Gądecki, Jacek. 2012. "Gating Warsaw: Enclosed Housing Estates and the Aesthetics of Luxury." In *Chasing Warsaw. Socio-Material Dynamics of Urban Change since 1990*, edited by M. Grubbauer and J. Kusiak, 109–32. Frankfurt: Campus.

Gagnon, Valère P. 2004. *The Myth of Ethnic War: Serbia and Croatia in the 1990s.* Ithaca, NY: Cornell University Press.

Galasińska, Aleksandra, Michał Krzyżanowski, Sue Wright, and Helen Kelly-Holmes, eds. 2009. *Discourse and Transformation in Central and Eastern Europe: Language and Globalization.* Basingstoke: Palgrave Macmillan.

Gallagher, Tom. 2005. *Theft of a Nation: Romania since Communism.* London: Hurst & Company.

Garton Ash, Timothy. 1990a. "Apres le deluge, nous." *Transit. Europäische Revue* 1: 11–34.

———. 1990b. *We the People: The Revolution of '89 Witnessed in Warsaw, Budapest, Berlin and Prague.* Cambridge: Granta Books.

———. 2009. "1989!" *New York Review of Books*, November 5: 4–9.

Geppert, Dominik. 2002. *Thatchers konservative Revolution. Der Richtungswandel der britischen Tories 1975–1979.* Munich: Oldenbourg.

Gieseke, Jens. 2012. "Der entkräftete Tschekismus. Das MfS und seine ausgebliebene Niederschlagung der Konterrevolution 1989/90." In *1989 und die Rolle der Gewalt*, edited by M. Sabrow, 56–81. Göttingen: Wallstein.

Ginsborg, Paul. 1989. *Storia d'Italia dal dopoguerra a oggi. Società e politica 1943–1988.* Milan: Einaudi.

Girthler, Roland. 2006. *Abenteuer Grenze. Von Schugglern und Schmugglerinnen, Ritualen und "heiligen" Räumen.* Vienna: Lit-Verlag.

Główny Urząd Statystyczny. 2012. *Dochody i warunki życia ludności Polski (raport z badania EU-SILC 2011).* Warsaw: GUS.

Goedicke, Anne. 2006. "A 'Ready-Made State': The Mode of Institutional Transition in East Germany after 1989." In Diewald, Goedicke, and Mayer 2006, 44–64.

Gorzelak, Grzegorz. 1996. *The Regional Dimension of Transformation in Central Europe: Regions and Cities.* London: Routledge.

Gorzelak, Grzegorz, John Bachtler, and Maciej Smętkowski, eds. 2010. *Regional Development in Central and Eastern Europe: Development Processes and Policy Challenges.* London: Routledge.

Grabbe, Heather. 2006. *The EU's Transformative Power: Europeanization through Conditionality in Central and Eastern Europe*. Basingstoke: Palgrave Macmillan.

Grabowska-Lusińska, Izabela. 2010. *Poakcesyjne powroty Polaków*. CMR Working Papers 43/101. Warsaw: Ośrodek Badan nad Migracjami.

Grubbauer, Monika, and Joanna Kusiak, eds. 2012. *Chasing Warsaw. Socio-Material Dynamics of Urban Change since 1990*. Frankfurt: Campus.

Habermas, Jürgen. 1990. "What Does Socialism Mean Today? The Rectifying Revolution and the Need for New Thinking on the Left." *New Left Review* 1(183): 3–21.

Hall, Peter A., and David Soskice, eds. 2001. *Varieties of Capitalism: The Institutional Foundation of Comparative Advantage*. Oxford: Oxford University Press.

Hann, Chris. 2002. *Postsocialism: Ideals, Ideologies and Practices in Eurasia*. London: Routledge.

Harter, Michael, and Reiner Jaakson. 1997. "Economic Success in Estonia: The Centre versus Periphery Pattern of Regional Inequality." *Communist Economies and Economic Transformation* 9(4): 469–90.

Harvey, David. 2005. *A Brief History of Neoliberalism*. Oxford: Oxford University Press.

Haupt, Heinz-Gerhard. 2012. *Gewalt und Politik im Europa des 19. und 20. Jahrhunderts*. Göttingen: Wallstein.

Haupt, Heinz-Gerhard, and Jürgen Kocka, eds. 1996. *Geschichte und Vergleich: Ansätze und Ergebnisse international vergleichender Geschichtsschreibung*. Frankfurt: Campus.

Havel, Václav. 1990. *Do ruzných stran*. Prague: Lidové noviny.

Hobsbawm, Eric. 1994. *The Age of Extremes: The Short Twentieth Century, 1914–1991*. London: Michael Joseph.

Hrytsak, Yaroslav. 2009. "On the Relevance and Irrelevance of Nationalism in Contemporary Ukraine." In *A Laboratory of Transnational History. Ukraine and Recent Ukrainian Historiography*, edited by G. Kasianov and Ph. Ther, 225–48. Budapest: Central European University Press.

Hunt, Lynn, ed. 1989. *The New Cultural History*. Berkeley: University of California Press.

Huntington, Samuel P. 1991. *The Third Wave: Democratization in the Late Twentieth Century*. Norman: University of Oklahoma Press.

Hunya, Gabor. 2007. *Shift to the East: WIIW Database on Foreign Direct Investment in Central, East and Southeast Europe*. Vienna: WIIW.

IHK Berlin and Handwerkskammer Berlin. 2009. *Berliner Wirtschaft in Zahlen. Ausgabe 2009*. Berlin: Heenemann. Accessed May 2014. http://www.ihk-berlin.de/linkableblob/bihk24/standortpolitik

/ZahlenundFakten/downloads/1890712/.5./data/Berliner _Wirtschaft_in_Zahlen_2009-data.pdf.

Investitionsbank Berlin. 2008. "Gründungsaktivitäten im Städtevergleich." *Berlin aktuell*, February 28, 2008. Accessed May 2014. https://www.ibb.de/portaldata/1/resources/content/download /newsletter/berlin_aktuell/kn_ba_gruendungen_080228.pdf.

Jajdek, Joanna. 2002. "Der mittelbare Nachbar. Österreichvorstellungen in Polen 1970–1995." In Rathkolb, Maschke, and Lütgenau, 647–76.

James, Harold. 2003. *Europe Reborn: A History 1914–2000*. London: Routledge.

Janos, Andrew C. 2000. *East Central Europe in the Modern World: The Small States of the Borderlands from Pre- to Postcommunism*. Stanford, CA: Stanford University Press.

———. 2001. "From Eastern Empire to Western Hegemony: East Central Europe under Two International Regimes." *East European Politics and Societies* 15(2): 221–49.

Jarausch, Konrad H. 2008. "Zwischen 'Reformstau' und 'Sozialabbau'. Anmerkungen zur Globalisierungsdebatte in Deutschland 1973–2003." In *Das Ende der Zuversicht? Die siebziger Jahre als Geschichte*, 330–52. Göttingen: Vandenhoeck & Ruprecht.

———. 2015. *Out of Ashes: A New History of Europe in the Twentieth Century*. Princeton, NJ: Princeton University Press.

Jarosz, Dariusz. 2013. "Problemy z peerelowską modernizacją." *Kwartalnik Historyczny* 120: 365–84.

Jasiecki, Krzysztof. 2002. *Elita biznesu w Polsce. Drugie narodzniy kapitalizmu*, Warsaw: IFIS.

Joffe, Grigoriy, Tatyana Nefedova, and Ilya Zaslavsky, eds. 2006. *The End of Peasantry? The Disintegration of Rural Russia*. Pittsburgh: University of Pittsburgh Press.

Judt, Tony. 2005. *Postwar: A History of Europe since 1945*. New York: Penguin.

Kaelble, Hartmut. 2007. *Sozialgeschichte Europas. 1945 bis zur Gegenwart*. Munich: C. H. Beck.

Kaelble, Hartmut, and Jürgen Schriewer, eds. 2003. *Vergleich und Transfer. Komparatistik in den Sozial, Geschichts- und Kulturwissenschaften*. Frankfurt: Campus.

Kalotay, Kálmán. 2007. "Investment Creation and Diversion in an Integrating Europe." In *The Future Competitiveness of the EU and Its Eastern Neighbours: Proceedings of the Conference*, edited by P. Vahtra and E. Pelto, 49–65. Turku: Pan-European Institute.

Kappeler, Andreas, ed. 2011. *Die Ukraine. Prozesse der Nationsbildung.* Cologne: Böhlau.

Karpiński, Andrzej, Stanisław Paradysz, Paweł Soroka, and Wiesław Żółtkowski. 2013. *Jak powstawały i jak upadały zakłady przemysłowe w Polsce.* Warsaw: Muza.

Katzenstein, Peter. 2003. "Small States and Small States Revisited." *Political Economy* 8(1): 9–30.

Keane, John. 2000. *Václav Havel: A Political Tragedy in Six Acts.* New York: Basic Books.

Keane, Michael P., and Eswar S. Prasad. 2001. "Poland: Inequality, Transfers, and Growth in Transition." *Finance & Development: A Quarterly Magazine of the IMF* 38(1). Accessed May 2014. http://www.imf .org/external/pubs/ft/fandd/2001/03/keane.htm.

Keat, Preston. 2003. "Fallen Heroes: Explaining the Failure of the Gdansk Shipyard, and the Successful Early Reform Strategies in Szczecin and Gdynia." *Communist and Postcommunist Studies* 36: 209–30.

Kenney, Padraic. 2002. *A Carnival of Revolution: Central Europe 1989.* Princeton, NJ: Princeton University Press.

———. 2006. *The Burdens of Freedom: Eastern Europe since 1989.* Black Point, NS: Fernwood.

King, Lawrence. 2002. "Postcommunist Divergence: A Comparative Analysis of the Transition to Capitalism in Poland and Russia." *Studies in Comparative International Development* 37(3): 3–34.

King, Lawrence, and Iván Szelényi. 2005. "Post-Communist Economic Systems." In *Handbook of Economic Sociology*, 2nd ed., edited by N. J. Smelser and R. Swedberg, 206–29. Princeton, NJ: Princeton University Press.

Knyt, Agnieszka, and Alicja Wancerz-Gluza, eds. 2001. *Prywaciarze 1945–89.* Warsaw: Karta.

Kochanowski, Jerzy. 2010. "Pioneers of the Market Economy? Unofficial Commercial Exchange between People from the Socialist Bloc Countries (1970s and 1980s)." *Journal of Modern European History* 8: 196–220.

———. 2013. *Jenseits der Planwirtschaft. Der Schwarzmarkt in Polen 1944–1989.* Göttingen: Wallstein.

Kocka, Jürgen. 2016. *Capitalism: A Short History.* Princeton: Princeton University Press.

Kocka, Jürgen, and Wolfgang Merkel. 2014. "Neue Balance gesucht. Gefährdet der Finanzkapitalismus die Demokratie?" *WZB-Mitteilungen*

144: 41–44. Accessed May 2014. http://www.wzb.eu/sites/default /files/publikationen/wzb_mitteilungen/s41-44_kocka_merkel.pdf.

Kołodko, Grzegorz. 2000. *From Shock to Therapy: The Political Economy of the Postsocialist Transformation*. Oxford: Oxford University Press.

Kończal, Kornelia. 2008. "Vom Schreckgespenst zum Dressman. Le plombier polonais und die Macht der Imagination." In *Der Europäer—ein Konstrukt. Wissensbestände und Diskurse*, edited by K. Patel, V. Lipphardt, and L. Bluche, 299–325. Göttingen: Wallstein.

Kornai, János. 2006. "The Great Transformation of Central Eastern Europe: Success and Disappointment." *Economics of Transition* 14(2): 207–44.

Korosteleva, Elena. 2012. *The European Union and Its Eastern Neighbours: Towards a More Ambitious Partnership?* London: Routledge.

Korzeniowski, Katarzyna, and Elżbieta Tarkowska, eds. 2002. *Spojrzenia na biedę w społecznościach lokalnych*. Warsaw: Wydawnictwo Instytutu Filozofii i Socjologii PAN.

Kostinskiy, Grigoriy. 2001. "Post-Socialist Cities in Flux." In *Handbook of Urban Studies*, edited by R. Paddison, 450–85. London: Sage.

Kotkin, Stephen, with a contribution by Jan T. Gross. 2009. *Uncivil Society: 1989 and the Implosion of the Communist Establishment*. New York: Random House.

Kovács, János M., and Violetta Zentai, eds. 2012. *Capitalism from Outside? Economic Cultures in Eastern Europe after 1989*. Budapest: CEU Press.

Kralinski, Thomas. 2000. "Die neuen Ostdeutschen." *Berliner Republik. Das Debattenmagazin* 4. Accessed May 2014. http://www.b-republik .de/archiv/die-neuen-ostdeutschen.

Kramer, Andrew E. 2014. "Ukraine Turns to Its Oligarchs for Political Help." *New York Times* March 2, 2014. Accessed May 2014. http:// www.nytimes.com/2014/03/03/world/europe/ukraine-turns-to-its -oligarchs-for-political-help.html.

Kramer, Mark. 2003. "The Collapse of East European Communism and the Repercussions within the Soviet Union (part 1)." *Journal of Cold War Studies* 5(4): 178–256.

———. 2004. "Ukraine and the Czechoslovak Crisis of 1968 (part 2): New Evidence from the Ukrainian Archives." *Cold War International History Project Bulletin* 14(15): 273–368.

Krapfl, James. 2013. *Revolution with a Human Face: Politics, Culture, and Community in Czechoslovakia, 1989–1992*. Ithaca, NY: Cornell University Press.

Krastev, Ivan. 2014. "Putin's World." Accessed May 2014. http://www .iwm.at/read-listen-watch/transit-online/putins-world/.

Krücken, Georg, and Gili S. Drori, eds. 2009. *World Society: The Writings of John W. Meyer*. New York: Oxford University Press.

Krugman, Paul. 1991. "Increasing Returns and Economic Geography." *Journal of Political Economy* 99(3): 483–99.

Kühl, Jürgen. 2014. "25 Jahre deutsche Einheit. Annäherungen und verbliebene Unterschiede zwischen West und Ost." *Bundeszentrale für Politische Bildung* 2014. Accessed February 2015. http://www.bpb.de /politik/innenpolitik/arbeitsmarktpolitik/55390/25-jahre-deutsche -einheit?p=all.

Kundera, Milan. 1991. "The Tragedy of Central Europe (April 26, 1984)." In G. Stokes 1991, 217–23.

Kurczewski, Jacek, Mariusz Cichomski, and Krzysztof Wiliński. 2010. *Wielkie bazary warszawskie*. Warsaw: Trio.

Kuznets, Simon. 1955. "Economic Growth and Income Inequality." *American Economic Review* 45: 1–28.

Kuzyk, Boris, and Yuriy Yakovets. 2004. *Rossiya 2050. Strategiya innovatsion- nogo proryva*. Moscow: Ekonomika.

Lavigne, Marie. 2007. *The Economics of Transition: From Socialist Economy to Market Economy*. 2nd ed. Basingstoke: Palgrave Macmillan.

Lawson, George. 2004. *Negotiated Revolutions: The Czech Republic, South Africa and Chile*. London: Ashgate.

Lawson, George, Chris Armbruster, and Michael Cox, eds. 2010. *The Global 1989: Continuity and Change in World Politics*. Cambridge: Cambridge University Press.

Leffler, Melvin, and Odd Arne Westad, eds. 2010. *The Cambridge History of the Cold War*, 3 vols. Cambridge: Cambridge University Press.

Leshchenko, Serhii. 2014. "Hinter den Kulissen. Eine Typologie der ukrainischen Oligarchen." *Transit. Europäische Revue* 45: 102–17.

Lindner, Bernd. 2014. "Begriffsgeschichte der Friedlichen Revolution. Eine Spurensuche." *Aus Politik und Zeitgeschichte* 24–26: 33–39.

Linz, Juan J., and Alfred Stepan. 1996. *Problems of Democratic Transition and Consolidation: Southern Europe, South America, and Post-Communist Europe*. Baltimore: Johns Hopkins University Press.

Lipton, David, and Jeffrey D. Sachs. 1990. "Poland's Economic Reform." *Foreign Affairs* 69(3): 47–66.

Macours, Karen, and Johan F.M. Swinnen. 2007. "Rural-Urban Poverty Differences in Transition Countries." LICOS Discussion Paper 169. Accessed May 2014. http://www.econ.kuleuven.be/licos /publications/dp/dp169.pdf.

Maddison, Angus. 1995. *Monitoring the World Economy, 1820–1992*. Paris: OECD.

Marcon, Giulio, and Mario Pianta. 2013. *Sbilanciamo L'economia: Una via d'uscita dalla crisi*. Rome: Laterza.

Martens, Bernd. 2010. "Der Zug nach Westen—Anhaltende Abwanderung." *Bundeszentrale für politische Bildung*, March 30, 2010. Accessed May 2014. http://www.bpb.de/geschichte/deutsche-einheit/lange -wege-der-deutschen-einheit/47253/zug-nach-westen?p=all.

Mayer, Karl Ulrich. 2006. "After the Fall of the Wall: Living through the Post-Socialist Transformation in East Germany." In Diewald, Goedicke, and Mayer 2006, 1–28.

Mazower, Mark. 2000. *Dark Continent: Europe's Twentieth Century*. New York: Vintage.

Mazurek, Małgorzata. 2010. *Społeczeństwo kolejki. O doświadczeniach niedoboru 1945–1989*. Warsaw: Trio.

Merkel, Wolfgang. 2007. "Gegen alle Theorie? Die Konsolidierung der Demokratie in Ostmitteleuropa." *Politische Vierteljahresschrift* 48(3): 413–33.

———. 2010. *Systemtransformation. Eine Einführung in die Theorie und Empirie der Transformationsforschung*. Wiesbaden: VS Verlag für Sozialwissenschaften.

Milanovic, Branko. 2013. "Reform and Inequality in the Transition: An Analysis Using Panel Household Survey." In *Economies in Transition. The Long Run View*, edited by G. Roland, 84–108. London: Palgrave.

Minh, Pham Quang. 2003. *Zwischen Theorie und Praxis. Agrarpolitik in Vietnam seit 1945*. Berlin: Logos-Verlag.

Mirowski, Philip, and Dieter Plehwe, eds. 2009. *The Road from Mont Pèlerin: The Making of the Neoliberal Thought Collective*. Cambridge, MA: Harvard University Press.

Modzelewski, Karol. 2013. *Zajeździmy kobyłę historii. Wyznania poobijanego jeźdźca*. Warsaw: Iskry.

Mueller, Wolfgang, Michael Gehler, and Arnold Suppan, eds. 2014. *The Revolutions of 1989: A Handbook*. Vienna: Verlag der ÖAW.

Müller, Jan-Werner. 2011. *Contesting Democracy: Political Ideas in Twentieth-Century Europe*. New Haven, CT: Yale University Press.

Müller, Katharina. 1998. "Vom Staat zum Markt? Rentenreformen in Mittelosteuropa." *Staatswissenschaften und Staatspraxis* 9(2): 163–89.

Naím, Moisés. 1999. "Fads and Fashion in Economic Reforms: Washington Consensus or Washington Confusion?" October 26, 1999. Accessed May 2014. http://www.imf.org/external/pubs/ft/seminar /1999/reforms/Naim.HTM.

Niemirska, Izabela. 2010. "Migracje zarobkowe Polaków w dobie kryzysu." In *Młodzi ekonomiści wobec kryzysu. Gospodarka. Finanse. Rynek Pracy*, 221–32. Szczecin: Uniwersytet Szczeciński.

N. N. 1994. *130 Lat Statystyki Warszawy 1864–1994*. Warsaw: Wojewódzki Urząd Statystyczny w M. St. Warszawie.

Norkus, Zenonas. 2012. *On Baltic Slovenia and Adriatic Lithuania: A Qualitative Comparative Analysis of Patterns in Post-Communist Transformation*. Budapest: Central European University Press.

Offe, Claus. 1994. *Der Tunnel am Ende des Lichts. Erkundungen der politischen Transformation im Neuen Osten*. Frankfurt: Campus.

Oltay, Edith. 2013. *Fidesz and the Reinvention of the Hungarian Center-Right*. Budapest: Századvég Verlag.

Orenstein, Mitchell A. 2008. *Privatizing Pensions: The Transnational Campaign for Social Security Reform*. Princeton, NJ: Princeton University Press.

Orenstein, Mitchell A., Stephen Bloom, and Nicole Lindstrom, eds. 2008. *Transnational Actors in Central and East European Transitions*. Pittsburgh: University of Pittsburgh Press.

Ost, David. 2005. *The Defeat of Solidarity: Anger and Politics in Postcommunist Europe*. Ithaca, NY: Cornell University Press.

Otáhal, Milan, and Miroslav Vaněk. 1999. *Sto studenských revolucí. Studenti v období pádu komunismu - životpisná vyprávení*. Prague: Lidové noviny.

Palmer, Robert R. 1959. *The Age of the Democratic Revolution: A Political History of Europe and America, 1760–1800*. Princeton, NJ: Princeton University Press.

Palska, Hanna. 2002. *Bieda i dostatek. O nowych stylach życia w Polsce końca lat dziewięćdziesiątych*. Warsaw: Wydawnictwo Instytutu Filozofii i Socjologii PAN.

Paqué, Karl-Heinz. 2009a. *Die Bilanz. Eine wirtschaftliche Analyse der Deutschen Einheit*. Munich: Hanser.

———. 2009b. "Transformationspolitik in Ostdeutschland: ein Teilerfolg." *Aus Politik und Zeitgeschichte* 28: 22–27.

Parker, David, ed. 2000. *Revolutions and the Revolutionary Tradition in the West 1560–1991*. London: Routledge.

Patočka, Jan, and Vera Schifferová. eds. 1997. *Komeniologické studie: Soubor textů o J. A. Komenském. Texty publikované v letech 1941–1958*. Prague: Oikoymenh.

Pavlínek, Petr. 2004. "Regional Development Implications of Foreign Direct Investment in Central Europe." *European Urban and Regional Studies* 11(1): 47–70.

Peterlik, Marcin. 2000. *Handel targowiskowy w roku 1999*. Warsaw: Instytut Badań nad Gospodarką Rynkową.

Plehwe, Dieter. 2009. "Introduction." In Mirowski and Plehwe 2009, 1–44.

Plokhy, Serhii. 2014. *The Last Empire: The Final Days of the Soviet Union*. New York: Basic Books.

Przeworski, Adam. 1991. *Democracy and the Market: Political and Economic Reforms in Eastern Europe and Latin America.* New York: Cambridge University Press.

Pullmann, Michal. 2011. *Konec experimentu. Představba a pad komunismu v Československu.* Prague: Scriptorium.

Putnam, Robert D. 1995. "Bowling Alone: America's Declining Social Capital." *Journal of Democracy* 6: 65–78.

———. 2000. *Bowling Alone: The Collapse and Revival of American Community.* New York: Simon & Schuster.

Puttkamer, Joachim von. 2011. "Die ungarische Nation und ihre Geschichte. Blicke auf ein gespaltenes Land." *Osteuropa* 61(12): 9–28.

Ramet, Sabrina P., and Davorka Matić, eds. 2007. *Democratic Transition in Croatia: Value Transformation, Education & Media.* College Station: Texas A&M University Press.

Rathkolb, Oliver, Otto M. Maschke, and Stefan August Lütgenau, eds. 2002. *Mit anderen Augen gesehen. Internationale Perzeptionen Österreichs 1955–1990.* Vienna: Böhlau.

Richter, Sándor. 2011. "Im Würgegriff des Populismus. Ungarns Volkswirtschaft." *Osteuropa* 61(12): 213–24.

Ritter, Gerhard A. 2006. *Der Preis der deutschen Einheit: Die Wiedervereinigung und die Krise des Sozialstaates.* Munich: C. H. Beck.

Robinson, Neill. 2013a. "The Context of Russia's Political Economy." In *The Political Economy of Russia*, edited by N. Robinson, 15–50. Lanham, MD: Rowman & Littlefield.

———. 2013b. "Introduction." In Robinson 2013a, 1–14.

*Rocznik Statystyczny Województwa Warszawskiego 1991.* 1991. Warsaw: Wojewódzki Urząd Statystyczny.

Rödder, Andreas. 2009. *Deutschland einig Vaterland. Die Geschichte der Wiedervereinigung.* Munich: C. H. Beck.

Rumpler, Helmut, and Peter Urbanitsch, eds. 2010, *Die Habsburgermonarchie 1848–1918. Band IX/1: Von der Feudal-Agrarischen zur Bürgerlich-industriellen Gesellschaft.* Vienna: Verlag der ÖAW.

Rupnik, Jacques. 2008. "1968: The Year of Two Springs." *Eurozine*, May 16, 2008. Accessed May 2014. http://www.eurozine.com/articles /2008-05-16-rupnik-en.html.

———, ed. 2014. *1989 as a Political World Event: Democracy, Europe and the New International System in the Age of Globalization.* London: Routledge.

Sachs, Jeffrey. 2005. *The End of Poverty: Economic Possibilities for Our Time.* New York: Penguin.

Safranskaya, Svetlana. 2013. "The Opening of the Wall, Eastern Europe, and Gorbachev's Vision of Europe after the Cold War." In *Imposing,*

*Maintaining, and Tearing Open the Iron Curtain: The Cold War and East-Central Europe, 1945–1989*, edited by M. Kramer and V. Smetana, 335–54. Lanham, MD: Lexington Books.

Samuels, Warren, Jeff Biddle, and John Davis. 2003. *A Companion to the History of Economic Thought*. Oxford: Oxford University Press.

Sapper, Manfred, and Volker Weichsel, eds. 2009. *Osteuropa* 59(2–3): *Freiheit im Blick. 1989 und der Aufbruch in Europa*.

Sarotte, Mary Elise. 2014. *The Collapse: The Accidental Opening of the Berlin Wall*. New York: Basic Books.

Sassen, Saskia. 2001. *The Global City: New York, London, Tokyo*. Princeton, NJ: Princeton University Press.

Schenk, Frithjof B., and Martina Winkler, eds. 2007. *Der Süden. Neue Perspektiven auf eine europäische Geschichtsregion*. Frankfurt: Campus.

Schmidt, Helmut. 2000. *Die Selbstbehauptung Europas. Perspektiven für das 21. Jahrhundert*. Munich: DVA.

Schmitter, Philippe, and Nicolas Guilhot. 2000. "From Transition to Consolidation: Extending the Concept of Democratization and the Practice of Democracy." In *Democratic and Capitalist Transitions in Eastern Europe*, edited by M. Dobry, 131–46. Dordrecht: Kluwer.

Schröder, Gerhard. 2000, "Die zivile Bürgergesellschaft. Zur Neubestimmung der Aufgaben von Staat und Gesellschaft." *Neue Gesellschaft* 4 (2000): 200–207.

Schwintowski, Hans-Peter. 2005. "Berliner Bankenskandal—und was wir daraus lernen könnten." In *Humboldt Forum Recht* 7: 60–184. Accessed May 2014. http://www.humboldt-forum-recht.de/druckansicht/druckansicht.php?artikelid=8.

Sebestyen, Victor. 2009. *Revolution 1989—The Fall of the Soviet Empire*. New York: Random House.

Segbers, Klaus. 1989. *Der sowjetische Systemwandel*. Frankfurt: Suhrkamp.

Segert, Dieter. 2013. *Transformation in Osteuropa im 20. Jahrhundert*. Vienna: Facultas.

Sekulić, Duško, and Željka Šporer. 2000. "Croatia: Managerial Elite Circulation or Reproduction?" In *Elites after State Socialism: Theories and Analysis*, edited by J. Higley and G. Lengyel, 143–62. Lanham, MD: Rowman & Littlefield.

Shevtsova, Lilia. 2007. *Russia: Lost in Transition. The Yeltsin and Putin Legacies*. Washington, DC: Carnegie Endowment.

Shleifer, Andrei, and Daniel Treisman. 2014. "Normal Countries: The East 25 Years after Communism." *Foreign Affairs* 93. Accessed March 2015. http://www.foreignaffairs.com/articles/142200/andrei-shleifer-and-daniel-treisman/normal-countries.

Siani-Davies, Peter. 2005. *The Romanian Revolution of December 1989*. Ithaca, NY: Cornell University Press.

Sinn, Gerlinde, and Hans-Werner Sinn. 1992. *Kaltstart. Volkswirtschaftliche Aspekte der deutschen Vereinigung*. 2nd ed. Tübingen: Mohr.

Skinner, Quentin. 1970. "Conventions and the Understanding of Speech Acts." *Philosophical Quarterly* 20(79): 118–38.

Skocpol, Theda. 1994. *Social Revolutions in the Modern World*. Cambridge: Cambridge University Press.

Smith, Graham. 1994. "The Resurgence of Nationalism." In *The Baltic States: The National Self-Determination of Estonia, Latvia and Lithuania*, edited by G. Smith, 121–43. New York: St. Martin's Press.

Smolar, Aleksander. 2010. *Tabu i niewinność*. Kraków: Universitas.

Staniszkis, Jadwiga. 1982. *Pologne. La révolution autolimitée*. Paris: Presses universitaires de France.

———. 2001. *Postkommunizm. Próba opisu*. Gdańsk: Wydawnictwo słowo.

Stedman Jones, Daniel. 2012. *Masters of the Universe: Hayek, Friedman, and the Birth of Neoliberal Politics*. Princeton, NJ: Princeton University Press.

Stiefel, Dieter, and Schumpeter Gesellschaft, eds. 2010. *Der "Ostfaktor": Österreichs Wirtschaft und die Ostöffnung 1989 bis 2009*. Vienna: Böhlau.

Stiglitz, Joseph. 2010. *Freefall: America, Free Markets, and the Sinking of the World Economy*. New York: Penguin.

Stöcker, Lars Fredrik. 2013. "Bridging the Baltic Sea: Networks of Resistance and Opposition during the Cold War Era." Ph.D. dissertation. EUI Florence: Department of History and Civilization.

Stokes, Gale, ed. 1991. *From Stalinism to Pluralism. A Documentary History of Eastern Europe since 1945*. New York: Oxford University Press.

Stokes, Raymond G. 2006. "Von Trabbis und Acelyten—die Technikentwicklung." In *Überholen ohne Einzuholen. Die DDR-Wirtschaft als Fußnote der deutschen Geschichte?*, edited by Andre Steiner, 105–26. Berlin: Ch. Links Verlag.

Stöver, Bernd. 2011. *Der Kalte Krieg. Geschichte eines radikalen Zeitalters, 1947–1991*. Munich: C. H. Beck.

Strubelt, Wendelin. 2008. "'Stadt und Land'—The Relation between City and Countryside. (Non-Urban Territories) The German Case—A German Case? Reflections and Facts." In *City and Region: Papers in Honour of Jiří Musil*, edited by W. Strubelt and G. Gorzelak, 233–67. Opladen: Budrich UniPress.

Suk, Jiří. 2003. *Labyrintem revoluce. Aktéři, zápletky a křižovatky jedné politické krize (Od listopadu 1989 do června 1990)*. Prague: Prostor.

Sulima, Roch. 2012. "The Laboratory of Polish Postmodernity: An Ethnographic Report from the Stadium Bazaar." In Grubbauer and Kusiak 2012, 241–68.

Sundén, Annika. 2006. "The Swedish Experience with Pension Reform." *Oxford Review on Economic Policy* 22: 133–48.

Sundhaussen, Holm. 2012. *Jugoslawien und seine Nachfolgestaaten 1943–2011.* Vienna: Böhlau.

Suny, Ronald G., and Terry Martin, eds. 2001. *A State of Nations: Empire and Nation Making in the Age of Lenin and Stalin.* Oxford: Oxford University Press.

Suppan, Arnold. 2014. "Austria and Its Neighbours in Eastern Europe, 1955–89." In Mueller, Gehler, and Suppan, 419–36.

Szacki, Jerzy. 2005. *Liberalism after Communism.* Budapest: CEU Press.

Szczepanowski, Stanisław. 1888. *Nędza Galicji w cyfrach i program energicznego rozwoju gospodarstwa krajowego.* L'viv: Gubrynowicz und Schmidt.

Szporluk, Roman. 2000. *Russia, Ukraine and the Breakup of the Soviet Union.* Stanford, CA: Hoover Institution Press.

Tamás, Pál, and Helmut Steiner, eds. 2005. *The Business Elites of East Central Europe.* Berlin: Trafo.

Taylor, Charles. 1992. *The Ethics of Authenticity.* Cambridge, MA: Harvard University Press.

Thelen, Tatjana, Andrew Cartwright, and Thomas Sikor. 2008. *Local State and Social Security in Rural Communities: A New Research Agenda and the Example of Postsocialist Europe.* Halle/Saale: Max-Planck-Institut für ethnologische Forschung.

Ther, Philipp. 2007. "Milan Kundera und die Renaissance Zentraleuropas." *Themenportal Europäische Geschichte.* Accessed May 2014. http://www.europa.clio-online.de/site/lang___de-DE/ItemID___153/mid___11428/40208214/default.aspx.

———. 2009. "Das 'neue Europa' seit 1989. Überlegungen zu einer Geschichte der Transformationszeit". *Zeithistorische Forschungen* 6: 105–14.

———. 2010a. "Comparisons, Cultural Transfers and the Study of Networks: Towards a Transnational History of Europe." In *Comparative and Transnational History: Central European Approaches and New Perspectives,* edited by H.-G. Haupt and J. Kocka, 204–25. New York: Berghahn.

———. 2010b. "1989—eine verhandelte Revolution." *Docupedia-Zeitgeschichte,* February 11, 2010. Accessed May 2014. http://docupedia.de/docupedia/index.php?title=1989&oldid=75064.

Thieme, H. Jörg. 1998. "Notenbank und Währung in der DDR." In *Fünfzig Jahre Deutsche Mark: Notenbank und Währung in Deutschland seit 1948*, edited by Deutsche Bundesbank, 609–54. Munich: C. H. Beck.

Tilly, Charles. 1992. *European Revolutions 1492–1992*. Oxford: Oxford University Press.

Tocqueville, Alexis de. (1856) 2011. *The Ancien Régime and the French Revolution*, edited by John Elster, translated by Arthur Goldhammer. Cambridge: Cambridge University Press.

Tomka, Béla. 2013. *A Social History of Twentieth-Century Europe*. Abingdon: Routledge.

Tsai, Kellee S. 2007. *Capitalism without Democracy: The Private Sector in Contemporary China*. Ithaca, NY: Cornell University Press.

Vachudova, Milada. 2005. *Europe Undivided: Democracy, Leverage and Integration after Communism*. Oxford: Oxford University Press.

Vachudova, Milada, and Timothy Snyder. 1997. "Are Transitions Transitory? Two Models of Political Change in East Central Europe since 1989." *East European Politics & Societies* 11: 1–35.

Vaněk, Miroslav. 2009. "Der 17. November und seine Ursachen in den Erzählungen kommunistischer Funktionäre." In *Die samtene Revolution. Vorgeschichte—Verlauf—Akteure*, edited by N. Perzi, B. Blehová, and P. Bachmeier, 147–64. Frankfurt: Peter Lang.

Verdery, Katherine. 1996. *What Was Socialism and What Comes Next?* Princeton, NJ: Princeton University Press.

Villaume, Paul, and Odd Arne Westad, eds. 2010. *Perforating the Iron Curtain: European Détente, Transatlantic Relations, and the Cold War*. Copenhagen: Museum Tusculanum Press.

Wagener, Hans-Jürgen. 2011. *Wirtschaftsordnung im Wandel. Zur Transformation 1985–2010*. Marburg: Metropolis Verlag.

Wandycz, Piotr. 1992. *The Price of Freedom: A History of East Central Europe from the Middle Ages to the Present*. London: Routledge.

Wasiak, Patryk. 2015. "Komputeryzujemy się!" In *Społeczeństwo polskie w latach 1980–1989*, edited by N. Jarska and J. Olaszek, 159–69. Warsaw: IPN.

Weber, Ursula. 2002. *Der Polenmarkt in Berlin: Zur Rekonstruktion eines kulturellen Kontakts im Prozess der politischen Transformation Mittel- und Osteuropas*. Neuried: Ars Una.

Wendland, Anna Veronika. 2014. "Hilflos im Dunkeln. 'Experten' in der Ukraine-Krise: eine Polemik." *Osteuropa* 9–10: 13–34.

Whitman, Richard G., and Stefan Wolff, eds. 2010. *European Neighbourhood Policy in Perspective: Context, Implementation and Impact*. London: Palgrave Macmillan.

Wiener Institut für Internationale Wirtschaftsvergleiche. 2013. *WIIW Handbook of Statistics 2012*. Vienna: WIIW.

Williamson, John, ed. 1989. *Latin American Readjustment: How Much Has Happened*. Washington, DC: Institute for International Economics.

———. 2004. "A Short History of the Washington Consensus." Accessed May 2014. http://www.iie.com/publications/papers/williamson0904 -2.pdf.

Wirsching, Andreas. 2012. *Der Preis der Freiheit. Geschichte Europas in unserer Zeit*. Munich: C. H. Beck.

Wolff, Larry. 1994. *Inventing Eastern Europe: The Map of Civilization on the Mind of the Enlightenment*. Stanford, CA: Stanford University Press.

Wolfrum, Edgar. 2013. *Rot-Grün an der Macht. Deutschland 1998–2005*. Munich: C. H. Beck.

Yekelczyk, Serhii, and Oliver Schmidtke, eds. 2008. *Europe's Last Frontier? Belarus, Moldova, and Ukraine between Russia and the European Union*. New York: Palgrave.

Yevtushenko, Yevgeni. 1995. *Don't Die before You Are Dead*. New York: Random House.

Zantovsky, Michael. 2014. *Havel: A Life*. New York: Grove Press.

Zielonka, Jan. 2006. *Europe as Empire: The Nature of the Enlarged European Union*. Oxford: Oxford University Press.

# INDEX